Incentivized Development in China

China's economy, as a whole, has developed rapidly over the past 35 years, and yet its richest county is over 100 times richer in per capita terms than its poorest county. To explain this vast variation in development, David J. Bulman investigates the political foundations of local economic growth in China, focusing on the institutional and economic roles of county-level leaders and the career incentives that shape their behavior. Through a close examination of six counties complemented by unique nationwide data, he presents and explores two related questions: *What is the role of county Party secretaries in determining local governance and growth outcomes?* and *Why do county Party secretaries emphasize particular developmental priorities?*

Suitable for scholars of political economy, development economics, and comparative politics, this original study analyzes the relationship between political institutions, local governance, and leadership roles within Chinese government to explain the growing divergence in economic development between counties.

David J. Bulman is an economist at the World Bank and an adjunct lecturer at the Johns Hopkins School of Advanced International Studies. He is a core author of the *World Development Report 2017* and contributed to *China 2030* and *Urban China*. Bulman has been a visiting scholar at the Hopkins-Nanjing Center, a University of Chicago and Ford Foundation New Generation China Scholar, and an inaugural China Public Policy Postdoctoral Fellow at the Ash Center for Democratic Governance and Innovation at Harvard Kennedy School.

Incentivized Development in China

Leaders, Governance, and Growth in China's Counties

DAVID J. BULMAN

CAMBRIDGE
UNIVERSITY PRESS

CAMBRIDGE
UNIVERSITY PRESS

One Liberty Plaza, 20th Floor, New York, NY 10006, USA

Cambridge University Press is part of the University of Cambridge.

It furthers the University's mission by disseminating knowledge in the pursuit of education, learning and research at the highest international levels of excellence.

www.cambridge.org
Information on this title: www.cambridge.org/9781107166295

First published 2016

Printed in the United States of America by Sheridan Books, Inc.

A catalog record for this publication is available from the British Library

Library of Congress Cataloging in Publication data
Names: Bulman, David Janoff, author.
Title: Incentivized development in China: leaders, governance, and growth in China's counties / David Janoff Bulman.
Description: New York, NY : Cambridge University Press, 2016. |
Includes bibliographical references and index.
Identifiers: LCCN 2016026216 | ISBN 9781107166295 (hardback)
Subjects: LCSH: China–Economic conditions–Regional disparities. |
Regional economics–China. | Provincial governments–China. |
Central-local government relations–China. | Economic development–China. |
BISAC: POLITICAL SCIENCE / Government / International.
Classification: LCC HC427.95 .B86 2016 | DDC 338.951–dc23
LC record available at https://lccn.loc.gov/2016026216

ISBN 978-1-107-16629-5 Hardback

Contents

Tables

Figures

Acknowledgments

The research for this book began in 2010, and over the past six years I have accrued debts to numerous individuals and organizations. I first started exploring county-level variation in China as a PhD student at the Johns Hopkins School of Advanced International Studies (SAIS). At SAIS, Mike Lampton mentored me and molded my understanding of the Chinese political system, and he has continued to be a source of inspiration and support since I graduated. A student could not ask for a more helpful and gracious advisor. Pieter Bottelier's enthusiasm for sharing his unparalleled expertise and insights made study of the Chinese economy both fascinating and enjoyable. Monica Martinez-Bravo helped generate many of the ideas related to promotion incentives through our original work on China's county leaders, and she provided critical methodological suggestions and advice throughout the research process. Along with helpful comments when this book was still a dissertation, Aart Kraay has been my mentor at the World Bank and, more than anyone, has influenced the way that I approach academic and policy questions. Kellee Tsai asked challenging questions that shaped my research during its early stages, and her comments helped move the project from dissertation to book manuscript. During the long research process, fellow SAISers Greg Fuller, Khalid Nadiri, John Gans, Ross Herbert, Amanda Kerrigan, and Selina Ho provided important camaraderie and an invaluable sounding board for ideas, albeit at the occasional expense of short-term productivity.

Tony Saich and Edward Cunningham gave me the opportunity to develop my dissertation into a book manuscript by inviting me to be one of two inaugural China Public Policy Postdoctoral Fellows at the Ash Center at Harvard Kennedy School. Tony's expertise on local governance in China is unparalleled – the book already reflected his research before I joined the Ash Center – and many improvements to the manuscript reflect comments and suggestions I received from Tony as a fellow. Edward was generous with his time guiding me through the book writing process and helping me shape my arguments to make them more compelling and reach a wider audience. Kaori Urayama offered support and guidance. Kyle Jaros, the other inaugural fellow, gave the book and various chapters multiple close readings, adding essential insights every time. Other fellows and seminar participants at the Ash Center were an important source of tough questions and suggestions.

Several other individuals and institutions deserve my thanks. The Hopkins-Nanjing Center hosted me as a visiting scholar in fall 2012, for which I am extremely grateful. Scholars at the Center and at Nanjing University, particularly Bu Maoliang and Qi Lingling, provided key insights as well as friendship. The University of Chicago and Ford Foundation New Generation China Scholars Program provided financial resources essential for my fieldwork and provided a venue to present and discuss early work. At these discussions, Dali Yang, William Parish, Tao Ran, and student participants provided important insights for developing my argument. Bo Zhiyue and Zhang Xiaobo were extremely generous in sharing data. The librarians at the Library of Congress and research assistants at SAIS, with the help of a grant from the SAIS Economics Department, helped collect data on tenures of county leaders. An early version of material in Chapter 5 and Chapter 6 was presented at the Association of Asian Studies 2013 conference, and I thank participants at the conference, particularly Dorothy Solinger, Lynette Ong, and Fubing Su, for their helpful comments, questions, and encouragement. At Cambridge University Press, Robert Dreesen gave an opportunity to a first-time author, and, along with Brianda Reyes, guided me through the entire process. Three anonymous reviewers read the manuscript closely and provided helpful suggestions.

The ideas and conclusions in this book were generated over the course of many months of fieldwork in Jiangsu and Anhui, and my greatest debt is to those who gave their time helping me understand economic and institutional development in their counties. These individuals must remain anonymous, but I thank them for everything they taught me and for providing friendship that prevented fieldwork from becoming a lonely experience.

Finally, I thank my family. My parents and my sister instilled in me a love of learning that made the research process interesting and rewarding. They have provided unwavering support for this and for all things, and I cannot thank them enough. Cassandra, you came into my life during the process of researching and writing this book, and you've made my life so much better. Thank you for supporting me and inspiring me. Isaac, you were lucky enough to miss this entire process, but your imminent arrival provided the incentive I needed to hurry up and finish.

1

Introduction

In November 2012, Xi Jinping officially became general secretary of the Chinese Communist Party (CCP), the country's "first-in-command" (*yibashou*, 一把手). Soon after entering office, as a precursor to a broader and bolder anticorruption campaign, Xi initiated a campaign to combat government waste, with a particular emphasis on excessive eating and drinking at official banquets. The campaign was part of a larger initiative to improve cadre culture and reduce negative perceptions of government leaders, particularly at the local level.

Prior to Xi's campaign, in September 2012, I arrived in China to conduct fieldwork in central Anhui Province and coastal Jiangsu Province on the underlying causes of county-level developmental variation, with a particular focus on three pairs of counties situated directly across from each other on the shared provincial border. During this first phase of fieldwork, the developmental divergence between the three Jiangsu counties and the three Anhui counties was readily apparent in industrial and urban development as well as in the attitude of local cadres. Despite sharing similar geographic and cultural histories, and despite having similar levels of wealth and industrialization in the mid 1990s, the Jiangsu counties now outshined their Anhui counterparts. Yet a common theme continued to characterize all six counties: feasting was a no-holds-barred exercise in over-ordering and general gluttony.

I returned to the same six counties in April 2013 for a second round of fieldwork and rapidly discovered a highly indicative change: feasting culture in the three Anhui counties remained unchanged, but feasting culture in Jiangsu had evolved. While officials still tended to over-order, in Jiangsu they made a point of referencing Xi's dictum and doggy-bagging every unfinished dish. In Anhui, references to Xi were often made as well, but these references were followed by guffaws, not "to-go" bags.

I will argue in this book that what may at first seem like a trivial throw-away comparison represents a larger pattern of divergent cadre behavior, with important developmental implications. Jiangsu's cadre promotion institutions have created pro-growth incentives for county leaders, and these leaders have translated their personal promotion incentives into bolder and more creative local development ideas as well as stricter control of local cadres in an effort to improve local investment environments. In Anhui, provincial authorities have been more concerned with stability maintenance (*weiwen*, 维稳) in local counties, leading to less courageous and less innovative county-level approaches to governance and economic policy. Largely as a result of these contrasting provincial emphases, counties in Jiangsu have vastly outperformed their Anhui counterparts since the mid 1990s, in terms of both economic and institutional development. In the six case study counties, the three counties in Jiangsu were on average slightly poorer than their three Anhui counterparts in 1994, the first year of the analysis; by 2007 they were over 60 percent wealthier. Although not the only factor explaining these outcomes, I argue that different governance and growth environments influenced by provincial variation in promotion emphases explain a significant share of the divergence.

Explaining the Developmental Orientation of Local Governments

The developmental orientation and effectiveness of China's local governments in recent decades presents a quandary. Local governments have intervened frequently in local economies, with rampant opportunities for rent-seeking and inefficient obstruction of markets. Corruption has been widespread, and the incidence and perceptions of corruption increase at lower levels of government. And yet in the past 35 years, increased levels of decentralization have been accompanied by the highest sustained economic growth in modern economic history. During this "growth miracle," many governments have had "helping hands" that benefit local businesses and help produce local growth. Other local governments have instead wielded "grabbing hands" that prey on local residents and businesses and stunt economic development. This variation in local government behavior is reflected in economic outcomes: although China as a whole has grown rapidly, this growth has been uneven. China's richest county is over 100 times richer in per capita terms than its poorest county, the difference between Singapore and Liberia.

Existing theories go a long way in explaining the pro-development orientation of China's local governments; they also go a long way in explaining predatory behavior. Yet these theories do not sufficiently explain the variation in behavior across local governments. As I discuss below, many of these existing theories concentrate on the incentives created by decentralization. For instance, theories based on fiscal federalism highlight the incentives for revenue maximization at the local level as spurring developmental approaches to nurturing local industry. Alternatively, theories based on implementation bias and authoritarian fragmentation that focus on pathological local government behavior highlight the lack of control over local actors within a highly decentralized system. These models do not focus on variation beyond that created by underlying economic conditions created by history or geography: in other words, local governments may be *a priori* pro-development or corrupt due to a combination of fiscal decentralization and political centralization, but the consequences of these incentives vary with initial conditions.

This book seeks to explain the variation in local government behavior that is left unexplained by existing theories. By focusing particular attention on the economic and institutional roles played by local leaders, I explain why so many governments have had "helping hands," and why other local governments have not performed similar roles. I argue that significant variation in developmental orientation, and thus developmental outcomes, arises as a result of regionally varying incentives for promotion faced by county leaders as well as the formal and informal institutional roles that these leaders play.

Decentralization, Federalism, and Developmentalism

A key theme of the reform-initiating 11th Central Committee Third Plenum in 1978 was to devolve economic power to localities. Following the Plenum, local economies grew rapidly. Improvements in agricultural productivity gave way to rapid growth of local industry, particularly in township and village enterprises (TVEs).[1] While a conventional view sees China's growth as a market-driven process resulting from a relaxation of government controls, a more compelling understanding of China's growth attributes rapid growth to an increasingly pro-development orientation

[1] Many in-depth accounts of this growth experience have been written. See, for instance, Bramall (2006).

of many local governments.[2] With decentralization in a state-dominated economy, local governments in China have assumed highly interventionist roles, often taking on characteristics of a local developmental state.[3] Local governments often have more direct control over the economy than national counterparts, and the interventionism of Chinese local governments seems to increase as one moves down the administrative hierarchy. In one of the most cited accounts of developmentally minded local governments in China, Jean Oi's "local state corporatism," local governments act like corporations in their management of state firms while utilizing a "combination of inducements and administrative constraints characteristic of a state corporatist system" to both encourage and control the private sector (Oi 1999, 99). The local developmental state idea in China also finds a champion in the discussions of local development "models," and particularly the South Jiangsu or "Sunan" model (*sunan moshi,* 苏南模式).[4]

Analyses of China's growth often attribute this local "developmentalism" to incentives for revenue maximization following from increased fiscal decentralization. In the 1980s, the Party-state devolved expenditure and revenue collection authority to local levels in order to promote growth and facilitate the transition to a market economy (Shirk 1993).[5] Consequently, according to "market-preserving federalism," the central government committed itself to fiscal reforms that allowed local governments to keep marginal revenues, aligning local government incentives

[2] The conventional view comes in different forms, from the neoclassical market reforms perspective of Pei (1994) and Steinfeld (1998) to a structural reform and factor accumulation perspective that minimizes the role of government reforms, including Krugman (1994) and Young (2003), as well as to the peasant-led revolution idea of Zhou (1996). For a review of the debate on China's economic success as dependent on non-capitalist institutions versus fundamental market reforms, see Wu (2002) and Woo (1999), as well as Wu's response (Wu 2003).

[3] See Blecher and Shue (1996), Walder (1998), Oi (1999), Blecher (1991), Vogel (1990), Duckett (1998), and Thun (2006), among others. For a discussion of developmental states more broadly, see Johnson (1982) and Woo-Cumings (1999).

[4] The Sunan model was first identified in the mid 1980s, with the basic idea of development through rural collective industrialization. As described by Liu (2005), this was a "government intervention model" (*yizhong zhengfu ganyu moshi,* 一种政府干预模式) and a "local government corporatist model" (*difang zhengfu gongsi zhuyi moshi,* 地方政府公司注意模式). The Sunan model is often contrasted with a "Wenzhou model" emphasizing private sector development, but even this "private industry" model had a strong local government role: see Nolan and Dong (1990) and extended discussion in Bramall (2006). See Zhang (2009) and Tsai (2007) for more in-depth discussion of these models.

[5] According to Oi (1992), the tax-sharing systems of the early 1980s gave local finance officials no incentive to work hard, and localities only became entrepreneurial once fiscal authority was devolved.

with revenue maximization and leading to pro-market and pro-growth policies and behavior (Montinola, Qian, and Weingast 1995). Federalism induced competition among jurisdictions, leading to experimentation and imitation and increased factor mobility through competition for capital and migrant labor.[6]

Scholars in more recent years have questioned the fiscal federalism framework. Fiscal federalism "with Chinese characteristics" helps induce interjurisdictional competition, but without political centralization governments are as likely to have corrupt "grabbing hands" as developmental "helping hands," regardless of revenue imperatives.[7] As per Robert Klitgaard's famous formula, "corruption equals monopoly plus discretion minus accountability": with increasing discretion as a result of decentralization, failure to increase accountability will tend to result in increased corruption, all else equal (Klitgaard 1988, 75). Arguments that fuse local economic autonomy with enhanced political centralization thus have more explanatory power in terms of the China local growth success story. Xu (2011) and Landry (2008) describe a decentralized authoritarian regime that combines political centralization with economic decentralization, helping to explain both the alignment of local incentives with national goals as well as the responsiveness of localities to national reforms, albeit with "implementation bias."[8] In China's economically decentralized and

[6] Montinola, Qian, and Weingast (1995, 58) contend that competition induces local governments to secure property rights and "provide a hospitable environment for factors," while Qian and Roland (1998) argue that competition punishes corruption with capital flight, similar to the way that international capital markets discipline national governments through the threat of capital outflow (Obstfeld 1998). For additional market-preserving federalism arguments, see also Qian and Weingast (1997), Weingast (1995); Mckinnon (1997), and Jin, Qian, and Weingast (2005).

[7] Blanchard and Shleifer (2001) use this terminology in contrasting the performance of local governments in China and Russia. They argue that the degree of political control, as opposed to differences in intergovernmental fiscal relationship, explains why China's local governments favor growth and Russia's do not. For more on the "grabbing hand" and growth-hindering rent-seeking, see Shleifer and Vishny (2002), Krueger (1974), and Bhagwati (1982). Others have challenged market-preserving federalism on its own (technical) terms, maintaining that levels of fiscal decentralization did not actually increase during the reform era (Bramall 2008); that China is not de facto federal and that local governments have less autonomy than the market-preserving federalism paradigm suggests (Tsui and Wang 2004); that constraints to free factor mobility are still imposed by protectionist local governments (Young 2000; Naughton 2003; Bai et al. 2004; Tsai 2004); and, perhaps most importantly, that there is no constitutional constraint on altering the degrees of marginal revenue held by local governments, and that these sharing percentages have changed frequently and arbitrarily (Yang 2006, 143–147).

[8] In China's hierarchical system, central policies are distorted as they move down the hierarchy, with decisions increasingly reflecting the preferences of implementing local governments

politically centralized regime, officials are upwardly accountable, with little direct downward accountability above the village level. The key means by which the CCP maintains political centralization in an economically decentralized state is hierarchical control through personnel management. During the reform era, explicit rule-based personnel management has evolved considerably. Administratively, since the late 1980s and particularly the mid 1990s, the center has attempted to formalize and control the cadre management system through increased institutionalization.

Institutionalization of cadre management enables the central government to transmit priorities throughout the administrative hierarchy through control over personnel decisions. This hierarchical personnel management system enables yardstick competition for advancement between local leaders, and there is considerable evidence that the CCP emphasizes economic growth in these performance contracts.[9] Indeed, the "GDP worship" of local officials is often perceived as common knowledge (Zhuang 2007), and many studies have uncovered a relationship between growth and promotion, implying that performance management serves an effective development role.[10] This is the basis of the "tournament promotion" (*jinsheng jinbiaosai,* 晋升锦标赛) hypothesis: if growth is a key target, then meritocratic promotions will incentivize faster growth and enhance actual growth outcomes. According to this logic, the combination of economic

and agents: "by the time one has moved through six, seven, or more layers of the system, the cumulative distortion … can be great. Almost invariably, unanticipated and unwelcome consequences are part of the implementation process from the Center's perspective" (Lampton 1992, 57). This gives rise to what Naughton (1987) describes as "implementation bias."

[9] Landry (2008) quotes a State Planning Commission official (cited originally in Yin 2001): "The current government stresses that development is the fundamental principle. Economic development becomes a criterion for assessing local officials. The current cadre assessment overstresses the economic growth of the region led by the assessed officials. Moreover, the criteria for assessing economic growth are essentially superficial: the number of projects and enterprises established, and the growth rate of the local economy."

[10] Most influentially, Li and Zhou (2005) find that over 1979–1995, the likelihood of provincial leader promotion increases with economic performance. Similarly, Chen, Li, and Zhou (2005) demonstrate that not only are provincial leader promotions based on their own economic performance, but that the difference of per capita GDP growth relative to predecessors significantly predicts provincial promotion prospects. This finding is similar to that of Hsu and Shao (2014), who find that GDP performance relative to predecessors is a much more important determinant of provincial promotions than performance relative to other provinces. Bo (2002) finds that between 1978 and 1998, provincial leader promotions are sensitive to central revenue contributions. Additionally, Xu, Wang, and Shu (2007) find that cross-regional governor transfer increases GDP growth. Wu et al. (2013) find that GDP growth relative to predecessors is the best predictor of promotions of prefecture-level leaders.

decentralization and local policy autonomy with hierarchical compliance through political centralization helps provide an understanding for local developmentalism. In other words, economic and fiscal decentralization provide local governments with the *ability* to promote economic growth, and centralized political control provides local cadres with the *incentive* to promote economic growth.

Unexplained Regional Variation in Local Developmental Orientation

Yet a puzzle remains. Not all local government economic intervention has been positive; China has produced predatory local states that stand in stark contrast to the local developmental state idea. As Chalmers Johnson has noted, "The state *can* structure market incentives to achieve developmental goals ... but it can also structure them to enrich itself and friends at the expense of consumers, good jobs, and development" (Woo-Cumings 1999, 48). Some "developmentally" minded behavior can quickly become predatory, and many behaviors in an interventionist mode can become more predatory as time progresses (Tsai 2002, 250). For instance, the Asian Financial Crisis led many Asian countries that had previously been considered "developmental" to be defined as "crony capitalist." Variation can also be seen between local developmental states. Thun (2006) identifies three local development models in China: local developmental states, laissez-faire local states, and centrally controlled SOEs. More broadly, local governments often play distinctly nondevelopmental roles, and studies of local Chinese governments have utilized a wide range of definitions across the "developmental" and "predatory" spectrum.[11] Corruption is endemic, and much of this corruption is distinctly antidevelopment.[12]

[11] Blecher (1991) distinguishes between China's local "development states" and local "entrepreneurial states." In the former, entrepreneurship lies within enterprises, and the role of governments is to create the conditions for market-based development: the state "stays above the competitive fray but works to keep that fray vibrant" (Blecher 1991, 286). In the entrepreneurial state, the state is actively involved in productive activity. Similarly, Duckett (1998) documents the emergence of an "entrepreneurial state" in Tianjin in the early 1990s as local state agencies responded to structural constraints and growing market opportunities. For a discussion of different typologies of China's local states, see Saich (2002), Tsai (2002), and Baum and Shevchenko (1999).

[12] It is of course possible that corruption and development complement each other. Wedeman (2002, 177) notes that local governments may have a vested interest in local development, even if this interest is simply "for the crass purpose of increasing the size of the local economic pie from which they can extract a slice." Yet most literature highlights the antigrowth effect of corruption, an issue I return to in Chapter 3.

Why have some governments been more "developmental" than others? The authoritarian decentralization argument fusing economic decentralization with political centralization can explain away cases of predation and low growth as those in which political incentives fail to work. Local outcomes would be expected to vary if incentives for economic growth do not always travel down administrative ranks due to weak incentives or a lack of monitoring. However, this would only explain random variation in outcomes. As I show in this book, however, the variation in government approaches is systematic and varies by region. Current explanations for local developmentalism do not account for this systematic regional variation. Decentralization and local autonomy have resulted in high variation in county economic outcomes both across provinces and within provinces. There has been strong regionalism in economic outcomes; during most of the reform era, counties in coastal provinces have grown much faster than counties in other regions, and as a result poor counties are now concentrated in western and central provinces (see Figure 1.1).

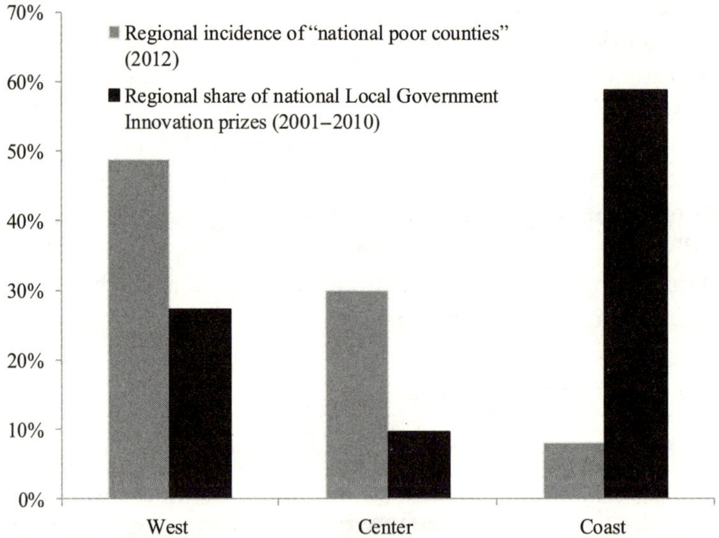

FIGURE 1.1. Regional variation in poverty and government innovation
Regional national poor counties (国家级贫困县) and Local Government Innovation Prize (中国地方政府创新奖) winners
Source: State Council Leading Group Office of Poverty Alleviation and Development (2012); Innovations & Excellence in Chinese Local Governance (中国地方政府创新奖), 2013 handout; author's calculations.

This economic regionalism can perhaps be explained by geographic conditions and local opportunity, but in addition to economic variation across regions, there has also been less-discussed variation in local governance across regions with regard to levels of corruption, institutional innovation, and government-business relations, as I demonstrate in later chapters (see Figure 1.1 for the regional contrast in Local Government Innovation Prize winners). I argue that these governance outcomes have been related to economic outcomes in virtuous and vicious circles; they are not merely consequences of growth outcomes, but also contributors to growth outcomes.

As a consequence of regional variation, an analysis of local government development orientation must take a sub-national perspective. Given China's vast regional differences in geography, culture, and institutions, applying a uniform national model to explain development outcomes is potentially misleading; this is especially true given that provinces and prefectures establish their own rules for fiscal transfers and criteria for personnel management. Much of the literature referenced above has a tendency to look at China as a single case rather than a set of regions/localities, which is problematic given that much national-level research necessarily involves national means, masking internal variation and leading to "mean-spirited" analysis (Snyder 2001, 98).[13] Sub-national comparison is thus important for studying China, a large country in which many policies and institutions have explicit regional variation, and in which the central Party-state often implements regional strategies that explicitly favor one region over another.[14] There is thus no reason to expect that the personnel management institutions and criteria for promotion that incentivize local leaders should be identical across regions and provinces; indeed, the central documents focused on local performance measurement are explicit about regional and local variation in targets.[15] Variation in incentives will lead to variation in outcomes,

[13] As King, Keohane, and Verba (1994, 208) write, "what may appear to be a single-case study, or a study of only a few cases, may indeed contain many potential observations, at different levels of analysis, that are relevant to the theory being evaluated." For more on "whole nation bias" see Rokkan (1970, Chapter 2) and Snyder (2001).

[14] Wang and Hu (1999) show how China's regionally divergent development paths have been a direct (and intentional) consequence of national policies. Similarly, Zweig's idea of "segmented deregulation" shows how central decision-makers as opposed to market forces determined regional comparative advantages in an increasingly open economy (Zweig 2002, 50).

[15] In observing regionally distinctive local government behavior, I follow Thun (2006, 9): "It is, of course, not unusual or new to focus on the developmental role of local government. It is less common to focus on systematic patterns of institutional *differences*

assuming that local actors have the autonomy and power to affect these outcomes; indeed that is the argument of this book.

Argument of the Book

Ask a Jiangsu county-level official why neighboring counties in Anhui have failed to develop, and nine times out of ten you will receive the same answer: "they're backwards" (*tamen de suzhi luohou*, 他们的素质落后). These assertions of cultural determinacy are made boldly and flippantly, representing an apparent long-term historical stereotype. Yet there are no ethnic or religious differences between these bordering counties, and cross-border migration is common and relatively unimpeded. Indeed, in the late 1990s, local interviews in Southern Jiangsu pointed to culture as a major reason for Northern Jiangsu's developmental challenge, in particular a "Central Plains stereotype" of a simple, satisfied people lacking drive (Jacobs 1999). As Northern Jiangsu has developed, the stereotype has slowly disappeared. However, while observed "cultural differences" seem to be a perceived consequence of economic development rather than a determinant of this development, "cadre culture" and local governance do differ in growth-affecting ways across the two provinces. Provincial institutions have interacted with local conditions to alter local institutional cultures. Cadres interact with each other, with businesses, and with local citizenry in ways that have been largely shaped by these provincial institutions. I argue that this behavior is a direct consequence of central policies that work their way down the administrative hierarchy in oft-unanticipated ways. The consequent corruption and low-growth economic environments, i.e., "backwardness," result not from a lack of upward accountability and control, but rather from high levels of upward accountability with inconsistent objectives and no local oversight in the form of downward accountability.

More broadly, in this book I explain regional variation in county development outcomes by analyzing the relationship between provincial political institutions, local governance, and leadership roles. I focus on two related questions: *What is the role of county Party secretaries in determining local governance and growth outcomes? Why do county Party secretaries emphasize particular developmental priorities?* These

between localities. There is no single dominant approach to development at the local level, whether it be market-led growth or local state corporatism, but rather multiple patterns ... There is no one-size-fits-all development approach, but a mosaic of local patterns within the national framework."

questions are interrelated. Much of the variation in county economic outcomes, and particularly in pro-growth governance as a condition for high growth, stems from the differing roles and abilities of county Party secretaries in creating pro-growth institutional environments, and these leadership roles are themselves explained by the incentives given to county leaders by provincial authorities. Here, I briefly elaborate on these questions and provide the basic arguments that I will flesh out in later chapters.

What is the Role of County Party Secretaries in Determining Local Governance and Growth Outcomes?

As a starting point for analyzing how leader actions affect local governance and growth, it is essential to understand the variation in county growth and the relationship between governance and growth. The developmental state literature has identified many ways in which governments can intervene proactively and positively, and in China the importance of local governments is usually taken as a given.[16] Yet reform and openness along with socioeconomic development have altered the bases for local growth and the role of local governments. As China has recentralized fiscal revenues since the mid 1990s, the local revenue/expenditure gap has expanded and the importance of intergovernmental fiscal transfers for local government finances has increased dramatically, with important implications for expenditure priorities.[17] Fiscal reforms have not taken place in a vacuum: China's socioeconomic conditions have changed rapidly, altering local incentives and capabilities. In particular, a growing private sector and reduced barriers to mobility have increased the relative importance of private mobile capital. As the private sector has grown, the role of local governments has necessarily changed, with less potential for direct management of firms. Fiscal reforms have increased incentives for local industrialization in order to generate local revenue sources, and

[16] As Walder (1998) writes, "... the question is not really whether the role of local government has been large; the question is why and how local governments have played the role that they have ..."

[17] Fiscal reforms include tax and fee reform, tax sharing, "budgetizing" extra-budgetary funds, etc. Formerly, extra-budgetary funds provided the greatest degree of freedom and autonomy for county governments (Blecher and Shue 1996), but national laws have worked to bring these funds on-budget, with varying degrees of success across different regions (Zhan 2011). For the incentive effects of targeted and general transfers, see Baretti, Huber, and Lichtblau (2002) and Bird and Smart (2002). Zhang (2009)

the growth of private capital has enabled counties to attract industrial investment.

In this context, China's counties, along with the country as a whole, have become more capital-intensive, particularly over the past decade, and investment has become the dominant source of growth. This compares to the 1990s, when labor and capital (particularly foreign direct investment) flowed to large cities, and county-level growth was led by productivity increases, predominantly through restructuring. As the ability to attract capital has become the most important determinant of county growth, the policies of successful local governments have focused on improving local investment environments. The most important determinant of the ability to attract investment has shifted from preferential policies, which have largely become equalized across counties and provinces, to county reputation, infrastructure, and service-oriented government, referring to government that is both pro-business in the sense of preventing *government failures* of corruption and excessive fee collection, and also service-oriented in its ability to assist firms through correction of *market failures* and more direct "developmental state"-type interventions.

I will argue that local leaders determine the effectiveness and direction of local governance. A strong individual role is an important, but unexplored, aspect of the pro-growth "authoritarian decentralization" literature described above. One well-known combination of economic/fiscal decentralization and political centralization applies a multidivisional "M-form" corporate hierarchy to China's intergovernmental relations, which sees each branch (local government) division as a semi-autonomous unit under central control: the leaders of each branch compete in tournament competitions for recognition and promotion.[18] Note that the incentives and behavior of individuals within the branch are assumed to respond to the branch (local government) leader. In other words, local leaders are seen as branch CEOs. Oi (1999) describes the county Party secretary as "akin to a 'hands-on' chairman of the board, who sets policy direction, decides development strategy, and makes long-term plans." Indeed, as a result of this interventionist role, county leaders are often referred to as

provides a discussion of provincial rules regarding sub-provincial revenue assignments. See also Ning, Li, and Tian (2012).

[18] The "M-form" hierarchy was initially developed in the firm literature by Chandler (1962) and Williamson (1975). Williamson's taxonomy includes three types of corporate structure: unitary "U-forms" with complementary (nonindependent) business functions, multidivisional M-forms comprised of related self-contained U-form organizations, and holding companies (H-forms). Several authors have utilized this conception in relation

"mom and dad officials" (*fumuguan*, 父母官) (Zhong 2003).[19] Yet while a strong role is observed and, often, assumed, implying that local Chinese leaders are likely to have systematic effects on economic outcomes, these effects have not been explored systematically in the literature in the way that CEO personal effects on firm outcomes have been.[20] Moreover, many studies see recent institutional trends in China as weakening the power of local Party secretaries, both as a consequence of strengthened bureaucracies and as a consequence of institutional reforms to limit individual power.[21]

I argue instead that China's local leaders continue to wield significant amounts of power through formal and informal institutions, and they are able to affect growth outcomes through both policy control and personnel

to China: Qian and Xu (1993); Maskin, Qian, and Xu (2000); Qian, Roland, and Xu (2006).

19 Vogel (1990), speaking of the Inner Delta Counties, argues that while all made rapid advances, "the speed and thoroughness with which they took advantage of their situation appeared to depend most on the sixiang (thought, i.e., attitude) of the county leaders." Similarly, in explaining differentials in city-level growth, Zweig (1997) focuses on "the entrepreneurship and strategies of its leadership" in addition to central/provincial preferential policies, path dependence, and opportunities (endowments and comparative advantages). Song and He (2003), cited in Guo (2009), quote a county mayor telling the mayor of New Haven, Connecticut: "The biggest difference is that you do not seem to manage the economy much. When I was mayor of Shouguang my main effort was on grasping the economy, everything from fiscal growth to enterprise profit, peasant income, private economy, structural adjustments ..."

20 Systematic leadership effects on growth have been assumed but empirically elusive in much of the international economics literature, with the important exception of Jones and Olken (2005). The "political budget cycle" literature identifies strong effects on government expenditure and individual manipulation of monetary and fiscal policy to ensure individual reelection, particularly in autocracies (as opposed to democracies). See Drazen (2001); Franzese (2002); Brender and Drazen (2005); Jones and Olken (2005). The economic literature on firm performance also suggests a strong role for individual CEOs in determining firm outcomes, and shows that where decision-making is concentrated, leader effects are amplified (i.e., there is greater variation in outcomes) (Adams, Almeida, and Ferreira 2005). Brady and Spence (2010) note that, "Although practitioners emphasize the role of leaders in economic growth, the social sciences have been slow to measure and include leadership in their economic growth models, largely because of the endogeneity problem." Bunce (1981, 14), in looking at leader transitions in the Soviet Union and western democratic states, remarks: "What counts in succession, then, is not so much the appearance of new faces, but rather the fact that these new faces may do new things. Ironically enough, this rather obvious point has been lost on political scientists."

21 As China's bureaucracy has become more professionalized, the role of leaders has potentially diminished, with policy interventions gaining a bureaucratic logic. This argument is implicit in Blecher and Shue (1996). Similarly, Zhong (2003) argues that in recent years the expansion of power of prefecture authorities has partially hollowed out county governments. Many county government bureaus and offices have been "verticalized,"

control over the local bureaucracy. Local leaders affect growth outcomes through system bargaining for fiscal transfers and investments, and they can affect local investment environments as well as firm efficiency through direct firm-level interventions, control over development zone policies, and instilling more pro-growth local governance. Leaders' personal characteristics determine their personal capacity to allocate resources, promote firm efficiency, attract investment, and bargain within the system. I propose that four broadly defined characteristics determine their growth-effectiveness: connections (system bargaining as well as relationships, or "*guanxi*," with private businesses), creativity (local innovations and entrepreneurialism), control (ensuring cadre compliance and responsiveness), and courage (daring to implement controversial reforms). When leaders have connections, creativity, control, and courage, the counties they lead exhibit effective governance and have achieved economic successes; counties whose leaders do not have these characteristics have fallen behind.

Why Do County Party Secretaries Emphasize Particular Development Priorities?

If leaders differ in their approach to local economic growth, is this dependent simply on random variation in personal characteristics, or are leader actions and policies shaped by institutions? County Party secretaries decide whether and how to promote growth in order to maximize personal utility; in other words, they behave in a strategic way so as to maximize attainment of their preferences.[22] Constrained in the tools they can use, leaders' solutions to personal utility maximization are based on the institutions in which they operate. Leaders both create and are subject to what Tsai (2002, 14–18) calls the "local logics of economic possibility," and their approaches to local growth and governance depend on evolving economic and fiscal constraints as well as personal incentives provided by cadre management systems. Officials in China are upwardly accountable, with little direct downward accountability; therefore, the personnel management system has become the most important institution for explicitly shaping local leader incentives.[23] Personnel management is designed to ensure

i.e., removed from authority of county government and placed under higher government offices.

[22] This "calculus approach" is distinguished from a "cultural approach" that emphasizes behavior bounded by actor worldview, focused on routines or patterns of behavior to "satisfice" rather than maximize utility (Hall and Taylor 1996).

[23] Downward accountability consists of leadership accountability not only to citizens but also to lower level officials. While China's leaders face no direct downward accountability,

compliance in a principal-agent framework with asymmetric information and limited monitoring capacity.[24] By helping the center achieve local compliance without the need for constant monitoring, the personnel management system provides a partial solution to the principal-agent problem.[25]

Although the number of formal institutions and rules guiding China's cadre management system have increased significantly over the reform period, questions remain regarding the degree to which these formal rules are followed as well as the priorities that are embedded in the system (direction of control) and the effectiveness of the system (degree of control). In terms of direction, performance evaluation systems need to be constructed with an eye towards specific goals, yet at the most basic level a debate remains over whether the underlying rationale behind China's system is development or political control, or whether these two goals can exist simultaneously. Cadres also face incentives outside of the cadre management system. While ideology has decreased in importance, privatization in a growing economy has provided potential career possibilities for cadres who seek to "jump into the sea" (*xiahai,* 下海) of private business. These outside opportunities may have changed the efficacy of promotion incentives: although the cadre management system includes bonuses, monetary opportunities outside the system, particularly in wealthy regions, are no doubt greater.[26]

it can factor indirectly through performance evaluations. Elections at the village level have introduced responsiveness of village officials, who may now demand more of their county superiors than in the past, as demonstrated by evidence that village elections positively influence local public goods provision. See Martinez-Bravo et al. (2011).

24 The principal-agent problem is integral to the analysis in this book and more broadly to analyses of central-local relations in China and elsewhere. The basic "problem" lies in identifying how principals can ensure compliance by agents given asymmetric information that tends to favor agents and results in the potential for shirking behavior. For a discussion of the development of the principal-agent model as part of the new economics of organization, as well as its applicability to public bureaucracies, see Moe (1984). For early applications of the principal-agent model to Chinese political actors, see Rozelle (1994), Huang (1996), and Oi (1999).

25 Note that there is no full solution to the principal-agent problem: the structure of personnel management gives power to the center, but there are still procedural implementation and monitoring problems. This is one of the key contributions of the "fragmented authoritarianism" literature, which highlights problems of implementation bias and bureaucratic decision-making, combining a central rational-actor approach with a local cellular process-based approach (Lieberthal and Lampton 1992). While institutions provide a structure that incentivizes and constrains agents, "bounded-rational" agents still make decisions based on personal considerations and personal psychology – in other words, agency matters and institutions are not wholly determinant.

26 These personal wealth-generating opportunities can be both legal ("retiring" into a private business) or illegal (corruption). For instance, one prosecutor investigating a

Despite the changing socioeconomic environment, I argue that personnel management institutions are highly effective at transmitting political and economic priorities down the administrative hierarchy, and that the strength of the cadre management system in providing promotion incentives to county leaders has not declined as private sector opportunities have increased. Where many others agree that upward accountability remains effective, the originality of my argument is that although cadres are equally responsive to promotion incentives across regions, regional goals and incentives themselves differ, resulting in regional variation in cadre behavior and local development outcomes. In particular, I will demonstrate that the incentives provided to county leaders focus predominantly on CCP goals of growth and stability, with the emphasis differing by region: poorer central provinces have emphasized stability maintenance in their management of country-level cadres, while wealthy coastal provinces have emphasized economic growth.

To return to the overarching question: Why have certain regions in China had virtuous circles of growth and governance improvement while others have experienced vicious circles of low growth and poor governance? I argue that local leaders head highly interventionist governments and have large personal systemic effects on outcomes. They are incentivized by a hierarchical promotion system whose criteria are based largely on performance, but these performance criteria differ between regions and provinces as part of a national strategy to maintain both high rates of growth as well as social and political stability. This system has incentivized leaders in poorer regions to emphasize stability maintenance, leading to less effective government-business relations and lower institutional capacity, and it has incentivized leaders in wealthier regions to emphasize economic growth, which has in turn incentivized these leaders to pursue effective government-business relations and heightened control over local cadres. Given the high degree of power wielded by county Party secretaries, this incentive system has been partly responsible for producing regional inequality in outcomes. Three decades after Deng's famous

sensitive local case, speaking about a corrupt county Party secretary, describes him as "just a businessman; in his hands power is simply a money-making tool (*zhuanqian de gongju*, 赚钱的工具)" (Wang, Liu, and Wang 2010). Montinola, Qian, and Weingast (1995) argue that cadres in advanced regions "no longer care to be promoted to posts in the higher level government ..." Similarly, Zhong (2003) finds that most county level officials do not expect promotions, as the system is pyramid-shaped, with fewer positions at the top. This is the opposite conclusion of Guo (2007, 382), who finds that cadres have no viable career options outside of the political hierarchy, as "the job market for them in the private sector hardly exists."

aphorism to let some get rich first, China's hierarchical cadre management system is still helping some get rich faster.

Research Design

The arguments in this book are based on research findings from fieldwork in six bordering counties in Jiangsu and Anhui provinces as well as quantitative analyses using unique county-level economic and biographical data. In-depth county cases are complemented by broader provincial and nationwide analyses. The primary focus is on top leadership (county Party secretaries) in rural counties (*xian,* 县) and county-level cities (*xianjishi,* 县级市), excluding county-level urban districts (*shixiaqu,* 市辖区).[27] Counties are arguably the most important hierarchical level in China with regard to economic growth as well as political stability.[28] As the center of the rural-urban nexus, counties have comprehensive economic responsibilities and are also key for social and political stability, with county governments responsible for managing many of the major social contradictions in China's development (Zhu 2011). Decentralization in the reform era has increased county government involvement in local economic and industrial development, and by concentrating local power has also strengthened the hands of local county Party secretaries.[29] These

[27] As sub-divisions of urban cities, districts have less autonomy than counties and county-level cities, making comparisons difficult. While counties and county-level cities have slightly different administrative responsibilities, they differ predominantly in levels of industrialization and urbanization, making comparison important. Of the 2853 units at the county-level in China, there are 1456 counties, 369 county-level cities, and 857 urban districts. In addition, there is one special district (*tequ,* 特区), one forestry district (*linqu,* 林区), 117 autonomous counties (*zizhixian,* 自治县), 49 banners (*qi,* 旗), and three autonomous banners (*zizhiqi,* 自治旗). These other categories are almost entirely located within minority/autonomous regions.

[28] China's administrative hierarchy is divided into five official levels: the center, provinces, prefectures, counties, and townships. Villages are an unofficial, albeit very important, unit beneath townships, which, according to the 1982 Constitution, are self-governing units (Joseph 2014). The county-level government structure and function has been remarkably persistent over time. The "county" has survived without interruption for 2700 years, beginning as the lowest level of government in imperial times, and nearly one-third of China's counties have existed for more than 1000 years (Tian, Luo, and Zeng 2005).

[29] According to Barnett (1967, 117), the county is "the most important administrative unit in rural China now, as in the past... Most counties have tended to be relatively stable administrative units, because more often than not they have constituted natural centers of transportation, communications, industry, and commerce. Traditionally, the county seat has served not only as an administrative headquarters but also as the economic and social center of a fairly well-defined region." Oi (1999, 103) adds that "this description remains apt today in many respects, with the exception that the county has now taken on a much more active role in fostering local economic development ..."

county "first-in-command," or *yibashou*, are frequently seen as unchallenged bosses of "independent kingdoms"; the leader of no other level of administration in China has the same degree of unchecked power.

In selecting counties for analysis, I controlled for initial conditions, geography, culture, and history in order to examine how variation in provincial institutions leads to variation in local government behavior and developmental outcomes.[30] I therefore sought out a border between two regions in which counties on both sides of the border had similar levels of development in the early 1990s. Selection of a set of six bordering counties in northwest Jiangsu Province and eastern Anhui Province enabled matching along these terms.

In selecting provinces, Jiangsu and Anhui are in many ways ideal comparative cases for county-level analysis. The two provinces have the same number of county-level units (105) and similar numbers of rural counties and county-level cities (58 and 61, respectively), as well as large populations (5th and 8th largest, respectively) densely packed in small areas (24th and 22nd in land area). Border regions in the two provinces have similar geography. Importantly, the two provinces are representative of China's coastal and central regions. China's economic regions are clearly defined, and provinces within regions tend to share highly similar economic outcomes.[31] As shown in Figure 1.2, the coastal region includes Beijing, Tianjin, Shanghai, Jiangsu, Zhejiang, Fujian, Shandong, and Guangdong, and central China includes Shanxi, Anhui, Jiangxi, Hunan, Henan, and Hubei.[32] In 2010, these provinces were home to 59 percent of China's population and accounted for 68 percent of China's GDP. Respectively, the coastal region accounted for 48 percent of

[30] Here I follow North (1990) in defining institutions as "the rules of the game in a society" and "the humanly devised constraints that shape human interaction." This institutionalist perspective facilitates an examination of the institutional foundations of economic outcomes, treating the state and governance as variables rather than idealized assumptions. Rather than assume either a benevolent government or an autocratic leviathan, I instead seek to understand how states with enough strength and capacity to reduce transaction costs and promote growth can limit themselves from acting predatorily and abusing their authority (Weingast 1993).

[31] Several studies have highlighted systematic differences between central and coastal provinces in terms of fiscal capacity and economic outcomes. See, for example, Fan (1997); Wei et al. (1997); Wei, Wang, and Bai (2013).

[32] Hainan and Hebei are borderline cases that are often included in coastal China, but both are much more similar to central China in terms of per capita wealth and levels of economic development. For instance, while no other coastal province has per capita GDP under 40,000 RMB, Hebei per capita GDP is only 28,351 RMB, and Hainan per capita GDP is only 23,770 RMB, much closer to the central region average of 24,123 RMB. In the analyses in this book, I exclude Hainan and Hebei, focusing instead on the core coastal and central regions of provinces with similar characteristics.

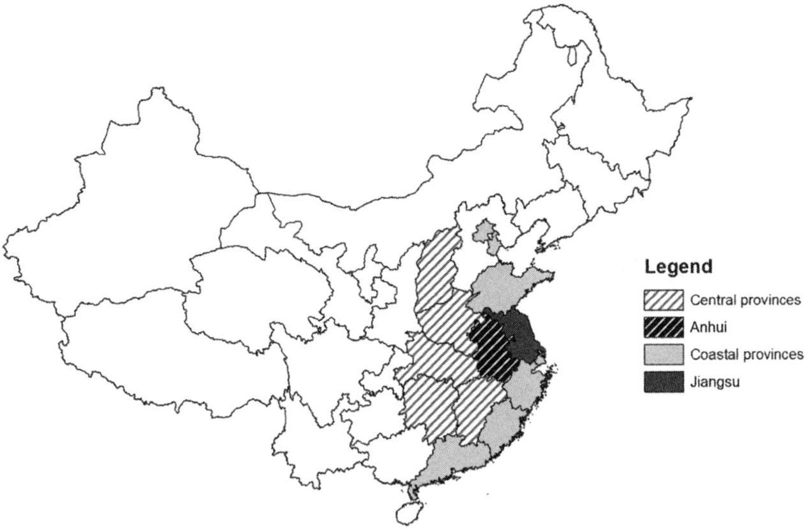

FIGURE 1.2. Map of coastal and central provinces

China's GDP and 32 percent of the population, while the central region accounted for 20 percent of GDP and 27 percent of the population. With a per capita GDP of 20,749 RMB, Anhui in 2010 was slightly poorer than the central region average (24,123 RMB); with a per capita GDP of 52,642 RMB, Jiangsu was slightly richer than the coastal region average (49,194 RMB). In other words, the coast is approximately twice as wealthy as the center, and Jiangsu and Anhui are representative of this divergence.[33]

Although Jiangsu is much richer than Anhui overall, wide variance in sub-provincial county income means that there are many counties with similar per capita income and similar levels of industrialization. In 1995, counties in Southern Jiangsu were already comparatively rich, but income in Northern Jiangsu and Anhui was similarly distributed, as seen in the upper panel of Figure 1.3. However, the provinces diverged over the past two decades. By 2010, every one of the poorest category counties was in Anhui.[34] And while per capita growth and investment have consistently been above the national mean in Jiangsu, they have consistently been below the national mean in Anhui, although Anhui has closed the investment gap in recent years (Figure 1.4).

[33] In recent years, Anhui has grown slightly faster than Jiangsu, but in 2013 Jiangsu's per capita GDP (74,607 RMB) remained 2.4 times greater than Anhui's (31,684 RMB).

[34] Here, "categories" are determined by Jenks optimization, divided into eight bins.

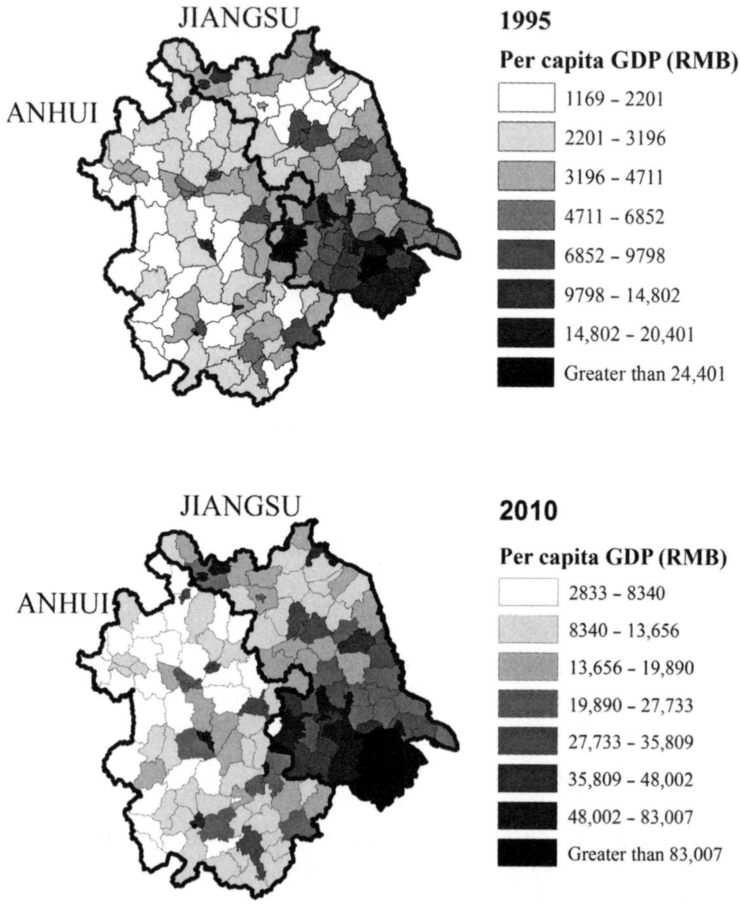

FIGURE 1.3. Jiangsu and Anhui county income distribution, 1995 and 2010
Note: Cut-off values are calculated using Jenks (natural breaks) optimization method, which minimizes the average deviation from the category mean while maximizing each category's deviation from other category means, seeking to minimize within-category variation and maximize between-category variation.

Within these two provinces, fieldwork focused on six neighboring counties in northeastern Anhui and northwestern Jiangsu.[35] The counties selected are "typical" within their province but also "most similar" (or matched) to the neighboring counties from the other province across

[35] In addition to interviews in these six counties, I conducted shorter-term fieldwork and interviews in neighboring counties and the prefecture-level cities administratively above these counties, as well as interviews in Nanjing and Beijing.

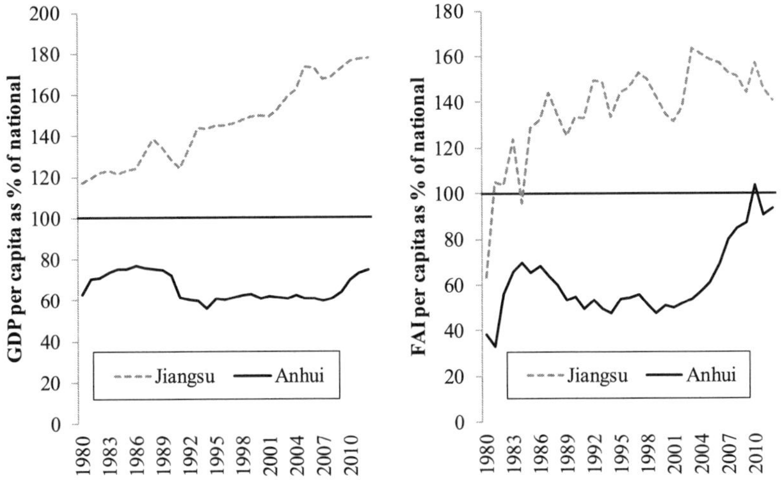

FIGURE 1.4. Per capita GDP investment in Jiangsu and Anhui, 1980–2012
Ratio of provincial to national GDP (left) and FAI (right) per capita (100 = equality), %
Source: China Data Online; author's calculations.

dimensions of geography, shared history, and initial conditions at the start of the analysis in the mid 1990s.[36] All six counties are located along the shared provincial border. Interestingly, and of considerable importance for ruling out historic and persistent provincial differences between the cross-provincial county pairs, two of the three Jiangsu counties were historically part of Anhui. Mingguang City in Anhui and Xuyi County in Jiangsu were a unified single county (Xujia County) under Anhui jurisdiction until the mid twentieth century. Similarly, Sihong County in Jiangsu was formerly under Anhui jurisdiction. All six counties have similar climates, dominated by plains and surrounded by water. The geographic location of the six counties is shown in Figure 1.5.

By selecting northwest Jiangsu counties and eastern Anhui counties, counties were matched across initial wealth, geography, and history,

[36] Seawright and Gerring (2008) divide potential case study selection strategies into seven types: typical, diverse, extreme, deviant, influential, most similar, most different. For large N analysis, "typical" case study selection is based on residual minimization; "most similar" is based on matching. Random sampling of the counties is not ideal for selecting a small sample from a large population; such a strategy can produce a sample that does not represent the population (Seawright and Gerring 2008). Purposive selection becomes necessary, and it is key to find not only a representative sample, but a sample with useful variation across the dimensions of interest.

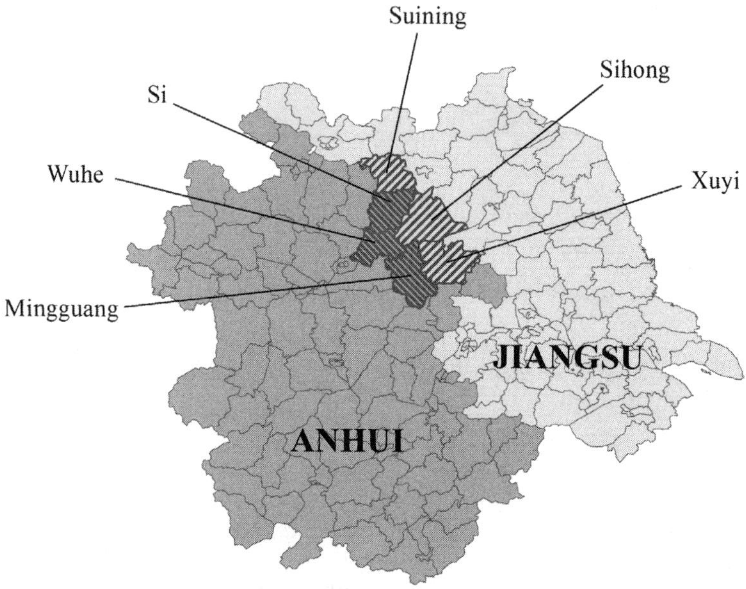

FIGURE 1.5. Sample counties in Jiangsu and Anhui

with variation coming from provincial institutions and local initiative, enabling an examination of how provincial institutions lead to variation in the dependent variable, economic and institutional development over 1994–2010. Looking at the data presented in Table 1.1 (or finding the counties in Figure 1.3), it is clear that in the mid 1990s, the three Anhui counties were on average wealthier than their Jiangsu counterparts. But by 2010, the Jiangsu counties were all much more economically successful. This is similar to the larger story of Jiangsu and Anhui. Both sets of counties have grown at or near their respective provincial averages over 1994–2010, although this growth rate has been lower in Anhui counties (9.2 percent) than Jiangsu counties (12.5 percent). Across many of the categories presented in Table 1.1, the Anhui counties match the provincial average, while the Jiangsu case counties are less developed than the provincial average (less urban, more agricultural, less wealthy), but similar to the average for Northern Jiangsu. In other words, these counties are not outliers, and are in fact fairly representative of their provinces (or, in the Jiangsu case, representative of a region within the province). While many counties in Anhui and Jiangsu could have been selected to match initial wealth, the geographic proximity of these six counties and the

TABLE 1.1. *Case county statistics and provincial county averages, 2010 (except where noted)*

	Jiangsu				Anhui			
	Xuyi	Sihong	Suining	Prov avg	Mingguang	Wuhe	Si	Prov avg
Area (sq. km)	2493	2731	1767	1476	2359	1595	1787	1828
Population (1000)	659	909	1039	905	533	622	799	647
Urban population (%)	43.8	41.4	41.0	48.6	38.4	31.2	18.5	33.7
Per capita GDP, 1994 (RMB)	2168	2235	1838	5093	2545	1840	1610	2124
Per capita GDP, 2010 (RMB)	20,032	17,797	15,034	52,080	10,492	12,912	9,512	14,543
Real GDP growth, 1994–2010 (CAGR)	12.7	11.4	11.9	12.5	6.5	10.3	9.5	9.3
Revenue share of GDP (%)	9.0	7.3	6.5	7.2	7.5	5.1	3.8	9.6
Expenditure share of GDP (%)	14.6	16.4	14.2	10.9	18.2	15.7	16.8	19.5
Primary sector share of GDP (%)	19.6	22.8	21.2	12.5	32.1	37.8	38.4	23.6
FAI share of GDP, 2006–2010 avg. (%)	111.9	81.9	62.1	52.2	47.4	44.9	40.7	46.9

historic fluidity of the provincial border around these counties helps to allay concerns of divergent geographic, historical, and cultural influences.

In these counties, fieldwork consisted of six months of fact-finding interviews from October to December 2012 and April to June 2013. In addition to interviews with local officials and citizens, case study analysis also benefited from the collection of local documents and media related to finance, local economic conditions, and government work plans. Appendix 1 describes the interview process.

The qualitative case studies are complemented by quantitative analyses at both the national and regional level based on a unique dataset that includes general economic data, detailed fiscal data, census data, geographic data, and county leadership biographies. Appendix 2 describes data sources and presents descriptive statistics. The most original and important data are biographical data covering all counties and county-level cities in Jiangsu and Anhui over 1994–2010.[37] Biographical data include age, gender, ethnicity, year of party entry, hometown, education, previous employment experience, and subsequent employment. In total, the Jiangsu and Anhui database consists of 2023 county-year observations of county Party secretaries between 1994 and 2010. These data enable analysis of the sources of economic growth, the systematic economic roles of county leaders, and the promotion incentives faced by these leaders.

Structure of the Book

The book proceeds as follows. Chapter 2 analyzes county growth variance and provides evidence on the correlates of growth at the county level, demonstrating the importance of provincial policies and institutions. A discussion of China's evolving factor markets, particularly for land and labor, demonstrates the developmental trajectory of China's county growth over the reform era: from TVE-based rural industrial growth in the 1980s to city-led growth in the 1990s, followed by robust county development based on investment attraction over the past decade. Growth accounting exercises and growth regressions identify correlates of growth and support this general story. Chapter 3 then argues that

[37] The year 1994 is selected as a starting point because of the fiscal and administrative reforms of the early 1990s. Insufficient data are available pre-1994 to enable a comparison of these two broadly defined reform era periods, so starting in 1994 maximizes the time period over which I expect to observe a relatively stable tournament promotion system.

much of the variation in economic outcomes across counties can be explained by differences in local governance. Government effectiveness determines the attractiveness of a region for mobile capital, and government approaches to private capital help boost productivity. Quantitative analysis highlights the relationship between government effectiveness and growth, while case studies highlight the pro-growth nature of combating government failures (corruption and excessive fees) and correcting market failures through proactive state-business relations.

Chapter 4 turns to the individual: China's county Party secretaries are given high degrees of formal and informal power and autonomy, extending from cadre management to direct economic intervention. After demonstrating that county Party secretaries have systematic growth effects, the chapter looks at cases from the six sample counties to generate a framework through which local leaders affect local economic outcomes, finding that the most important local leader characteristics are connections, creativity, courage, and control. Chapter 5 looks at promotion incentives, finding that in Jiangsu and coastal counties more broadly, county leaders are promoted based on economic growth, while in Anhui and central provinces they are not. Moreover, growth itself is based on leader initiative rather than patron ties, implying that in China's coastal areas, a "tournament promotion hypothesis" holds, meaning that yardstick competition of local leaders based on economic outcomes helps to explain rapid economic growth. Chapter 6 analyzes this dichotomous regional approach to promotions, providing further evidence that counties in Anhui and other central provinces emphasize stability maintenance over economic development. This surprising phenomenon can be explained by the developmental interaction and contradiction between the central Party-state's dual objectives of stability and growth. I conclude by tying all of these findings together into a unified framework for local institutional and economic development, and by discussing the implications and importance of this research.

2

Understanding China's County-Level Economic Growth

Scientific development is all about development: the key is discovering and scientifically confronting the relevant contradictions that impede further development at the current stage of development. Xuyi is currently at the beginning stages of industrialization. At this stage, the most important contradiction is the need to speed up industrialization despite weak economic foundations. This contradiction manifests itself in needing to find outside help – the difficulty of attracting investment.

– *Former Xuyi County Party Secretary Wang Youfu (Wang 2005, 79)*

The economic historian and the local industrial promotion agency are both interested in economic growth. Perhaps they should compare notes more often. A sound and useful body of general principles of economic development must be derived at least partly from studies of specific local situations. Conversely, a sound and useful approach to specific problems of promotion and development in a community or a region requires an understanding of general principles.

– *Hoover and Fisher (1949, 175)*

In May 1994, China's State Council approved Anhui Province's application to upgrade the administrative status of Jiashan County (嘉山县) to a county-level city (*xianjishi*, 县级市). Along with the administrative upgrade, Jiashan got a new name: Mingguang (明光), the city of bright light. As its new name implied, Mingguang in the early 1990s was a developmental success story with a seemingly bright future. Per capita GDP in 1993 was 2383 RMB, 25.4 percent greater than Anhui's county average. Mingguang was geographically well situated, directly on the rail line from Bengbu City to Chuzhou City (and on to Shanghai), and only an hour and a half from Nanjing on the #104 National Highway. The local ground was blessed with abundant clay minerals (palygorskite/attapulgite, *aotubang,* 凹凸棒) with uses in pharmaceuticals, pesticides, and fertilizer. Wang Daohan (汪道涵), the county's most famous son and a former Shanghai mayor (and mentor/patron to General Secretary Jiang Zemin), had recently become the president of the Association for Relations Across the Taiwan Straits (ARATS) and continued to encourage Shanghainese investors to target funds at his hometown (Interview AH104). The new administrative "county-level city" status gave Mingguang more favorable tax treatment and more direct access to provincial authorities.[1]

Xuyi County in Jiangsu Province borders Mingguang to the east. Belonging administratively to Huaian Prefecture, Xuyi is part of Jiangsu's "backwards" northern region, Subei (苏北). Despite being less than a two-hour drive from Jiangsu's capital city, Nanjing, and the outskirts of the Shanghai metropolitan area, Xuyi had been left behind. Per capita GDP in 1993 was only 51 percent of the provincial average, and while both Xuyi and Mingguang were poorer than the national county average, Mingguang was 6 percent richer per capita than Xuyi in 1994.

Mingguang in 1994 seemed to have a brighter future than Xuyi, but by 2010 Xuyi had nearly twice as much income on per capita terms as Mingguang (14,330 RMB versus 7579 RMB). Multiple industrial development zones in Xuyi now host highly profitable domestic and foreign manufacturing firms. While Mingguang has the same basic city plan that it did two decades ago, Xuyi's county seat has developed multiple "city" centers that have become increasingly modern as they have progressively moved east, with wide roads and tree-lined streets. For the past decade, Xuyi has branded itself as the crawfish capital of China, hosting a "Crawfish Festival" (*longxia jie,* 龙虾节) each summer that attracts tens of thousands of visitors and serves as an annual occasion for proactive investment promotion. Investors from the region praise high levels of local administrative efficiency and efficacy as well as the "helping hand" provided by the Xuyi government. Some of these same investors and many others identify the unhelpful attitude of Mingguang's officials as a major deterrent to investment. Mingguang is most famous for a set of cases of corruption "nests" (*wo'an,* 窝案) discovered and rooted out over the past twenty years.

1 County-level cities earn this status through a combination of economic success (GDP in the entire county as well as in the county seat itself) and bargaining. Once the status is attained, these cities become a half-step higher in administrative grade and can deal with provincial authorities directly. See Jacobs (1999).

The Mingguang and Xuyi divergence is not unique: lying just north of Mingguang and Xuyi, respectively, Wuhe (Anhui) and Sihong (Jiangsu) share a similar albeit less extreme story, and even further north, Si (Anhui) was left behind by Suining (Jiangsu). These six case counties are not outliers; more generally, Northern Jiangsu counties outgrew neighboring Anhui counties that had had similar levels of income in the mid 1990s.

What happened? I posed this question to dozens of economic officials, entrepreneurs, and investors in the six case counties. Their responses diverged in specific details, but almost unanimously highlighted several similar themes: cultural and historical differences, geography, provincial policies, local governance, and good leadership. It is worth quoting at length from one Jiangsu county deputy finance bureau chief who tried to explain why Northern Jiangsu (Subei) is backwards compared to Southern Jiangsu (Sunan) and why Anhui is backwards compared to Jiangsu:

> We need to look from a historical perspective. There aren't many land resources in Sunan, so they developed other industries. It's also close to Shanghai. And then there's the Suzhou-Singapore connection, which brought in new management methods and human capital. There's also the historical Silk Road. This is to say that that area has always been developed. On the other hand, Subei from a historical perspective has been just one big agricultural plain with lots of land and people all dependent on the land. Subei's development really started with [Jiangsu Province Party Secretary] Li Yuanchao who wanted to close the gap. This was done in two ways: fiscal transfers and Sunan enterprises moving north to Subei. The latter happened because Subei had lots of land which it could offer cheaply, and also lots of migrants were returning and labor was cheap and plentiful. In deciding where to locate, enterprises have to consider people's overall quality (*ren de pubian suzhi,* 人的普遍素质) and the local environment as well as preferential tax policies. Anhui can't give away land as cheaply or support enterprises enough, but the bigger problem is the people's lack of quality. The cadre environment is entirely different (*ganbu suzhi dou buyiyang,* 干部素质都不一样). This cadre environment means that enterprises don't want to invest there and banks don't want to support them. If local funds can't support a good investment environment, then no one wants to come. (Interview JS286)

This official highlighted several themes: historical/cultural differences, the role of provincial policies and provincial leaders; changing dynamics in factor prices (cheaper land and cheaper labor); and the role of governance and cadre "quality" as opposed to just preferential policies. In exploring the dynamics and causes of county-level growth in China, and particularly in Jiangsu, Anhui, and the six sample counties, this chapter examines the first three of these themes; I examine the final theme, governance, in the subsequent chapter.

The first half of the chapter examines broad economic growth trends at the county level during China's reform period, focusing in particular on the transition from relatively slow growth based largely on productivity enhancements in the 1990s to rapid growth based on capital accumulation in the 2000s. Understanding *how* counties grow enables an analysis of the determinants of county-level variation and serves as a building block for creating a framework of the channels through which county leaders themselves affect local growth outcomes. The second half of the chapter examines existing alternative explanations for why some counties have grown rapidly while others have not. Traditional explanations of growth that rely on geography and natural endowments help explain broad regional trends in China's counties, but they cannot help explain the difference in outcomes among bordering counties. Provincial policies and institutions have resulted in large border effects that help determine outcomes, but also have widely varying sub-provincial effects. Changing factor price dynamics have made counties more attractive as destinations for mobile capital and have changed local approaches to growth, but the ability of counties to take advantage of this transformation has differed greatly both across and within regions.

Broad Trends in County-Level Growth

Counties constitute an important economic tier in China's administrative hierarchy. They are not only responsible for agricultural and rural development, but are also at the nexus of urbanization and industrialization, frequently centered around the county seat (*xiancheng*, 县城), resulting in "comprehensive" (*zonghexing*, 综合性) regional economies.[2] The vast majority of counties are *xian*, often translated as "rural county," which is a misnomer given the rising importance of counties as urban and industrial centers; most urbanization is actually township development (*chengzhenhua*, 城镇化) at the county level more than it is a true city-level process (*chengshihua*, 城市化), and "rural counties" have now become China's major growth engine, with higher relative urban, investment, and economic growth in recent years than the urban cores of prefecture-level cities.[3]

[2] County economic "comprehensiveness" refers to economic systems that include production, distribution, consumption, and allocation across primary, secondary, and tertiary industries (Yao 2010).

[3] The view of counties as "rural" often includes an implicit assumption that as China develops, these small rural units will become increasingly marginalized by population growth and economic growth in China's larger urban centers (i.e., the urban cores of

During the post-Mao era, China's counties have evolved through three broad developmental eras, changing their role within the national economy; while not exact, these three eras can be divided by decade into the 1980s, 1990s, and 2000s. Much of the transformation of China's economy over this period has resulted from the impact that ownership restructuring, sectoral reallocation (industrialization), openness, and migration patterns have had on factor markets (land, labor, and capital), with inconsistent county-level effects during the separate broadly defined periods. In the 1980s, counties led China's growth as agricultural productivity increases generated local capital and surplus labor that created conditions for rural industrialization. The 1990s saw a move towards coastal cities, with a hollowing out of rural counties; the counties that did grow did so with the help of foreign capital (in a few lucky coastal counties) or productivity increases through industrial restructuring (predominantly TVE privatization). The trend towards county hollowing-out was replaced by a return to counties in the 2000s, as labor out-migration slowed and investment searched for high returns outside of increasingly expensive major cities. Counties in this period, like the rest of China, grew through capital accumulation.[4]

This book focuses on China's county growth in the late 1990s and 2000s, as the emphasis switched from industrial restructuring to investment attraction, but brief background on the growth story of the 1980s

prefecture-level cities). However, given China's size and population density in central and coastal regions, even rapid expansion of prefecture-level cities will not marginalize counties, especially given a current growth and urbanization model that focuses on township development within counties.

[4] The openness story of the 1980s/1990s and the "return to counties" story of the 2000s is a sign of China's maturing domestic industrial structure and can be seen as a variation (or continuation) of the "flying geese" theory. A common historical experience of today's advanced countries has been concentration of urban industry followed by concentration of urban services as manufacturing and heavy industrial firms move to small cities, suburbs, and rural areas (World Bank 2009). In a framework tied to East Asian industrial development patterns, the rise of China's counties can be seen as a natural continuation of the Japanese "flying geese" theory popularized by Saburo Okita in 1985, which looks at stages of productive development across countries in East Asia: as early moving countries move up the industrial value-added chain, next-in-line countries fill the gap. Because of China's size and spatial inequality, it makes sense to consider China's advanced industrial cities as separate from more "backwards" rural counties. While recent discussions of China's economic development highlight growing costs in Shenzhen, Shanghai, and other manufacturing powerhouses, conclusions that these plants will move to Vietnam or other countries slightly lower down on the development spectrum overlooks the role of China's counties. Note that these counties are not all "inland," so this is not simply a story of firm migration to inland China.

is useful. China's growth in the 1980s hinged on agricultural productivity growth that enabled the creation of industrial TVEs. The introduction of the household responsibility system in the early 1980s rapidly boosted agricultural productivity, leading to local industrial growth in "non-state" collective and private enterprises; many farmers left the land without leaving the village (*litubulixiang,* 离土不离乡). National growth in the 1980s was largely a rural phenomenon centered in China's counties. Indeed, some authors attribute the rapid growth of the 1980s entirely to rural farmer initiative, divorced from (or in spite of) local state structure.[5] TVEs were very flexible and had few institutional constraints, allowing them to compete favorably with unwieldy and inefficient state-owned enterprises (SOEs) that also had social welfare responsibilities and minimal profit motives. Rural industrial employment grew from 28 million in 1978 to over 100 million by the early 1990s, over 20 percent of the rural workforce (Bramall 2008). While nearly all counties benefited from the household responsibility system reforms, some counties were better positioned to take advantage of industrialization.

By the mid 1990s, however, continued economic opening and reform generated conditions that challenged rural industry. Deng's Southern Tour (*nanxun,* 南巡) in 1992, followed later that year by the 14th National Party Congress, set the stage for deeper reforms en route to a "socialist market economy."[6] Special economic zones (SEZs) became more important and foreign investment, particularly from Hong Kong, Taiwan, and Singapore, flowed in. Inefficient SOEs were restructured, creating more efficient private firms, a process that accelerated following the "grasping the large and releasing the small" (*zhuada fangxiao,* 抓大放小) strategy introduced at the 1997 15th CCP National Congress.[7] This emerging growth pattern, emphasizing foreign direct investment (FDI) attraction and the growth of large private enterprises, favored coastal cities and an elite subset of geographically well-positioned coastal counties that could take advantage of this environment.

The 1990s thus witnessed a hollowing out of county industry. As SOE reform deepened and China entered the global economy, low efficiency and low technology TVEs could not compete with larger industrial firms

[5] See, for instance, Zhou (1996).

[6] The Third Plenum of the 14th Central Committee in 1993 introduced the idea of the "socialist market economy," which boosted the nonstate sector role, leading to growth in private enterprise and foreign investment. See Suliman (1998).

[7] Between 1995 and 2001, SOEs in China shed over 40 million workers. For the effect of this restructuring on urban employment, see Giles, Park, and Cai (2006).

in coastal prefecture-level cities, which also benefited from centrally determined preferential policies.[8] Migrants flowed into industrial cities with large FDI inflows, and county shares of total industrial production fell. China's net annual urban population growth increased from 11.1 million residents annually during 1981–1990 to 15.7 million during 1991–2000, and most of this was to cities (as opposed to "urban" county townships). In the 1990s, FDI as a share of total gross fixed capital formation surged: this share remained under 3 percent throughout the 1980s before jumping to 17 percent by 1994. The county share of total fixed asset investment declined from 36.7 percent in 1996 to 31.5 percent by 2001;[9] as more investment came from outside the country, less investment went to counties (see Figure 2.1). With capital and labor exiting, factor accumulation was not a reliable growth source, and counties had to rely on productivity increases through TVE restructuring. The speed at which privatization occurred differed across provinces and prefectures depending on upward pressure, but even in Jiangsu, traditionally seen as a leader of the collective/TVE economy, 79 percent of TVEs had undergone "property rights reform" by the end of 1997 (Bao, Zhang, and Wang 2000).[10]

In the 2000s, China as a whole has increasingly relied on capital-intensive growth. Factor market conditions have changed rapidly, "pulling" investments into many counties and also "pushing" investments away from many cities. Counties re-emerged through private domestic investment and industrialization. In more recent years, competition, rising domestic demand, and slower growth of foreign demand have added competitive pressures on the supply side while gearing more production towards domestic markets. Despite concerns that "the state advances, the

[8] See discussion in Wang (2003). One scholar of China's county development writes: "Following the deepening of reforms of large SOEs and large-scale foreign capital inflows, rural industry lost the bulk of its market space (*shichang kongjian*, 市场空间). The scattered nature of TVEs, high-input-low-efficiency (*gaohao dixiao*, 高耗低效) and low-technology production began to restrain TVE competition, and in the face of this competition many collapsed" (Liu 2005, 43). For a discussion of the centrally determined regional favor given through preferential policies, see Wang and Hu (1999).

[9] Reliable data on county-level investment does not exist before the mid 1990s.

[10] This is similar to the Ministry of Agriculture national estimate that 80 percent of TVEs had privatized or restructured by 1998 ("converted into SCs, shareholding companies, partnerships, proprietorships, or had been reformed through merger, leasing, collateral contracting, or bankruptcy") (Yuan 2000). For a discussion of the regional/spatial variation of privatization in the 1980s and 1990s, see Han and Pannell (1999). In Xuyi County, one of the case counties, by 2000, TVE reform was basically completed, with over 98 percent reformed, attracting over 990 million RMB in the process (Xuyi Yearbook 2001).

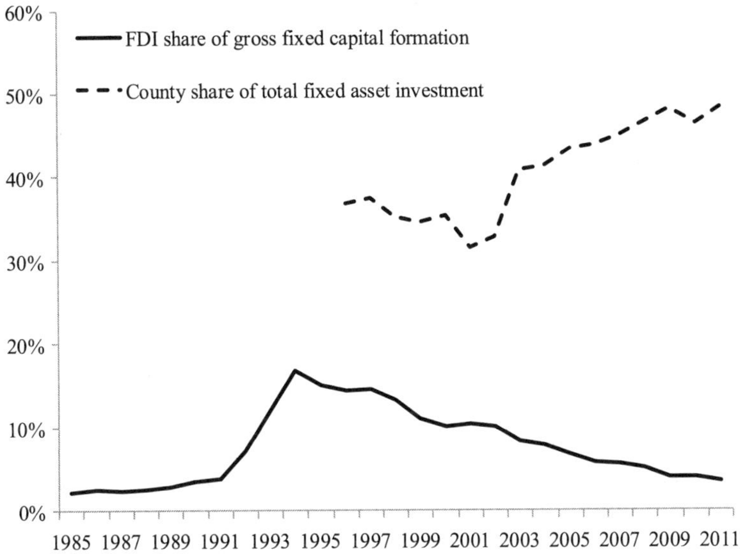

FIGURE 2.1. Trends in county-level and foreign shares of investment
Source: China Statistical Yearbook, various years; China City Statistical Yearbook, various years; author's calculations.

private sector retreats" (*guojin mintui,* 国进民退), privatization has continued, and more and more of China's domestic industrial output and investment comes from private domestic firms (Lardy 2014). The mobile capital of firms and investors has fled high city prices to invest in counties; investment and industry flowed out of cities and into counties with cheaper land, lower wages, and more helpful (and desperate for revenues) local governments. As the 2000s progressed, growing domestic demand and growing *expectations* of domestic demand made noncoastal counties more attractive.[11] One young but already very successful real estate investor in Sihong County, Jiangsu, described how he had previously worked his way up several export industry firms in both Shenzhen and Southern Jiangsu, but returned to Subei after the financial crisis:

> Investing in Shenzhen and other first and second tier cities is now impossible. Small eastern cities at the county and prefecture level have more growth potential. And once these markets are saturated, investment will move west. For instance, there are tons of Anhui and Sichuan workers in Sihong right now, and

[11] In other words, investments began to be targeted at inland areas in anticipation of new demand, even if some of this demand has yet to materialize.

when they make enough money, they'll go home and get those economies moving. (Interview JS240)

The data support these trends. The 1990s trends towards growing importance of FDI and growing city share of FAI were reversed: the county share of FAI shot up to over 48 percent by 2011 while the FDI share of gross fixed capital formation fell to only 3.5 percent (see Figure 2.1). The county shares of FAI in Anhui and Jiangsu rose from 26.0 percent and 46.3 percent in the 1990s (average over the decade) to 39.4 percent and 53.0 percent, respectively, in the 2000s, and rising to 44.1 percent and 63.6 percent, respectively, in 2010.[12] China's urbanization and industrialization in this period relied more on county growth than city growth, contrary to common perceptions. Manufacturing employment in China's counties rose by 23.4 million people between 2000 and 2010, rising from 41.0 percent of China's total manufacturing employment to 49.5 percent.[13] The manufacturing share of total county-level employment rose in 23 out of 31 provinces over 2000–2010, while the share at the prefecture level *decreased* in 20 out of 31 provinces. And as counties have industrialized, they have also urbanized. Between 2000 and 2010, China's urban population grew by 217 million people: 56 percent of this increase was in China's counties, while only 44 percent was in cities (urban districts).[14]

Accounting for Growth: Productivity versus Capital Accumulation

Increased levels of investment have enabled counties to grow rapidly and become centers for manufacturing and urbanization. A growth accounting exercise enables a more rigorous examination of the changing

[12] Note again that the rural-urban distinction is misleading. According to national statistics, the "rural" share of investment actually fell from 21.9 percent in 1995 to 13.2 percent in 2010. While counties generate a larger share of investment in Jiangsu than in Anhui, the shift away from cities has been more pronounced in Anhui.

[13] Migration patterns have changed, increasingly favoring counties and inland provinces. In 2012, 65.0 percent of rural migrants worked in cities (prefecture level cities, municipal provinces, and provincial capitals) and 23.6 percent worked in counties (11.4 percent worked in towns and other areas). The share working in counties has increased rapidly in recent years: in 2009, the share was only 18.5 percent. Intra-provincial migration has also increased, from under 47 percent in 2009 to over 53 percent in 2012, reflecting a similar pattern. Increasingly "local" migration patterns reflect more rapid inland growth and more rapid county development.

[14] From 1982 to 2010, according to census data, the rural population in China's counties shrank by 131 million people while the urban population within counties grew by 248 million. The urban population in prefecture-level cities grew by 219 million.

determinants of county growth in the 1990s and 2000s, and in particular facilitates an identification of the relative importance of productivity improvements (intensive growth) versus higher levels of investment and hours worked (extensive growth). The appendix to this chapter describes the growth accounting framework in depth. The basic idea is to separate GDP growth into four general sources: capital accumulation, labor accumulation, labor/capital reallocation, and productivity gains. Most growth accounting exercises focus only on capital and labor accumulation and residual total factor productivity (TFP) growth. In other words, a standard aggregate growth accounting exercise identifies aggregate TFP growth as the difference between total output growth and this aggregate share-weighted (by sector) average of capital and labor growth. Such an approach subsumes reallocation effects into the TFP term. In looking at a nationwide county sample, limited data necessitates this approach, focusing on capital accumulation, labor accumulation, and TFP contributions to growth over 1998–2010. I also conduct a more precise analysis that includes labor reallocation effects for Anhui and Jiangsu counties over 1994–2011.[15]

The key results from the nationwide exercise, showing averages across counties, are presented in Figure 2.2. Over 1998–2010, China's counties have on average relied on capital accumulation for over 68 percent of total growth (7.3 percentage points out of 10.6 percent average annual real GDP growth). Over the whole period, labor accumulation has had a negligible negative contribution, which reflects widespread out-migration to cities that has been somewhat counteracted by a demographic dividend that has boosted the working age population. The remainder of growth, 3.4 percentage points, has come from TFP.[16] The nationwide sample is restricted to data from 1998 to 2010, but even in this period, counties experienced a large and steady increase in the capital accumulation contribution to growth, as expected from the discussion above. In the three years from 1998 to 2000, county real GDP growth averaged only 7.6 percent, and 48 percent of this growth (3.6 percentage points) came from TFP growth, more than the share from capital accumulation (3.4 percentage

[15] The major shortcoming of the national series is the lack of a consistent FAI or GFCF series at the county level and thus the need to proxy overall investment: as explained in the chapter appendix, this is done by dividing total county investment within each prefecture based on loan and expenditure growth. These assumptions make individual observations/estimates less robust, but the overall averages still represent real trends.

[16] This is a relatively large growth residual, but similar to other estimates at the national level in China.

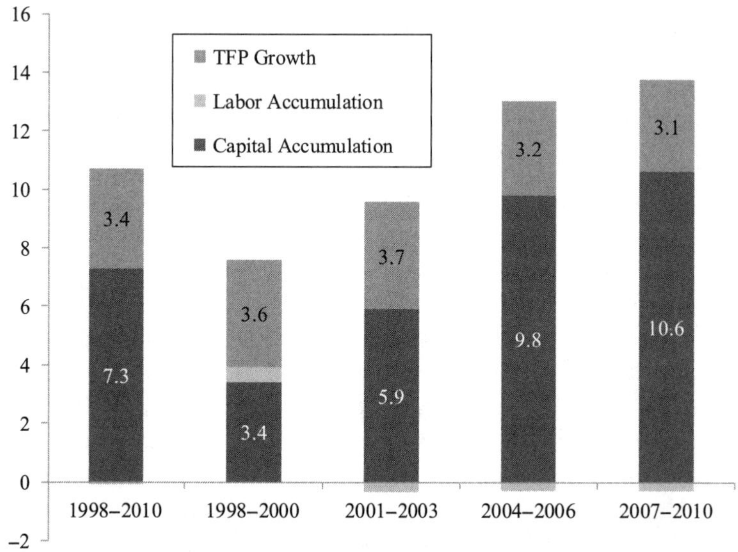

FIGURE 2.2. Average county growth contributions over time, 1998–2010
Average nationwide contributions to total county GDP growth, %
Source: See data appendix.

points). Between 2007 and 2010, capital contributed nearly 80 percent of faster growth (10.6 percentage points of 13.4 percent GDP growth). In other words, in the 1998–2000 period, TFP contributed nearly half of growth, while from 2004 to 2010 it contributed less than one-quarter of growth. This trend tracks the experience of China's national economy; the capital accumulation contribution to growth has likewise increased from 50 percent during 1991–2000 to 66 percent during 2001–2008 (Bulman and Kraay 2012), but it differs from developed country experiences that see a rising share of TFP in total growth as income rises. Note also that while the TFP contribution as a percentage of total growth has halved, TFP growth itself has remained high and fairly constant at 3–3.5 percentage points of growth.

Turning to Jiangsu and Anhui, greater data availability enables a more rigorous analysis that includes labor reallocation effects. Reallocation of labor and capital consists of the movement of factors of production from low productivity areas (agriculture) to higher-productivity areas (e.g., manufacturing). A worker who moves from tilling a field to building computers adds to growth through higher labor productivity, but there is no labor/capital accumulation, nor is there an increase in technological

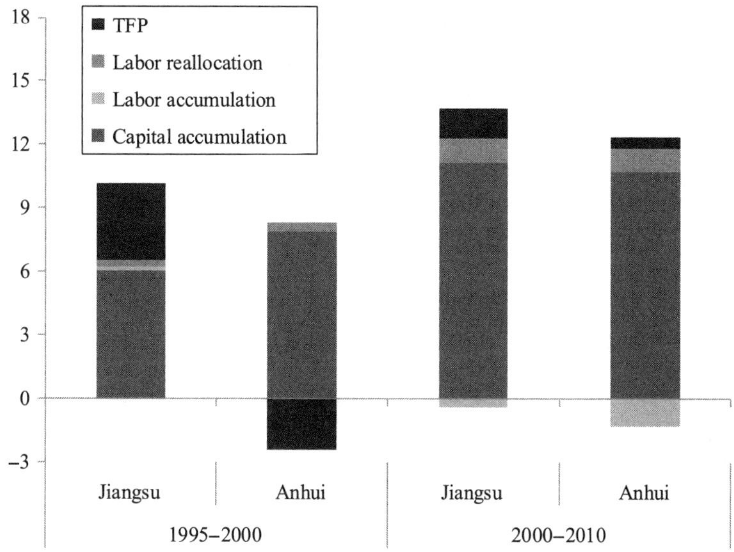

FIGURE 2.3. Growth contributions in Anhui and Jiangsu counties
Source: See data appendix.

productivity.[17] A decomposition of output growth across sectors enables a distinction between productivity growth at the disaggregated level and the contribution of factor reallocation across sectors. Because capital cannot be divided between primary and nonprimary sectors due to a lack of relevant investment data, the decomposition looks only at the role of labor reallocation out of agriculture.

Results are presented in Figure 2.3. Similar to the results presented in the nationwide exercise, both Jiangsu and Anhui experience a large increase in the capital accumulation contribution to growth. Including labor reallocation diminishes the pure TFP growth contribution: in the more recent period, as the shift from agriculture to industrialization has accelerated, labor reallocation contributes over 1 percentage point of growth annually in both provinces. In Jiangsu, the TFP contribution to growth fell from 3.6 percentage points in 1995–2000 to 1.4 percentage points in 2000–2010, while the capital accumulation share rose from 6.1 to 11.1 percentage points. Anhui had a *negative* TFP contribution in 1995–2000, but the capital accumulation contribution similarly changed, contributing 7.9 percentage points of growth in 1995–2000 versus 10.7 percentage

[17] This is a simplification; the key is whether the marginal productivity of a worker in one sector is lower than the marginal productivity of a worker in another sector.

points in 2000–2010. One interpretation is that restructuring in Jiangsu in the 1990s contributed to productivity increases, while Anhui had no similar capacity for development in the 1990s due to a less developed TVE sector. Both Anhui and Jiangsu have relied on rapid capital accumulation for growth, while labor accumulation and reallocation combined only provided an additional 1 percentage point of growth annually. In sum, both nationally and in the provincial sub-samples, counties at the turn of the millennium switched from productivity-led growth, partially as a result of lowered barriers (SOE restructuring) that enabled labor reallocation, towards growth based predominantly on capital accumulation. The inclusion of labor reallocation effects diminishes the TFP contribution to 10.6 percent and 5.0 percent of total growth, respectively, in Jiangsu and Anhui. A similar national-level analysis shows that pure TFP growth at the national level added 19.6 percent of total growth from 2000–2008.[18] In other words, counties have been much more capital-intensive and had much lower productivity gains than the national-level economy. The six case counties highlight the changing growth emphasis and capabilities of counties. Investment data shows that in all six counties, while investment grew over the late 1990s, it exploded in the mid 2000s (see Figure 2.4).

Yet as Figure 2.4 shows, in the case counties, efforts to industrialize have proved much more effective in Jiangsu than in Anhui. The subsequent section of this chapter looks more in depth at the changing *average* conditions for county growth; the second half of the chapter returns to the variation in county level outcomes represented here by the different outcomes between the Jiangsu and Anhui case counties.

Growing County Attractiveness: Push and Pull Factors

What accounts for increased county-level investment? Here, I look in more depth at the factors that enabled the re-emergence of counties as industrial units in the 2000s through increased investment, setting up a discussion in the subsequent section of what differentiates counties from each other. These factors had to do with changing conditions in cities and counties as well as national and provincial reforms to the financial system, fiscal system, and industrial structure. Rising factor prices and

[18] This figure is calculated based on Bulman and Kraay (2012), and includes both pure TFP and capital reallocation effects; as the exercise here cannot distinguish capital between sectors, the capital reallocation effect is subsumed under the TFP term.

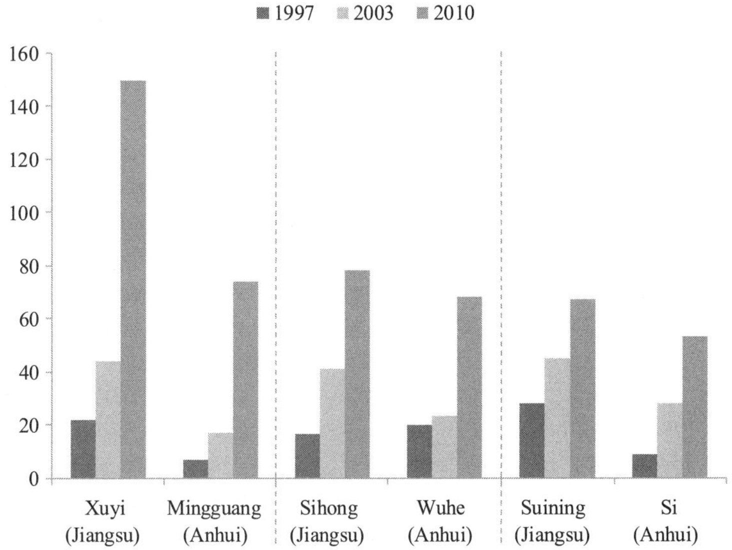

FIGURE 2.4. Rising investment in sample counties
Fixed asset investment as share of GDP (%)
Source: See data appendix; author's calculations.

changing investment conditions pushed firms and investment out of large cities at the same time that counties faced added incentives to seek outside investment as a result of changing local fiscal conditions. Counties were able to capitalize on lower relative factor prices to pull firms from cities. Additionally, in recent years domestic demand has made counties more attractive, pulling investment away from coastal cities that produced for external demand, and infrastructure investments have made counties more accessible with lower transportation costs (measured in both time and money).

Pushing Investment Away from Cities

Changing factor market conditions and rising factor prices in cities have "pushed" firms and investors to seek alternative investment opportunities. Rising wages, rising land prices, fewer preferential policies and greater levels of regulation have diminished profit margins in cities, and counties have attempted to capitalize on this development. Hu Qiwang, a former county Party secretary in Wuhe, notes that, "Industry from developed coastal regions is relocating, especially labor-intensive (*laodong mijixing*, 劳动密集型) and resource-intensive (*ziyuan mijixing*, 资源密集型), and they're looking for places to settle down (*luojiao didian*, 落脚地点). Anhui is close to the Yangtze River Delta and is a good place to invest, with a low level of development but lots of advantages for relocating" (Hu 2010). Relative land and labor prices have risen rapidly in major cities. Low land prices have been a major factor in China's industrial expansion and high rates of fixed asset investment, spurring growth.[19] With high incentives to convert rural farmland, the urbanization of rural farmland has vastly outpaced the urbanization of people, particularly in sub-tier one prefecture-level cities, reducing the potential for continued conversion (World Bank 2014). However, competition in major cities is beginning to focus on quality as much as quantity, particularly given growing incentives to switch towards tertiary industries.[20] Nationally mandated minimum transfer prices for industrial land are staggered by region as well as city size and income, with benchmark prices based on average local conditions.[21] For 2007, the Ministry of Land and Resources issued minimum industrial land prices in 15 categories that ranged from 60 RMB per square meter in poorer western areas (Tibet and Yunnan) to 840 RMB per square meter in Shanghai's nine downtown districts – land in Shanghai had a 1400 percent premium (Cai 2006). Even within localities, prices differ by assigned grades, which are determined by pseudo-market means.[22] Additionally, particularly in large cities, increasing media attention has

[19] Land in China is owned and allocated by the state, although long-term leases can be bought and sold and convey many of the benefits of property ownership. In converting rural land to urban land, local governments can expropriate farmland while compensating the rural land-rights holders for only the agricultural value of the land, typically only a fraction of the urban value of the land. Particularly when this land is converted as part of an industrial development park, the local government takes responsibility for land grading and building out infrastructure. As the industrial firms will pay taxes, it benefits the local government to sell land at bargain or zero cost. Even when sold at nationally mandated minimums, such land transfers entail a one-time loss for local governments that must be recouped through multiple years of taxation. Tao et al. (2007) discuss the race-to-the-bottom competition for low land prices in some of China's most successful prefecture-level cities in Southern Jiangsu. According to Tao et al. (2007), in one quarter of city development zones, the land leasing price is less than half the land requisition and preparation costs. Wujiang and Wuxi (in Jiangsu) lowered their average leasing prices to a fraction of the price in neighboring Suzhou in order to compete; all cities incurred revenue loss from this land price competition.

[20] For instance, Keng (2010) discusses policies in Kunshan City in Jiangsu Province to free up land and kick out labor-intensive industries.

[21] For instance, in 2001, two technical regulations were promulgated: *Regulations for Gradation and Classification on Urban Land* and *Regulations for Valuation on Urban Land*, which set benchmark land prices based on average regional conditions.

[22] Prices should be determined by proximity to business centers, road quality, public traffic, level of urban planning, population, parks, hospitals, and schools, as well as previous

been paid to farmer rights, leading many provincial and city governments to crack down on local land conversions and sales.[23] All this has led to rising city land prices, which in turn make counties, particularly in coastal and central provinces, more capable of competing for industrial investments through low land prices.[24]

Additionally, labor costs in advanced industrial cities have risen rapidly, following rising costs of living, particularly for housing, combined with lack of *hukou* (household registration) provision for labor migrants, which makes non-hometown employment more costly. Regional variation in wages is seen in provincial minimum wages; as of the end of 2013, Shenzhen's minimum wage was 1808 RMB per month, while Anhui's minimum wage was only 1260 RMB per month (MOHRSS 2013).[25] Since 2008, in China's major manufacturing cities, wages have grown faster than industrial output, reversing a decades-old trend.[26] With wages at one half the value of nearby cities, as highlighted by local businesses in multiple interviews, counties are increasingly attractive to industry.[27]

real estate transactions, leading to high price variation within localities. For instance, in 2011 Guangzhou Grade One industrial land sold for 1419 RMB per square meter, while Guangzhou Grade Seven industrial land sold for only 309 RMB per square meter (Dong 2013).

[23] In 2002 and 2003, the central government put limits on land use quotas (*yongdi zhibiao*, 用地指标) to slow down over-conversion of arable land to urban use (Keng 2010). More recently, in Jiangsu, as of 2013 all local land conversion decisions must be approved by the National Land Bureau (Wang 2013).

[24] Such diversity in land prices across counties and cities in China helps explain why rising average land prices have not undermined China's industrial competitiveness. For instance, the Boston Consulting Group notes that the national average price of industrial land in China has reached 10.22 USD per square foot, higher than industrial land in Alabama, Tennessee, and North Carolina, which ranges in price from 1.30 USD to 7.43 USD per square foot (Sirkin, Zinser, and Hohner 2011). But much of China's industrial land remains well below these prices.

[25] According to China's Employment Promotion Plan, minimum wage levels should not be lower than 40 percent of average local salaries (Chen 2012).

[26] Much of this has to do with the slowdown in industrial growth, but the important factor in firm relocation is the relative speeds of the growth in input costs and output value. Based on simple calculations using Shanghai, Wuxi (Jiangsu), Suzhou (Jiangsu), Hangzhou (Zhejiang), Ningbo (Zhejiang), Wenzhou (Zhejiang), Guangzhou (Guangdong), and Shenzhen (Guangdong), while average wages grew 13.2 percent annually over 1997–2007, industrial output grew 22.4 percent; from 2008 through 2011, wages grew 11.2 percent annually while industrial output growth slowed to 10.7 percent. (Data from China Data Online, using "urban districts" under the city.)

[27] The former county Party secretary of Xuyi, Wang Youfu, characterizes the county-city difference as the "five lacks and two manys" (*wuque liangduo*, 五缺两多) versus the "two lacks and five manys" (*liangque wuduo*, 两缺五多): cities have lots of projects, lots of money to invest, high levels of technology, high management experience, and

Pulling Investment Towards Counties

As costs have risen in cities, county projects have become more economically viable at the same time that local fiscal incentives have changed. Following SOE/TVE restructuring and changes to the fiscal system, counties have become increasingly dependent on the taxation of private industrial enterprises for local revenue. From the late 1990s, counties were increasingly pressured to generate local industrial revenue. Not only did upper-level governments impose more expenditure requirements on local governments, but traditional revenue sources, mainly fees and agricultural taxes, were eliminated.[28] At the same time that traditional revenue sources were eliminated, central mandates for increased local social outlays led to higher government expenditure: counties in Jiangsu and Anhui had expenditures of 4.5 percent of GDP and 5.8 percent of GDP, respectively, in 1996, but by 2010 these shares had more than doubled to 10.9 percent and 19.5 percent. Although transfers increased as well, revenue had to rise to keep up, and revenue became increasingly dependent on industrial taxes: the share of business VAT, business sales taxation, and enterprise taxation rose from 21.3 percent of all revenue in Anhui in 1996 to 45.5 percent in 2006, while in Jiangsu the combined share rose from 40.1 percent to 53.2 percent.

In response to these pressures, county governments devoted increasing efforts towards attracting industrial investment.[29] Changing emphases in county economic strategies from restructuring to investment promotion are clear in annual development plans, as seen in an analysis of the evolving economic emphases in annual government work reports (*zhengfu gongzuo baogao*, 政府工作报告). Industrialization remains a constant

high human capital, but few agricultural sideline products and rural labor (Wang 2005). This means that counties should focus on their comparative advantage: cheap and abundant labor.

28 For the impact on township governments of tax-for-fee reform and the abolition of agricultural taxes, see Kennedy (2007). See also Li (2005); Yep (2004); Yang (2004). Formerly, extra-budgetary funds provided the greatest degree of freedom and autonomy for county governments (Blecher and Shue 1996), but national laws have worked to bring these funds on-budget, with varying degrees of success across different regions (Zhan 2011). This was particularly the case in agricultural counties. For instance, Siyang County is explicit in noting that agricultural tax elimination provided the impetus for it to develop industrial development parks. Siyang is an agricultural county, so agricultural tax reform (*nongye shuifei gaige*, 农业税费改革) in 2001 decimated local finances, leading to a one-year decline in revenue from 106.37 million RMB to 39.94 million RMB. As a consequence, the county had to rely on industrial growth, leading to the 2002 opening of the Western Industrial Park (*xiqu gongyeyuan*, 西区工业园) and the 2003 opening of the Eastern Industrial Park (*dongqu gongyeyuan*) (Tai 2004).

29 See Liu et al. (2008); Li, Li, and Zhang (1998).

theme, but in the early and mid 1990s, the means to achieve industrialization focused on rural upgrading and privatization/restructuring, with some attention to FDI attraction in richer counties. For instance, the Xuyi 1995 work report, delivered by County Magistrate Wang Shigao (王士高) emphasized the "central plan" of "grasp the opportunity (*zhuazhu jiyu*, 抓住机遇), deepen reform, (*shenhua gaige*, 深化改革), expand openness (*kuoda kaifang*, 扩大开放), promote development (*cujin fazhan*, 促进发展), maintain stability (*baochi wending*, 保持稳定)." This 20-character phrase appears throughout the 1995 Xuyi Almanac.[30] The work report focused on industrial growth, with a particular emphasis on the growth in private enterprise, whose industrial output tripled from the year before, although it was still less than one-eighth the value of TVE output (101 million RMB versus 830 million RMB). The 1995 government work report includes an entire section on enterprise reform, with a major emphasis on leasing (*zulin*, 租赁) and "publicly owned, privately run" (*gongyou minying*, 公有民营) management to enliven (*gaohuo*, 搞活) enterprises.[31] Similarly, in the 1996 Xuyi Almanac, an entire section is devoted to a discussion on enterprise restructuring, with adherence to "selling first and shareholding after" (*xianshou hougu*, 先售后股). However, in more recent years, "investment promotion" (*zhaoshang yinzi*, 招商引资) has become the most important economic pursuit of counties. According to County Party Secretary Hu Qiwang of Wuhe: "We need to soberly recognize that a small economy remains Wuhe's most important reality, an undeveloped economy is Wuhe's most important county situation, speeding up development and seeking investment from beginning to end are Wuhe's main goals and most pressing mission" (Hu 2012).

Investment promotion has worked based on cheaper costs of land and labor as well as the creation of local development zones, effective preferential policies (*youhui zhengce*, 优惠政策), and enhanced government efforts through outside promotion efforts and local assistance. These government efforts are discussed in more depth in the subsequent chapter. At the center of county investment promotion efforts are

[30] Xuyi in 1994 also continued the "three foci, three breakthroughs" (*san weizhu, san tupo*, 三为主，三突破) economic development strategy to focus on industry, rural income, and privatization. The 1995 goals demonstrate the lack of attention to investment: while the GDP growth goal is 8.6 percent, the FAI growth goal is only 6 percent, a far cry from a decade later when FAI growth is expected to outpace GDP growth by a 2:1 ratio.

[31] In 1995, the county completed property rights reform (*chanquan zhidu gaige*, 产权制度改革) for 490 firms, of which 220 were leased (*zulin*, 租赁), generating over 15 million RMB.

industrial development zones, which serve as foci for preferential policies. Development zones have long been an important part of China's development, and in the past decade they have taken off at the county level. At the end of 2003, China had 3837 development zones, with only 6 percent approved by the national government and 27 percent approved by provinces; by the end of 2006, there were 6015 development zones, and each of the 2862 county-level administrative units in China has on average over two development zones (Zhai and Xiang 2007).[32] This national trend is seen in the sample counties, all of which introduced provincial-level development zones in the 2000s. On the Jiangsu side, Xuyi established a provincial-level development zone in October 2001, the earliest in the sample. Begun in eastern Xuyi in a space of 3 square kilometers, in 2003 this was expanded to 17.1 square kilometers.[33] The Sihong Economic Development Zone was established in March 2003 and has attracted over 300 investments. Suining had the latest Jiangsu start, with a provincial-level zone established in April 2006, but has developed the fastest, with seven industrial parks with total area over 100 square kilometers. The major zone is the Suining Economic Development Zone to the west of downtown Suicheng Zhen.[34] Anhui has seen slower development, with all three counties getting their first provincial-level development zone approval in 2006.[35]

Development zones have benefits in terms of agglomeration, specialization, and scale economies, including concentrated skilled and semi-skilled labor, and they also serve as focal points for preferential policies, particularly regarding land and taxation. According to a former Wuhe County Party secretary, "development zones are the vehicle/medium (*zaiti,* 载体), and the quality of enterprises a county attracts depends on the quality of its development zone" (Hu 2010). Preferential policies are a key aspect of development zone attractiveness. A CEO of one large Jiangsu plastics

32 See also discussion in Lin, Liu, and Tao (2013).

33 By the end of 2003, 321 firms had already invested, paying taxes of 11 million and employing over 6000 people.

34 The planning area is 60 square kilometers, while the core region is 10 square kilometers. Within the zone, the population is 32,000, with three schools, two private hospitals, and 43 enterprises above designated size (in 2012).

35 Of these, Wuhe is the most developed. At the end of 2012, it had two industrial parks with 263 companies, 136 already in operation, 69 being built, and 58 contracted (Wuhe Government 2013). This includes three investments over 1 billion RMB, and 20 over 100 million. Si County's provincial development zone in 2009 attracted 13 new projects, 9 of which were industrial. Contracted FAI was 524 million RMB, and completed investment attraction was 469.3 million RMB (Wang and Hui 2010).

manufacturer attributed recent growth in Northern Jiangsu to the provincial willingness to allow looser preferential policies in recent years, particularly those related to immigration, land, and tax: lower prices for land sales were allowed as were greater tax rebates and subsidies for newly investing businesses. These "good policies" (*haode zhengce*, 好的政策) have enabled northern counties to develop (Interview JS172).

Basic preferential policies cover land, taxes, and fees, and are generally graded by size of investment. Land and tax rebates are key. For instance, in Suining, big investments can get land prices cut drastically, from 25,000 per *mu* to 10,000, and even larger investments are decided on a case-by-case basis. Local taxes are fully refunded for the first two or three years, and personal taxes for managers are waived. There are no fees imposed for this time. In Suining, while some policies are explicit, the general determination is "one project one discussion" (*yishi yiyi*, 一事一议), "according to the investment scale, investment intensity and industrial promotional effects," so long as the investment is greater than 50 million RMB (Suining Investment Promotion Office 2012). Preferential policies are given to industrial projects with average tax per *mu* greater than 1.8 million RMB. On taxes, Suining rewards (*jiangli*, 奖励) companies a set percentage of the VAT and enterprise income tax retained by the county (i.e., the portion not transferred upward) for three years (longer if the company is in the Fortune 500 or if the initial investment is greater than 100 million RMB). The reward/rebate range for industrial projects depends on the size of the tax base, and during the first three years ranges from 40 percent (2–5 million in taxes) to 70 percent (10–30 million in taxes), with ten additional percentage points to government-promoted (high-tech) projects. Individual investors and outside management do not have to pay personal income tax for the first three years.[36]

Preferential land policies in the sample counties highlight cheap and negotiable industrial land prices, and interviews with investors in the region make clear the attractiveness of these policies. The lowest price is based on the legal national standard (Suining Party Committee and Suining Government 2012). With cheap land and easy rural-urban land conversion, land can also be given out as a reward. One real estate investor in Northern Jiangsu took me to several project sites 5–10 kilometers

[36] Similarly, in Wuhe, industrial investments of 100 million and above get the entire period's fees returned to them; investments of 30–100 million RMB get 50 percent returned. Industrial land is sold at the minimum national lowest price for all investments greater than 1.5 million RMB per *mu*. For these and other similar policies in Wuhe, see Wuhe Government (2012).

outside of the county seat, showing off an eight-story complex meant to attract rural workers that was built on 20 *mu* of the 80 *mu* that he had been given for free for doing "pro-bono work," consisting of setting up cheap brick housing to house workers in a government-supported agricultural production space (Interview JS153). In other words, for setting up minimal low income housing he received free land for profitable housing.[37] The same plastics manufacturing CEO quoted above argues that the major reason Subei has started to grow more rapidly than Sunan is that "Subei also has more land and thus more land expropriation (*zhengdi*, 征地) possibilities, as long as this is done smartly" (Interview JS172).

Preferential policies have also helped to attract back migrant workers, which has combined with a virtuous circle of more local opportunities and greater levels of local human capital: these changing labor conditions in counties have made them more attractive, and have resulted from both national trends and general socioeconomic development as well as specific county policies. Counties have seen a transformation with regard to both the quantity and quality of labor. In the 1990s urbanization model, counties were largely drained of surplus agricultural laborers who moved to cities in the coastal belt. In successful counties, this flow has begun to reverse: not only are many migrants returning to their home counties with enhanced levels of human and financial capital, but successful counties themselves are becoming employment magnets for migrants from poorer counties and provinces. Part of this process has arisen based on the central government's urbanization model, which focuses on small-scale urbanization in townships (*chengzhenhua*, 城镇化) rather than city urbanization (*chengshihua*, 城市化), and thus has accelerated local county rural/urban *hukou* unification prior to city unification (World Bank 2014). Also, married and older individuals with deeper local roots and family ties and responsibilities are reluctant to move too far, as was readily apparent in discussions with factory workers and basic service employees in Jiangsu. Many of these individuals migrated from neighboring counties in Anhui and returned home very frequently. They were unwilling to migrate to larger cities further away, despite the potential wage premium gained from doing so. At one Chinese medicine farm in Suining, all of the laborers were from Anhui (mostly from neighboring Si) and were all at least 40 years old.

Reversing migration flows by attracting back migrants, or at least stemming the outward flow, is essential for maintaining a sufficient labor

[37] This was not industrial land, and should not have been given out for free (even if it were industrial it should not have been), but the "pro bono" work was identified as a payment.

force. In the city-led urbanization model of the 1990s, out-migration made more sense: TVEs were losing their competiveness against well-financed larger enterprises with economies of scale, and county-level SOEs were rapidly being privatized, restructured, or simply shuttered, as discussed above. In this environment, labor outflows prevented local unemployment.[38] But as counties began to compete for industrial investments with rising labor, land, and capital prices in cities, the lack of local employment turned into a liability, spurring local governments to provide incentives to migrants to return. In Anhui Province, all three case counties have explicit policies to attract back migrants, with varying degrees of success. Of Mingguang's 330,000-person workforce, for much of the past decade 150,000 workers have worked outside the city annually. But starting in 2005, Mingguang began to evolve from an "emigrating to work tide" (*waichu dagong chao,* 外出打工潮) to a "return to open a business tide" (*fanxiang chuangye chao,* 返乡创业潮) (Yang 2012). Much of this change can be attributed to the local government: since 2005, policies have attracted back 551 enterprises, of which 10 had investments over 10 million RMB.[39] Returned-migrant enterprises had 165.3 million RMB in sales in 2011, and contributed 56.85 million RMB in taxes, 10.1 percent of the city total. They employed 11,600 people.[40] Similarly, in Si County, township governments are responsible for giving seed capital to returning migrants who want to start local businesses.[41]

In addition to attracting back migrants, counties still have large populations of surplus labor, and many counties have taken advantage, setting up programs to train these laborers. Considerable room remains for within-county labor reallocation. In Suining in 2007, of

[38] Remittances were also an important source of local income. In many poorer provinces, remittances can account for 15–30 percent of net rural income (Bramall 2006).

[39] Almost half of all returned-migrant enterprises are in mining and services rather than manufacturing.

[40] In February 2012, the government also released *Implementation Methods for Mingguang City to Encourage Returnees to Establish Industrial Enterprises,* 《明光市鼓励返乡创办工业企业实施办法》, to clarify supporting policies and encouragement, including reduced taxation, employment requirements, and land use, as well as assistance in finding funding channels.

[41] One interviewee who himself had been enticed to return and open a photography store, said the government assistance was helpful, and that it was also easy to get a bank loan if you were a returning worker (Interview AH136). However, the economic impact of returning migrants is unclear. Wang and Fan (2006) find that returnees are more often those who fail in the emigration destination than those who succeed, and therefore do not bring back strong skills or investment. De Brauw and Rozelle (2008) find that these returnees do not substantially increase rural investment.

a total population of 1.33 million people, the rural labor force was 724,500, over 300,000 of whom had migrated outside of the county to work, with an additional 124,900 (29 percent) migrating to work in townships within the county.[42] The local government identifies outmigration as hurting the local economy and has thus opened 32 professional training schools, which in 2007 trained 24,149 people. Of the 724,500 rural labor force, 297,000 are still employed in primary industry, working on 150,000 *mu*. The local government calculates that based on factors including current levels of mechanization, operational standards, and agriculture adaptability to new technology, every rural laborer should have 10 *mu* of arable land, meaning that the county should have 150,000 primary sector laborers overall, which in turn implies that the rural labor force is still 42.8 percent over-capacity and should shed another 127,000 workers who can work in industry and services in local townships (Qin 2009).

In addition to preferential policies and labor conditions, conditions for capital and financing have also made counties more suitable for investment, with higher levels of expenditure on infrastructure and greater capacity for local lending. Local capital consists not only of outside investment, but also of local self-financed investment, lending, and revenue. An increasing share of China's investment comes from self-raised funds and retained profits rather than loans that have in the past favored large SOEs: the state budget has consistently accounted for only 2–7 percent of total FAI, and the domestic loan share of FAI has declined from over 20 percent in the 1990s to 15 percent in 2010,[43] at the same time

[42] Barriers still remain to rural workers coming to urban areas: although *hukou* restrictions have been largely removed, systemic deficiencies create additional migration obstacles, as rural migrants still do not receive equal social services and insurance (unemployment, health, pension, and childhood education social security).

[43] It is difficult to determine at the local level the share of investment from domestic credit. Lending is complicated given the difficulty in pinning down location of loan origination. Many loans for investment in sample counties were taken out from larger city banks. Conversely, many local loans were meant for investment outside of the county. In looking at formal statistics on aggregate local bank lending, we can look at either outstanding loans or year-on-year changes in loans – the relevant statistic depends on what proportion of loans are repaid in a year. Either way, there is a decrease in the importance of lending to total local FAI. While outstanding loans were over 200 percent of FAI in all sample counties in 1997 (the first year with loan data), the outstanding loan-to-FAI ratio in 2010 had fallen to under 75 percent in all counties (as low as 37 percent and 42 percent in Xuyi and Wuhe, respectively). Over the whole period, the average share of the growth in annual loans to total FAI ranged from 5.9 percent in Xuyi to 10.4 percent in Sihong – not much variation, and not much change over time. Even on a per capita basis, deposits are not much larger in Jiangsu, but loans are twice as large. But lending is not

that the foreign investment share has fallen to less than 2 percent. Taking up the slack, self-financing has risen from 65 percent to nearly 80 percent of total FAI.[44] While foreign investment favored more convenient and "developed" coastal cities and state capital favored large heavy industrial investment or large city investment, private capital is more malleable and has less geographic (coastal) preference in addition to more local knowledge.

Local financing options at the county-level have also greatly expanded. Local banks have evolved out of rural cooperatives into rural commercial banks (*nongcun shangye yinhang,* 农村商业银行) with large and growing portfolios. These rural commercial banks have become important sources of local lending, with larger annual lending volumes in individual counties than the local branches of China's four major national banks. For instance, in Xuyi in 2011 the Xuyi Rural Commercial Bank had 3.66 billion RMB in outstanding loans, more than the next three largest banks combined: the Bank of China (1.34 billion RMB), the Industrial and Commercial Bank of China (1.23 billion RMB), and the Agricultural Bank of China (969 million RMB) (Xuyi Yearbook 2012). These local rural commercial banks do not have to receive permission for lending from higher levels, as the four big banks do, and they therefore are able to extend much more local lending (Interview JS192). With the development of these local banks, local financing capacity has increased greatly.

Informal lending is also very important for local development (Tsai 2002), although also very difficult to quantify. In Sihong a high-interest loan bubble (pyramid scheme) made national news in 2011. Loans had been 7–8 percentage points above bank rates, and thousands of people in the county were making money. At one point, an epicenter of the lending, Shiji Township (石集乡), became known as "BMW town" (*baoma xiang,* 宝马乡) due to all the BMWs on the streets. According to a local PBOC employee, the central bank efforts to control lending to the real estate market had led to a decline in official bank loans of almost fifty percent, and the informal high-interest markets naturally rose to meet the unfulfilled demand. A local saying arose: "if you don't lend (*fang zhuazi,* 放爪子) you're an idiot (*lengzi,* 愣子)"; by one estimate, as many as 95 percent of local citizens in two particularly loan-friendly villages (Xinbian, 新汴

the whole story: Mingguang has a higher loan-to-GDP ratio (55.4 percent in 2010) than any county in the sample except for Sihong (57.4 percent in 2010) but has low returns to capital and low levels of productive investment.

44 Note that much of this self-financing likely comes from informal and secondary loan markets outside the formal system.

村, and Shiji, 石集村) were not "idiots." The situation eventually blew up, making national news. At its height, according to the local Politics and Law Committee secretary, Xu Yijun, the informal person-to-person financing had reached 2 billion RMB, although 1.5–1.7 billion RMB of this total was legitimate and not at usury type rates, possibly providing an indication of a massive "normal" size of local informal financial markets (Money Weekly 2011).

In addition to local bank development and informal finance, local governments play a major role in securing loans for infrastructure investment and company loan guarantees, and the rise of local government debt has boosted infrastructure expenditure and direct financing that have helped counties grow. Local government financing vehicles (LGFV) play a quasi-fiscal role that allows for expanded infrastructure investment without commensurate fiscal balance sheet increases. By the end of 2010, these LGFV at all administrative levels in China had debt of nearly 5 trillion RMB, equal to two-thirds of total local revenue and transfers (Lu and Sun 2013). In one of the Jiangsu case counties, the LGFV started operations in 2008 and is run by a deputy county Finance Bureau chief.[45] While this LGFV helps support local enterprises, the vast majority of its loans are for urban development and "other government needs," which are off-budget and do not show up on the government balance sheet. The "company" has between 1 and 2 billion RMB (*shijiyi*, 十几亿) in loans, which is "nothing compared to Sunan counties with 20 billion or more."[46] As an example of one loan (the largest individual loan), the LGFV has a 100 million RMB loan from the China Development Bank that is supposed to be used for small-and medium enterprise (SME) development; 40 million RMB has indeed been loaned to the 18 businesses that the company supports, but 60 million RMB of this loan has been added to general government funds. Much of the remaining loan volume is used not only for potentially positive-return infrastructure projects, but also for paying salaries and covering other gaps – in other words, investments with no return potential.

45 This paragraph is based on Interview JS254 and Interview JS230 with employees of the LGFV.

46 All of this lending is short term, usually one year, but this is automatically rolled over as long as interest payments are met, which they invariably are. According to the official, the banks have nothing to worry about, as local governments have lots of assets (mostly land) that can be sold if need be, and also have the backing of the city, province, and national governments if worst comes to worst.

Unexplained Variation in County Economic Outcomes

Preferential policies and changing factor market conditions increase the attractiveness of county investment relative to city investment, but they do not explain why certain counties have been more successful than others. Preferential policies are largely the same across counties, and therefore do not explain why particular development zones are more attractive than others.[47] Most counties have engaged in a race to the bottom: industrial land is basically free (or as close to free as national and provincial authorities will tolerate),[48] so while trends in land prices can help explain the transition from city industry to county industry, they cannot help to explain differentiation among counties. Changing migration patterns and labor dynamics help explain differentiation between cities and counties but do not explain differentiation between counties: wages, policies on returning migrants, and volumes of surplus rural labor are all fairly undifferentiated across the sample counties.

In terms of local finance, conditions differ greatly across counties as a result of varying development of local banks, informal finance, and LGFVs. Yet rules governing the creation of banks, LGFVs, and informal financial markets do not differ by county, although the extent of financial development clearly does. Local deposits for formal lending and rules on banking are relatively equalized across counties. Tsai (2002) discusses the need for development-minded local governments to support informal financial markets, but again, this is not a rules-based cross-county distinction. In terms of LGFVs, they operate in a semi-market environment, securing loans based on perceived capacity to repay – the largest loan for the LGFV identified above was from a national institution, not a provincial institution. Banks provide 8.5 trillion of the 10.7 trillion RMB in outstanding local government debt, and base lending decisions to LGFVs

[47] In the words of Hu Qiwang, former county Party secretary of Wuhe: "Regional competition for investment increases by the day, causing the 'price tag' for good projects and the cost of investment attraction to increase as well ... There are four kinds of good projects: (1) large investments; (2) strong industry-pull effect; (3) high value-added (and thus large potential for taxation); (4) and mature firms or firms with high potential. These types of projects are the targets everyone is striving for, so the price tag continually rises. The rising price tag manifests in the following aspects: free industrial land, matching real estate and infrastructure development, fiscal subsidies, and assistance in factory construction. The rising price tag necessitates a new approach and a new level of investment promotion work" (Hu 2010).

[48] Basically, industrial land is sold at the lowest possible value – either the nationally mandated minimum or lower in the (illegal) case of "one project one discussion." Most land transfers do not simply include land, but also land grading and infrastructure.

largely on the projected value of local land and a county's ability to grow (Lu and Sun 2013). Similarly, revenue is an important determinant of growth potential, with the potential to boost infrastructure investment and support investing enterprises, but despite perceptions of Northern Jiangsu counties developing based on greater fiscal support, there is minimal evidence for this. Revenue comes from both local capacity and upper-level transfers, and while Jiangsu county local revenue is higher (a function of higher local output), the Anhui share of transfers is much higher than the Jiangsu share of transfers. Most of these transfers cannot be used on "productive investment" in poorer counties.[49] In other words, while local financial development and LGFV size clearly impact developmental possibilities and the attractiveness of the investment environment, local government approaches to finance and the endogenous perceived potential for growth seem to determine this financial development.

In sum, the growth accounting exercise and the discussion above of push and pull factors contributing to counties' emergence as centers for industrial investment both demonstrate a general shift towards capital-intensive industrial growth in the 2000s but do not explain regional and county-level variation in growth and productivity. And there is a lot of explaining to do. China's richest county in 2010, Kunshan (county-level) City in Jiangsu (295,273 RMB per capita GDP), had 116 times more per capita income than China's poorest county, Dongxiang Autonomous County in Gansu (2545 RMB per capita GDP). To repeat: *116 times.* With a GDP per capita of nearly 44,000 USD at market exchange rates, Kunshan would have been one of the richest 20 countries in the world, while Dongxiang, with a GDP per capita of 376 USD would have been among the 10 poorest, with lower per capita income than the Central

[49] Most government expenditure, particularly at the county level, is nonproductive and intended for social services, predominantly education and health. China's county expenditure share is much higher than its revenue share, leading to a large local government revenue-expenditure gap that must be filled by upper level fiscal transfers or debt. When local budgetary revenue increases, this can offset transfers while keeping overall expenditure the same. Even when increased own revenue does not offset transfers, it is most likely to be used for social spending, security spending, or administrative spending. There are many laws about specific centrally mandated local expenditure increases: the 1993 Agricultural Law (农业法) mandated that agriculture expenditure increases should be higher than increases in revenue; the 1994 Education Law (教育法) mandated that education expenditure increases should reach 4 percent of GDP; the 1996 State Council Decision on Issues Concerning Environmental Protection (国务院关于环境保护问题的决定) mandated that environmental protection expenditures should reach 1.5 percent of GDP (Yin and Zhu 2011). When revenue is only a small share of GDP, there is little freedom in the uses to which it can be put.

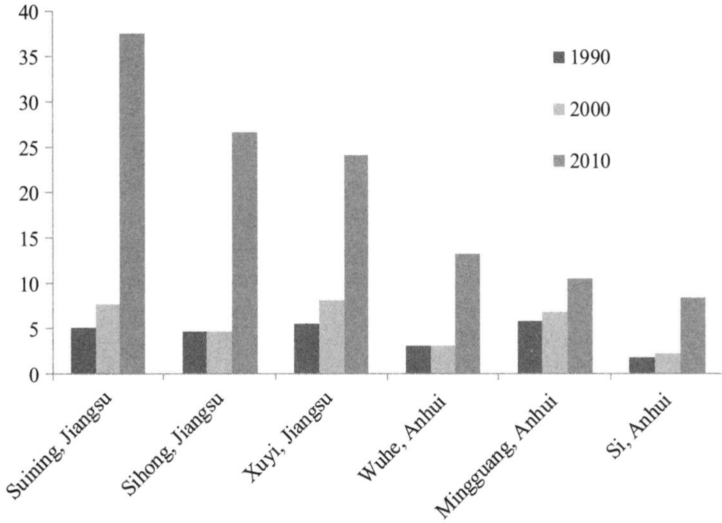

FIGURE 2.5. County industrial employment growth is a 2000s phenomenon
Industrial employment share of total employment (%)
Source: Census data, various years.

African Republic, Sierra Leone, and Guinea.[50] China's inter-county inequality is much starker than provincial differences: the richest province, Jiangsu (52,840 RMB per capita) is only four times richer than the poorest, Guizhou (13,119 RMB per capita).[51] The six case counties do not demonstrate as much variation as Kunshan and Dongxiang, but they have nonetheless achieved very different outcomes. Table 1.1 in the previous chapter demonstrates the wide differences in per capita GDP as of 2010; differences that did not exist 20 years ago. Similarly, the Jiangsu case counties have industrialized and urbanized at a much more rapid clip. In 1990, all six case counties had agricultural employment shares over 85 percent and industrial employment shares ranging from only 2 to 6 percent; by 2010 industry accounted for 38 percent of employment in

[50] These calculations are made comparing all 188 countries with available data for 2010 from the World Bank World Development Indicators. Note that a purchasing power parity (PPP) comparison of per capita income would better reflect local conditions; however, price differences in Kunshan and Dongxiang are likely to be as different as price differences between countries, so applying one PPP conversion in both areas yields extreme results: namely, in 2010 PPP terms, Dongxiang would have been the fifth poorest country in the world and Kunshan would have been the third richest with nearly $90,000 per capita GDP, behind only Qatar and Macao.

[51] Including province level municipalities instead of simply provinces, Guizhou is 5.8 times poorer than Shanghai (76,074 RMB per capita).

Suining, 27 percent in Sihong, and 24 percent in Xuyi (the three Jiangsu sample counties), but only 13 percent, 11 percent, and 8 percent, respectively, in Wuhe, Mingguang, and Si (the three Anhui sample counties), as shown in Figure 2.5.[52]

County economic outcomes have been highly variable; the following sections demonstrate that economic outcomes are not determined solely by history, initial conditions, or geography, as frequently asserted. More than geography, provincial borders, and thus province-level policies and institutions, play an important role.

Initial Conditions and Geography

Do particular county conditions help predict particular growth outcomes? An important place to start is to see if geography or initial conditions influence growth outcomes. Arguments for such pre-determined growth are common and varied. The most common sentiment expressed in both Jiangsu and Anhui interviews for the difference in outcomes came down to "backwardness" (*suzhi luohou,* 素质落后). When pressed on an explanation for this, most interviewees expounded on the historical differences between the counties, regions, and provinces. One Jiangsu county finance bureau official described the fait accompli of culturally determined growth paths as "a cultural issue with deep roots (*genshen digu,* 根深蒂固) going back hundreds or thousands of years" (Interview JS245). He referred to the example of the Qing Dynasty Emperor Qian Long traveling to Southern Jiangsu (*qianlong xia jiangnan,* 乾隆下江南) to observe government behavior, noting that "his advisors wouldn't let him go to a backwards place like Anhui. This shows that these regions have had their same reputations for centuries." More broadly, economic growth cannot be separated from geographically determined comparative advantages and previously determined economic legacies and structures. Natural factors including geography clearly affect the attractiveness of a region, as noted by former Suining County Party Secretary Wang Tianqi:

> From a geographic perspective, Suining has three important conditions: from a climate perspective, Suining is the closest region to the Yangtze River Delta with winter vegetable production; from a potential consumption perspective, Suining

[52] The most rapid increases in all six counties occurred from 2000 to 2010; in fact, during the 1990s, when further industrialization (from the 1980s) remained largely a prefecture-level city and advanced county phenomenon, these sample counties saw little or no additional movement out of agriculture: the minor restructuring and initial inward investment in industry were largely counteracted by TVE closures in a large-firm-led industrialization process in which smaller TVEs were no longer competitive.

is in the midst of the Yangtze River Delta and Huiahai and the four-province border region with 100 million people; and from a transportation perspective, it has a first class airport nearby and a rail line connecting all four directions. (Li 2010)

The high-income level of many counties in Shanxi, Inner Mongolia, and Xinjiang, among other places, demonstrates the importance of natural resource endowments, with local economies based entirely on coal and oil/gas.

Perceptions of cultural determinism exist despite historical and geographic similarities between the sets of case counties. Some of the geographic factors can vary sub-provincially and influence intra-provincial inequality; however, if we look at Jiangsu alone, geography is fairly equal, and the case counties in both provinces have very similar geographic conditions. Xuyi and Mingguang both have attapulgite (*aotubang*, 凹凸帮) reserves, yet while Mingguang relies on these reserves for growth, Xuyi has branched out into more value-added industry. Sihong and Xuyi have taken full advantage of their lakeside location, focusing on crab and crawfish development, respectively. But Wuhe's Lake Tuohu (沱湖) and the five rivers of the county name (Wuhe, 五河, literally translates as "five rivers") are famous for plentiful freshwater delicacies that have not been as well developed. As for historical industrial composition, Xuyi and Mingguang were a merged county (Xujia County, 盱嘉县) until 1949, and Xuyi remained part of Anhui until 1955. Similarly, Sihong was created out of several Anhui districts in 1949 and was initially under Anhui jurisdiction; it too was placed under Jiangsu jurisdiction in 1955. In other words, while culture may play a role, this is not a "deep-rooted" role.

In addition to geography, historical institutional development and industrial composition inherited from the Maoist era have had a large impact on the ability of private firms and collective firms to grow, as well as on degrees of societal integration and cohesion. Maoist legacies have been found to determine local government approaches to informal finance (Tsai 2002) as well as degrees of reform-era rural industrialization, particularly in Jiangsu (Bramall 2008).[53] Using census data and current economic data, scatter plots of industrial employment shares in 1982 (the closest observation to the beginning of the reform era using census

[53] The slogan "the priority is to develop heavy industry" (*youxian fazhan zhonggongye*, 优先发展重工业) was adopted in Jiangsu in the 1950s as part of the first five-year plan. Similarly, Zhang (2006) finds that the agricultural share of the population in 1993 predicts growth over the subsequent decade. For another industrial legacy argument, see Whiting (2000).

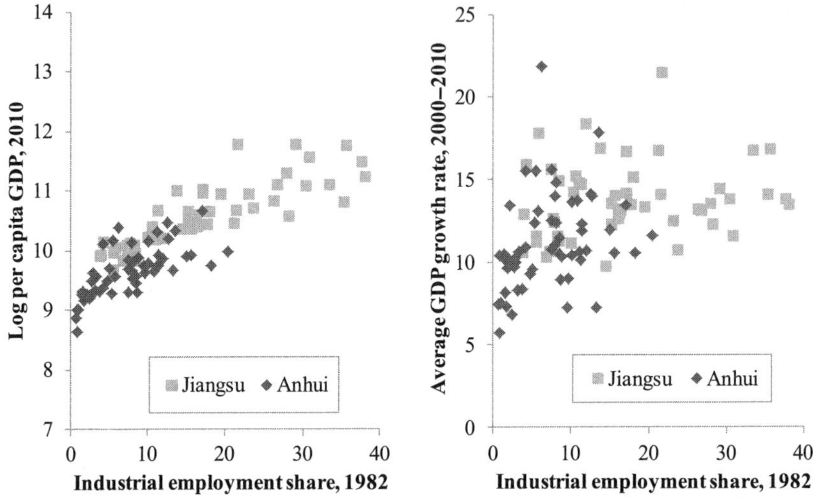

FIGURE 2.6. Mao-era industrial legacy predicts current income but not recent growth
Source: China County Statistical Yearbook; author's calculations.

data) versus current GDP per capita show that initial industrialization strongly predicts per capita GDP three decades later, seen in Figure 2.6 using data for Jiangsu and Anhui. However, industrial employment shares do not strongly predict growth rates over 2000–2010 (see the right panel of Figure 2.6) – in other words, initial industrial structures and income are persistent, but in the past decade other factors have become more important.

More broadly in China, it is clear that geography plays a role in economic development. At the most simple level, coastal regions have developed much faster than inland regions. Given the importance of foreign capital and foreign trade to China's growth, it is not surprising that this geographical correlation holds more broadly: proximity to Shanghai is a good proxy for county economic development throughout the country (see Figure 2.7).[54] And even within Anhui and Jiangsu, two provinces in close proximity to Shanghai, GDP per capita is negatively correlated with distance from Shanghai: on average, every additional kilometer distance is associated with a 31 RMB lower per capita GDP in Anhui and 168 RMB lower per capita GDP in Jiangsu (both significant at 99 percent).

[54] Mining and oil counties in western China are among China's richest, explaining some of the observations in the upper right quadrant.

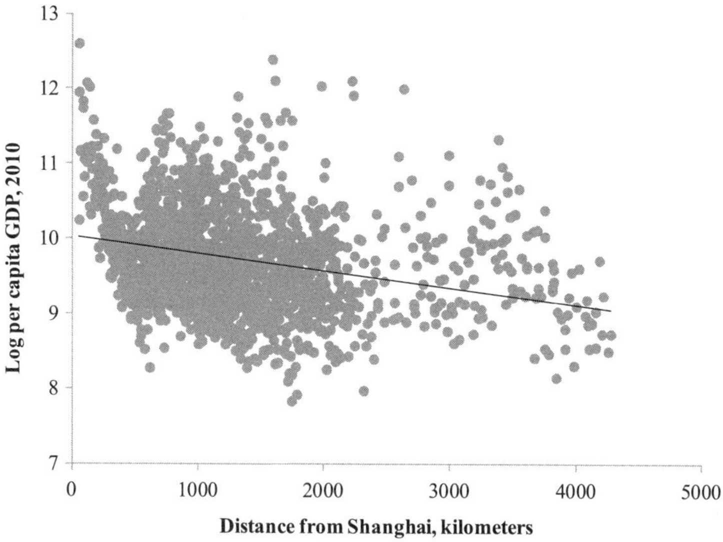

FIGURE 2.7. Geography as a determinant of income
Distance from Shanghai versus per capita GDP
Source: China Data Online; census data; author's calculations.

Feng County in the northwest tip of Jiangsu is 592 kilometers from Shanghai, implying that if it abutted Shanghai its 2010 GDP would be 108,754 RMB rather than 9221 GDP, a nearly 12-fold difference. Part of this effect is likely related to the existence of transportation routes and toll roads, which determine the ability to get products to market cost- and time-effectively, and which are likelier to be better developed closer to coastal urban centers.

To look more rigorously at the importance of geography and initial conditions, Table 2.1 shows results for regressions of recent growth and income on previous period conditions, using as controls static variables from 1982 and 2000, geographic variables, and provincial fixed effects.[55] Looking at columns (1) and (2) that regress 2010 GDP and recent growth rates on 1982 static variables, high-income counties in 1982 remained high income, although they grew more slowly over 2000–2010, indicating recent convergence. Conditions in 1982 explain 64 percent of variance in 2010 GDP per capita but only 21 percent of GDP growth over 2000–2010. Looking more recently, column (3) reports coefficients and

[55] These are the years that census data at the county-level are released. Census data are also released in 1990, but those results are not reported here.

TABLE 2.1. *Preconditions and geography as determinants of income and growth*

	(1)	(2)	(3)
Dependent variable:	**Log per capita GDP, 2010**	**GDP growth avg 2000–2010**	**GDP growth avg 2000–2010**
	Independent variables lagged 28 years (1982 values)		*Ind. variables lagged 10 years (2000 values)*
Log per capita GIAO	0.254*** (7.58)	−0.489 (−1.53)	
Log per capita GDP			−1.460*** (−4.19)
Agricult. employment share	−0.0160*** (−4.12)	−0.0259 (−0.70)	−0.0268 (−1.22)
Industrial employment share	−0.00499 (−1.08)	−0.0260 (−0.59)	0.0547* (1.85)
Population	−2.33e−07*** (−4.20)	−1.01e−06* (−1.93)	−8.70e−07* (−1.81)
Dependency ratio	−0.00631*** (−2.90)	0.00472 (0.23)	0.0285 (1.28)
College ed. (% working age)	−0.453*** (−4.14)	2.311** (2.23)	0.194 (1.48)
Illiteracy (% working age)	−0.0106*** (−7.36)	0.0106 (0.77)	−0.0345* (−1.88)
Urbanization rate			−0.0394*** (−2.76)
Population density	−1.99e−05 (−0.27)	−0.000288 (−0.42)	1.37e−05 (−0.02)
Distance from Shanghai	−9.94e−05 (−1.28)	0.000462 (0.63)	0.000809 (1.17)
Distance from prov. capital	−0.000770*** (−8.48)	−0.00214** (−2.49)	−0.00385*** (−4.59)
Distance from pref. city	0.000272 (1.04)	0.00803*** (3.25)	0.00440* (1.78)
Revenue share of GDP			0.273*** (5.04)
Expenditure share of GDP			0.0571** (2.53)

	(1)	(2)	(3)
Dependent variable:	**Log per capita GDP, 2010**	**GDP growth avg 2000–2010**	**GDP growth avg 2000–2010**
	Independent variables lagged 28 years (1982 values)		*Ind. variables lagged 10 years (2000 values)*
Loan share of GDP			0.0103***
			(4.47)
County-level city dummy	0.213***	0.237	0.788**
	(6.55)	(0.77)	(2.46)
Constant	10.85***	13.95***	22.00***
	(20.42)	(2.77)	(4.72)
Observations	1546	1546	1,603
R-squared	0.642	0.207	0.278

t statistics in parentheses. All regressions include provincial fixed effects.

*** $p<0.01$, ** $p<0.05$, * $p<0.1$

standard errors for a regression of the ten-year per capita growth average over 2000–2010 on a set of static variables from 2000 and geographic variables. Here, initial conditions account for only 28 percent of variance in growth over the past decade. In other words, geography and preconditions matter, but they are far from determinative. Generally, we see convergence, but counties with higher levels of human capital, higher revenue shares, and more industrial employment were able to partly offset this convergence – in other words, strong preconditions for growth were more important than geography. Moreover, growth in 2000–2010 is largely unexplained by preconditions; in this period of rapid investment and mobile capital, factors unrelated to preconditions have most influenced growth patterns.

The Role of the Province

Understanding the dynamics of county-level inequality through a comparison of the relative contributions of inter-provincial and intra-provincial inequality helps determine the role of geography and provincial borders in explaining county-level growth outcomes. The Theil index enables a disaggregation of inequality into *within* and *between* components, treating counties (rather than individuals) as the unit of analysis.[56] China has extremely high variance in county per capita incomes, with an overall Theil index in 2010 of 0.28. For comparative purposes, in the United States, a similarly sized geographic area with a relatively similar number of counties and states/provinces, the county-level Theil index is only 0.03; China has nine times higher county-level inequality (see Figure 2.8).[57] In China, county inequality both between and within provinces is nearly an order of magnitude larger than in the United States. In contrast, it is interesting to note that national individual-level Gini coefficients in both countries are relatively similar (and high), although the data are insufficient to determine what degree of individual inequality in each country stems from within-county versus between-county inequality.[58]

County development in China has varied not only by region and province; intra-provincial variation is also high. The degree of inequality within provinces differs widely, with the intra-province Theil index ranging from 0.044 in Hainan to 0.433 in Gansu, and no easily identifiable provincial characteristic predicts within-province levels of inequality,

[56] The basic expression for the index, first proposed by Theil (1967), is:

$$T_T = \frac{1}{N}\sum_i \left(\frac{x_i}{\bar{x}} \cdot \ln \frac{x_i}{\bar{x}} \right)$$

where N is the population size, x_i is the unit of measurement across i individual units of analysis (usually individual wealth, but in this case county average GDP per capita), and $\bar{x}$ is average county GDP per capita in the entire country. The Theil index can be decomposed as:

$$T_T = \sum_j s_j T_{T_j} + \sum_j s_j \ln \frac{\bar{x}_j}{\bar{x}} \qquad (2.1)$$

where T_T is the total Theil index, s_j is the county share of total GDP, T_{T_j} is the Theil index within province/state j, $\bar{x}_j$ is average GDP per capita in province j, and $\bar{x}$ is average county GDP per capita in the entire country. The left-hand term represents the within-province component of inequality, while the right-hand term represents the between-province component.

[57] Note from the Theil index equation in footnote 56 that the greater number of counties in the US should result in higher inequality as measured by the Theil index, all else equal.

[58] In the latest official Gini coefficients reported for each country, China reached 0.47 while the US reached 0.45.

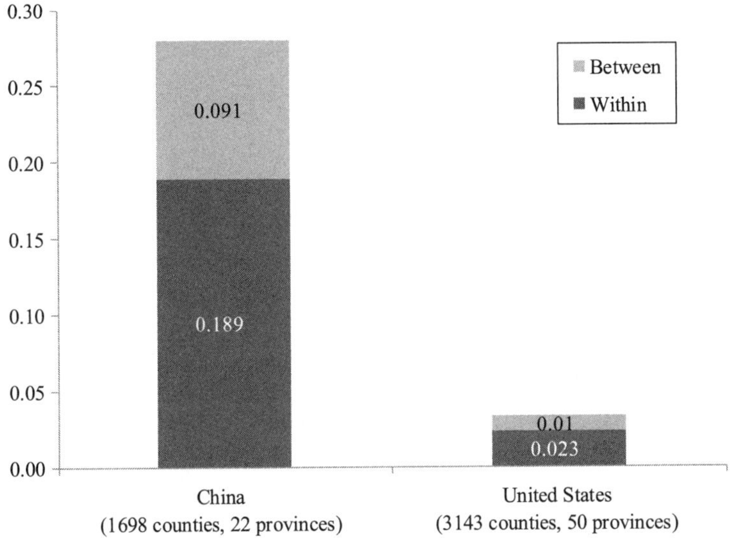

FIGURE 2.8. China has high inter-provincial and intra-provincial inequality
Theil index decomposition for counties in China and the United States
Source: China Statistical Yearbook; author's calculations.

implying that specific local factors, policy choices, and institutional differences explain variability in intra-provincial inequality.[59] Anhui and Jiangsu are at opposite ends of the within-province inequality spectrum. Largely as a consequence of a historical development gap between north and south Jiangsu, Jiangsu is extremely unequal; its internal Theil index is larger than that of the nation as a whole, and this is not an artifact of its size (number of counties or population) or its high income.[60] A rising

59 Although one might expect higher inequality in wealthier coastal regions that have seen certain areas develop rapidly or might expect greater inequality in provinces with more counties, none of these hypotheses holds on a strictly correlative basis. Moreover, as discussed in Acemoglu and Dell (2010) and elsewhere, a neo-classical growth model would attribute most income differences to variability in physical capital: China's provinces could exhibit variation in inequality due to differences in physical capital stocks. This hypothesis does not hold either, using provincial capital stocks from Wu (2009) (results not shown).

60 Shandong and Zhejiang, China's two richest provinces apart from Jiangsu, have much lower levels of inequality. Poor Qinghai and Gansu have the highest levels of internal county inequality, while Anhui, just as poor as these two provinces, has one of the lowest levels of internal inequality.

tide apparently does not lift all boats.[61] Given that Northern Jiangsu is the poorest part of the province, it is natural to conclude that geography is at play. Southern Jiangsu is a historically rich area with high population density and close proximity to Shanghai, and as shown previously, distance from Shanghai is a strong predictor of GDP per capita.

However, while geography plays some role, provincial boundaries and thus provincial institutions are important determinants of growth. Continuing with the US-China county comparison, it is informative to compare border dynamics in Jiangsu and Anhui to border dynamics in the US states of Virginia and West Virginia. These two states share many similarities with Jiangsu and Anhui. Geographically, they are in the country's central-east, with the richer province on the coast and the poorer bordering to the west (see Figure 2.9). While Washington, DC, is not quite the economic growth engine for the US that Shanghai is for China, distance from DC is nevertheless a very good income proxy for both Virginia and West Virginia. Virginia (Jiangsu) is one of the richest states (provinces) in the US (China), while West Virginia (Anhui) is one of the poorest, and the West Virginia-Virginia border is the most unequal state border in the US.[62] Even the number of bordering counties is similar: 14 Virginia counties border 11 counties in West Virginia, while 13 Jiangsu counties border 11 counties in Anhui.[63]

[61] Several authors have tried to describe why Jiangsu is so unequal. Wei and Kim (2002) look at within-province inequality in Jiangsu from 1950 through 1995, finding that while inequality between Jiangsu's sub-regions grew during the Mao era, inequality took off both within and between sub-regions post-1984, as growth switched from extensive agriculture to intensive industry. Inequality in the 1984–1995 period was driven by shares of SOE assets, levels of foreign direct investment, human capital levels, and agglomeration effects. Ho (1994) and Wei (2000) further discuss the advantages of Sunan in achieving agglomeration effects and attracting FDI, not only as a result of geography, particularly proximity to Shanghai, but also as a direct result of national and provincial preferential policies. Similarly, Rozelle (1994) finds rising inter-county inequality in Jiangsu between 1984 and 1989 based on varying speeds of rural industrialization. Long and Ng (2001) identify several factors as contributing to increasing intra-provincial inequality in Jiangsu: not only regional preferential policies (e.g. Nantong and Lianyungang were designated as open port cities, and Zhangjiagang became the only inland river port free trade county in 1993), but also historical factors, including Subei Huaihe flooding and pre-Ming Dynasty conflict!

[62] This is calculated by taking the per capita GDP ratios of all US states that share a border. The Maryland-West Virginia border is actually slightly less equal, but there are only three counties bordering West Virginia on the Maryland side, making the comparison less useful.

[63] Unfortunately rounding out the similarities, negative stereotypes of the poorer counterpart in both countries abound.

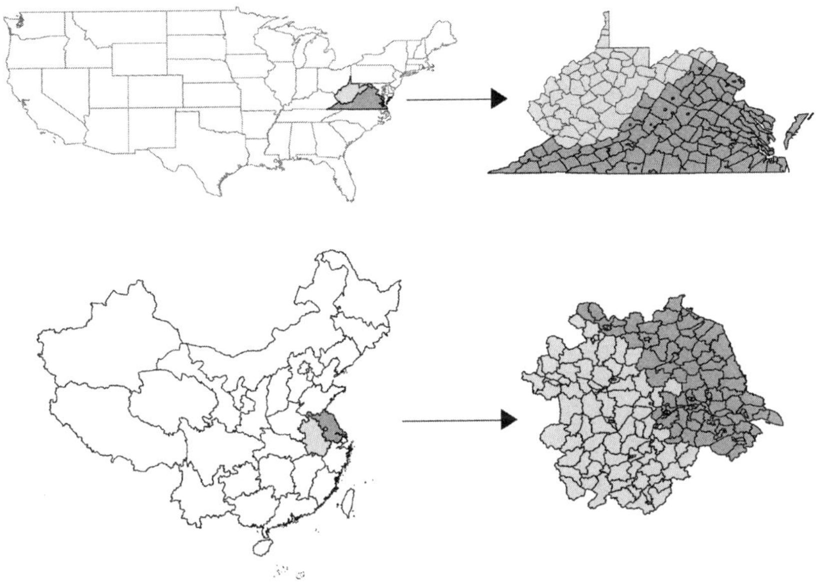

FIGURE 2.9. Geographic position of West Virginia and Virginia versus Anhui and Jiangsu

However, a comparison of income ratios of bordering counties between the province/state pairs in the two countries shows that while in the federalist United States the state boundary has minimal impact on determining per capita GDP, in China the provincial boundary deeply influences economic outcomes. This is shown graphically in Figure 2.10. The light gray line represents the state (province) overall per capita income ratio, and the dark gray line represents equality. The dots represent the ratio of each border county to the average per capita income of the counties (in the adjacent state) that it borders. For the richer state/province counties, these ratios are inverted. If province/state policies were largely irrelevant and geography determined outcomes, then counties bordering each other across provincial/state lines should have income ratios approaching equality; in terms of the graph, points would be expected to lie close to the light gray line, or at least between the dark gray line and the light gray line. The charts show that in the US, bordering counties trend towards equality: geography dominates state policy. In China, however, nearly half (10 out of 24) of the border counties are *more* unequal than the provincial average. Put another way, the average gap closes by more than half for counties in West Virginia-Virginia, while it closes by less

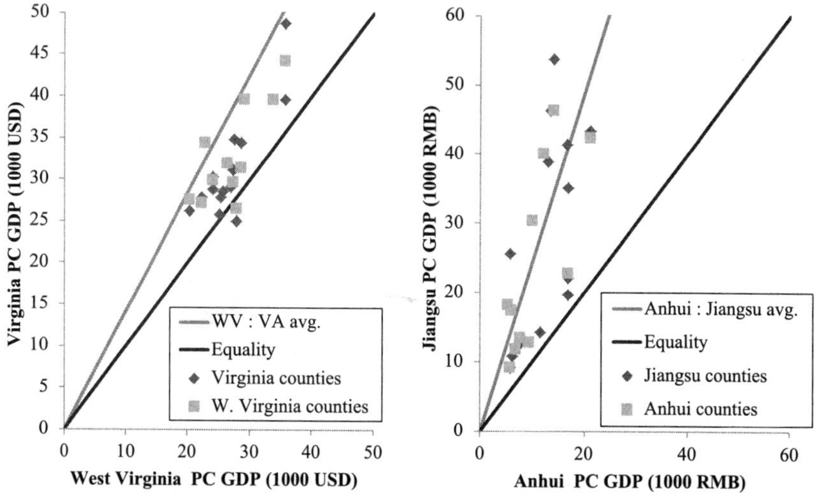

FIGURE 2.10. Provincial (state) borders more determinant of growth in China than the US

Per capita income ratios between bordering counties

A. West Virginia v. Virginia

B. Anhui v. Jiangsu

Source: China County Statistical Yearbook; US census data; author's calculations.

Note: The light gray line represents the overall per capita income ratio in each state (province). The dark gray line represents equality. The dots represent the ratio of each border county to the average per capita income of the counties that it borders in the adjacent state or province. For the richer counties, these ratios are inverted.

than one-sixth for counties in Anhui-Jiangsu. In a perhaps more intuitive way, Figure 2.11 shows that for any given distance from Shanghai, Jiangsu counties have considerably higher per capita income than Anhui counties. Given the above results showing the importance of distance from Shanghai in determining growth, the results here are especially striking, and imply that provincial-level institutions have a large effect on county growth outcomes.

Conclusions

As factor market conditions across labor, land, and capital have changed, counties have emerged in the 2000s as attractive destinations for mobile capital. This broad transformation is easy to document: changing factor

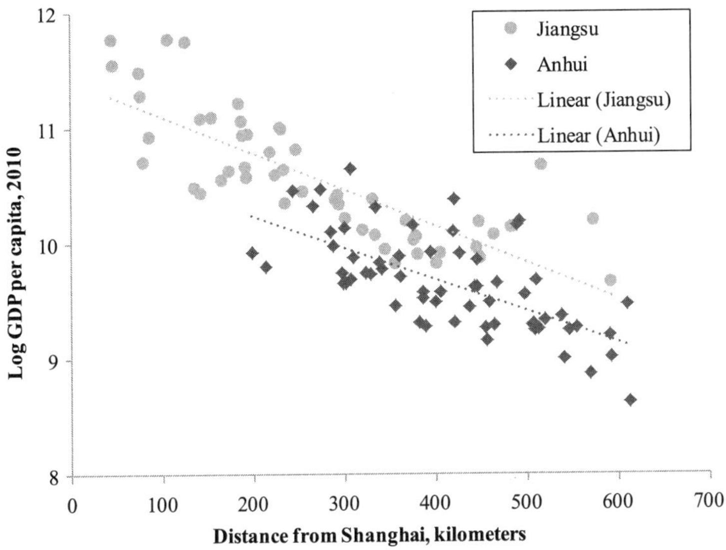

FIGURE 2.11. County income, provincial borders, and distance from Shanghai
Distance from Shanghai versus per capita GDP in Jiangsu and Anhui
Source: China Data Online; Census Data; author's calculations.

market conditions have made counties increasingly attractive relative to larger cities. But what differentiates counties from each other? In a new economic environment in which mobile capital is king, many counties have thrived. Others have been left behind. Why are some counties able to attract more investment than their neighbors? And why do some counties seemingly stagnate, unable to attract investment or boost productivity? Traditional explanations relying on initial conditions and geography are insufficient; even structurally similar counties with similar histories and geography have achieved very different growth outcomes. Intra-provincial inequality is extremely high and varies across provinces; inter-provincial inequality is also high, and provincial boundaries are important determinants of growth. In other words, provincial institutions appear to play an important role in determining the variation in outcomes. The following chapters attempt to explain capital differences and productivity differences between counties using a political economy framework. In the following chapter, I argue that governance and administrative quality and efficiency are important determinants of local growth, helping to attract finance both through investment promotion and through increased lending.

Chapter Appendix: Growth Accounting Data and Methodology

This section describes the data and methodology used in the growth accounting exercise whose results were reported in the text above. The data come from Chinese local statistical yearbooks, compiled for convenient analysis by the China Data Center at the University of Michigan. The data is for all counties (*xian,* 县) and county-level cities (*xianjishi,* 县级市), excluding urban county-level districts (*qu,* 区) over 1996–2010. As national county-level data in 1996 is partially incomplete, I select 1997 as the first year of analysis, and thus 1998 is the first year in which growth rates are calculated.

GDP and Value Added. Current RMB GDP data is available on an annual basis at the county level. To convert to constant 2000 RMB, several potential concerns arise. First, significant debate exists over whether China's official deflators overestimate growth; however, with no consensus on a superior deflator I opt to use official statistics. Second, the most robust analysis would use county-level deflators, but these do not exist for China. Therefore, to convert to constant prices, I use the annual GDP deflator from the prefecture-level to which the county belongs. This data is unavailable for many prefecture-years; when it is unavailable, I use provincial GDP deflators. Figure 2.12 shows how average constant price county GDP growth compares to national GDP growth over 1998–2010. While county growth is higher from 2002 to 2010, this does not necessarily imply a problem with the data (either over-reporting by local authorities or a too-low GDP deflator); rather, counties may have grown faster than the national average over this period, as the discussion above highlighted. The lower-than-national county growth prior to 2002 supports this argument.

Employment. For the growth accounting analysis, I focus on total employment rather than working-age population or an education-weighted human capital measure. Adjusting employment for human capital gains would tend to lower the TFP estimates. For the national data, I focus only on total employment. For Anhui and Jiangsu, I can disaggregate further to look at primary sector employment, enabling an analysis of the growth contribution of labor reallocation out of agriculture. For primary sector employment, I use data on employment in rural farming. When rural farming data is missing and only rural total employment data is available, I proxy primary sector employment by assuming the rural farming share of rural employment in the proximate year.

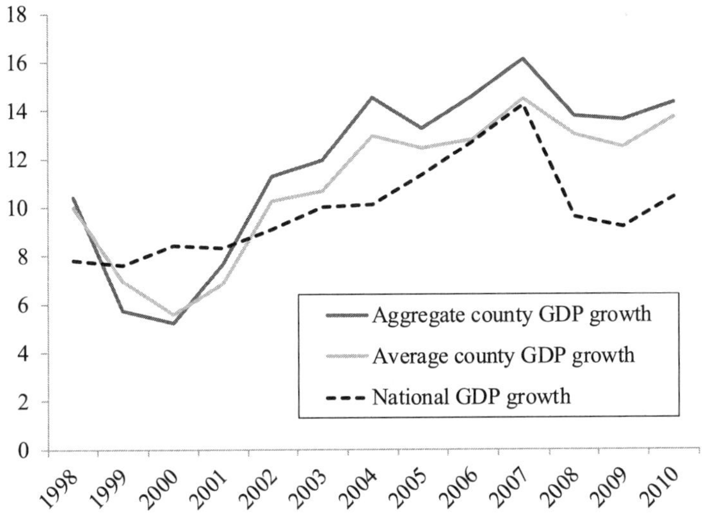

FIGURE 2.12. County GDP growth versus national GDP growth, 1998–2010
Note: Aggregate county growth is the aggregate weighted growth rate of all counties in the sample. Average county growth weight is the unweighted mean of county GDP growth in the sample. All three GDP growth rates represent real GDP growth.
Source: China Data Online; author's calculations.

Fixed Capital Stock. To calculate local fixed capital stock estimates, I use annual investment data and a perpetual inventory method, assuming annual depreciation of 10 percent. For Anhui and Jiangsu, I use official county-level annual fixed asset investment (FAI) data reported in provincial statistical yearbooks. No county-level investment data exists in the national county data, requiring broad estimations. The approach I take is to use FAI data at the prefecture and urban district (within prefecture) level; the difference between these two is the within-prefecture county sum of investment.[64] To generate individual county shares of this within-prefecture county sum of investment I calculate the within-prefecture

[64] Ideally, the annual investment series would use gross fixed capital formation (GFCF) rather than fixed asset investment, as this series more accurately reflects total investment levels across large- and small-scale projects, excluding land sales, but GFCF data is only available at the provincial level. The National Bureau of Statistics (NBS) counts the value of purchased land and expenditure on used machinery as part of FAI, and also excludes survey data for small investments (only investments over 500,000 RMB are included after 1997). See Bai (2008).

county share of annual loan growth and government expenditure, which serves as a loose proxy for total investment, and divide the investment by these shares:

$$I_{cpt} = \left(I_{pt} - I_{dpt}\right) \cdot \left(\frac{L_{cpt} - L_{cpt-1} + Exp_{cpt}}{\sum_{c} \left(L_{cpt} - L_{cpt-1} + Exp_{cpt}\right)} \right) \quad (2.2)$$

where I_{cpt} is investment in county c in prefecture p in time t; I_{pt} is investment in prefecture p; I_{dpt} is investment in urban districts, d, within prefecture p; L_{cpt} is county loans in time t, and Exp_{cpt} is county government expenditure in time t. Without access to a county or prefecture level FAI or GFCF deflator, I choose to deflate these investment data using the same GDP deflators described above. To generate a capital stock estimate based on this constant price county-level investment estimate, I apply a perpetual inventory method of the form:

$$K_t = (1 - \delta) \cdot K_{t-1} + I_t \quad (2.3)$$

Here, K_t is the capital stock in time t; δ represents the depreciation rate (assumed to be 10 percent), and I_t represents investment. I suppress county subscripts for convenience. For the initial capital stock in 1997, K_0, I use two estimates, one that assumes capital is equal to GDP and one that assumes capital is two times GDP. The former approach is taken as a baseline – while a capital-output ratio of one seems low, China's counties received very little investment and were predominantly agricultural in the mid 1990s. Given rapid investment in the late 1990s and 2000s, the choice of the initial capital stock does not have a large effect on the growth accounting exercise outcomes.

Capital share. The final ingredient in the growth accounting exercise is an estimate of the output elasticities of capital and labor. Most studies for China assume a constant and arbitrarily imposed capital share over time and across sectors (typically a value ranging from 0.4 to 0.6). Here, I use the sectoral capital shares calculated in Bulman and Kraay (2012), which impose the assumption of constant returns to scale at the level of sectoral production functions, so that the capital output elasticity is one minus the labor output elasticity. The national sectoral capital shares assume competitive factor markets, so that the labor output elasticity is approximated by the share of labor compensation in value added. For data, that analysis relied on Hsueh and Li (1999) for provincial-level sectoral value added and compensation for 1978–1995 and input-output table figures for 1997, 2000, 2005, and 2007, with intervening years estimated. Similar to the GDP price deflators discussed above, capital shares will differ across localities, and a more robust analysis would include separate capital shares for each province, but this is impossible due to data limitations.

For the growth accounting analysis, I take the annual growth rate of GDP, capital stock, and employment. Summary statistics for these data as well as the capital share data and growth in the alternative capital stock estimate are presented in Table 2.2. For the analysis, I focus on a limited sample including only county-year observations for which data exist for the full set of variables, and also excluding outlying observations below the first percentile or above the ninety-ninth percentile of each variable (except the capital share, which is assumed constant across counties). The unrestricted sample 1% and 99% observations thus represent the minimum and maximum variable values for the limited sample.

Methodology

Following Jorgenson (1991), World Bank (1997), and Bulman and Kraay (2012), I begin by assuming a constant-returns production function at the level of each sector, with aggregate output as the sum of the value of output across sectors and ownership forms:

$$Y_i = \sum_j Y_j = \sum_j A_{ij} F_{ij}\left(K_{ij}, L_{ij}\right) \tag{2.4}$$

Here, Y_i is county value added and Y_{ij} is value added in county *i* and sector *j*. In the nationwide analysis, there is only one sector (the whole local economy), so the *j* subscript is omitted. In the Anhui and Jiangsu analysis, j indexes agriculture and nonagriculture. I assume that value added in each sector is produced using a constant returns production function $F_{ij}(\cdot)$ using capital and labor (K_{ij} and L_{ij}), and A_{ij} is a measure of Hicks-neutral technological progress. Time subscripts are suppressed for notational convenience.

County aggregate GDP growth can be written as a share-weighted sum of growth in each sector:

$$g_{Y_i} = \sum_j s_{ij}\left(g_{A_{ij}} + \alpha_j g_{K_{ij}} + \left(1 - \alpha_j\right) g_{L_{ij}}\right) \tag{2.5}$$

TABLE 2.2. *Summary statistics for variables used in national growth accounting analysis*

Variable	Total Obs.	Mean	Std. Dev.	Min.	Max.	1% cutoff	99% cutoff	Sample Obs.	Sample Mean	Sample Std. Dev.
GDP growth	25,570	10.77	14.85	−333.2	320.8	−34.58	52.77	19,050	10.70	9.00
Capital growth	21,498	17.54	16.32	−254.3	320.8	−10.49	63.44	19,050	16.80	12.91
Capital growth (alt.)	21,500	13.25	15.88	−254.3	392.6	−10.49	61.76	19,050	12.26	12.33
Employment growth	25,631	-0.09	2.14	−104.6	107.3	−4.93	4.66	19,050	−0.14	1.54
Capital share	27,707	0.41	0.09	0.12	0.65	0.12	0.65	19,050	0.43	0.08

Note: The alternative capital measure is based on K=2Y in 1997 (versus K=Y in 1997 in the baseline). The sample for analysis is based on county-year observations for which data exist for the full set of variables, excluding observations below and above, respectively, the 1st and 99th percentile of each variable (except the capita share, which is assumed constant across counties, and only varies by year). The unrestricted sample 1% and 99% observations thus represent the minimum and maximum variable values for the limited sample.

where s_{ij} is the constant-price share of sector j in county i GDP, and α_j is the output elasticity of capital in sector j (as discussed above, I am unable to differentiate capital shares at less than a national level, so these shares do not differ by county). A useful decomposition of output growth is as follows:

$$g_{Y_i} = \alpha g_{K_i} + (1-\alpha) g_{L_i} + \sum_j s_{ij}(1-\alpha_j)\left(g_{L_{ij}} - g_{L_i}\right) + \sum_j s_{ij}\alpha_j\left(g_{K_{ij}} - g_{K_i}\right) + \sum_j s_{ij} g_{A_{ij}} \qquad (2.6)$$

where g_{K_i} and g_{L_i} are the growth rates of the county stocks of capital and labor; $g_{K_{ij}}$ and $g_{L_{ij}}$ are the growth rates of capital and labor in sector j; s_{ij} is the share of county GDP in sector j; and $\alpha = \sum_j s_j \alpha_j$ is the weighted average of the output elasticity for the economy as a whole.

The first two terms can be interpreted as the contributions of capital and labor accumulation to output growth. A standard aggregate growth accounting exercise would identify aggregate TFP growth as the difference between total output growth and this aggregate share-weighted average of capital and labor growth. Such an exercise would not distinguish between productivity growth at the disaggregated level, and the contribution of factor reallocation across sectors, to overall growth; these are captured by the third and fourth terms. The final term is a share-weighted average of TFP growth across sectors. Note that for the national analysis, excluding the sector terms results in a simplified one-sector analysis that groups the final three terms into a TFP growth measure that also includes all reallocation effects. The other two terms, representing the growth contributions of capital and labor accumulation, remain the same. For the Jiangsu and Anhui analysis, while I can disaggregate labor and output across sectors, I cannot disaggregate capital, so the residual TFP estimate includes the final two terms: sectoral capital reallocation and pure TFP growth.

Table 2.3 presents growth contributions under the baseline for the national sample as well as the coastal and central regional samples, and also presents results using the alternate capital and labor estimates.

TABLE 2.3. *Robustness check of national growth accounting exercise*

		National	National	National	Coast	Center
		Baseline	*Alternate capital estimate*	*Alternate labor estimate*	*Baseline*	*Baseline*
Whole period	Total growth	10.6	10.6	11.8	11.3	9.9
	Capital accum.	7.3	5.4	8.8	7.6	7.6
	Labor accum.	−0.1	−0.1	−0.1	−0.1	−0.1
	TFP growth	3.4	5.3	3.1	3.7	2.4
	Observations	19,464	19,489	14,092	4290	7741
1998–2000	Total growth	7.6	7.5	5.9	8.9	5.7
	Capital accum.	3.4	1.4	2.0	3.4	2.7
	Labor accum.	0.5	0.5	−3.9	0.1	0.4
	TFP growth	3.6	5.6	7.8	5.4	2.6
	Observations	5806	5833	323	1101	1885
2001–2003	Total growth	9.2	9.2	9.2	10.4	8.4
	Capital accum.	5.9	3.1	5.9	6.7	5.6
	Labor accum.	−0.3	−0.3	−1.7	−0.1	−0.3
	TFP growth	3.7	6.5	5.0	3.8	3.1
	Observations	4114	4124	4123	955	1762
2004–2006	Total growth	12.7	12.7	12.7	12.8	12.6
	Capital accum.	9.8	7.6	9.8	10.6	10.2
	Labor accum.	−0.3	−0.3	0.4	−0.1	−0.3
	TFP growth	3.2	5.4	2.6	2.3	2.7
	Observations	4086	4092	4120	956	1755
2007–2010	Total growth	13.4	13.4	13.4	12.8	12.4
	Capital accum.	10.6	9.7	10.6	9.6	11.1
	Labor accum.	−0.3	−0.3	1.0	−0.1	−0.3
	TFP growth	3.1	4.1	1.9	3.3	1.6
	Observations	5458	5440	5526	1278	2339

3

Governance for Growth: Investment Attraction and Institutional Development

In recent years, the Suining Development Zone has made "emphasize trust, high efficiency, excellent service" the objective, further establishing the theory of "government creates the environment, businesses create the wealth," and adhering to the work plan of "select people based on trust, keep projects based on service, win people's hearts based on relationships"...

– Wu and Wang (2013)

*The goal of reform in Suining is to make cadres clean (*rang ganbu ganjing, *让干部干净) and to make cadres administrators (*rang ganbu ganshi, *让干部干事) ... We gave cadres lots of targets. At first they didn't get it, complaining that the entire pressure of development shouldn't be placed on cadre shoulders, and that you can't rely on administrative strength to promote economic development. But afterwards they slowly began to accept the responsibility. Why? Because no matter the time or place, politics and economics cannot be separated (*zhengzhi he jingji, zai renhe shihou, renhe guojia dou shi fenbukaide, *政治和经济，在任何时候、任何国家都是分不开的).*

– Suining County Party Secretary Wang Tianqi

In the spring of 2013, I spent time in Suining County (Jiangsu) and Si County (Anhui) speaking with investors and local officials to learn about preferential policies and local investment climates. In both counties, I wanted to learn how the county presented itself and tried to appeal to potential investors. In particular, building off of ideas from the previous chapter, I wanted to see how development zone preferential policies differed, and, when these policies converged, how counties differentiated themselves from the competition, i.e., neighboring counties. My experiences in the two counties were starkly different. In Suining, the deputy head of the investment promotion bureau (*zhaoshangju*, 招商局) eagerly met me in a large conference room, located in a new building directly next to the county government headquarters. He graciously met me in his office and apologized for not having a translator on hand. I was offered tea and small talk. I asked him to speak to me as he would a potential investor, and to explain why a company facing rising costs elsewhere in China should consider relocating in Suining. The deputy bureau chief handed me a glossy 58-page booklet introducing Suining's investment climate and advantages in both Chinese and English and talked me through the preferential policies that businesses could receive based on how large their investments were. He also handed me a print-out from the previous month with all updated policies, but said that with a large investment all policies would be up for discussion. I pushed him a bit: why invest in Suining, especially since it seems like the preferential policies were equal in all nearby localities? He concurred:

> Preferential policies are largely the same in all the surrounding areas. The reason we [in Suining] get more investment [than Si] is government service (*zhengfu de fuwu*, 政府的服务), which is much more important for investors than preferential policies. The government's service mentality means that you can be confident that the government will help your company develop (*bangzhu nide qiye fazhan*, 帮助你的企业发展). (Interview JS290)

I asked him to explain, and he discussed government provision of labor services, partnering with local firms, financial assistance, infrastructure provision, lack of red tape, one centralized contact point for firms to avoid excessive fees, assistance selling the factory were it ever to close, and technological and worker training assistance. He was a gracious host with a lot of information, treating a foreign researcher with the same openness and helpfulness that might be extended to an actual investor, and he differentiated his county on the merits of its service mentality.

A week later I went to Si County in Anhui. Si and Suining border each other, and, as I discovered, their official preferential policies are practically identical, but the presentation of these policies is entirely different. The investment promotion bureau refused to grant me an audience, although the preferential policies were listed online, albeit in a much less professional and less detailed manner than in Suining. In Si, I encountered a closed and suspicious environment that was worlds away from the environment directly across the provincial border. One official in Jiangsu had described the reason for Subei's emergence relative to neighboring Anhui in one word: "openness," which he elaborated upon as an eagerness to invite in outside ideas, people, and capital (Interview JS281). I began to give credence to this attitudinal difference. The deputy director of the

Suining investment promotion bureau, when I thanked him for meeting with me, further demonstrated the contrast, mentioning that as a foreign researcher I could potentially provide a reputational boost to his county that would help attract future foreign investment (a grandiose view of academic readership to which I admit I did not overly object). The suspicious Si atmosphere could of course have rationally resulted from confusion as to my research goals, but the county contrast is nevertheless stark.

My experience in Suining and Si does not serve as a rigorous controlled comparison, but if I were a real investor, I would invest in Suining rather than Si. Actual investors agree: between 1997 and 2010, Suining received 69 percent more investment than Si. Currently in Si there are no western companies, and only a few Japanese companies investing in make-up and clothing. As one investor mentioned based on his experience in real estate markets in Si, Wuhe, and Lingbi (three counties that border each other in northeast Anhui), "In Suining County, the government is my partner. In Anhui, several county governments all tried to get me to invest, but the conditions were terrible and the governments were corrupt and just wanted my money" (Interview JS240). The previous chapter demonstrated that investment is the primary source of growth in China. Holding all else equal, if Si had received 70 percent more investment over 1994–2010 (the same amount as its Jiangsu neighbor), its expected growth rate would be 35 percent higher and its per capita GDP today would be nearly 60 percent larger than its actual value.[1]

This chapter explores local governance and local economic development in China's counties, using the case counties to demonstrate that governance and institutional capacity differ widely at the local level and are extremely important for determining growth outcomes. China's counties are in stark competition with one another for resources, particularly outside investment, and they must search out some form of competitive advantage; given low variability in factor and demand conditions, local governance becomes an important potential competitive advantage. The chapter begins by discussing what "governance" means, particularly as it relates to local economic development, paying attention to problems of endogeneity as well as the difference between local governance and national governance. The subsequent section looks at governance as it relates to government failures and market failures, using the case counties to develop an understanding of the ways that pro-growth governance

1 This calculation is based on Si's 9.5 percent average annual growth rate and an assumed coefficient of 0.5 on investment growth for GDP growth.

oss counties as well as the direct ways that these differences n different growth outcomes through enhanced investment ess. I then quantify some of these effects using county-level all counties in Jiangsu and Anhui. In combination with the analysis in the previous chapter, the findings presented here suggest that differences in local governance and government-business relations explain a significant portion of the variation in county-level investment outcomes and economic growth. The subsequent chapters seek to explain the reasons for differences in local governance by analyzing the roles and incentives of local leaders.

Pro-Growth Local Governance

"Governance" is notoriously difficult to define. One British newspaper described the concept as "slippery as an eel swathed in Swarfega" (Flinders and Matthews 2007). Its use across fields and issue areas gives rise to concerns that the term suffers from "concept stretching" that undermines theory-building based on the term (Sartori 1970).[2] Nevertheless, governance remains a key concept that is important to understand. According to Shah (2006), "Local governance is a broader concept and is defined as the formulation and execution of collective action at the local level," encompassing "the direct and indirect roles of formal institutions of local government" as well as informal norms, networks, community organizations.[3] In this chapter I refer only to the roles and institutions of local governance, looking at public governance rather than the mix of public-private governance. I build off the influential definition of governance behind the World Bank's Worldwide Governance Indicators, namely, "the traditions and

[2] In settling on a definition for governance, there are several approaches, for instance structure versus process and bureaucratic versus political economy. The majority of the literature on growth and governance applies to this latter definition/approach, and that is the approach used here. Flinders and Matthews (2007) differentiate between "structure" and "process" approaches to governance, as well as "vertical" and "horizontal" approaches. Fukuyama (2013) discusses different ways to measure governance: process, capacity, and output.

[3] Shah goes further, arguing that, "Good local governance is not just about providing a range of local services but also about preserving the life and liberty of local residents; creating space for democratic participation and civic dialogue; supporting market-led, environmentally sustainable local development; and facilitating outcomes that enrich the quality of life of local residents." Recent literature highlights the large network of non-government entities that provide local services (Bailey 1999). However, in China these local organizations and civil society have been less apparent, helping motivate a focus on government itself.

institutions by which authority in a country is exercised," including "the process by which governments are selected, monitored and replaced," "the capacity of the government to effectively formulate and implement sound policies," and "the respect of citizens and the state for the institutions that govern economic and social interactions among them" (Kaufmann, Kraay, and Zoido-Lobatón 1999, 1). The Worldwide Governance Indicators operationalize this definition through six composite governance indicators representing voice and accountability, government effectiveness, rule of law, control of corruption, political stability, and regulatory quality.[4]

How do government quality, constraints on government action, and the relationship of government to citizenry affect economic outcomes? The relationship between governance and growth has long been hypothesized and explored. Much economic analysis of government tends towards two extremes: a welfare economics perspective stressing government action for the public interest and a public choice perspective that sees government as an agglomeration of actors acting in their own private interest.[5] From a public choice perspective, pro-growth governance consists of the government controlling itself, while from a welfare economics perspective, governments should proactively address market failures to eliminate Pareto sub-optimal outcomes. In the 1950s, modernization theory took a welfare perspective and equated governance with democratization, perceiving economic development and governance enhancements as two sides of the same coin. In the 1980s, governance was seen as secondary: state reform was an essential component, but structural adjustment would itself lead to state reform by removing incentives for rent-seeking and corruption (Khan 2008); in other words, a public choice perspective that identifies government itself as the problem took over.[6] As the structural adjustment approach failed, the 1990s saw the mainstream emergence of theoretical and empirical studies of governance and growth, largely as a part of New Institutional Economics. These approaches were more nuanced, identifying both positive and negative roles for the exercise of

4 Similarly, as early as 1993 Knack and Keefer developed IRIS at the University of Maryland based on the International Country Risk Guide and consisting of six indicators: corruption, rule of law, bureaucratic quality, repudiation of government contracts, ethnic tensions, and expropriation risks.

5 More nuanced views see a spectrum, with governments able to act more or less in the public interest while also fulfilling personal aims. See Besley (2007) for a more in-depth discussion.

6 Many of these ideas were part of the development of "new political economy" that included Krueger (1974); Posner (1975); Bhagwati (1982); Bardhan (1984); Colander (1984); Alt and Shepsle (1990); Lal and Myint (1996). See Khan (2008) for a discussion.

public authority. In this perspective, good governance was identified as an essential component of enhancing growth through the promotion of markets and the elimination of government failures.

Institutional approaches to economics and politics have theorized on the linkages between governance and growth. Particularly popular have been theories explaining virtuous circles of good governance and growth and vicious circles of bad governance and stagnation or decline. Recently, several books have looked at institutional and political foundations of long-term growth. North, Wallis, and Weingast (2009) distinguish between "natural states" that create and extract rents, and "open access" states that are vulnerable to political entry and thus embrace public interests; these latter states develop and prosper, whereas natural states trend towards violence. Similarly, Acemoglu and Robinson (2012) distinguish between "extractive" and "inclusive" institutions, with the first resulting in exploitative, low growth, violence-prone vicious circles, and the latter resulting in pro-development virtuous circles. In both of these approaches, the idea of vicious circles of low institutional quality and low growth contrast with virtuous circles of high institutional quality and high growth.[7] Khan (2008) presents theoretical policy linkages between governance and growth: stagnant economies lead to unaccountable governments, rent-seeking and corruption, and therefore weak property rights; weak property rights lead to high transactions costs, which lead to stagnant economies, completing the vicious circle. Conversely, where markets are efficient, growth follows, making governments accountable, reducing rent-seeking and corruption, and thus leading to stable property rights and rule of law, which combine to make markets efficient.

Empirical evidence tends to support the positive relationship between governance conditions and economic growth, and there is now abundant research from both political science and economics demonstrating how a state's governance quality can improve economic outcomes.[8] While many empirical studies focus on the correlation between growth and governance and do not reject reverse causality, limited evidence exists that the governance-to-growth pathway has more empirical validity than the growth-to-governance pathway.[9] Using instrumental variables

[7] Similarly, Gradstein (2004) presents a model showing that economic performance and enforcement of property rights are complementary and tend to reinforce one another.

[8] See, for example, Knack and Keefer (1995); Mauro (1995); Barro (1997); Evans and Rauch (1999); Aidt (2009); Holmberg and Rothstein (2012).

[9] Empirical evidence demonstrates a high correlation between wealth and growth, but there has been a long debate on the direction of causality between governance and

to control for the endogeneity problem, whereby higher incomes could lead to better governance rather than vice versa, several papers still identify causal effects running from governance to wealth.[10] Going even further, Kaufmann and Kraay (2002) find evidence confirming not only the importance of good governance for economic development, but also the absence of "virtuous circles" in which higher incomes lead to governance improvements; in other words, causality runs in only one direction.[11]

However, this strong empirical linkage between governance and growth does not hold closely with every country: in the China case, without effective democracy and institutionalized downward accountability, the governance-to-growth chain seems broken, and yet China has achieved rapid growth. Indeed, many see China as a case in need of explanation: how has China grown so fast despite such poor governance? As Keefer (2007) writes, "Fast growth, and in the Chinese case, extraordinary growth, have been accompanied by strictly average governance indicators. From the 1980s to the present, international risk rating firms report that investors have confronted frequently arbitrary government decision making and insecure contractual and property rights."[12] High levels of corruption and minimal downward accountability are identified as particularly problematic.[13]

China's governance shortcomings are widely identified as becoming amplified at the local level. Keefer (2007) discusses the microeconomic evidence of corrupt collusion between firms and local governments that "reinforces the conclusion that growth has proceeded despite a somewhat challenging governance environment."[14] Pei (2006) discusses in depth the

growth. Does higher growth lead to better institutional quality and better governance, or does better governance enable higher growth? The correlation between governance and growth could indicate causation from one to the other or result from an omitted variable that causes both. For instance, Sachs et al. (2004) show that when taking initial incomes into account, governance quality has no relationship with growth in Africa.

[10] See, for example, Hall and Jones (1999); Kaufmann, Kraay, and Zoido-Lobatón (1999); Acemoglu, Johnson, and Robinson (2001); Easterly and Levine (2003).

[11] The paper uses worldwide governance indicators for 175 countries over 2000/2001, speculating that elite influence and state capture help account for the surprising negative effects of per capita income on governance.

[12] Note that Keefer still concludes that governance is important for explaining China's growth, arguing that governance in China was better than that in other poor countries and that significant governance improvements in the late 1970s and early 1980s were a prerequisite for China's growth take-off.

[13] For a discussion of the antigrowth consequences of corruption in China, see Pei (2006).

[14] For instance, Cai, Fang, and Xu (2005) find that firms make large payments to government officials in order to prevent opportunistic local government behavior and bureaucratic burdens, rather than to create rents. Nee and Opper (2006) find that CEOs engaged in political activity have significantly better access to credit.

capture of local government. If satisfaction with government can indicate governance quality, then localities are significantly worse than the center: Saich (2013) finds that while 92 percent of respondents in China were relatively or extremely satisfied with central government work in 2011, only 64 percent were satisfied at the local level.[15] As Saich explains:

> ... one could argue that many of China's core problems arise from deficiencies in governance. The system is riddled with corruption, a sure sign of poor governance, with officials abusing official position for personal gain and with the sale of government positions undermining the notion of promotion based on meritocratic principles. Many, if not most, of the local protests are caused by the improper or illegal actions of local officials. This includes the poor implementation of good national regulation at the local level (leading to environmental pollution or sale of substandard products), the illegal transfer of land that dispossesses or undercompensates farmers, and restricting access to public goods and services.

Interestingly, however, many theories of China's growth rely on decentralization and autonomy given to local governments, as highlighted in the introductory chapter, so on the one hand China's local governments are seen as privately motivated and lacking good governance, and on the other hand they are seen as capable of producing the world's fastest sustained growth over the past three and a half decades. This seeming contradiction has two explanations. First, there is variance in governance quality at the local level in China: some localities have better governance than others, so it is not helpful to discuss "good" or "bad" local governance as a nationwide local constant. Second, and more compellingly given that even "bad governance" localities in China have achieved growth rates above the global average, governance itself can be broken into components representing a broad range of government roles and government-society interactions.[16] China's local governments have performed very well on some of these governance components and very poorly on others; in particular, they have often performed well on governance dimensions that are most directly related to local growth.[17]

[15] Similarly, while the China Survey 2008 on trust in leaders finds that 45 percent had high levels of trust in the central leadership, only 17 percent had high levels of trust in county and township leaders. A Horizon Survey Group 2003 survey showed that four out of seven county magistrates failed to meet a 50 percent target of public support (if asked to vote for their magistrate), while just one level up 13 of 13 prefecture city mayors reached more than 50 percent (Yang 2004).

[16] Rothstein (2013) identifies a third explanation, namely that while China's formal institutions exhibit poor governance, informal institutions may yield good governance. For instance, high levels of social trust may offset the negative effects of corruption (Li and Wu 2010). *Guanxi* relationships can ensure honesty in transactions (Huang and Wang 2011).

[17] Rothstein (2013) argues that definitions of the quality of government institutions have been "conceptualized by mostly western scholars," which is "specifically detrimental

The "local economic development" (LED) literature provides a useful starting point for identifying some of these components of local governance that are beneficial for local growth. LED evolved in the 1970s as a policy approach as municipal governments realized that businesses were seeking to move between locations to gain competitive advantages (Swinburn, Goga, and Murphy 2006, 1–2).[18] In response, these local governments attempted to understand the local obstacles to investment and how to facilitate capital entry. LED consists of policy responses to create conditions conducive to job growth and investment attraction by maximizing the potential of finance, infrastructure, technology, industrial structure, quality of life, human resources, etc. (Abrams and Murphy 2005, 232). LED highlights that governance can enhance both inputs and efficiency through agency coordination, firm connections, worker training, labor and technology matching, as well as other mechanisms requiring government involvement. OECD (2004) focuses on the government's role in boosting efficiency and productivity through skilled labor, entrepreneurship, and innovation polices. Innovation policies require governments to build local knowledge bases by providing risk capital (particularly for SMEs) and attracting talented researchers and labor, as well as exploiting production and distribution advantages by becoming "technology brokers" and sharing of equipment as well as researchers for firm-to-firm and firm-to-institute networking (Giguere 2004, 13–15). The policy-intervening capacity of local authorities/agencies is important to LED, and a major focus is on the "welcome mat" effect provided by the incentives and relocation packages provided by local development agencies (Wong 2002).[19] Note also that LED

to the Chinese case," concluding that China's special form of public administration, "cadre organization," can produce superior outcomes to Weberian rule-of-law based bureaucracies.

18 The World Bank examines the evolution of LED through three phases since the 1960s (Swinburn 2006, 6). From the 1960s to the 1980s, the focus was on attracting mobile capital from outside the area through big firm subsidies, grants, tax breaks, hard infrastructure investment, and recruitment of cheap labor. This process was public sector only. From the 1980s to the mid 1990s, a public sector driven process involved attracting capital from specific sectors and retaining local businesses through direct payments, business incubators, technical advice and SME support, and hard/soft infrastructure investment. Finally, the past two decades have focused on making business environments more favorable, soft infrastructure (human resources, knowledge sharing, regulatory rationalization), leveraging the private sector, improving quality of life, and highly targeted/specialized investment attraction.

19 This effect has been especially apparent in explaining cross-border FDI decisions. For instance, Munday (1990) describes the "welcome mat" incentives provided by Wales and their effectiveness at enticing Japanese investment.

strategies and pro-growth governance requirements differ across levels of development. At early stages the focus is simply on attracting capital, but later stages of development require a shift towards efficiency and rational/selective investment seeking/approval, which requires more attention to pro-clustering policies to enhance localization economies.[20] In other words, the role of governance in developing and developed countries may be different.[21]

Looking at the LED literature, government "effectiveness" (i.e., the quality of the civil service and the quality of policy formulation and implementation) and regulatory quality should have the strongest relationship to local growth. However, despite theoretical reasons to believe that local governance in the form of institutional capacity and government efficiency affects growth outcomes, the quantitative evidence is limited, more as a result of the difficulty in assessing local institutional capacity than as a consequence of contradictory evidence.[22] Traditional governance indicators related to the rule of law and corruption would seem to have a second-order relationship in helping to improve government effectiveness and quality, while indicators related to accountability may have little direct relationship to short-term local growth. Voice and accountability are likely important for long-term growth through ensuring continued government effectiveness and rule of law, but may be orthogonal to short-term growth. Accountability generally refers

[20] Much of the efficiency/productivity benefits of local governance depend on localization and urbanization economies. The relative weight of urbanization and localization economies remains highly contested, but the policy implications are important (Parkinson 2004). Localization economies require pro-clustering policies, related firms, inter-firm connections, perhaps through creation of highly specialized industrial districts. Urbanization economies benefit all firms, and focus more on the public goods of infrastructure, education, research and development, as well as making livable cities good environments, social cohesion, and high service quality. Policies that work for urbanization economies tend to also work at boosting inputs; this is not as relevant for localization economies.

[21] For instance, Khan (2008) makes a distinction between market-enhancing and growth-enhancing governance, with the latter more suited to developing countries in which market-enhancing governance is often unachievable. Growth-enhancing governance requires three interrelated governance capabilities/processes: managing nonmarket asset transfers, disciplining learning process and managing rents in order to acquire technology, and political stability.

[22] For instance, Wong (2002, 1843) includes institutional capacity as one of 11 factors essential for local development, but not among her 29 indicators: "Due to the qualitative nature of institutional capacity, it is not possible to devise any reliable and valid measure for this factor."

to downward accountability towards citizens, but the accountability that matters in the local government capacity framework in China comes from within-institution horizontal and vertical accountability; in other words, do agencies and bureaus coordinate in policy formulation and implementation? I will argue later that where upward accountability mechanisms lead to pro-growth "good governance," by which I mean high levels of government effectiveness and good regulatory quality, corruption declines as growth (and government effectiveness) rises. Similar limited definitions of governance have been used before. Fukuyama (2013), for instance, defines governance as "a government's ability to make and enforce rules, and to deliver services, regardless of whether that government is democratic or not," and he complains that most measures of governance concentrate more attention on "checking" institutions than on "power-deploying" institutions. Within this power-deploying framework, governments may perform better or worse: "governance is thus about execution, or what has traditionally fallen within the domain of public administration, as opposed to politics" (Fukuyama 2013, 4).

Thought about in this way, the apparent puzzle of poor local governance and rapid economic growth in China is less puzzling: there is a low level of downward accountability and a high level of corruption, but governments have at times been highly effective and implemented pro-growth regulations and policies. In cross-national comparison, as shown in Figure 3.1, China is an outlier on the voice and accountability indicator, but performs as expected on government effectiveness.[23] Similarly, China's local governments perform well in government effectiveness and regulatory quality, less well in corruption control and rule of law, and worst in downward accountability. Indeed, China has its own definitions of governance that focus on economic efficiency, control of corruption, and policy implementation, in addition to trust in government (Dimitrov 2013). And over the reform period, while explicit political reforms that would significantly alter citizen voice and improve downward accountability have been limited, there have been deep institutional reforms at

[23] Note also that not a single country with above-average government effectiveness has per capita GDP below US$3800 (and only seven are below the global median of US$7957), whereas many countries with high voice and accountability rankings have very low incomes (lower right quadrant), and many rich countries have low levels of voice and accountability (upper left quadrant).

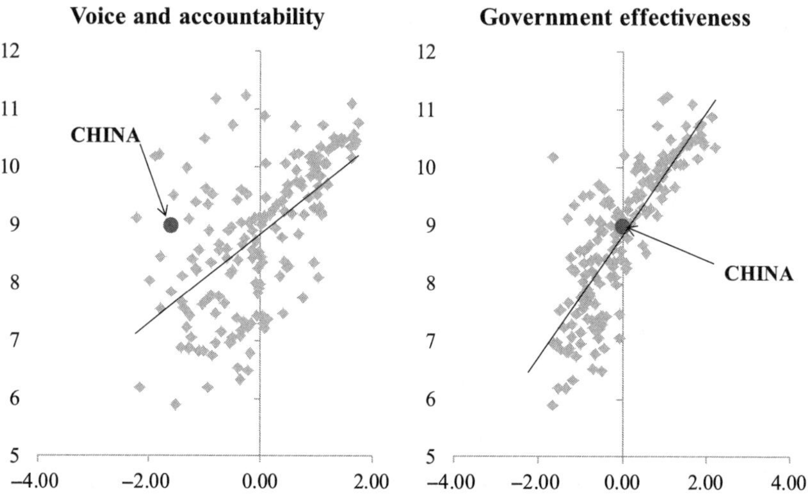

FIGURE 3.1. China is an outlier in "accountability" but not "effectiveness"
Log per capita GDP versus governance indicator component, all countries, 2010
Source: Worldwide Governance Indicators 2013; World Development Indicators 2013; author's calculations.

all levels of government focused on administrative restructuring, cadre competency, and institutional capacity.[24]

Looking at China's local governance and growth, China's governance capacity matches those that the World Bank identifies as important for developing an effective "five process" LED framework (Swinburn, Goga, and Murphy 2006). These five processes include organization of the LED effort, assessment of the local economy, development of a strategy, implementation, and review. Organizing the effort requires institutional arrangements that enable coordination. At the national level and cross-hierarchy levels in China this is highly problematic, but local governments have had more success ensuring horizontal accountability and coordination, as well as proactive interactions with businesses themselves. This coordination and interface is supported by a highly institutionalized process of assessments, strategy making, and review, identified most clearly through government work reports that highlight the major difficulties of previous years and goals moving forward. These plans/reports are the result of multi-month processes of consultation between bureaus: each bureau submits its own annual report to the government work office, which reviews and adjusts

[24] Brodsgaard (2010) discusses many of these institutional reforms. For more in-depth accounts, see Shambaugh (2008) and Yang (2004).

and then makes county-level plans based on all inputs (Interview JS281). Finally, while reporting and implementation problems continue to exist, the formal framework is very strong, and at the local level, implementation of *local* strategies is less problematic, particularly where county Party secretaries can ensure high levels of compliance (see Chapter 4). In other words, China's local institutions seem to be designed for managerial efficiency and governance capacity along the lines that have been identified as important for local economic development and growth.

A useful way to look at the characteristics of pro-growth governance in China's counties and understand the variance in government efficiency and capacity involves looking at local economic development as a policy response framework for correcting *government failures* and *market failures*. The former includes corruption, excessive regulations, high transaction costs, and risks for local investors, while the latter involves increasing the efficiency of factor markets (Abrams and Murphy 2005). In their use here, government and market failures correspond to the ideas of "grabbing hands" and "helping hands" of governments; "grabbing hands" are government failures, while "helping hands" alleviate market failures. Similarly, and more descriptively, in Suining County the government differentiates the pro-business role of government into "bodyguarding" (*baobiao*, 保镖) and "nannying" (*baomu*, 保姆); "bodyguarding" refers to preventing the government from collecting fees and harming enterprises, similar to the idea of government failure here, while "nannying" refers to proactively helping enterprises, similar to the market failure approach here. The government failure approach in some ways corresponds to a public-choice conception of government as an accumulation of actors with private interests that can oppose public interests; the market failure approach sees governments as acting in the public interest. In the government failure area, pro-growth governance implies prevention, or a diminution/elimination of certain types of government behavior. Eliminating the government from areas in which it should not engage can lower business costs and decrease waste (measured in time and money); enhancing "good" behavior can boost productivity and performance. All of this makes localities more attractive to investors and makes local firms operate more efficiently. In the market failure area, pro-growth governance requires proactively enlarging, enhancing, or refining certain types of government behavior. These relate to many of the government roles identified in the developmental state literature.[25]

[25] For instance, Evans (1995) identifies four major roles that government can play in the economy: custodian (protecting, policing, and regulating); midwife (creating new

Local Economic Development and Government Failure

Government failure comes in many forms. Often the term is used to describe bad policies, or policies that lead to the inefficient allocation of resources compared with the absence of policy: "Government failure, then, arises when government has created inefficiencies because it should not have intervened in the first place or when it could have solved a given problem or set of problems more efficiently, that is, by generating greater net benefits" (Winston 2006, 3). Coase (1964) used the term with regard to inefficient and harmful industrial regulations. Examples include regulatory arbitrage, regulatory capture, and economic crowding out of private sector spending and investment. Whereas a market failure is a Pareto-inefficient equilibrium allocation of resources, a government failure is a sub-optimal allocation of resources resulting from government efforts to correct market failures.[26] Here I focus on behavior rather than policy and take a slightly more expansive view of government failure, looking at government pathologies that lead to inefficient outcomes, with particular attention to corruption and excessive fee collection, corresponding to the "grabbing hand" idea of government failure.

Corruption in Chinese counties is rife, although it comes in different forms, only some of which appear to have strong antigrowth implications.[27] In the country as a whole, corruption is seen as hindering growth, and several authors have estimated costs of corruption that reach as high as 13–16 percent of GDP.[28] The incidence of corruption seems to have

businesses in specific sectors); husbandry (cultivating and nurturing entrepreneurial forces); and demiurge (becoming directly involved in production). And indeed, all four of these roles are played by China's local governments.

[26] Kreuger (1990, 10) distinguishes between government failures of "omission" and "commission": failures of commission include government involvement in a variety of economic activities not generally associated with the public sector (state marketing boards, SOEs monopoly rights, inefficient government investment programs, price controls, etc.). These failures of commission are failures of policy, not a priori failures (e.g., some SOE monopolies work). Failures of omission included deteriorating infrastructure, refusing to eliminate exchange controls and fixed exchange rates, low nominal interest rates.

[27] Manion (2004, 96–110) provides a taxonomy of the most common forms of corruption in China: bureaucratic commerce (businesses of government agencies, basically the "entrepreneurial state"), predatory extraction ("excessive compulsory and irregular nontax charges"), corrupt exchanges (basic bribery), use of public funds as private capital, and illegal privatization of state enterprise assets. This taxonomy largely ignores the buying and selling of offices, although this appears to be the most common type of corruption at the county level.

[28] Hu and Guo (2001) estimate 13.2–16.8 percent. According to Wu and Zhu (2011), counties with higher anticorruption efforts have higher income levels based on data for

been relatively constant over time: China's corruption perception index has not changed significantly since the mid 1990s.[29] But the relationship between corruption and growth is not entirely clear, and others note the potential for positive-sum corruption. For instance, Kang (2002) argues that corruption in South Korea and the Philippines has been relatively similar, but that South Korea has been able to develop due to the greater power of business groups relative to the government. Leff (1964) and Huntington (1968) suggested ways in which corruption could actually enhance growth: corruption in the form of "speed money" enables businesses and individuals to avoid bureaucratic red tape and delay. Additionally, if corruption is seen as a payment, then it can incentivize those government employees who levy bribes. However, more arguments focus on the negative consequences of corruption,[30] and Rose-Ackerman (1978) notes that even if certain forms of corruption have pro-growth consequences, limiting corruption only to these areas may be impossible. In other words, the key is identifying the type of corruption and its effects. "Speed money" may be pro-growth, or at the very least not anti-growth, while assigning government positions based on bribes may lead to an unqualified and incapable bureaucracy; these are not contradictory conclusions. Corruption as a deterrent to local investment is bad, while corruption to entice local investment may not have negative short-term consequences.[31]

Corruption has been very common at the county level in Jiangsu and Anhui. In the six case counties, over the past 20 years, four have had county Party secretaries convicted of corrupt behavior, and all have had multiple cases of corruption lower down the administrative ranks.[32] But the negative consequences of corruption in the counties have differed, and the timing and degree of corruption has differed across Jiangsu and

2003. Indicators are the number of audits, number of auditors, and illegal funds uncovered in the year before (2002).

29 Transparency International Corruption Perceptions Index: www.transparency.org/cpi2011/results.

30 See, for example, Shleifer and Vishny (1993).

31 Most literature now highlights the negative growth effects of corruption. Kaufmann and Wei (1999) find that "speed money" (what they refer to as "efficient grease") does not exist empirically: firms that pay bribes spend more time dealing with bureaucrats and have higher costs of capital than firms that do not.

32 Si and Suining, the poorest sample counties in Anhui and Jiangsu, respectively, had no documented cases of corruption at the highest level – this may simply be because of poor oversight in less institutionalized environments. Note that if this explanation is correct, then the higher prevalence of corruption in poorer Anhui described below is likely even more extreme than identified.

Anhui counties more broadly. In the two Jiangsu case counties with past corrupt leadership, one county Party secretary and one county magistrate in Sihong and Xuyi, respectively, were arrested for corruption in the early to mid 1990s. In Sihong, a magistrate in the early 1990s, Li Yuanzhang (李元章), was found guilty for accepting 49,000 RMB in bribes from eight people. The Xuyi County Party secretary from 1995 to 1997, Xin Lizhong (欣立忠), accepted cash, a color TV, a microwave, and jewelry worth 274,070 RMB (including during his final two years as the propaganda bureau chief in Huaiyin City). These are not trivial amounts, but in both cases the frequency and volume of bribes was relatively low. Moreover, these cases, with the most recent concerning bribery in 1997, preceded the switch in growth emphasis from restructuring to investment promotion described in the previous chapter.

In Mingguang and Wuhe in Anhui, corruption at the highest level has been more systematic, larger in magnitude, and more recent – both have had county Party secretaries arrested for corrupt behavior as recently as 2007. In Wuhe, two successive county Party secretaries who served from 2001 to 2007 were convicted of corruption. Zhang Guiyi (张桂义) served as Wuhe magistrate from January 1999 to March 2002 and Party secretary from November 2001 to February 2004. During his time in office he accepted 245,199 RMB and 4000 USD for appointments, promotions, recommendations, personnel transfers, and project development.[33] More recently, Xu Shexin (徐社新) spent six years as an official in Wuhe, becoming known as an "official position retailer" (*guanmao shouhuolang,* 官帽售货郎) who "wasted time away" selling all important bureau and township head positions. According to one local official, it was an "open secret" (*gongkai de mimi,* 公开的秘密) that the only way to get promoted was to pay a bribe (Li 2010). While in office Xu accepted 3.1 million RMB, 13,789 USD, 500 Euros, 5000 HKD, and 55,000 RMB worth of shopping cards. The largest single "briber" was Yang Jingxue, the CEO of a local beer company, who between 2003 and 2006 paid Xu over 650,000 RMB. In order to get a low auction price for a Tianjing Beer Factory in June 2006, Yang gave Xu 100,000 RMB, along with a further 40,000 RMB to convince Xu to arrange the auction as soon as possible.

[33] In November 2000, he told the Finance department head (Sun Liping) to take 800,000 RMB from the department coffers and transfer it to a land bureau account to substitute the Xinghua Company land transfer fund. The land bureau then transferred 800,000 RMB back to the county finance department, as if it had come from a transfer. For a much more in-depth discussion of this case, see the court judgment: Yuhui District People's Court (2005).

Two of the four Mingguang Party secretaries who served over 1992–2007 were convicted of corruption. Xue Xianzao (薛贤早) and Zhang Songjian (张松坚) served collectively for nine years (not successively), and both left legacies of entrenched corruption. Indeed, corruption was frequently identified in interviews as the key reason for Mingguang's backwardness since the mid 1990s. One well-informed interviewee identified corruption (*tanwu fubai,* 贪污腐败) as the most problematic issue in Mingguang's development, and particularly the corruption case under Party Secretary Xue in the early 1990s that resulted in convictions of over 130 people, including the Party secretary, magistrate, two other department-level (*chuji,* 处级) cadres, and 15 section-level (*kejuji,* 科局级) cadres (Ming 1998). The incident became known as the "Mingguang nest case" (*mingguang wo'an,* 明光窝案), and if you ask a local about the "nest case," they know exactly what you are talking about. Indeed, in one academic survey of corruption in China, the "corruption nest" under Party Secretary Xue is identified as the archetype (*dianxing,* 典型) of a process that evolves from "self-initiated individual corruption" (*zhudongxing geti fubai,* 主动型个体腐败) to "group corruption" (*qunti fubai,* 群体腐败), particularly "between-bureau group corruption" (*bumenjian qunti fubai,* 部门间群体腐败), and on to "regional corruption" (*quyuhuai fubai,* 区域怀腐败) (Xu and Wang 2000). This case involved the buying and selling of offices, and it negatively affected government operations for years to come, for multiple reasons. First, almost the entire government structure had to be re-staffed. Second, local government lost the people's trust. And third, no qualified officials wanted to go to Mingguang, so Chuzhou City and Anhui Province itself basically wrote the county off (Interview JS133; Interview AH104; Interview AH138).

More recently, Zhang Songjian (张松坚) is remembered for having further undermined the cadre system, permitting and promoting a lawless culture of corruption. In selling off state assets at bargain basement prices for personal gain and in appointing only cadres who paid bribes, Zhang undermined local revenue sources and permanently damaged state-society and state-business relations. Zhang was convicted of corruption, involving enterprise restructuring, cadre appointments, and land transfers, after he accepted bribes from 162 people worth 4.3 million RMB, with an additional 70,000 RMB worth of shopping cards. One factory CEO gave him over 100,000 RMB on one occasion, but he was not above accepting as little as 800 RMB (Wu 2010). There was a popular saying while Zhang was in office: "Zhang Songjian, County head Zhang, after one year on the job, the sky over Mingguang grew a foot" (张松坚,

张知县，走马上任才一年，明光高出一尺天): Zhang sold off land with alacrity, meaning all the land lost a foot and the sky gained a foot. While Zhang accepted nine bribes from local CEOs, the vast majority (132) of the bribes came from other cadres. When he fell, many of these other cadres were ousted as well.[34]

One particular bribe was frequently mentioned in local interviews, with considerable still-festering anger: the below-value sale of Old Mingguang Liquor (老明光酒). The factory dated to the Southern Song dynasty (1127–1279 AD), and by the turn of the millennium it had four major brands and over 100 varieties, employing over 3000 workers. For several years running it was one of China's 500 biggest industrial enterprises, with fixed assets of 460 million RMB and a factory covering 600,000 square meters. Zhang controversially decided to auction off the factory, and in 2006 sold it to Wang Zhenshuang (王振爽), a Wenzhou (Zhejiang) businessman, for well below its market price (as confirmed later in court). According to local accounts, another offer from Zhejiang was made for over 200 million RMB, but Zhang sold the factory to Wang for only 60 million RMB.[35] Zhang, in addition to the deputy Party secretary Lin Changyou, the liquor factory restructuring leading small group head Sun Hong (孙红) and the Price Bureau chief Li Jianhua (李建华), took nearly 2 million RMB in bribes for this transaction: in other words, for 2 million RMB in private gains, they gave away 140 million RMB in potential public county revenue.

A comparison of these cases in Wuhe and Mingguang to those in Xuyi and Sihong suggests that corruption in the Anhui counties is more systematic and has covered a longer period than corruption in the Jiangsu counties.[36] To repeat the local official quoted above, "everyone" in these

[34] Several of these ousted cadres held some of the county's most important positions, including Party Committee member Li Luguang (李鲁光), Vice Mayor Zhu Bin (朱彬), Urban Construction Bureau Chief Yuan Xiuzhong (袁秀忠), Water Conservancy Bureau Chief Wang Guoli (王国利), County Grain Bureau Chief Zhang Jingui (张金贵), Land Bureau Chief Li Jinheng (李金衡), Public Health Bureau Chief Zhang Xuemin (张学民), Public Security Bureau Chief Zhang Jiawang (张家旺), Radio and Television Bureau Chief Hu Xuebiao (胡学彪), and Education Bureau Chief Zhao Yang (赵祥).

[35] To make matters worse, Wang had no intention of running a liquor factory, but wanted to use the good location of the land for commercial purposes: he turned the land from industrial use into commercial use. After selling the factory, the employees collectively petitioned at the higher level (*jiti shangfang*, 集体上访), but Zhang accused them of "gathering to disturb public order."

[36] However, this interpretation should be taken with a grain of salt. As with all studies of corruption, there is a problem with using prosecution data. Another possible explanation is that prosecutors and investigators are more active in the Anhui counties, or that

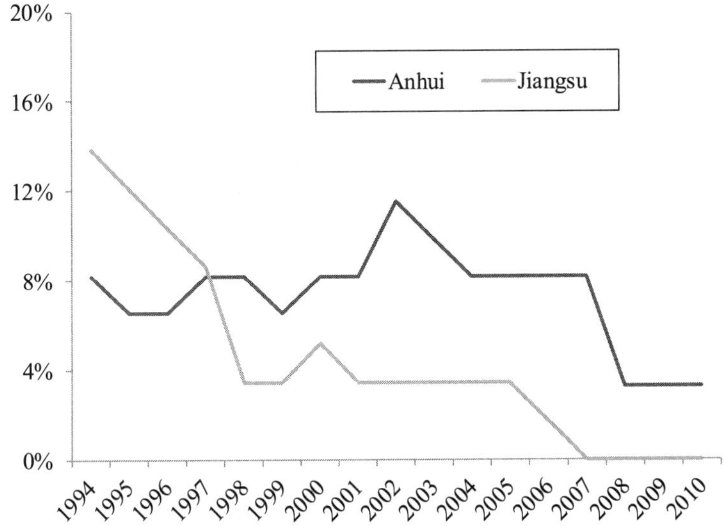

FIGURE 3.2. Corruption more prevalent in Anhui than Jiangsu
Share of county Party secretaries eventually convicted of corruption
Source: Biographical database; author's calculations.

counties knew that bribery was the only means of promotion. In Xuyi and Sihong, the volume of cases was low enough that while bribery clearly greased the wheels, it was not a prerequisite for getting everything done. The corruption in Wuhe and Mingguang undermined trust in the system, eliminating meritocratic promotions and harming county revenue collection.

More broadly in the two provinces, corruption at the county Party secretary level has been higher in Anhui than Jiangsu, in terms of both perceptions and convicted cases. Much has been written about local corruption in Anhui, including *One Hand Blocks the Sky* (2006) about 18 corrupt Party Secretaries as well as Chen Guidi and Wu Chuntao's *Will the Boat Sink the Water?* (2006), an exposé of brutal treatment of Anhui's peasantry by local cadres. Using the biographical data compiled for this project and looking at cases of corrupt county Party secretaries between 1998 and 2010, over this period 7.3 percent of all county-year observations in Anhui had a corrupt county Party secretary, while the corresponding number in Jiangsu was 2.4 percent, three times lower. As shown in Figure 3.2, although in the mid 1990s Jiangsu actually had more

the Anhui leaders are simply less skilled at corruption and therefore more likely to get caught.

cases of corruption among its county leaders than Anhui, in more recent years Jiangsu has become much "cleaner" while Anhui has stayed similarly corrupt.[37] Not only are the number of cases higher, but *perceptions* of corruption are also higher in Anhui than in Jiangsu, with interviewees frequently identifying a "culture of corruption" (*fubai wenhua,* 腐败文化) in Anhui, characterized by local lack of control over local cadres.[38]

This lack of trust hints at the negative effect of local corruption on growth. The generally accepted channels by which corruption hinders growth are through negative incentives for businesses to invest and through distorting the allocation of human capital.[39] This latter effect harms growth by making government itself less effective by decreasing the capability of the civil service. In the case counties, the most prevalent form of local corruption seems to be the buying and selling of official positions (*maiguan maiguan,* 买官卖官), which creates a bureaucracy based on money rather than meritocracy and impedes the positive roles that the state can play. It also implies that positions themselves will be used to gain money (otherwise why pay for the position?). The buying and selling of offices "de-institutionalizes the state" by transforming public authority into a form of private property (Zhu 2008). Buying and selling office cases can reverberate throughout the entire administrative hierarchy: for instance, in a famous case in Heilongjiang, a provincial leader sold the position of Party secretary of Suihua, a prefecture-level municipality, who sold the Suiling county Party secretary position to Li Gang, who then sold many positions under him. Similarly, in Mingguang, as mentioned above, the behavior of former Party Secretary Xue has been identified as the epitome of a corruption process by which individual leader corruption leads to corruption throughout the bureaucratic hierarchy and then to corruption within an entire local region (Xu and Wang 2000).

37 Note that the recent data do not mean that there was no corruption – there is generally a lag in corruption convictions, so many corrupt leaders in 2008–2010 are likely to be prosecuted later than 2012–2013 (when this research was conducted).

38 Myrdal (1968) discusses the "folklore of corruption," a concept that Manion (2004) has applied to problems of anticorruption work in China: "anticorruption reform in a setting of widespread corruption is a problem not only of reducing corrupt payoffs, but also of changing the shared expectations of rank venality that define a 'folklore of corruption.'" Such a "folklore" can dominate even when the actual practice diminishes (Oldenburg 1987, 532–533). This "folklore" has grown to surround the Anhui case counties, extending to locals and investors alike, and consequently diminishing levels of trust.

39 See Aidt (2009). Mauro (1995) finds that corruption lowers private investment, as it acts like a tax on investment proceeds, lowering the private marginal product of capital.

Alternatively, firm bribery and favors can have different consequences. Corruption should be differentiated from wining and dining, but the two overlap. In a culture that prizes personal connections, some wining and dining is unavoidable.[40] On investment promotion, the problem becomes even trickier. In *The English Constitution*, Walter Bagehot differentiated between two components of government: the dignified part, dealing with matters of ceremony and state occasions, and the efficient part that actually governs. But in the case of investment attraction, the two may not be differentiable. According to Jiang Guoxing, the former county Party secretary of Suining: "The locals said that I'd brought 'eating and drinking culture' (*chihe feng,* 吃喝风), but that implies sitting around doing nothing – to attract investment, you may need to wine and dine, but this isn't 'eating and drinking culture' – you have to spend money to make money (*xianhuaqian houzhengqian,* 先花钱后挣钱)" (Wang 2006). Sometimes, as in the Sihong corruption case identified above, the goal is to help an industry or firm, and involves a transfer from state coffers to individual coffers, but less overall cost for the firm. Other gift-giving may in effect be "speed money." One official described entrenched "legal" corruption in a Jiangsu county:

> Assume there are 5000 cadres in County X, with 500 leaders and 1000 minor section chiefs (*xiao kezhang,* 小科长), and then gradations all the way down. The lowest level cadres, like myself, make 40,000 RMB a year but spend 60,000. The rest of this money comes in the form of meals, gas, etc. charged to the bureau's account, as well as gifts from companies and individuals. It's not convenient (*bufangbian,* 不方便) to give a physically large gift, and cash gifts are expressly forbidden, so most gifts come in the form of store gift cards. So assume a low level cadre makes 20,000 a year in 'legal corruption.' And if you work your way up the chain, county magistrates make 20 million in corruption and Party secretaries make 50 million. If you add this all up, we're talking about a few "100 millions" (*yi,* 亿) in County X alone. (Interview JS254)

The "legal" and semi-legal corruption described in this interview blurs the line between out-and-out corruption and administrative red-tape. China is a country of diverse and plentiful overlapping codes and regulations, as well as diverse and plentiful overlapping state organizations assigned to administer and implement these codes and regulations. To get an official signature, or turn on the water, or transfer land use rights,

40 In addition, study tours and investment tours are often seen as wasteful, but they can prove productive. For instance, Foster (2006) finds that the Yantai study trip to Hong Kong led to administrative innovations and reforms based on the Hong Kong governance model.

companies must interface with these bodies. Many counties have moved to unilaterally remove red tape as an incentive for investment (see below), but other counties have added corruption to the mix, creating a "disorderly fee collection" (*luan shoufei,* 乱收费) environment.

This out-of-control fee collection is a clear deterrent to outside investment, but local dependence on industrial enterprises for revenue has made its elimination difficult. As Whiting (2004) has documented, dependence on rural enterprises has spawned an array of metaphors, including "money trees" (*yaoqianshu,* 摇钱树) and "flesh of a Tang monk" (*tangsengrou,* 唐僧肉), a reference to the mythological belief found in *Journey to the West* that consuming a monk's flesh will let one live forever. The former magistrate of Mingguang, Gong Ronggang (龚荣刚), acknowledges the problem, noting that eliminating "disorderly fee collection" is essential in order to "improve investment attraction work and create a positive investment environment" (Gong 2000). Fees are a strong deterrent to investment with high levels of interjurisdictional competition for investment, preventing industry from locating locally. Such red tape is problematic in China as a whole: in the World Bank "Doing Business" rankings, China ranks in the top half of the 2013 rankings in terms of getting credit, trading across borders, enforcing contracts, and resolving insolvency, but it ranks in the bottom half of starting a business, dealing with construction permits, getting electricity, and paying taxes – in other words, red tape categories.[41] This red tape was highly apparent in the same Anhui counties that exhibited higher degrees of corruption; in both cases the problem is one of government failure. This was readily apparent in interviews: "No one wants to invest in Anhui. Instead of helping companies, every bureau just collects fees from companies" (Interview JS128).[42]

What is the effect of corruption in the sample provinces and case counties? In Jiangsu, corrupt counties (i.e., those with corrupt county Party secretaries in the given year) tend to be poorer at the start of the sample (3469 RMB per capita GDP versus 6147 RMB per capita GDP), an artifact of the greater prevalence of corruption in Subei rather than

[41] See: www.doingbusiness.org/data/exploreeconomies/china/.

[42] Note that the problem of fee collection in China is compounded by a fiscal system that does not allow local governments the discretion to modify taxation or create new sources of taxation. While such fee collection that drives away enterprises seems irrational (killing the goose that laid the golden egg), it can be seen as a collective action problem: fee collecting makes sense from the perspective of each individual bureau and each official within the bureau, even if not from the perspective of the county as a whole.

Sunan. In Anhui, however, corrupt counties are insignificantly different from noncorrupt counties at the start of the period (2411 RMB per capita GDP versus 2589 RMB per capita GDP). By 2010, however, corrupt counties in Anhui are much poorer: 7699 RMB per capita GDP versus 11,774 RMB per capita GDP. To look at this slightly more rigorously, I construct a measure for the degree of corruption in each county, defined as the share of years in the sample in which either a corrupt county Party secretary or county magistrate hold office. This variable ranges from 0 to 65 percent. Note that this variable attempts to capture the effect of entrenched cultures of corruption more than the effect of a corrupt leader in a single year. Regressing growth on this "degree of corruption" variable while controlling for initial wealth and population, corruption has a negative correlation with average growth over the 17-year two-province sample, as seen in Table 3.1. Separating the regression into individual province regressions, the effect in Anhui is large and significant, with the coefficient implying that an additional leader-year of corruption results in 0.24 percent lower annual growth. Of course, this does not imply causality; rather, it is likely that a lack of growth opportunities incentivizes corrupt behavior, which in turn lowers growth, resulting in a vicious circle.[43] The effect in Jiangsu is small in magnitude and insignificant, implying that corruption has little effect on growth. One interpretation of these results is that corruption in Jiangsu has been of a different type that has less effect on growth; the other possibility is that Jiangsu's corruption was concentrated in early years of the sample, during which corruption had fewer negative effects given the lack of importance of attracting investment during that period.

Antigrowth corruption and fee collection are not culturally determined, but stem from county-level institutions and control of local cadres. From a rational-choice institutionalist perspective, these government failures – corruption and excessive fee collection – are the original sin of government, and institutional reforms must attempt to disincentivize and successfully monitor such behavior. Case counties have explicitly experimented with such institutional reforms, including mechanisms

[43] Indeed, that is my conjecture. Chapters 5 and 6 will show that Jiangsu focuses more political attention on achieving economic growth, thus incentivizing increased investment seeking, and this investment seeking itself is likely to lower corruption. Several authors have documented how openness to trade is associated with less corruption (Bhagwati 1982; Ades and Di Tella 1999; Treisman 2000; Knack and Azfar 2003). Similarly, investment seeking should disincentivize many types of corruption.

TABLE 3.1. *Corruption and growth in Anhui and Jiangsu*

Dependent variable = Growth	(1)	(2)	(3)
	Full sample	**Anhui**	**Jiangsu**
Degree of corruption	−4.616***	−5.120***	0.986
	(−2.88)	(−2.91)	(0.56)
1994 log per capita GDP	0.961**	−3.081***	0.134
	(2.51)	(−3.23)	(0.41)
1994 population	0.00470	−0.0252***	−0.00648
	(0.76)	(−2.89)	(−0.97)
Constant	2.261	34.86***	11.04***
	(0.70)	(4.49)	(3.68)
Observations	116	61	55
R-squared	0.137	0.312	0.029

Note: degree of corruption defined as the share of years that a county has a corrupt county Party secretary or county magistrate (identified by subsequent conviction). *t* statistics in parentheses.

*** p<0.01, ** p<0.05, * p<0.1

to enhance control over lower levels cadres, create "one-stop shops" for businesses, and increase transparency, with varying degrees of success.

In Sihong, in order to instill and provide a customer-oriented ("everything for the customer, for the customer everything," 一切为了客商、为了客商一切) environment, the county government created the Administrative Service Center (*xingzheng fuwu zhongxin*, 行政服务中心) that combines examination and approval, fee collection, firm assistance, and complaint services into one location, provided at zero cost (Sihong Economic Development Zone Regulatory Commission 2013). Additionally, in order to control government-business interfaces, Sihong has set up a firm responsibility system by producing a list of the 100 most important companies and their corresponding contact person/unit for management assistance (*bangban lingdao ji bangban danwei*, 帮办领导及帮办单位) (Sihong County Government 2013). The top 38 firms on the list all have individual contact people listed, while the rest have associated government bodies. The top firm on the list[44] has Xu De (徐

[44] Jiangsu Shouyi (江苏首义薄膜有限公司), involved in plastic membrane manufacturing, was established in 2008 as an investment from the Zhejiang Shouyi Corporation, with registered capital of over 200 million RMB, total investment of 1 billion RMB, and annual output value of over 2 billion RMB.

德), the Party secretary, listed as the contact person, while the county magistrate, Xu Qinzhong (徐勤忠), is listed as the contact person for the second largest firm.

Similarly, in Suining, the government created a large new government Service Center in the middle of downtown which now houses representatives from over ten departments who were put in the same place to make firm services easier. The Center was a bustling place with good internal propaganda: huge character signs hung on every wall about speed and ease and good service, for instance "handle affairs for common people with zero obstruction" (*baixing banshi ling zhang'ai,* 百姓办事零障碍). Suining prides itself as having "the fewest approval procedures in the province; the lowest charges in the province; the easiest process in the province." The "bodyguarding" (*baobiao,* 保镖) of firms mentioned above refers specifically to the work of the #110 Economic Office in ensuring that enterprises are not bothered about local fees and problems – they have one number to call to solve any interference (Li 2010). Complementary to the #110 office, Suining has instituted a rule whereby functional bureaus can only interface with enterprises on one predetermined day in each month, which limits unnecessary fees and time wasting (Interview JS290).

Suining has also gone the furthest in controlling local cadres through increased transparency. In March 2009, the county began a "county power transparency" (*xianquan gongkai,* 县权公开) campaign with several complementary laws and regulations designed to rein in the negative behavior of local bureaus as well as the Party Committee itself. The "County Standing Committee Advance Notice System 《县委常委会提前预告制度》 specifies rules on publishing pre- and post- meeting reports and plans, and every town and bureau has to publish work goals (*gongzuo de mubiao renwu,* 工作的目标任务) in the local newspaper and local television (Yi and He 2012). Complementary reforms range from "not speaking official-ese" (*bushuo guanhua,* 不说官话) to regulations requiring all bureaus to have an online spokesman who answers all queries within 48 hours. As former Party Secretary Wang Tianqi noted, "Supervision is necessary in order to correctly use Party Committee power, and transparency is the foundation of supervision." These reform initiatives have received national attention (see further discussion in Chapter 4). The county recognizes that this supervision and transparency is conducive to attracting investment. In the Suining Guide, under the service and policy and investment cost section, the first sentence is "Suining is one of the three pilot counties which make the county authority open and transparent determined by the CCDI and the CCP's Organization Department."

Counties that have combated their own government failures have been able to reduce the "grabbing hand" nature of local administration. In the Anhui counties such one-stop shopping and institutionalized transparency have been much less apparent. Attempts to rein in control do not always work. A former magistrate of Mingguang discussed efforts in the early 2000s to rein in fee collection, including the release of a "Fee Clarification Outline" (*shoufei mingbai ka,* 收费明白卡) and greater punishment for units engaging in excessive fee collection: "Units that engage in disorderly fee collection will have the responsible leader lose his position and the responsible person lose his 'rice bowl' (*fanwan,* 饭碗) [secure employment], which will improve the investment attraction environment and improve Mingguang's ability to attract investment" (Gong 2000). But Mingguang's efforts to actually rein in such behavior have been relatively ineffective. Indeed the effectiveness of reining in government failures in the Jiangsu case counties relative to the Anhui case counties helps explain their different economic outcomes. Subsequent chapters provide an explanation for this cross-provincial difference by exploring the role of county leaders and the incentives that these leaders face; most importantly in this context, weaker pro-growth incentives in Anhui have led to diminished efforts to monitor and control local cadre behavior.

Local Economic Development and Market Failures

The above "grabbing hand" approach to local governance has its counterpart in the "helping hand" approach: local governments frequently and proactively step in where imperfect information and externalities create Pareto-sub-optimal outcomes, taking on pseudo-developmental roles and acting as service-oriented agents of local industry. In many ways these local governments are acting in market-enhancing ways – cutting down red tape, as described above, is a move towards markets – but they also operate in market-defying ways. Below, I focus mostly on development zone policy. Interviews with both officials and private sector investors confirmed the importance of "helping policies." Counties often have different names, different content, and different capabilities when it comes to these policies, but the general idea is to go beyond explicit preferential policies and provide government assistance to firms in legal but highly specialized ways by using government monopoly power, information advantages, and economies of scale. The ability and demeanor of local officials and investment promotion offices are good indicators of the ability to attract outside capital. While the preferential policies with regard to land and taxation were nearly identical in all sample counties, the government-business relationship was highly variable. As the Suining investment bureau deputy director argued, the difference is "government service" (*zhengfu de fuwu*, 政府的服务).

"Management assistance," or *bangban* (帮办), best summarizes much of the "helping hand" content, although counties often have their own terminology. No county among my cases had a dedicated *bangban* office, but others in the Subei region do.[45] Several aspects of government assistance are related to *bangban*: employment matching, sales and product placement, technological support, financial guarantees, and bankruptcy protection. Other government roles are county-wide rather than firm-based: for instance, supporting informal finance and employment training. Local governments have different approaches to firms as well as different levels of capacity. Tsai (2002) refers to the "local logics of economic possibility," highlighting the developmental orientation of local governments towards the private sector, and how this translates into varying degrees of support for informal finance. Today, the general role of local governments in helping private industry is more universal, but government developmental perspectives and capacities still vary.[46]

The three Jiangsu case counties have highly institutionalized approaches towards creating a pro-business and pro-growth government service environment. In Xuyi officials are urged to adhere to the "101 percent service concept" and follow the "three relations" role (*sanqin*, 三亲) by "treating businesses as close as parents, treating businessmen as dear as brothers, and treating projects as close as children" (对待企业亲如父母，对待客商亲如兄弟，对待项目亲如子) in order to give projects "full process" (*quan guocheng*, 全过程), "omni-directional" (*quan fangwei*, 全方位), and "all-weather" (*quan tianhou*, 全天候) management assistance service (*bangban fuwu*, 帮办服务) (Xuyi Almanac 2011). These policies are implemented through economic development zones: "*Bangban* is the key to development zone attractiveness, along with local infrastructure. The zone is run by a deputy Party secretary who wears two hats (*xianzhi*,

[45] For example, Shuyang County has a dedicated *bangban* office, whose specific policies and roles can be found online at http://sykfq.cn/bangbanfuwu/713.jhtml.

[46] Governmental support for local private business is one of the clearest "developmental state" examples. Blecher and Shue (1996) document county government involvement in the development of private commerce, particularly the creation of local markets in which the county invested, sought other investors, gave zoning permits, and set up stalls to rent. They argue that this planning and execution was an example of a successful "developmentally oriented state."

兼职), and under him is an entire microcosm of the county level government; nearly every bureau has a sub-bureau under the development zone which reports to both the county level bureau as well as the deputy Party secretary in charge of the development zone" (Interview JS169).

In Sihong, *bangban* is formalized, with required government behavior based on the "Sihong Economic Development Zone Complete Personnel Service Implementation Plan" 《泗洪经济开发区全员服务工作实施方案》. According to the document, the economic service bureaus must publish *bangban* notifications (*tongzhi,* 通知) based on work plans; relevant *bangban* personnel must implement and provide feedback on the completion conditions; and the bureau along with the supervising office (*jiancha shi,* 检察室) must conduct monthly and quarterly evaluations. All *bangban* personnel should provide "start-to-finish, face-to-face, nannying-style" (全过程、零距离、保姆式) *bangban* service. Through these requirements, Sihong aims to achieve a "service environment" for attracting investment through five service mechanisms (*fuwu jizhi,* 服务机制): namely, a start-to-finish *bangban* mechanism (*quancheng bangban zhi,* 全程帮办制), employment guarantee mechanism, (*yonggong baozhang zhi,* 用工保障制), inspection and reporting mechanism (*jiancha shenbao zhi,* 检查申报制), advanced claims settlement mechanism (*yuxian lipei zhi,* 预先理赔制), and service appraisal mechanism (*fuwu pingyi zhi,* 服务评议制) (Sihong Development Zone Regulatory Committee 2013).

In Suining, "nannying" refers to ensuring that large projects can operate smoothly, with government assistance across diverse categories including administrative approval, technology financing, children's education, etc. In other words, in the words of former Suining County Party Secretary Wang Tianqi, "We'll take care of all those things that enterprises used to run and break their legs over in order to achieve." The official Suining development zone mentality is: "the government creates the environment, businesses create the wealth," which is obtained through "restaurant-style service" (*jiudianshi fuwu,* 酒店式服务), and can turn the intangible "soft environment" (*ruan huanjing,* 软环境) into a tangible "hard strength" (*ying shili,* 硬实力). Suining has explicit policies to help small and medium size enterprise (SME) development through three platforms: a science and technology information platform (*keji xinxi pingtai,* 科技信息平台), mostly by establishing cooperation with national level universities and research institutes; an intermediary service platform (*zhongjie fuwu pingtai,* 中介服务平台), namely legal, accounting, and patent mechanisms; and a human capital and financing platform, which consists of expert centers and uniting firms with banks and providing loan guarantees (Wu and Wang 2013).[47]

These three Jiangsu counties demonstrate many specific approaches to proactive government-business partnership. Along with general service orientation, they have developed many specific approaches towards local employment; finding business partners and product placement; and significant financial assistance, including loan guarantees, financial assistance, and assistance with bankruptcy.[48] Successful county governments take on explicit roles in helping firms secure employment and train employees. Investors are guaranteed that if they invest, the government will ensure that their factory is staffed with qualified employees on day one. One investor in Xuyi noted the employment assistance as the most helpful role, arguing that once he invested he was not forgotten, but rather the government continued to help him find employees (*zhaogong*, 招工), publicize employment ads (*zhaogong xuanchuan*, 招工宣传), and train workers (*peixun gongzuo*, 培训工作) (Interview JS143). In Suining, the local government identifies out-migration as hurting the local economy, and has thus opened 32 professional training schools which in 2007 trained 24,149 people to make them locally employable (Qin 2009). These governments also help establish business partners and find sales venues and complementary upstream parts. One Zhejiang businessman with two factories in Xuyi explained how these factories were no longer profitable for him, and how the local government had been proactively reaching out to other investors on his behalf who wanted to buy the factories; they had recently brought in a group from Shanghai, and negotiations were in progress. He waxed eloquent about the government's role in helping him do this, saying that nowhere else he had invested in the past (Zhejiang, Sunan, Shanghai) provided nearly as much support – in those places, once they had your money they just forgot about you (Interview JS259). To boost sales for local products, governments seek out specialty branding and certification, lobbying prefecture-level, province-level, and national governments for brand and product certification. For instance, in Sihong, the government has subsidized "national organic farming" standardization for over half of the county's arable land, and there are

[47] These policies seem effective: at the end of 2012, the Suining development zone had 131 SMEs with 21,000 employees (55 percent of total employment in the zone) (Qi 2013).

[48] According to the Suining Guide, "The government provides the platform for the cooperation of bank and enterprises. It funds Xingqi Guarantee Company (兴企担保公司) and Runqi Investment Company (润企投资公司) to help enterprises solve financing problems and improve the financial environment."

now 306 county products branded with one of the three organic standards (Xu 2013).[49]

Within this framework, quality and efficiency are key. Any government can make these promises (although many do not), but firms have to believe that the government has sufficient capacity and the will to follow through. The Suining investment promotion bureau official emphasized that the government "makes good on all of its promises" (*duixian chengnuo,* 兑现承诺): Suining has done its best to establish a "government of integrity" (*chengxin de zhengfu,* 诚信的政府), and this government ability and honesty is what makes Suining a good place to invest, summarized as the government's "work style" (*gongzuo zuofeng,* 工作作风). Many interviews with the private sector supported this. An owner of one of the most successful factories in Suining says that in Jiangsu, the government and cadres are extremely hardworking (*ting nuli,* 挺努力), which is lacking in Anhui (Interview JS172).

Local Growth Effects of Good County Governance

This focus on efficient and proactive government service provision can be seen as pro-growth "good governance," and it directly encourages outside investment while also boosting revenue and making banks more likely to lend.[50] Mauro (1995) finds that the specific components of investment most associated with growth are closely associated with bureaucratic efficiency, and that private investment is more closely associated than public investment with bureaucratic efficiency.[51] Governance improvements of this sort can also help explain better infrastructure and revenue outcomes.[52] And governance quality differs across counties and

49 Similarly, Xuyi Crawfish branding, discussed in Chapter 4.

50 One county finance bureau official described Anhui's continued backwardness as largely stemming from the unwillingness of banks to lend: many national lenders (banks and financial organizations) and mobile direct investment are turned off from investing in Anhui due to perceptions of government inefficiency and corruption (Interview JS172).

51 He looks at equipment investment, whose relationship with growth is documented by DeLong and Summers (1991), and private investment, whose relationship with growth is documented by Barro (1991).

52 Zhang et al. (2007) find a large role of governance in explaining growth in local infrastructure spending: controlling for the level of development and financial depth, among other variables, they find that FDI-driven competition and governance are both significant in providing incentives to local governments to improve infrastructure. The variance in local revenue (extraction) capacity differs not only in the local economic size and structure, but also in the institutionalization of the tax collection agencies. As the head of the Si County (Anhui) State Tax Bureau complained in 1995, Si County has a "sliding economy, feeble markets, and enterprises and tax bureaus that have created a

regions, helping to explain investment variation. Thun (2006, 9) notes that because different institutional arrangements vary in their capacity to help develop different industrial sectors, it is possible to define a "locality's comparative institutional advantage." Foresight and quality of economic strategic planning matters, particularly in the sense of deciding which firms to target; this becomes increasingly important for richer counties that have the leisure of being selective.[53]

While it is difficult to determine growth effects beyond the anecdotal experiences within the case counties, two exercises provide initial supportive evidence: evidence from fiscal expenditure on administration, which can loosely proxy for government quality, and correlations between perceptions of "government effectiveness" and growth using data collected from Anhui. In analyzing fiscal data, it is likely that increases in administrative expenditure are associated with increases in administrative quality: according to the Chinese expression, "cheap goods aren't good, and good goods aren't cheap" (*pianyi mei haohuo, haohuo bu pianyi,* 便宜没好货, 好货不便宜): you get what you pay for.[54] The regression results reported in Table 3.2 show that increases in government expenditure on administration in year *t-1* positively predict higher GDP growth and higher capital accumulation growth, although this effect is concentrated in Jiangsu and is insignificant in Anhui. This is true regardless of the controls used (a full set of controls are reported here; other results are not shown). In the growth regression, even controlling for lagged growth and lagged revenue, administrative expenditure growth remains positive, and lagged nonadministrative expenditure (which generally accounts for ~90 percent of total expenditure) is generally insignificant. In other words, it does not seem that the effect is merely a correlation of past success translating into current success.

'you have, I have, we all have, only tax payments don't exist' and 'You owe, I owe, we all owe, those who don't owe are idiots' phenomenon, whereby lots of enterprises have small payments, but because enterprise leaders lack an understanding of taxation, tax payments are always in arrears, and overdue payments are impossible to collect." In other words, there is a sense that in low revenue areas, vicious circles make it tough to break out.

53 For example, Kunshan has become very selective in attracting firms, and has attempted to promote industrial concentration and agglomeration effects. After 1996, the focus became concentration (*san zhuan ju,* 散转聚), particularly of Taiwanese firms in information technology and precision machinery (Zhang and Zhang 2008, 15–30).

54 This contrasts with a view that administrative expenditure increases indicate waste and even corruption, and it is true that the central government tries to rein in administrative expenditures. Administrative expenditure is thus at best a weak proxy for administrative quality, and may simply reflect patronage.

The explanation that I pursue here is that the addition of government employees (or pay increases for talented employees) allows the government to more effectively manage the economy; for instance, creating a development zone requires an entirely new administrative apparatus. Additionally, and perhaps more importantly, pay increases may induce cadres to behave more proactively. Bonuses are given for meeting promotion targets, so concurrent growth should clearly be associated with administrative expenditure growth, but there might also be a lagged motivation effect.[55] The insignificant correlation in Anhui may result from administrative expenditure being wasted or focusing on improving aspects of administration with no relation to economic growth, an explanation explored in Chapter 6.

Additional evidence for the channel from government capacity to growth comes from Anhui. A group of official Anhui provincial research institutes collaborated to put out the *Anhui County Economic Competitiveness Report 2011–2012* that ranks Anhui's 61 counties and county-level cities according to several components and correlates of economic development (Zhou, Zhu, and Zhang 2012).[56] Of interest here, the authors create a measure of "government capacity competitiveness" (*zhengfu nenglixing jingzhengli*, 政府能力性竞争力) that includes public services investment, organizational structure, quality of investment attraction work, and several other categories.[57] Zhou, Zhu, and Zhang (2012) also report competitiveness rankings for infrastructure, human capital, social development, and geography and natural resources. Regressing GDP per capita and recent GDP growth on these other scores, including government capacity, enables an identification of the correlates of economic competitiveness. As the charts and regression results below show, geographic and natural resource characteristics have a negative relationship with economic competitiveness, while infrastructure, human

[55] An alternative possibility is that there is no causation, and that an omitted variable increases administrative expenditure in the current period and GDP growth in the subsequent period; for instance, if investment is channeled into greater administrative expenses. One final possibility is that in the current period, officials recognize that next period growth will be higher, and therefore preemptively raise administrative expenditures.

[56] The same analysis is not conducted for Jiangsu, unfortunately.

[57] In justifying the potential accuracy of the "government capacity" variable, it is worth comparing the three case counties in Anhui. Mingguang, Si, and Wuhe ranked 53rd, 54th, and 49th out of Anhui's 61 counties in 2010. The low rankings coincide with the fieldwork findings, as does Wuhe's slightly superior ranking.

TABLE 3.2. *Administrative expenditure and future growth*

ALL IND. VARS. LAGGED ONE YR.	(1)	(2)	(3)	(4)	(5)	(6)
	GDP growth			Capital growth		
	Pooled	*Jiangsu*	*Anhui*	*Pooled*	*Jiangsu*	*Anhui*
Admin. exp. growth	0.0197	0.0537**	0.0210	0.0321*	0.0671**	0.00554
	(1.11)	(2.03)	(0.88)	(1.82)	(2.28)	(0.28)
Nonadmin. exp. growth	0.00931	0.0186	−0.0278	−0.0146	0.0239	−0.0162
	(0.41)	(0.63)	(−0.92)	(−0.70)	(0.67)	(−0.56)
GDP growth	0.153***	0.108*	0.124***	0.0190	0.132**	0.0661
	(5.14)	(1.84)	(2.68)	(0.56)	(2.31)	(1.28)
FAI growth	0.00526	0.0188	0.00791	0.041***	0.044***	0.0350**
	(0.86)	(1.33)	(1.07)	(3.10)	(3.02)	(2.32)
Log per capita GDP	−30.48***	−12.99***	−41.82***	0.280	−4.402	−4.707
	(−7.62)	(−3.82)	(−7.82)	(0.09)	(−1.40)	(−0.64)
Revenue growth	0.0347*	0.0147	0.0230	0.076***	0.0333	0.0712**
	(1.68)	(0.48)	(1.04)	(3.84)	(1.07)	(2.32)
Population	−0.579***	−0.564***	−0.653***	−0.595***	−0.780**	−0.556***
	(−3.86)	(−2.80)	(−3.34)	(−3.57)	(−2.56)	(−2.68)
Loan growth	−0.00112	0.0302	0.00186	0.021***	−0.0357	0.019***
	(−0.24)	(1.04)	(0.45)	(5.85)	(−1.01)	(4.15)
Secondary share GDP	0.152	−0.244	0.522***	0.293***	0.0791	0.385**
	(1.43)	(−1.62)	(4.15)	(2.66)	(0.56)	(2.32)
Constant	306.7***	200.1***	372.9***	51.31*	127.8***	90.48
	(7.95)	(4.79)	(7.21)	(1.67)	(2.77)	(1.41)
Years covered	1997–2006	1997–2006	1997–2006	1997–2006	1997–2006	1997–2006
Year fixed effects	Yes	Yes	Yes	Yes	Yes	Yes
County fixed effects	Yes	Yes	Yes	Yes	Yes	Yes
Observations	1013	464	549	963	450	513
R-squared	0.425	0.377	0.516	0.339	0.363	0.390

t statistics in parentheses.

*** p<0.01, ** p<0.05, * p<0.1

capital, and government capacity all have positive relationships. The largest positive effect (as well as the most significant effect) is for government capacity. The scatter plots in Figure 3.3 looking at bivariate correlations with log GDP per capita in 2010 support this, with low levels of dispersion across predicted values in the positive relationship between government capacity and economic competitiveness (top right chart).

TABLE 3.3. *Government capacity and other correlates of economic success*

Independent variables	(1) County log GDP per capita, 2010	(2) County GDP growth, 2000–2010 (CAGR)
Geography and natural endowment	−0.352***	−3.424***
	(0.089)	(1.040)
Government capacity	0.427***	1.958*
	(0.094)	(1.106)
Infrastructure	0.210*	1.892
	(0.109)	(1.279)
Human capital	−0.114	0.818
	(0.099)	(1.160)
Social development	0.109	2.928*
	(0.128)	(1.500)
Constant	9.652***	15.712***
	(0.034)	(0.398)
Observations	61	61
R–squared	0.635	0.527

Standard errors in parentheses; *** $p<0.01$, ** $p<0.05$, * $p<0.1$

Note: All independent variables are 2010 indexes over [−2,2] constructed by Zhou, Zhu, and Zhang (2012).

Conclusions

Governance matters for growth. It is important to re-emphasize that "good governance" here is defined in the very limited sense of "pro-growth governance"; downward accountability and responsiveness to citizens may not exist. The role of governments in local development has shifted in the reform era; as TVEs closed, a "cadre-led" growth model turned to a more market-led growth model. But the shift away from direct management of firms did not make government quality less important for growth. Feedback and endogeneity and virtuous circles are possible, but the arguments presented above suggest that there is also a causal direction from good governance to growth. Preventing government failures of corruption and excessive fee collection while setting up capable service-oriented governments helps counties attract investment and grow.

This chapter has helped explain some of the additional variation in county growth identified in Chapter 2. Pro-growth governance boosts

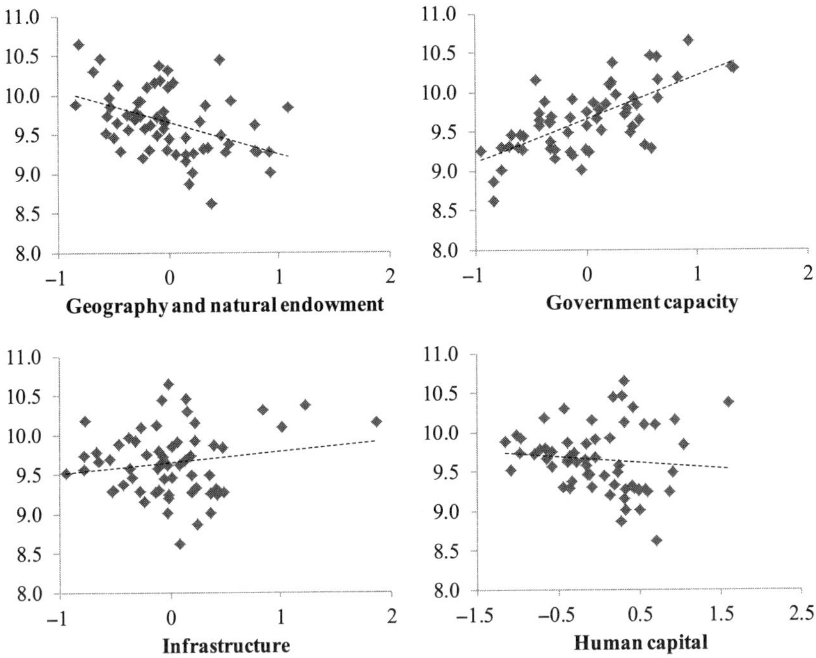

FIGURE 3.3. Correlates of economic success in Anhui counties, 2010
Scatter plots of [-2,2] competitiveness indices versus log per capita GDP
Source: Zhou, Zhu, and Zhang (2012); author's calculations.

productivity and attracts investment, the two most important components of growth at the county level. But *why* are some counties more pro-growth than others? And *why* do Jiangsu counties appear to have better pro-growth governance quality, controlling for initial income levels?[58] The argument in the following three chapters explores an

58 Governance is not perfect in Northern Jiangsu, by any means. I could fill pages with local cadre complaints and questionable (or even immoral) behaviors. One official in Subei opined on the lack of meritocracy, sneering at sycophants "with no ideas" but close relationships to superiors who were in line for major promotions. He had a lot of disgust about promotions and having to brown-nose (*paimapi*, 拍马屁) local leaders. He was still positive about the capacity and civic duty of younger cadres, although he whined about older cadres with "sweepover hair and dirty hick [*laotu*, 老土] western suits." When this official entered the finance bureau in 1995, the leaders just wanted to get drunk at lunch and play cards or go home and sleep in the afternoon, and they did. Now, he says, *guanxi* is still important, but you also need ability.

institutional explanation for pro-growth governance, demonstrating that county Party secretaries are largely responsible for local pro-growth institutional reforms (Chapter 4) and that the personnel management system determines how county Party secretaries act (Chapter 5 and Chapter 6).

4

First in Command: Leadership Roles for County Development

Cadre ability is essential. Why are Beijing and Shanghai so successful? Because they attract all the best cadres and people. If all of the Jiangsu local leaders replaced all of the Anhui local leaders, they [Anhui] would be much better off, but obviously this can't be done. As it stands, not much can be done and it will take time.

– *Jiangsu County Finance Bureau official, explaining why Anhui had worse economic outcomes (Interview JS245)*

The biggest difference is that you do not seem to manage the economy much. When I was mayor of Shouguang my main effort was on grasping the economy, everything from fiscal growth to enterprise profit, peasant income, private economy, structural adjustments ...

– *Li Qun, mayor of Shouguang (county-level) City, speaking to the mayor of New Haven about the difference in their job descriptions (Song and He 2003, cited in Guo 2009)*

Zhao Peng (赵鹏) became Xuyi County Party Secretary in February 1998, having served as county magistrate since September 1996. Zhao hailed from neighboring Hongze County, also located within Huaian Prefecture in Jiangsu, and started his career in Hongze as a teacher in the early 1980s before entering the Communist Party in 1985 and subsequently working his way up the ranks of the Hongze government office and Huaiyin Prefecture Organization Department. Zhao served as Xuyi County Party Secretary for nearly three years, transferring at the end of 2000. While he was in office, Xuyi's laggard economy took off. In the four years prior to his arrival (1994–1997) Xuyi's average annual GDP growth had been 5.0 percentage points below Jiangsu's county average over that period. During Zhao's three years in office growth averaged

20.5 percent at a time that provincial growth as a whole slowed down; Xuyi's average annual growth over this period was 9.3 percentage points above the provincial county average.

Xuyi residents and local officials have developed a narrative of local growth that credits Zhao with starting an economic boom; his successor, Wang Youfu, is credited with "courageously" taking the ball and running with it. Zhao "had the most personal impact," helping set up the economic development zone and also starting the Crawfish Festival (*longxiajie,* 龙虾节) in 2000, the year of the Dragon (Interview JS281). In Xuyi, the "general development strategy" has been in place since Zhao, who personally outlined the 16-character "four major strategy" (*sida zhanlüe,* 四大战略), a development path concentrated on industry (*gongyeqiang xian,* 工业强县), tourism (*lüyouxing xian,* 旅游兴县), urban construction (*chengjianju xian,* 城建举县), and the environment (*huanjingli xian,* 环境立县). The strategy focuses on promoting industrialization as the basis for development, because without industry there are no taxes; promoting tourism by focusing on Xuyi's long history and ecology, which creates a strong local reputation as well as employment without pollution; facilitating urbanization; and creating a good environment by creating a service-oriented government for a positive investment environment (*touzi huanjing,* 投资环境) and also creating a good living environment (*shenghuo huanjing,* 生活环境) by not allowing polluting companies to invest. These four broad guidelines for growth have been in place since 2000, surviving through three successive governments. During Zhao's three years in office, inward investment took off with the creation of the economic development zone along with new rules for cadres and stricter local evaluations. Tourism exploded with the Crawfish Festival and increased investments in eco-tourism, and urban development expanded rapidly, with the county seat's urban center moving east from its old location.

In neighboring Mingguang City, Anhui, Zhang Songjian (张松坚) became Party secretary in March 2003. He had a promising early career, becoming the mayor of Nanqiao County-level Urban District in 1997 at age 43, and soon after the Party secretary. During the four-year term of his predecessor, Chen Bingbing (1999–2002), Mingguang's average annual GDP growth was 5.2 percentage points above Anhui's county average, allowing Mingguang's economy to begin to converge after several years of falling behind provincial averages, largely as a result of the early 1990s [illegible]n nest described in the previous chapter. But during Zhang's five [illegible]re, growth was 10.7 percentage points below Anhui's county [illegible]veraging only 2.1 percent annually from 2003 to 2007 (Zhang transferred in May 2008). Zhang is remembered as a "spineless" (*mei poli,* 没魄力) leader who looked after only his own personal gains, halting or reversing the beneficial reform directions of Chen (Interview AH138). Perhaps more harmful than the immediate growth effects, Zhang is also remembered for having undermined the cadre system, allowing and contributing to a lawless culture of corruption as described in Chapter 3. In selling off state assets at bargain basement prices for personal gain and in appointing only cadres who paid bribes, Zhang undermined local revenue sources and permanently damaged state-society and state-business relations. Mingguang has yet to recover.

* * *

Individual cases do not demonstrate systematic leadership effects, but they help identify the channels through which individual leaders can enhance or undermine local economic growth. Xuyi Party Secretary Zhao provides a case study in how bold and innovative local leadership can improve local economic outcomes by enhancing investment environments and improving local governance. Mingguang Party Secretary Zhang demonstrates a cautionary tale of a leader's personal corruption trickling down the administrative ranks and ruining a county's reputation as a place to invest. This chapter argues that the power and initiative of county Party secretaries explains much of the county-level economic growth variation and local approaches to governance identified in the previous two chapters, and it lays out a framework describing the roles that county Party secretaries play in the local economy. By establishing the personal role of Party secretaries, the chapter sets up the discussion in the subsequent two chapters of the importance of the promotion incentives facing these leaders for determining county outcomes.

The chapter proceeds in several sections. First, I look at the power of Party secretaries in general – as *yibashou* (first-in-command) they wield awesome levels of control over local personnel, political, and economic decision-making. A quantitative assessment looking at systematic leadership effects on growth follows, demonstrating that individual leaders explain more variance in growth than either time or county fixed effects. Subsequently, I lay out a broad framework of leader/economy interactions. The goal here is not to look at every individual decision but rather to see what types of leader characteristics result in what types of economic outcomes through local decision making. A review of leadership roles in the six case counties demonstrates the overriding importance of four leader characteristics, here referred to as the "4 Cs": connections, control, creativity, and courage. These characteristics manifest in growth through the channels identified in the last two chapters: investment promotion, pro-growth policy decisions and innovations, and creation of pro-growth governance environments. Note that an important fifth "C," competence, is subsumed under these other characteristics: competent leaders are those who can effectively ensure compliance, generate and implement bold new ideas, and build and take advantage of their relationships. In elucidating the roles of county Party secretaries, this chapter relies on three approaches: the personal rhetoric of leaders in local media, interviews and analysis of county primary sources, and actual outcomes during leaders' terms in office. A discussion of leader backgrounds and how leaders come to power is reserved for the next chapter.

The Leadership Role of County Party Secretaries

County Party secretaries wield tremendous amounts of local power. Although county Party secretaries account for less than 1 percent of national department-level (*chuji*, 处级) and above leadership cadres, they are not "normal" (*yibande*, 一般的) department-level cadres, as they have "great power, responsibility, and influence" (*quanli da, zeren da, yingxiang da*, 权力大、责任大、影响大) (Wang et al. 2011). To understand the source of this power, it is important to differentiate between structure (i.e., the distribution of authority and resources) and process (i.e., how policies are actually formulated and implemented). China's formal decentralized structure endows counties and county leaders with considerable power, but the informal de facto process by which authority is exercised gives county Party secretaries considerably more power. Such informal "power" comes from two sources: the lack of effective monitoring and control by superiors and the ability to ensure compliance by subordinates. With regard to the former, county Party secretaries are largely given free rein locally. China utilizes a "police patrol" rather than a "fire alarm" approach to monitoring as a solution to principal-agent problems, which requires oversight from bureaucratic superiors.[1] But as highlighted by the fragmented authoritarianism model and its descendants, China has

[1] McCubbins and Schwartz (1984) discuss the preference of democratic politicians for [illegible] "fire alarm" approach to local monitoring of bureaucratic agents that depends [illegible] oversight. Shirk (1992) rightly notes that communist/authoritarian regimes [illegible]ned to empower nonstate actors to oversee the state, leading to a reliance on [illegible]trol" type mechanisms.

considerable difficulties monitoring and implementing policies at the local level.[2] Since the late 1980s, a popular saying in localities has been, "They [the center] have policies, and we [localities] have countermeasures" (*tamen you zhengce, women you duice,* 他们有政策，我们有对策). Media, books, and blogs frequently use the phrase *yi shou zhe tian* (一手遮天), literally "blocking the sky with one hand," to describe the local power of county Party secretaries, who wield the power to prevent upward information transmission while forging local reality. Counties are often perceived as "independent kingdoms," as they are microcosms of the national level, with similarly minimal levels of direct oversight.

But blocking out the sky with one hand goes beyond corruption: the sky can represent not only inspection bodies and hierarchical superiors, but also local bureaucracies, Party Committees, society, and media. With weaker Party Committees at the county level, county Party secretaries are masters of their domain, monopolizing important local economic and security decision-making. Such local control over jurisdictions is not a new phenomenon; for hundreds of years, county magistrates constituted the lowest official level of government, with high degrees of control over everything within their jurisdictions (Reed 2000). Mao Zedong once said that Party secretaries should be good "squadron leaders," adding that this was just a metaphor (*bifang,* 比方), and they should not behave as if they were actually in the military – but county Party secretaries today take the advice literally, behaving with strict authoritarian control (Zhao and Zheng 2006). In terms of control over local economies, the idea of county Party secretaries as chairmen of the board, identified by Oi (1999), was frequently repeated in local interviews.

Countervailing institutional reforms and trends have attempted to increase vertical (*tiao*) bureaucratic control and lessen the county Party secretary monopoly on power. The Party secretary of Shandong's Qufu county-level city, Zhang Shuping (张术平), argues that management mechanisms have weakened as many bureaus have implemented stricter

2 Fragmented authoritarianism combines three approaches to the study of Chinese politics: an elite-oriented rational actor approach in which top leaders are rational and wield control; a cellular approach focusing on decentralized power and ability to block upward flows of information; and bureaucratic structure and politics. See Lieberthal and Lampton (1992, 8): "The fragmented authoritarianism model argues that authority below the very peak of the Chinese political system is fragmented and disjointed. The fragmentation is structurally based and has been enhanced by reform policies regarding procedures. The fragmentation, moreover, grew increasingly pronounced under the reforms beginning in the late 1970s ..." For an updated version of fragmented authoritarianism that includes a greater role for non-state actors in policy formulation and implementation, see Mertha (2008).

tiao-tiao management, so the county is left with little actual strength (*shi quan,* 实权) even though responsibilities keep increasing (Dong, Zhang, and Zhang 2005). That argument echoes Andrew Mertha's discussion of "centralized management" (*chuizhi guanli,* 垂直管理), whereby "leadership relations" (*lingdao guanxi,* 领导关系) for offices within bureaucracies at the county and prefecture level were switched to vertical functional administrative superiors (*tiao*) from horizontal local governments (*kuai*), particularly since the late 1990s. As a consequence, in the fields of administrative regulation, financial regulation, and commodities management, sub-provincial governments "lose direct control over these bureaucracies and find it more difficult to manipulate provincial-level directives" (Mertha 2005). Similarly, decisions in the 1990s moved bank-lending decisions within branches up the hierarchy, requiring sign-off from upper-levels. Strengthening *tiao-tiao* arrangements at the expense of *kuai* control over local cadres is complemented by ever-expanding county governments; expanding administrations may increase the power of the state vis-à-vis the citizenry, but likely decreases the power of the county Party secretary vis-à-vis the administration.[3] In addition to reforms to the institutional/administrative system, activist local media and nonstate actors, the sources of informal bottom-up supervision that Nathan (2003) refers to as "input institutions," have begun to constrain the "anything goes" environment in which local governments and county Party secretaries operate. Local governments now feel increasingly obliged to publicize policy decisions and keep up-to-date websites informing local society of their activities, with activist media proactively seeking out corruption and illegal behavior of local officials. Many of these "activist media" are simply local citizens with internet access who have become part of the "human flesh search engine" (*renrou sousuo,* 人肉搜索).[4]

Yet despite these trends constraining the power of local leadership, evidence from the ground shows that while in some ways de jure power has

[3] County governments are the most overstaffed of all administrative levels, with over half of all "overfl[illegible]w" party and government employees at the county level. According to official [illegible], the number of county government agencies should be 24–26 for large [illegible]on plus), 22–24 for medium counties (0.5–1 million) and ~20 for small [illegible]n 0.5 million), but in reality nearly all exceed this, with most having [illegible]d some as many as 80. Of the half-million overflow party and govern- [illegible] the early 1990s, 60 percent were at the county level (Zhong 2003). [illegible]nts also swelled in 1990s, doubling from 1.36 million employees in [illegible]million in the mid 1990s (Bai 1995).

[4] [illegible]ghts this increase in bottom-up supervision. Wang et al. (2010) [illegible]e study of the "human flesh search engine" and its online-offline

diminished, local leaders' de facto power is largely undiminished, with county Party secretaries still wielding almost complete control over local decision-making.[5] Part of the explanation is that countervailing institutional trends have taken place: for instance, township and village mergers helped to centralize power at the county level, making oversight and control easier, and decreasing the nodes of administrative interface.[6] More importantly, though, institutional reform has not clarified the *tiao-kuai* matrix muddle that endows local leaders with both formal and informal power. In an authoritarian regime, local cadres are accountable only to their superiors, and the countervailing reforms have not reduced the major source of local county Party secretary power: a monopoly on political appointments. In personnel matters, the *yibashou* still has "one word worth the Nine Cauldrons" (*yiyan jiuding,* 一言九鼎), a symbol of uncontested imperial power.[7] County Party secretaries retain veto power (*yippiao foujuequan,* 一票否决权) on all local appointments: as one county Party secretary bluntly states, "If I don't agree, then you can't become an official" (Sheng 2011).[8] A Southern Weekend interview with the former national Organization Department head (Zhang Quanjing) makes this control "problem" clear. When asked why the "Party manages cadres" (*dangguan ganbu,* 党管干部) has turned into "*yibashou* manages cadres" (*yibashou guan ganbu,* 一把手管干部), Zhang admits that "right now there are indeed many places with the 'one person has the final say problem' (*geren shuolesuan de wenti,* 个人说了算的问题); this is unnatural (*buzhengchang,* 不正常) and must be corrected" (Zhao and Zheng 2006).

Despite institutionalization of the formal system, the informal personnel system still concentrates power in the hand of the *yibashou*. Following formal full Party Committee meetings, the *yibashou* frequently adds "guidance" (*yindao,* 引导) to make final decisions, thereby "fixing the tone with one hammer blow" (*yichui dingyin,* 一锤定音), though also violating regulations (Sheng 2011).[9] One former county Party secretary

5 This differentiates them from urban district (*shixiaqu,* 市辖区) leaders, who have much less independence and economic control.

6 Between 1989 and 1999, the number of townships fell from 55,800 to 44,500 (Yang 2004, 47). Coastal provinces, particularly Jiangsu, Shandong, and Zhejiang, led the way.

7 This is seen as a major reason for the numerous buying and selling of office (*maiguan maiguan* 买官卖官) cases (Sheng 2011).

8 Similarly, Zhou (2004) finds that the Party secretary has complete control over the local personnel system in an unnamed northwest county.

9 See, for instance *Party and Government Leading Cadre Work Appointment Selection Regulations* 《党政领导干部选拔任用工作条例》 released in 2002, which lays out rules for collective decision-making in promotions.

in Henan notes that, "When I make a decision, 99.99 percent of the time no one will object; when I object, no one dares endorse anyone else" (Sheng 2011). Mertha (2005) acknowledges that on the ground, many cadres admit that local governments maintain the upper hand – "in fact the transformation is only half complete." A former Party secretary of Mengcheng County lays it out clearly:

> Too much power is vested in the "first-in-command" (*yibashou*). If I'm the county Party Secretary, and I recommend someone for a post, will that carry the same weight as another county leader? I'm the Party Secretary, so all candidates who've been recommended or who are seeking posts will come knocking. Whatever I say, the Party Organization Bureau will obey. Procedures are there in name only. Lines of authority that are there on paper don't exist. These problems are systemic. (Chen 2006, cited in Smith 2009)[10]

Informal control over the personnel system undermines efforts to strengthen *tiao-tiao* management at the expense of *kuai-tiao* control, giving rise to "three one" (*sanyi,* 三一) cadres: appointments require one word (*yongren yiyantang,* 用人一言堂); spending money requires one pen (*huaqian yizhibi,* 花钱一支笔), and decisions require one sheet of paper (*juece yizhangzhi,* 决策一张纸). In other words, control over appointments also gives *yibashou* control over all aspects of local decision-making.

Such concentration of power in one individual can result in pathological behavior, both intentional (corruption) and inadvertent (irrational bureaucratic decisions).[11] Lack of effective monitoring undermines the control of a central/provincial principal over local agents and enables corrupt behavior. As the former Mingguang City magistrate highlighted after getting arrested for corruption: "Unrestrained power (*quanli meiyou zhiyue,* 权利没有制约) necessarily results in corruption" (Zhang 1997). Additionally, the lack of horizontal accountability to other agencies at the county level (as opposed to downward accountability to local constituents or upward accountability to higher level government) can undermine the effective operation of local institutions. Horizontal

[10] In a survey of 11,586 party members in Sichuan in 1999, one-third said local party bosses monopolized decision-making (Pei 2006). Landry (2008), in a survey of 245 local officials at deputy bureau chief level or higher conducted in four counties in Jiangsu, asked about 11 institutions/individuals at county, municipal, and provincial level, and how important they were for promotions, finding that county-level institutions are most important, followed by municipal, followed by provincial. The Party secretary himself is the most important individual or institution by far, followed by the county organization department and then the county Party Committee.

[11] See discussion in Jian (2003) and Smith (2009).

accountability "depends on the existence of state agencies that are legally empowered – and factually willing and able – to take actions ranging from routine oversight to criminal sanctions or impeachment in relation to possibly unlawful actions or omissions by other agents or agencies of the state" (O'Donnell 1998). Such horizontal accountability is violated by both corruption and by encroachment (when "one state agency trespasses upon the lawful authority of another"). In this sense, China's all-powerful local leaders obstruct the effective apolitical operations of local bureaucracies, undermining the rationality of these institutions.[12]

Concentration of power in one individual also results in highly variant economic outcomes. Group decision-making has a "diversification of opinions" effect, whereby more group involvement in decisions results in less extreme outcomes (Sah and Stiglitz 1986). Outcome variability should decrease when the number of executives consulted on decisions increases (Sah and Stiglitz 1991). With the lack of constraints in collective leadership at the county level, along with broad latitude to implement locally relevant development plans, more variant and unequal growth outcomes should result. This helps to explain both the large degree of county-level inequality and the large growth residual identified in Chapter 2. Similarly, the CEO literature highlights that in firms with CEOs who are personally responsible for important decisions, "the risk arising from judgment errors is not well diversified"; there is a higher likelihood for "either very good or very bad decisions" as compared with a firm in which multiple executives take part in the decision-making process (Adams, Almeida, and Ferreira 2005).[13]

China has developed norms that help to mitigate this volatility. One convention that mitigates the economic volatility is the replacement of county Party secretaries by concurrent county magistrates. According to one official:

> Even if we assume that the *yibashou* imposed his own policies during the previous five years, we still have to admit that the "second in command" signed off on

[12] The control over so many fields leads to a very busy, high pressure job, described by many county Party secretaries as a "pressure cooker" (*yali guo*, 压力锅): "On the surface we look happy and satisfied, but actually many of us have high blood pressure, and if you look closely we have bags around our eyes from working over 10 hours a day and not sleeping," according to Zhang Shuping (张术平), the Party secretary of Shandong's Qufu county-level city (Dong, Zhang, and Zhang 2005). In other words, taking these officials at their word, even assuming publicly minded, responsible, and capable county Party secretaries, control over so many fields may be impractical.

[13] Adams, Almeida, and Ferreira (2005) find that stock return variability increases with CEO power to influence decisions.

these ideas and helped implement them, so when he takes over he is unlikely to switch trajectories too drastically. On top of this, the decision to replace the county Party secretary with the county magistrate implies that the provincial organization department is "satisfied" (*manyi,* 满意) with the county's development, so changing paths would not be prudent from an individual perspective. (Interview JS281)[14]

In addition, central, provincial, and prefectural policy guidance can help unify and rationalize county decisions; despite implementation bias, localities remain at least partially responsive to upper-level policies. Nevertheless, it is clear that variance in economic outcomes due to personalized decision-making remains large.

Systematic Leader Effects on Growth Outcomes

Given the high degree of personalized leader control in China, leaders should have systematic personal effects on growth, assuming that their ability and incentives differ. The past two chapters have shown that policies and institutions help determine growth, highlighting a potential path for county Party secretary impact on economic outcomes, but leaders may still just be cogs in institutional systems. How different would local economic outcomes be in the counterfactual case of switching leaders, similar to the quote at the beginning of this chapter? Greenstein (1969) importantly distinguishes between action dispensability and actor dispensability: action dispensability refers to the circumstances under which individual actions are likely to have outsized influence, whereas actor dispensability is whether a given action can be explained in terms of an actor's personal characteristics. Greenstein (1969, 41) describes the distinction more illustratively: "The first is, as it were, the question of under what circumstances nations are likely to be saved (or lost) by the juxtaposition of the little Dutch boy's finger and the dyke; the second is addressed to whether we must take account of the psychology of the little boy." In his conception of the terms, both personal and environmental characteristics will determine the likelihood of individual impact.[15]

[14] The converse side of this is that when the magistrate does not replace the county Party secretary, this often implies that provincial authorities want a change, so economic volatility should be higher than normal. An example of this is Lianshui County. Li Yuanchao is originally from Lianshui County, and when he was Jiangsu Province Party secretary he selected an "extremely qualified" person to become the Lianshui County Party secretary and change the local development path (Interview JS284). In these cases, we should expect even higher variance.

[15] Greenstein argues that the likelihood of personal impact increases with the degree to which the environment permits restructuring, varies with the actor's location in the

This section provides quantitative evidence that in a system that empowers local leaders to take responsibility for and influence a wide range of economic decisions, differences in leader capabilities and incentives manifest in systematically different growth outcomes. Although case studies can demonstrate individual leader decisions that influence economic outcomes, it is more difficult to argue that leaders generally have significant effects on economic outcomes. There are two basic problems in identifying leader effects: first, leadership transitions are endogenous to local economic outcomes, and second, it is difficult to distinguish leadership effects from locational and temporal effects. In both democracies and autocracies, leadership transitions are highly endogenous to local growth; underlying economic conditions can drive leadership removal and appointment. Economic failure can lead to leader reassignment,[16] and indeed, in the China case the underlying generalized assumption is one of endogeneity: leaders with good economic outcomes will be rapidly promoted, while those with poor economic outcomes will be demoted or removed. If growth is in fact independent of leader effects, but high (low) achievers are rewarded (punished) through promotions (demotions), a quantitative analysis would nevertheless falsely identify leadership effects on growth (a Type I error).

In addition, leader effects are difficult to differentiate from geographic and temporal effects. When looking at growth in a given year in a given locality or country, some part of the variation will be determined by cross-sample temporal trends: a short-term economic boom or bust, for instance, as in the case of the Asian Financial Crisis and its negative effects on Chinese local growth in the late 1990s. These temporal effects influence all observations within the sample. Additionally, every local economy has its own "fixed effects" – institutions, cultural differences, geography, legacies – that are unique to the specific area and help predict annual variation. With data across several locations and several years, it is possible to identify both temporal fixed effects and locality-specific fixed effects, but identifying constant leadership fixed effects across time is impossible, as they will be inseparable from the other fixed effects.

environment, and varies with the personal strengths of the actor; in other words, personal and environmental characteristics.

16 Evidence in the US shows that incumbents are more likely to win reelection during booms than recessions. See Fair (1978); Wolfers (2002). Londregan and Poole (1990) find that high growth rates make coups less likely.

One way to overcome the endogeneity problem is to look for a source of exogenous variation in leadership transitions/successions. Cross-nationally, Jones and Olken (2005) provide the most compelling case. Using natural deaths of leaders while in office as an exogenous source of leadership transition (i.e., eliminating violent deaths and therefore looking only at leaders who ostensibly die from causes unrelated to local economic outcomes), they find robust evidence that leaders matter for growth outcomes, and also that leader personal effects are strongest in autocratic settings with fewer constraints on a leader's power. In China, county leaders tend to be relatively young and relatively healthy; death and poor health do not result in a sufficient number of career terminations to utilize a similar identification strategy. The CEO literature provides another approach, looking at CEOs who head multiple companies, which allows separation of time, company, and personal effects.[17] This is a similar approach to that employed by Denizer, Kaufmann, and Kraay (2013) in estimating the personal effects of task team leaders in determining World Bank project outcomes. Following leaders across multiple positions in multiple counties removes endogeneity concerns: leaders with successful or unsuccessful outcomes may still be transferred, but if this effect is persistent across multiple different jobs, this implies that the leader is influencing the local outcome rather than benefiting or suffering from "luck" that is exogenous to his personal effect.

Here, following from the CEO literature, in particular Bertrand and Schoar (2003), I analyze the impact of county leaders by parsing out the contributions of time, county, and personal fixed effects. In any given year, county-level growth (Y_{it}) is a function of county-independent year fixed effects (φ_t), time-independent county fixed effects (γ_i), personal effects of individual county leaders (λ_{CPS}), a vector of time-varying county-level control variables (X_{it}), and unobserved error (ϵ_{it}):

$$Y_{it} = \beta X_{it} + \gamma_i + \varphi_t \left(+\lambda_{CPS}\right) + \epsilon_{it} \qquad (4.1)$$

Running Equation 4.1 with and without leader fixed effects (λ_{CPS}) and analyzing the difference in the R-squared enables an estimation of the amount of growth variance explained by county leaders. An F test on the

[17] At the provincial level in China, Xu, Wang, and Shu (2007) use a similar approach. They construct a data set consisting of governors who serve in at least two provinces, and then explore the effect of governor transfer, finding that approximately 1 percentage point of economic growth is attributable to incumbent governors.

joint significance of the personal fixed effects provides further evidence of systematic leadership effects. A general problem with this approach in the leadership literature is that most leaders serve in only one location, which makes the leader and county fixed effects perfectly co-linear. In this data, however, 20 counties in Jiangsu and 23 counties in Anhui have leaders who serve in multiple counties, enabling a separation of the county and personal effects for this connected subset.[18]

The process specified in Equation 4.1 enables an identification of leader personal effects on growth. The general idea is to highlight the role of leader personal effects across a sample of counties connected by leader transitions. In Table 4.1, for the combined dataset as well as each province individually, results are shown for two regressions, one that includes year and county fixed effects, and another that also adds personal fixed effects. All regressions include log per capita income and population as additional controls. By comparing the adjusted R-squared from the regressions with and without personal fixed effects, we can see the increase in variance explained by the leadership personal effect. In all cases and across provinces, the effects are very large, significantly larger than corresponding figures in the CEO literature.[19] Leaders have a large effect in both provinces, explaining an additional 19.2 percent of GDP growth variation, 32.6 percent of capital growth variation, and 24.2 percent of TFP growth variation. In other words, leader effects explain nearly one-fifth of variance in GDP growth, one-third of variance in capital growth, and one-quarter of variance in total factor productivity growth. The F-test results for joint significance of the leadership personal effects are also presented (with p-values and degrees of freedom in parentheses); all are significant with 99 percent confidence. In Anhui, county leaders explain 15.7 percent of total county growth variation; in Jiangsu, they explain 16.9 percent.[20]

[18] See Yao and Zhang (2012) for a similar analysis at the prefecture level in China. They include both governors and Party secretaries. Note that if these leaders have different economic roles/impacts, this inappropriately conflates two separate leader fixed effects.

[19] Bertrand and Schoar (2003) find that manager fixed effects result in over 4 percent increases in adjusted R-squared's for a range of policy and outcome decisions. Here, there is a 69 percent increase in adjusted R-squared for the baseline (connected sample and combined provinces).

[20] General time trends in Anhui have more impact on individual counties – for instance, during the growth slowdown of the late 1990s, Anhui counties slowed down almost universally. This implies a greater role for provincial policies in influencing county outcomes, a process that is explained in Chapters 5 and 6.

TABLE 4.1. *Growth contributions of county leader personal effects (connected sample)*

	Number of obs.	Adjusted R2			F Statistic (p value)[a]
		Excluding leader effects	*Including leader effects*	*Addit. var. explained by leader effects*	
GDP growth					
Combined	708	0.277	0.469	0.192	486 (0.000)
Jiangsu	340	0.341	0.510	0.169	4686 (0.000)
Anhui	368	0.446	0.603	0.157	5418 (0.000)
Capital growth					
Combined	708	0.354	0.680	0.326	34,046 (0.000)
Jiangsu	340	0.622	0.756	0.134	85,097 (0.000)
Anhui	368	0.250	0.658	0.408	101,986 (0.000)
TFP growth					
Combined	708	0.165	0.407	0.242	4444 (0.000)
Jiangsu	340	0.273	0.452	0.179	2539 (0.000)
Anhui	368	0.365	0.562	0.197	279 (0.000)

[a] F statistic for joint significance of the county Party Secretary fixed effects. P-values are presented in parentheses.

A similar but more intuitive approach to looking at leader effects on growth involves analyzing the relationship between the growth outcomes that leaders are associated with in successive counties. In other words, do leaders achieve similar outcomes when they serve in multiple counties? The simple univariate regression results in Table 4.2, represented visually in Figure 4.1, look at all county leaders in the national biographical sample who serve in multiple counties, demonstrating that a positive and significant correlation exists for both average growth in successive counties and the average growth difference from the provincial average in successive counties. This latter specification partially deals with temporal effects that otherwise cannot be controlled for; in other words, if a leader switches counties in a year in which an entire province experiences a growth shock, this latter specification will look at the leader's effect relative to other counties rather than past performance. This exercise provides additional evidence that county Party secretaries have personal impacts on county growth outcomes.

TABLE 4.2. *Correlation between growth outcomes in successive county posts*

	(1)	(2)
	Second post average GDP growth	*Second post average GDP growth (provincial difference)*
First post average GDP growth	0.188***	
	(0.048)	
First post average GDP growth (provincial difference)		0.180***
		(0.049)
Constant	4.681***	−0.043
	0.452	0.257
R-squared	0.035	0.030
Observations	437	441

Standard errors in parentheses; *** p<0.01, ** p<0.05, * p<0.1

Note: Average GDP growth refers to the average real GDP growth over a leader's tenure in one county. Average GDP growth (provincial difference) refers to the annual difference of county GDP growth from the average growth of all counties in a given province-year, averaged over the leader's tenure in one county.

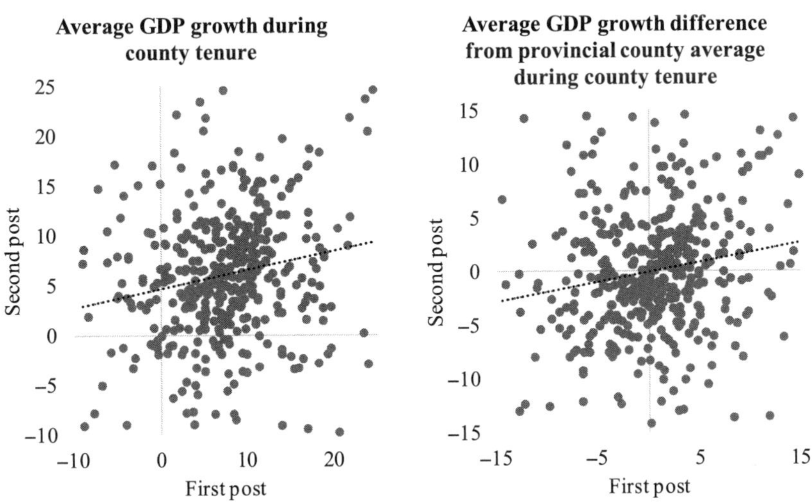

FIGURE 4.1. Relationship between growth outcomes in successive posts
Correlation between growth outcomes in successive county posts
Source: China Data Online; biographical database; author's calculations.

Leadership Characteristics to Influence Growth Outcomes: The Four Cs

What are the channels for these large leadership effects on growth, investment, and productivity? Leaders can have both direct and indirect effects on the local economy. Looking at the national level, Brady and Spence (2010) find four common issues that economically successful leaders must confront: "(1) creating national unity, (2) building good, solid institutions, (3) choosing innovative and localized policies, and (4) creating political consensus for long-run policy implementation." At the county level, national unity and political consensus for long-run policy implementation are less important, so the takeaway from Brady and Spence is that economically successful local leaders must choose pro-growth policies and build good institutions. In the China-specific context, Zweig (1997, 5–7) separates local leadership effects in China into upward hierarchical bargaining ("lobbying for open status or restructuring the community's relationship to upper level governments") and internal initiatives ("altering the political and economic climate within their community"). Choosing good policies and building strong institutions are part of this latter category. This section looks at these local leadership effects, focusing on the leader characteristics (i.e., Greenstein's "actor dispensability") that create these outcomes. In other words, what leader characteristics predict the ability to successfully bargain upwards, build good local institutions, and choose successful economic policies?

Through an analysis of leadership effects in the six case counties, four personal leadership characteristics stand out as helping to determine local economic outcomes. These "characteristics" are not necessarily innate, but rather are reflections of ability, circumstance, and emphasis. First, leaders have personal connections, or *guanxi*, in both private and public spheres. Connections to provincial or prefectural leaders can help leaders obtain preferential policies and fiscal transfers through effective upward bargaining, while connections to firm CEOs can help attract direct investment. Second, leaders differ in their creativity and capacity for innovation, particularly with regard to economic development tactics and strategies. In a highly competitive investment environment, these ideas predominantly relate to how to brand a county to distinguish it from other counties and how to improve the local investment environment through institutional reforms. Rarely are these innovative ideas new economic contributions, although economic policy choices do fall under this category. Third, leaders differ in their willingness to act. There is often talk of "bold vision" when discussing successful leaders: vision (i.e., the creativity just discussed) is a necessary but not sufficient condition; courage is essential, particularly in an authoritarian regime embedded in a culture that has generated such sayings as "the lead bird gets shot down" (*qiang dachu touniao,* 枪打出头鸟); it is often easier to react than to act, but in a highly competitive environment, the contrast can have important implications. Courage is key in both formulating and implementing local reforms, especially institutional reforms that could be deemed "innovative," as well as for challenging local vested interests. Finally, leaders differ in their degree of control over the local bureaucracy and local cadres. While the beginning of this chapter focused on the outsized power of county Party secretaries, the de facto level of control that cadres wield varies greatly on both societal and individual characteristics, and leaders have different approaches to how much control they exert through carrots, sticks, and oversight; this is often a result of choice as much as ability. These four categories, the "four Cs," are summarized and explained in Table 4.3 below.[21]

The subsections that follow highlight leadership roles across these personal characteristics using evidence from interviews in the six case counties, but it is worth highlighting first an archetype of leader economic impact across all four characteristics: Qiu He (仇和).[22] Before drawing national attention as Party secretary of Suqian (prefecture-level) City and eventually deputy Party secretary of Yunnan Province (and also before he was expelled from the Party and indicted on bribery charges in 2015), Qiu He served in the late 1990s for over four years as Party secretary of Shuyang County in Northern Jiangsu (in the same prefecture as Sihong County, one of the case counties). Qiu He had it all: connections to the top, new ideas, courageous reforms and managerial decisions, and complete control over the local government/party hierarchy as well as local society. These characteristics and their consequences brought Qiu national attention, both positive and negative, and brought Shuyang enhanced levels of investment and growth.

21 Any framework necessitates a simplification. These four leadership characteristics – connections, creativity, courage, and control – clearly overlap and even complement each other. These four Cs should not be confused with the "four Cs of communication" (clear, concise, complete, correct), although I strongly hope that this book abides by these latter Cs.

22 For in-depth accounts of Qiu He, see Bao and Xu (2009), Fewsmith (2006), Fewsmith (2013), and Kuhn (2010).

TABLE 4.3. *Leader characteristics influencing local economic outcomes*

Characteristic	Description	Manifestations
Connections	Ability to use personal or organizational connections to bureaucratic superiors, Party and government leaders, and outside business leaders	• Transfers/subsidies, preferential policies, public investment from upper government • Local private investment by outside capital
Creativity	Developing new ideas/policies, demonstrating either business acumen or organizational acumen	• Policies for enhanced county visibility and reputation • New cadre management institutions
Courage	Willingness to challenge vested interests and society, act without upper-level sign-off, and risk potentially "destabilizing" policies	• Controversial policy choices • Sticking to policies despite local opposition
Control	Gaining compliance from bureaucratic subordinates (and local societal interests)	• Successful policy implementation • Fulfillment of identified targets • Prevention of government failure

Qiu's connections are evidenced by his appointment: he was young and favored and was sent to Shuyang by provincial leaders explicitly to create change and turn around a lagging county. He had studied abroad at the University of Maryland just prior to his promotion as part of a "first senior managerial talents economic research class in Jiangsu Province." Such study abroad is a rarity for county leaders, particularly those in poor counties and particularly as early as the 1990s. In addition, he was sent to Shuyang as a "concurrently promoted" (*gaopei*, 高配) cadre, meaning that in addition to his appointment as Shuyang County Party secretary, he also was appointed to the Suqian City Party Committee. This concurrent position on the prefecture-level Party Committee gave Qiu direct access to his superiors and a direct voice in fiscal and policy decisions related to Shuyang's development.[23] One finance bureau official from a neighboring

[23] Chapter 5 explores the economic consequences of this phenomenon in more depth.

county (who had held the position since Qiu's time in Shuyang), recalled that Qiu's *guanxi* was excellent, noting in particular that Qiu was able to get much more financial assistance, particularly in the form of special purpose transfers from upper-level governments (Interview JS112).

Upon entering office, Qiu initiated innovative policies that required considerable courage. Many of the most effective of these policies related to reforms to cadre management, which gave Qiu significant personal control. He had a particular focus on corruption/crime and government transparency. Under Qiu's guidance, all departments had to openly publish "promises" (*chengnuo,* 承诺) to their constituents. At the village level, Qiu initiated "three reforms, four controls" (*sangai sizhi,* 三改四制), the most important of which were "public selection control" (*gongkai xuanze zhi,* 公开选拔制) and "two vote control" (*liangpiao zhi,* 两票制) which required that village officials were first approved by villagers before being voted on by the Party Committee (Bao and Xu 2009, 33). Under Qiu, the number of village-level cadres was cut by 45 percent, with over 5000 officials "retired" (*xiagang,* 下岗), saving the county 5 million RMB. These reforms were part of Qiu's stated goal to move from an "executive order system" to a "service system" (*you xingzheng mingling xing xiang fuwu xing zhuanhua,* 由行政命令型向服务型转化). Fewsmith (2013, 62) describes Qiu as a political reformer, noting in particular his policy innovations with regard to cadre appointments and the introduction of a cadre "public showing" (*gongshi,* 公示) system: whenever he made an appointment, Qiu would first notify the public through various broadcast and print media, giving people ten days to report any problems relating to the individual who was to be appointed. If the public identified severe problems, Qiu would not appoint the individual.

In addition to the implementation of new formal institutions, Qiu ensured enhanced bureaucratic/administrative control through informal reward and punishment mechanisms (*jiangcheng zhidu,* 奖惩办法).[24] Soon after entering office, Qiu's "strike hard" campaign focused on rooting out corruption in the police department as well as corruption left over from the previous administration. Additional control measures required significant micromanagement: after making bureaus publish promises, he personally would travel to random locations and place calls to the police to see if they could actually make it to him within five minutes (Bao and

[24] The punishments focused considerable attention on one-child policy enforcement, with extreme results: in the first year of the campaign, there were 73,000 family-planning surgeries (*jihua shengyu shoushu,* 计划生育手术), accounting for 56 percent of the total in all of Suqian.

Xu 2009, 29). He also made it a point to personally travel unannounced to township offices to see if cadres were playing cards. Qiu was "the personal sword of Damocles hanging over officials' heads." More broadly, Qiu was a micromanager of all aspects of Shuyang's development, and this extended to even the most basic local involvement, including the "famous" examples of chasing down a woman who illegally crossed the street and asking a restaurateur if anyone ever "ate and ran" (*chi bawang can*, 吃霸王餐) and then making sure they found the person who had.

With considerable local control and new institutions, Qiu was able to implement several bold and innovative local economic decisions. When he arrived, local finances were in terrible shape, with nearly 100 million RMB in budget deficits and wage arrears. Qiu decided to unilaterally withhold 10 percent of the wages of all public employees, and also mandated that one-third of cadres leave their posts and temporarily go into business. Part of Qiu's creative "new" approach was correct use of media, and more broadly his ability to create a cult of personality around himself that enhanced the county reputation as a place where "things got done." Qiu created an image of himself as willing to personally sacrifice for the county's development, setting himself up as a cadre to be emulated. This involved taking the lead in cadre-led "Saturday cleanups" and being the first cadre out in the morning shoveling snow after snowstorms. On his second day in office, Qiu spearheaded a clean-up campaign depending on 5000 cadres working overtime, with himself at the lead (and cameras in tow, of course).

Qiu's policy initiatives, particularly his authoritarian approach to ensuring local compliance and reining in government behavior, required significant courage in the face of growing national controversy. Strict implementation of new policies led to (correct) perceptions of Qiu as an extreme authoritarian leader, particularly due to his approach to the one-child policy, razing ancestral graves on arable land, and prohibiting people from playing mahjongg on the street. Fewsmith (2013, 52) argues that Qiu's approach to reform was a "top-down approach, one focused very specifically on economic development rather than on new institutional arrangements that might regularize state-society relations." Yet although Qiu's approach to economic development did not *regularize* state-society relations, his authoritarian control of local cadres did ensure greater administrative responsiveness to both formal and informal rules, an important aspect of institutionalization. In February 2004, the widely read Southern Weekend (*nanfang zhoumo*, 南方周末) published a long piece on Qiu, describing an autocratic leader who produced economic growth at all costs (and also implemented institutional and even democratic innovations despite his own authoritarianism). Qiu's controversial behavior also resulted in the national Focus Interview (*jiaodian fangtan,* 焦点访谈) television program reporting negatively on him three separate times.

Qiu was a controversial Party secretary – indeed, his local behavior was at times despotic – but his innovative policy approaches and institutional reforms, capacity for upward bargaining, and control over the local bureaucracy enabled Shuyang County to thrive economically under him, particularly as a result of increased investment. Qiu took up the helm at the beginning of 1997. In 1996, the year before Qiu arrived, fixed asset investment (FAI) reached 157 million RMB, or 5.3 percent of GDP. In 1998, Qiu's first full year in office, FAI had jumped to 1.32 billion RMB, 26.8 percent of GDP. In other words, in Qiu He's first full year in office, fixed asset investment was over *eight* times greater (in nominal terms) than in the year before his arrival. Upper level authorities were more inclined to give Shuyang funds, and mobile capital was also more likely to locate to Shuyang, both as a result of Shuyang's enhanced visibility as well as a result of perceived control of local cadres and prevention of the government failures mentioned above. Indicatively, in the two years after Qiu left office (2001–2002), fixed asset investment actually *shrank* by 13 percent. Clearly, Qiu's arrival sparked an investment boom, and this boom enabled higher GDP growth. In taking full advantage of his connections, courage, creativity, and control over all aspects of Shuyang's development, Qiu was an indispensable economic actor, and his successes even won over (some of) the local population: one local who previously petitioned against Qiu's policies said that he had stopped filing petitions; "It seems that at that time, I was backward. I couldn't see as far as Qiu He" (quoted in Fewsmith 2013).

Connections: It is Who You Know

Connections, or *guanxi*, provide direct paths to growth for local leaders. There are many different types of personal connections, and these different types of connections produce different outcomes.[25] Connections to bureaucratic superiors can boost transfer payments, public investment, and preferential policies. Connections to outside investors can entice them to invest in the local county, boosting private investment. Connections to "top" leaders can do all of these things, as top leaders themselves have

25 In the previous literature, connections have received considerable attention. See Friedman, Pickowicz, and Selden (2005) on Raoyang County. Also Zweig (1997).

ample bureaucratic and private firm connections. The informality of the economic system allows county leaders with personal connections to top provincial or national or even prefecture-level leaders to be more successful at attracting investments and preferential policies. There is a role for both formal (institutional) and informal connections. Most connections are informal: previous work, shared hometowns, graduation from the same university, experience in the same organization (e.g., non-CCP parties, CCYL, etc.). Formal connections consist of current institutional ties, as with Qiu He's "concurrent promotion" to the city Party Committee, discussed above. The high volume of central and provincial lobbying by county units hints at the importance of personal connections to superiors within the Party-state apparatus.[26] These units bargain for preferential policies as well as greater on-budget investment and transfers.

However, preferential policies have been diminishing in number over the past decade (Heilmann 2008), and a more important aspect of upward bargaining now consists of bargaining for fiscal transfers. Bargaining upward for budget is an expected part of the system,[27] and it is a part that has become more important following the tax-sharing system reforms in 1993–94 and the subsequent rise in importance of intergovernmental transfers. This is not merely an artifact of China's authoritarian hierarchical system; as Wildavsky (1964) explains in an analysis of the United States budgetary process, officers and executives reviewing budget decisions expect bureaus to argue aggressively for larger budgets – any lack of lobbying effort would make the determination of budgets more difficult, as it would reduce the information on which the determination is made.[28] China's fiscal system has come to rely more and more on transfers, and

[26] Peng (2006) describes the "craze" (*feng*, 风) of lobbying for money and appointments. Zou (2011) describes the proliferation of local government lobbying offices in Beijing despite the banning of such offices. According to Zweig (2002), this lobbying for concessions is a result of the segmented nature of policy experimentation that prevents collective action by local governments. Heilmann (2008) argues that the "atomistic character" of this lobbying bolsters the political authority of the center.

[27] According to Guo (2009), local cadres "visiting ministries to lobby for money [for projects] has become a reasonable activity that [their superiors] tacitly approve of and even solemnly stipulate in official documents with red headings as an important criterion in examining the capability and talent of local cadres." For the importance of bargaining within the Chinese political system more broadly, see Lampton (1987).

[28] As Wildavsky (1968) writes, "If the agencies suddenly reversed roles and sold themselves short, the entire pattern of mutual expectations would be upset, leaving the participants without an anchor in a sea of complexity. For if agencies refuse to be advocates, congressmen would not only have to choose among the margins of the best programs placed before them, they would also have to discover what these good programs might be."

in particular on special purpose transfers. Sub-national governments in 2009 had local ("own") budgetary revenue accounting for 53.8 percent of total revenue, with VAT, consumption tax, and income tax rebates (specified by sharing rules) accounting for an additional 7.2 percent. General purpose transfers accounted for 6.7 percent, and special purpose transfers accounted for 32.4 percent (Huang and Chen 2012). The vast majority of special purpose transfers are earmarked transfers.[29] The malleable and nonrules-based determination of volume and destination in the allocation of special purpose transfers adds an important role for personal relationships, as has been documented in China and elsewhere.[30] An interview with a finance section chief (*kezhang,* 科长) in a Jiangsu county confirmed this:

> Of the two major types of transfers [special purpose, *zhuanxiang,* 专项, and general purpose, *yibanxing,* 一般性] special transfers are both much larger and also much more subject to connections (*guanxi,* 关系). The other important transfer, "fiscal system settlement" (*tizhi jiesuan,* 体制结算), has no *guanxi* element, as it's predetermined. Basically, the process for special transfers is as follows. A bureau will draft a request for funds and submit it to the finance bureau, which will look it over and decide whether to change it and whether to pass it on. The finance bureau and the requesting bureau will then jointly send their request to the province. Here, the provincial finance ministry is paramount. While special transfers are supposed to have spending ratios determined between province and county or city and county, in reality most transfers are non-matched. When the county applies it will specify "empty" matching (*kong peitao,* '空' 配套), meaning that it has no money of its own to contribute. In this system, the personal relationships of the county leadership (*lingdaoren,* 领导人) and the finance bureau chief are paramount. The vast majority of all requested special transfers are rejected by the province, so having an inside track makes success much more likely. (Interview JS112)

This section chief then mentioned that the current county *guanxi* of both the finance bureau chief and the Party secretary were very good, explaining recent high volumes of special purpose transfers.

Connections to top leadership can spur growth through many channels: direct investments from firms, higher levels of transfers and

[29] Special purpose transfers come in two types: revenue replacement (fiscal capacity balancing transfers to compensate for lost revenues, e.g., wage adjustment, agricultural tax adjustment, tax-for-fee reform) and earmarked transfers.

[30] Huang and Chen (2012) construct a "Central Committee Leadership" index based on strength of politburo and Central Committee representation of provincial leaders, and find that this index significantly and positively explains central fiscal grants to provinces. Boex and Martinez-Vazquez (2005) document that allocation of intergovernmental transfers depends on both normative and political considerations. In the public choice literature, see Alperovich (1984) and Grossman (1994).

investments, and also the indirect effect of empowering local leaders and giving them more local control.[31] During the Wang Daohan era in Shanghai in the 1980s, Mingguang (then still Jiashan County) remained particularly strong – Wang Daohan was a native "Mingguang ren" and he did not want Shanghai's money going to Jiangsu, but rather to Anhui (Interview AH104).[32] Such a leader connection is obviously exogenous to the county leader's personal connections, and based simply on his appointment as a local leader while Wang was in office. Similarly, Li Yuanchao is originally from Lianshui County, and when he was provincial Party secretary he selected an "extremely qualified person" to become the Lianshui Party secretary, thus changing the local growth path (Interview JS284).

Although no other counties in the sample have high level hometown heroes, several county Party secretaries were able more proactively to generate personal connections with provincial leaders, or at least were able to give provincial leaders "skin in the game" of local development. Connections do not always have to do with hometown or previous work or formal institutional ties – they can also be developed and nurtured. For instance, Jiang Guoxing, a cadre in prosperous Southern Jiangsu, personally received a call from Jiangsu Provincial Party Secretary Li Yuanchao telling him to go north to become Suining County Party secretary. Jiangsu has a saying: "better to go ten feet south than one inch north" (*ningyuan xiangnan yizhang, buyuan xiangbei yicun,* 宁愿向南一丈，不愿向北一寸), and as Jiang notes, "No southern cadre wants to come north, but if you're told to, you do." Jiang responded quickly. As he says, "on April 6 Li Yuanchao gave me a call. I got to Xuzhou that afternoon, and at 9am on the 7th I was in Suining – at noon, without notice, Li himself came to Suining" (Wang 2006). In arriving personally on the same day as Jiang, Li provided support to Jiang, giving him more credibility and making him appear more powerful to locals, which helped with his policy implementation capacity.

31 China's one-level-down administrative management system means that the administrative level just above is most important; however, many public investment and fiscal transfer decisions are made two levels up (i.e., province to county), or directly from the central government to county governments. Additionally, top leaders can pressure lower leaders even within the "one-level-down" framework.

32 While many Mingguang interviewees referred to the positive effects on Mingguang of Wang's term as Shanghai Mayor, the fact that this took place over two decades before prevented anyone from recalling specific investments that Wang initiated. Nevertheless, this connection is still bearing fruit. Wang's son came to Mingguang in 2005 and initiated the building of a Wang Daohan Library (汪道涵藏书楼).

Or take the case of Dianhu Village (垫湖村) in Sihong County. A large modern memorial hall and museum has been built in the center of the village to commemorate the village's (contested) role as China's first to initiate the household responsibility system, and in 2012 Jiangsu Party Secretary Luo Zhijun visited as part of his "develop Subei" initiative. A year later, framed posters of Luo from the initial visit were scattered throughout the village. When Luo came, there was no sense that the county or county Party secretary had a previous relationship to him – but after his visit, he developed a connection and stake in the future prospects, continuing to check in to see how the village development was proceeding. This level of investment made the village more attractive for other investors (Interview JS203; Interview JS117; Interview JS220; Interview JS191).

Personal connections to firms and their CEOs can also be very important for helping to attract outside investment. The institutionalized "law of avoidance" (*diqu huibi,* 地区回避) means that all county Party secretaries hail from outside the county they lead; while this may make them less knowledgeable about local conditions, it also expands their *guanxi* base. A particularly strong case of this external *guanxi* comes from "Sunan cadres going North" (*sunan ganbu xiangbei,* 苏南干部向北) and bringing with them connections to firms with large investments in the south. As Suining County Party Secretary Jiang notes, "people follow people" (*ren genzhe ren zou,* 人跟着人走):

> I spent seven years in Jurong [in Southern Jiangsu] and learned how things work ... if an official isn't there to help, an enterprise won't succeed, in China's current development period this is tough to change. So I tell firms that I'll grant whatever's asked (*youqiu biying,* 有求必应), if you have a problem, make a call and we'll figure it out. This concept of service has been deeply ingrained locally... Right now, Sunan has problems with electricity use, finding employees, using land, and other issues, so a lot of Sunan enterprises have a strong desire to come north. Just now, a Taiwan bicycle manufacturer came called "Yasese" (雅瑟瑟), they produce here and sell abroad. When I was in Jurong, Yasese built a bicycle factory, and now they want to make their second investment here in Suining. There's another example, Bingyu Beer (冰语啤酒), with an investment of 195 million US dollars. They came to Jurong in 2003 to talk with me – when I left Jurong, the CEO didn't want to stay, and now he's started a factory here in Suining. This is to say that the reputation of a place's leader is very important. If you are an efficient, service-oriented, and productive leader, then one becomes ten and ten becomes 100 and then everyone will come, manifesting in an investment promotion network (*zhaoshang wang,* 招商网). (Wang 2006)

Creativity: Thought Leadership

One deputy county magistrate of Xuyi County, when asked the difference between Jiangsu and Anhui counties, replied immediately and succinctly: "leadership thinking" (*lingdaoren de sixiang,* 领导人的思想) (Interview JS294). Such leader "ideas" and "thinking" were highlighted in many interviews as the key to local development. While grandiose assessments of local thought leadership may be self-serving, innovative leadership can nevertheless have significant effects on county development. Creativity manifests in both direct policy/economic decisions as well as in ways to attract investment and achieve pro-growth governance, and over time these latter categories have become much more important. Effective policies including free land, tax incentives for migrant returnees, urban zoning, etc., are often applied broadly across entire regions, sometimes at the initiative of the province or prefecture, as discussed in Chapter 2, which highlighted the similarities in cross-county and cross-province development zone policies for investment attraction. In an environment in which localities do not actually control most laws and regulations and in which competition has led to policy and regulatory equalization through races to the bottom, localities must find ways to differentiate their counties from others. In the past, counties had a larger role in determining the speed of restructuring and local reform, but as growth priorities have switched to investment attraction, there has in turn been less variation in specific local economic policies. According to one local Party secretary, referring to China's "reform and opening up" (*gaige kaifang,* 改革开放): "reform is basically done, now it's just opening [i.e., to outside investment]." Indeed, because of the dependence on attracting mobile capital, the two most important "innovation" categories in which county Party secretaries can make economic contributions are enhancing county visibility and reputation for investment, often through attempts at county branding and through innovations in cadre management and control.[33]

County Party secretaries use county strategic development plans to highlight their innovative thinking: these plans are a means of visibility, meant as indicators of county leader vision as much as reflections of specific policy ideas. Every county government has an annual work conference discussing the previous year's achievements and the goals for the subsequent year. When the leadership determines that a new growth

[33] Implementation of policy can be more or less pro-growth, but new policy ideas are less important at the county level: for instance, in deciding to restructure firms, the possibilities are largely known.

direction is required, this is often the stage for unveiling such a change, and policy innovations can be identified through these reports. Certain "strategic plans" gain traction, but the quality of economic ideas in these plans is less original or insightful than the plans' ability to "brand" the county. For instance, Xuyi County Party Secretary Zhao's 16-character development plan described at the beginning of the chapter was grammatically more innovative than it was economically innovative: the focus, which many interviewees noted lasted for several administrations over the course of a decade, was on industry, urbanization, tourism, and creating a good investment environment. Zhao's early switch to investment rather than restructuring is perhaps noteworthy, but more noteworthy is how un-noteworthy this strategic direction really is. The key was instead the rhetoric (a catchy 16-character phrase), and supporting policies for branding and governance reform, as discussed below.

Similarly, in Sihong, the "three concentrations" (*sange jizhong,* 三个集中) plan developed by County Party Secretary Xu De (徐德) to solve the "three rural" (*sannong,* 三农) problems, has received considerable attention, but has more to do with Xu's ability to get this concept printed in media than originality of the concept.[34] The three concentrations relate to land, people, and industry. In describing the plan, County Party Secretary Xu uses technical economic language, arguing that land is a "capital resource," but concentrated land is a "high quality resource" (*youzhi ziyuan,* 优质资源), and noting that "only by increasing scale can you lower costs and improve economic efficiency." When the prefecture-level Party secretary visited Sihong in August 2012, Xu focused on the successes of his "three concentrations" policy, explaining how the policy was helping to create a middle-class *xiaokang* society (Pan 2012).[35] In Suining, County Party Secretary Han Zhenmei (韩振美) explains how Suining improved its fiscal situation by actively developing scale

[34] See, for example, Xu (2013). This is perhaps too cynical: beyond the rhetoric, some of the accompanying policies are somewhat innovative. A first step is concentrating housing construction and building these areas with low prices. Low income households get particular assistance moving in – for instance, in one village houses smaller than 60 square meters were sold below cost, which allowed 32 low-income households to move in. Once the people live in a concentrated area it is easier to concentrate land, which can then attract capital for large agriculture and agricultural processing. After selling off the land, the government still has to help provide insurance, technology, and capital. As one standing committee member says: "Transferring land doesn't mean the government can stand aside and do nothing."

[35] These "creative" undertakings not only help to attract outside investment, but also help to attract political attention toward the county Party secretary; the two are not mutually exclusive, and may be mutually supportive.

agricultural industry (*guimo nongye,* 规模农业) and supporting private industry, particularly by emphasizing the "2455" plan to generate 20,000 private/individual units, 4000 cooperative units, 5000 units paying at least 3000 RMB in annual taxes, and 500 units paying over 30,000 RMB in taxes (Z. Han 1995).

Compared to the Jiangsu counties, strategic plans from the three Anhui counties have been less innovative, even in rhetoric, with the partial exception of Wuhe in more recent years. An excuse made in these counties is that counties are constrained in policy decisions by the provincial government. "The Mingguang leaders aren't at fault for poor growth. They're very constrained. The biggest problem in Mingguang is that Anhui itself takes no initiative, but rather simply implements government policies" (Interview AH104).[36] But even in an environment where policies are determined by upper-level governments, there can be a strong role for creativity in innovative implementation. Indeed, the most successful leadership initiatives in Jiangsu have less to do with policy than with proactive county branding, and evidence from the three Jiangsu counties shows that county Party secretaries can be highly able marketers.

When preferential policies are similar across locales and counties have similar conditions, an effective means of attracting investment may just be getting the county's name into the public sphere. This branding can serve the purpose of both investment attraction as well as personal political motivations. Among the Jiangsu case counties, several "innovative" branding initiatives were established with direct personal involvement and commitment of county Party secretaries: the annual Crawfish Festival in Xuyi and the "Sui character" (*suizi,* 睢字) advertisements in Suining were the most effective. Sihong's "first county" and "crab" branding efforts have been innovative but somewhat less effective.[37] The strategic rhetoric described above is also very much part of county branding efforts.

In the late 1990s, Xuyi was looking for a way to distinguish itself. At the time Zhao Peng transferred to Xuyi County to become Party

[36] This interviewee explained how investment promotion work started late in Anhui: officially in 2001 in every county throughout the province. In 2004 the center allowed every county to have a province-level development zone, which were then developed over the next few years – but again there was no local decision or initiative, and there was also no major competition for investment.

[37] Popular wisdom credits Xiaogang Village (小岗村) in Fengyang County (凤阳县) in Anhui as the grassroots initiator of the household responsibility system, but Sihong has tried to give credit to Dianhu Village instead as the "first agricultural reform village" (*nongcun gaige diyicun,* 农村改革第一村). The village now has a large, modern museum/

secretary, the economy was almost entirely privatized, and the government was not sure how to develop further. Zhao decided to build up the local crawfish industry, searching for a "festival economy" (*jieqing jingji*, 节庆经济) commercial opportunity. As he said: "Qingdao had a beer festival, Weifang had a kite festival, Luoyang had a peony festival, so why can't Xuyi create a crawfish festival?" (Shangguan 2010). Zhao's idea was that such a festival would give Xuyi national recognition and serve as an opportunity to attract (and wine and dine) local investors. Indeed, the raison d'être of the festival was explicitly to attract investment. According to the Party secretary succeeding Zhao, Wang Youfu, attracting investment was identified as the solution to a "contradiction" of needing to speed up industrialization despite weak economic foundations, and the county put forth the concept of "small lobster [crawfish], big strategy" (*xiaolongxia, dazhanlue,* 小龙虾，大战略) in order to boost the local reputation given that "attracting investment difficulties are reflected in Xuyi's lack of reputation" (Wang 2005, 85).

Since initiation of the Crawfish Festival in 2000, the crawfish industry has grown to become an integral part of Xuyi's economy, with a brand value exceeding 4.13 billion RMB, 200,000 people employed in crawfish-related businesses, and annual market output value of 2 billion RMB. The festival serves as an opportunity to attract investment as an image ambassador for both domestic and foreign investment.[38] In 2000 only 11 percent of investment came from attracting outside investment, whereas in 2003, 98 percent did (Wang 2005, 100). Crawfish now serve as a major generator of Xuyi's tourism industry: in the year before the festival was established, according to festival promotional materials, "Xuyi was not known to many outsiders," attracting fewer than 80,000 tourists; by 2002 this number had already grown ten-fold to 800,000, and by 2009 nearly 3 million people visited Xuyi and tourism revenue topped 1.7 billion RMB. According to the 2010 Xuyi Yearbook: "During the 2009 Crawfish Festival, Xuyi brought in 86 projects, totaling 7.53 billion RMB, 135 million USD and 100 million Hong Kong dollars,

memorial full of supporting documentation, news articles, and 1970s/1980s agricultural equipment.

[38] As Xuyi's crawfish promotional documents claim: "Attracting foreign investment is one of the best ways to speed up development in some of the least developed areas." An investor locals are particularly fond of highlighting is Greg Williams, former mayor and current councilor of Bendigo, Australia, who invested 180 million RMB in the Sino-Australian Manjianghong Crawfish Industrial Park. As Zhang Lianzhen, chairwoman of the Jiangsu Provincial People's Consultative Conference noted, "It's amazing for a retired foreign mayor to farm crawfish in Xuyi."

against the background of international economic recession." Former Party Secretary Wang explains that the festival helped Xuyi rank number one in Huaian Prefecture for three years running in its "comprehensive economic evaluation" (Wang 2005, 80). Local festival documents state that the crawfish business has created over 20 billionaires, 200 millionaires, 2000 "hundred-thousandaires," and 20,000 rich households.

While Xuyi's geographic position and natural conditions make crawfish breeding possible, branding was a more important factor in this rapid development. Indeed, multiple interviewees admitted (often sheepishly) that most "Xuyi" crawfish were actually imports from Sichuan, where the quality was better and the fish more plentiful:[39] "Since at least 2007, most 'local' crawfish come from Anhui and Chongqing. They ran out here as the price rose from a few *mao* [0.1 RMB] to 60 RMB per *jin* [0.5 kilograms]. Even at the start [of the festival in 2000] there was nothing special about Xuyi crawfish – they were never as good as those in Sihong or Anhui – the key was Zhao's creativeness and Wang's courage" (Interview JS145). More recent Party secretaries have continued to promote Zhao's initial idea. In 2006, Party Secretary Cai Duncheng introduced the Xuyi crawfish to Stockholm, Sweden, which has held crawfish festivals for centuries and now holds an additional crawfish event annually at the same time as Xuyi. Cai also promoted the festival in Beijing, holding a festival at Peking University and becoming the first county Party secretary to give a speech at the university. Apparently, he also arranged to have a festival flag placed on Mt. Everest, although it is unclear how many intrepid climbers this stunt has enticed to Xuyi.

North of Xuyi, in Suining, Jiangsu, local leaders also tried to attract the notice of potential investors, this time through a series of attention-getting advertisements.[40] Despite a 4000-year history and an important role during the Three Kingdoms period (Zhang Liang is said to have encountered Cui Guang on the ancient Yi Bridge in Suining), outside recognition of the county was very low. In 2008, County Party Secretary Wang Tianqi led a government investment tour to Beijing, and was upset when none of the potential investors knew how to pronounce the first character of the county name, 睢 (*Sui*). In his words:

[39] Part of this was a result of overfishing, likely as a result of the festival craze. Shangguan (2010) discusses the collapse of local crawfish breeding by the late 2000s.

[40] The county leadership has also attempted to brand the county as "the realm of children's drawings" (*ertonghua zhi xiang*, 儿童画之乡), a designation supported by the Ministry of Culture, and local children's drawings have been given as gifts by the Ministry of Foreign Affairs and stored at the United Nations.

> In the process of seeking investment, we ran into a lot of embarrassment (*henduo ganga*, 很多尴尬) as many people didn't know Suining (*buzhidao suining*, 不知道睢宁). Some had never heard of the county, others just didn't recognize the character. While seeking investment, some read 'huai,' others read 'wei'; we heard everything (*du shenme douyou*, 读什么的都有). This was a really awkward situation, so we decided to use an advertisement to introduce our city. (Zhang and Lan 2009)

The "advertisement" consisted of four separate full page ads to "raise the local reputation" (*tigao defang zhimingdu*, 提高地方知名度). All four ads had a similar format. The first day had the 睢 character printed in a huge font, with a question below: "Do you recognize this character?" The second day had the same character, adding a huge exclamation point and exclaiming, "the people (*laobaixing*) here will tell you, it's easy to be a commoner, hard to be an official!" (*zuo baixing yi, zuo guan nan*, 做百姓易，做官难).[41] The third day had the same character and exclamation point and adding, "This city has seized the smile gene" (*zhangwo zhe weixiao de jiyin*, 掌握着微笑的基因). The final day included the full county name printed across the top and *Sui* written in pinyin above the 睢 character, helping readers pronounce the county name.

Party Secretary Wang intentionally placed the ads in Beijing newspapers during the annual National People's Congress and Chinese People's Political Consultative Conference, figuring that the "two sessions" representatives include many famous businessmen and business owners, and that it is also the time of year with the most media attention. All four ads included the cell phone number of Party Secretary Wang and the county magistrate. Wang notes: "My cell phone received lots of messages. There were also people who wanted to deeply discuss cooperating with us. This made me very happy." According to local interviews, the "Sui" advertisement was very successful at attracting attention and thus investment (Interview JS115), and indeed investment in 2009 and 2010 grew rapidly in Suining, and Suining was one of Jiangsu's fastest growing counties during Wang's years in office.

Beyond the county branding efforts spearheaded by local leaders, innovative institutional reforms have also had strong pro-growth effects through their effect on governance and through ensuring "good" behavior from subordinates. Informal control mechanisms are discussed below under the "control" section, but leader-initiated institutional reforms

[41] This preceded the more modern internet joke that "When the officials' bottoms are stable, society is unstable. When the officials' bottoms are unstable, then society is stable (官员稳腚了，社会就不稳定了；官员不稳腚了，社会就稳定了)."

are one of the most effective and creative areas for leader impact. For instance, as discussed above, Qiu He's "open government" transparency efforts were designed to win back trust in government and were a creative solution to an antigrowth challenge as well as an effective way to control cadres who ignored his diktats. Institutional reform requires not only an idea, but the courage and ability (control) to implement the idea, so this discussion carries over into the next two leadership characteristics.

Innovative institutional reform is frequently the brainchild of local leadership, not just in the case counties but in China's development more broadly. Leaders play a key role in initiating local government reforms, as Saich and Yang (2003, 205) describe in Shizhong with Zhang Jinming, a Party secretary who "played a key role in initiating and sustaining momentum for ORS [open recommendation and selection]" and who "persisted over the objections of some members of the party standing committee."[42] Similarly, Fewsmith (2009) describes how one of China's most innovative and bold local institutional experiments, participatory budgeting, was adopted in Xinhe Township in 2005 in large part because "the Party secretary was open-minded ... neither this nor the reform adopted in Zeguo was forced upon the townships by higher-level authorities." Foster (2006) similarly shows that the "service commitment system" in Yantai resulted from the influential role of enterprising local leaders. The China Local Governance Innovation Awards established jointly by the China Center for Comparative Politics and Economics, the Center of Comparative Studies on Political Parties of the Central Party School, and the Center of China Government Innovations at Peking University, provide additional evidence of the role of local leaders in initiating pro-growth governance reforms. Officials who have won awards "proudly state that the primary feature of their projects is 'originality, not a mere imitation of others or the simple implementation of instructions from above'" (Yang 2013). Credit is given to local leadership, with over half of award winners saying that the innovation idea was "first suggested by some knowledgeable leaders." Most recipients of the reward have approached governance innovation from a utilitarian pro-growth perspective, with a focus on pro-growth institutions, and citizens seem to agree that this is the correct angle.[43]

[42] He and Lang (2000) confirm this in their analysis of the Buyun election, describing the key role of the Party secretary who had an analytical and open mind as well as a pioneering spirit. See also Yang (2001).

[43] For more on leaders and local government innovation awards, see Chen and Huang (2010), Wang (2005), and He (2007).

In the case counties, the clearest example of innovative institutional reform comes from Suining and the government transparency and control initiatives described in the previous chapter. These reforms started in Suining under Wang Tianqi.[44] In September 2008, Wang attended cadre training in Beijing and presented his "only when cadres have it rough will the people be okay" theory, which in his telling attracted the attention of higher authorities. After that, Suining was selected as one of three trial counties for reform, but as Wang says, "really, the reforms had already started." In other words, these institutional reforms were made at the initiative of Wang, and he wanted to be given credit.[45] Perceptions of individual creativity are important to local leaders: Wang says that while he greatly admires Qiu He, "I'm my own man ... I never researched Qiu's 'administrative style' (*shizheng fengge,* 施政风格) or administrative measures (*shizheng cuoshi,* 施政措施). Everything I do is done based on my own personality and my own determinations. It's not only him [Qiu He], I've never deliberately imitated anyone else (*keyi mofangguo renhe ren,* 刻意模仿过任何人)" (Bian 2009).

The Anhui case counties have been largely lacking in brand/reputation building and formal institutional reforms. Wuhe has tried weakly to promote its aquatic products, but none have developed into brand names.[46] Mingguang had a famous liquor brand, but its national renown has diminished; if you ask most people in the region what they know of Mingguang, it is a culture of corruption. Si only made national news over the furor caused when a temple was razed (see Chapter 6).

Control: What I Say Goes

Innovations in cadre management tie in closely to the capacity of local Party secretaries to ensure subordinate compliance. Economically successful county Party secretaries ensure this compliance in order to implement policies and prevent antigrowth government failures. Good governance requires responsiveness and accountability, and implementing

[44] The experiment in local government transparency began in Suining, Hebei's Cheng'an County, and Wuhou District in Chengdu (Sichuan). An overview of the trial "opinions" (*yijian,* 意见) can be found in Che (2010).

[45] Actually, many of the institutional innovations were made under Jiang Guoxing, Wang's predecessor. Getting credit and gaining "political visibility" is a key incentive to initiate reforms, as Yang (2004, 35) describes with regard to Li Tieying in Liaoning's Haicheng, who introduced a program for comprehensive economic reform in mid 1995 that significantly reduced the role of the government in the local economy.

[46] These products include Tuo Lake Crabs (沱湖螃蟹), Wuhe Mandarin Fish (五河桂鱼), and Wuhe Whitebait (五河银鱼).

cadre management reforms requires high degrees of control over the local bureaucracy. County Party secretaries are personally responsible for the behavior of local bureaucracies. As the former head of the national Organization Department notes, "In many localities, the quality of work and the 'democratic mood' (*minzhu fengqi,* 民主风气) depend entirely on the work style (*zuofeng,* 作风) of the first party secretary" (Zhao and Zheng 2006). But beyond setting a personal example, local leaders differ greatly in their personal involvement and oversight, and particularly in their use of rewards and punishments through the local cadre responsibility system.

County Party secretaries themselves recognize the importance of good governance, administrative efficiency, and corruption prevention in generating a pro-growth investment environment. According to Wuhe County Party Secretary Hu Qiwang, "Investment promotion is the most important and most direct force for county economic development … Therefore we put forth a plan to grasp administrative effectiveness (*zhua xingzheng xiaoneng,* 抓行政效能), raise government service efficiency (*tigao zhengfu de fuwu xiaolü,* 提高政府的服务效率), and use administrative efficacy to attract bigger and bigger companies to Wuhe." He continues, "Before coming to Wuhe, Huafang Group (中国华芳集团) had already visited many places, some of which had more preferential policies. But after many comparisons, Huafang chose Wuhe. The company representative, in describing why they settled on Wuhe, from his heart (*cong neixin li,* 从内心里) said that administrative efficacy is more important than preferential policies."[47] More succinctly, Sihong County Party Secretary Xu De emphasizes that "assistance (*bangban,* 帮办) is service, assistance brings investment" (Sihong News Agency 2013).

Yet despite acknowledging the importance of local service and bureaucratic efficiency, leader control over local bureaucracies varies widely, both within and across regions. Burns and Wang (2010) note that despite laws, "efforts to impose tighter discipline and control on civil servants have been relatively ineffective."[48] In the discussion of corruption in the

[47] Hu acknowledges that achieving a goal of administrative efficacy is not simple: "Of course, raising administrative efficacy can't be achieved simply with a few campaigns (*yundong,* 运动) or documents. We need to continue to strive to make raising administrative efficacy a conscious idea (*zijue de linian,* 自觉的理念) and let it soak into our blood and genes (*jintou zai women de xueye he jiyin li,* 浸透在我们的血液和基因里)" (Hu 2012).

[48] Some of these control mechanisms include surveillance, e.g., the "supervisor responsibility system" (*shouzhang fuzezhi,* 首长负责制), and systems of reporting on the fulfillment of targets.

previous chapter, the focus was on cultures of corruption resulting from leadership corruption, but corruption also occurs against the will of the local leadership, and may indicate a lack of county Party secretary control. Especially in localities with histories of corruption and entrenched bureaucracies, local leaders may have little control, either by choice or by necessity. In one Anhui county, several officials in economic bureaus bemoaned local corruption, arguing that the county simply could not be controlled. "They [the provincial authorities] will send in a new *yibashou*, but he has no way to control subordinates, so everything remains corrupt" (Interview AH247). The local bureaucracy was simply too powerful and too corrupt to change. Such local corruption makes leaders less courageous and less willing to innovate, as discussed in the next section.

Cadre institutional innovation is one means of ensuring against such behavior, but many control mechanisms have more to do with willingness to exert control through existing means, and in particular the use of the personnel management system and target responsibility system (*mubiao zeren zhi,* 目标责任制) through enforced mechanisms for monitoring, rewards, and punishments. Qiu He, as described above, used not only "open government" reforms to ensure compliance and good behavior, but also micromanagement and appointment of trustworthy cadres. One Anhui cadre saw the establishment and enforcement of targets for subordinates as the most important role played by local leaders: "In terms of the major Party secretary role, basically he just accepts upper level guidance but can then tweak targets (*mubiao,* 目标) for subordinates in order to tweak directions" (Interview AH104). With ever more bureaucrats to control, often with their own vertical (*tiao*) reporting lines, problems of asymmetric information naturally ensue, with increasing difficulties in monitoring and local implementation. Managing cadres through targets deals with incentives of subordinates and lets them handle means: as former US President Eisenhower said, "Leadership is the art of getting someone else to do something you want done because he wants to do it."

In several of the case counties, individual leaders have had strong approaches to personnel management. As described above, Qiu He enforced control through random testing and calling of subordinates. In Xuyi, similar Party secretary hands-on involvement has become the norm. Under Party Secretary Zhao at the turn of the millennium, economic targets began to be seriously enforced, and under the current Party secretary, target achievement has become even more strictly enforced. Every year, the government work report will report not only last year's achievements, but also next year's targets. This is a very formal process. The targets are generated by asking each bureau to research potential targets, starting in November. Once set, the goals then become part of performance evaluation; if goals are not reached, then each cadre and bureau needs to explain why (Interview JS281). In the finance bureau, Xuyi is apparently much stricter than surrounding counties about hitting revenue targets within each bureau and section. When targets are missed, salaries are immediately docked, and "even worse," (*gengbuhaode,* 更不好的) cadres lose face when they have to go up in front of everybody and explain why they failed: "when you walk up to the podium, they play extremely unpleasant (*feichang buhaoting,* 非常不好听) music" (Interview JS112). In Xuyi, even for noneconomic functional bureaus, the bureau leaders have to hit six annual economic targets, of which investment attraction is by far the most important, accounting for 70–80 percent of the total score with an annual requirement of 28 million RMB per bureau. Leaders who do not hit this target have no chance of promotion (Interview JS192).[49]

This seems at first glance like an institutional effect rather than an example of leadership personal control and initiative, but a comparative look at one of the Anhui case counties demonstrates the leadership role. A bureau chief of a directly economics-related bureau specifically referred to the contrast with Jiangsu, noting that unlike in the neighboring Jiangsu county, not hitting investment targets in his county was irrelevant and "no one cared." In the Jiangsu county, this official argued, the county Party secretary had control – if a bureau missed its target, then that bureau chief was demoted, no questions asked. "In Jiangsu they see growth as more important. This is particularly clear in hitting investment promotion targets. I and others have targets, but it doesn't matter if we don't hit them" (Interview AH178). Another Anhui county official complained that in Jiangsu counties, the Party secretary will randomly call land lines to make sure that subordinates are dutifully at work, whereas in his county, "it's expected that people won't go to work!" (Interview AH247). This Anhui county highlights a common cadre problem that Deng highlighted in the 1980s (and was still highlighted in the 18th Party

[49] Former Xuyi County Party Secretary Wang describes his former emphasis on investment attraction, taking credit for 19 township Party secretaries and 41 department heads personally going on investment attraction trips for over one month each between November 2002 and June 2003, altogether attracting over 62 projects worth 5 million RMB or more, and signing 1.25 billion RMB in contracts (Wang 2005). Whiting (2004) looks at county promotions of township officials in the Shanghai suburbs and identifies a focus on positive (remuneration) incentives based on highly quantitative performance evaluations, with the greatest focus on industrial output and profits: bonuses for industrial output and profits accounted for 85 percent of a leader's income.

Congress Third Plenum Communique in Fall 2013): "cadres can't fall, they can only rise."[50] Such an incentive structure fails to prevent shirking and misbehavior.

Not all informal control mechanisms stem from control through the target responsibility system. Under Wang Tianqi, Suining did its best to establish a "government of integrity" (*chengxin de zhengfu,* 诚信的政府) and improve the government's "workstyle" (*gongzuo zuofeng,* 工作作风) to make Suining a good place to invest. In 2008, Wang initiated the "changes to two styles" (*liangfeng zhuanbian,* 两风转变): cadre style (*guanfeng,* 官风) and people's style (*minfeng,* 民风). The key for "cadre style" is integrity (*chengxin,* 诚信), steadfastness (*tashi,* 踏实), and service-mindedness (*fuwu xing,* 服务性). Accompanying this highly abstract rhetoric, Wang was known for directly punishing cadres for misbehavior. Most famously, he strictly implemented the "alcohol-free lunch" (*zhongwu jinjiu,* 中午禁酒) rule in 2008. Many local cadres thought this policy was just a rhetorical flair, but Wang proved them otherwise. In one extreme case, a township Party secretary went to Anhui for lunch to discuss an investment project and had a beer. When this was found out, he was fired, even though he had been in Anhui and following their customs (Interview JS290).

The control mechanisms described here have strong pro-growth implications along the lines discussed in the previous chapter: they help to prevent corruption and excessive fee collection while at the same time incentivizing lower-level cadres to behave in ways dictated by the county leadership. Given that county leadership frequently emphasizes growth, this results in more efforts to attract investment.[51]

[50] Burns and Wang (2010) speculate that "peer evaluations" (*minzhu pingyi,* 民主评议) have undermined the use of punishments to control subordinate behavior: "Because supervisors must go through peer evaluation in preparation for promotion, their subordinates become stakeholders. As a result, supervisors avoided using punishments for fear that their subordinates would renege during the peer evaluation." But punishments in Jiangsu seem serious, albeit based more on fines and loss of face rather than strict demotions.

[51] In discussing control over local society, it is also important to confront the literature on charismatic leadership and leading by example. Gardner (1965, 12) writes that, "Leaders have a significant role in creating the state of mind that is the society … they can conceive and articulate goals that lift people out of their petty preoccupations, carry them above the conflicts that tear a society apart, and unite them in the pursuit of objectives worthy of their best efforts." When Chinese local leaders make the news, more often than not it is as a result of corruption and immoral leadership, not exemplary moral behavior or a Confucian/Platonic ideal of demonstrating the right to lead through virtue. Yet this book attempts to overlook the natural cynicism surrounding local leaders. Despite upward accountability, it is clear that successful leaders are often those who can gain societal

Courage: Act First, Discuss Later

Innovative ideas and approaches to institutional management and reform require courage and a willingness to act. Many of the most prominent local reforms in China have had negative consequences for important interest groups and segments of the population, particularly in the short-term: restructuring firms challenges vested interests, urban development requires demolitions, and cadre institutional reform opens government up to criticism and attack. While there are signs of increasing central support for local institutional innovations, this support likely only extends to post facto *successful* innovations.[52] But in China's competitive and rapidly changing environment, passivity loses out to proactivity.[53] Lam (1999) finds that courage predicted the entrepreneurialism of county Party secretaries in Nanhai and Panyu and thus largely determined their divergent economic outcomes: "The importance of leadership in the early years of the reform era can hardly be exaggerated, because what was required when uncertainties abound was the courage to take political risks by stepping into uncharted territories. The county party secretary was therefore in a crucial position to determine the locality's approach to reform and development."[54] Saich and Yang (2003, 205) concur: "Leadership is also important in promoting or resisting change. In many localities, an insightful and strong-willed individual leader can play a crucial role in initiating and implementing reform." As discussed above, Qiu He's controversial innovations and control mechanisms brought him national attention: this attention had the potential to backfire.

support for innovative or disruptive policy shifts. This often has as much to do with courage as control: for instance, in the Qiu He case, there were initially lots of petitions but then society came on board. Wang Youfu in Xuyi had a similar experience.

[52] In 2002, the 16th National Congress of the CCP articulated "innovation" as a value and promoted the concept to an ideological level, concluding that "innovation is the soul that enables a nation to make progress, the inexhaustible power for a nation to be prosperous, and the source for a party to sustain its vitality." According to Yang (2013) since the 16th National Congress, "governance innovation has been received favorably by governments at different levels, as well as by all sectors in society." Additionally, the 11th Five Year Plan set governance innovation as a reform goal. Premier Wen Jiabao said in 2006: "The main task in the reform of the administrative system is to promote self-enhancement of the government and governance innovation. This is also the main [illegible]tent of reform of the economic as well as the political system."

[illegible] issue of proactivity versus passivity resurfaces in Chapters 5 and 6 when attempting [illegible]plain regional and provincial variance in promotion incentives.

[illegible] early 1980s, Nanhai had a much more entrepreneurial leader; this was reflected in [illegible]r of magnitude greater rural loans and much more rapid rural industrialization [illegible]yu.

Jiangsu has produced many courageous leaders who pursue economic growth and development without regard for local opinion. Wang Youfu served as county Party secretary in Xuyi from December 2000 through June 2006, a period that can be seen as Xuyi's "Golden Era" economically. Wang was known for his boldness and direct style, with his trademark phrase being *bulun xiangan* (不论先干), or "act first without discussion." Following his tenure, he even penned a book with this title, describing his leadership style. Naturally, this style created enemies and detractors as well as supporters. Wang introduced the phrase as a current manifestation of Deng's "crossing the river by feeling for stones," arguing that the key to development is acting: "When confronting a changing situation and changing development needs, you can't blindly rack your brains (*ming si ku xiang,* 冥思苦想) from the initial vantage point ... or waste lots of time deciding what to do. Instead, you need a 'keen sense of smell' (*lingmin de xiujue,* 灵敏的嗅觉) to act quickly and seize opportunities ... this starts right now with me (*cong wo zuoqi, cong xianzai zuoqi,* 从我做起，从现在做起)" (Wang 2005). A key example of Wang's courageous approach came when the Crawfish Festival was challenged in the early 2000s as an excessive waste. The controversy was aired on national television on July 28, 2004, on the popular show Focal Point (*jiaodian fangtan* 焦点访谈), with the title "Who Pays the Crawfish Festival Bill?" (*shei wei longxiajie maidan* 谁为龙虾节买单), and Wang was seen as losing crucial provincial support (Weng 2006). But even though the festival had not been Wang's idea, he committed to preserving and expanding it, and refused to back down (Wang 2005; Interview JS284). The consequent reputational and economic benefit of the festival was discussed above.

More generally, many economic decisions require courage, which actually serves to reduce the appeal of holding economic office. According to former Suining County Party Secretary Jiang Guoxing, "There's a saying in Suining official circles: past generations committed sins, this generation manages industry. Every cadre wants to be politics and law or discipline inspection leader because they like managing people (*guanren,* 管人) and have no interest in managing industry: with industry if you fail you're criticized, and if you get too close to enterprises you're implicated and questioned. This is a problem of official culture" (Wang 2006). Courage in the county economic environment of the past decade manifests largely in reforms that challenge local vested interests and force institutional change, but in the 1990s and early 2000s decisions on economic restructuring were put in the hands of local leaders. Privatization has occurred at varying speeds and times across provinces, and provincial aggregates mask significant variation in sub-provincial privatization reforms – these reforms depended on local conditions and leader decisions.[55] Xuyi's Wang discusses some of these tough decisions (Wang 2005, 87): Xuyi in the second half of 2001 forced the closure of over 100 quarries and attapulgite factories, resulting in an immediate loss of over 10 million RMB, nearly 5 percent of total revenue (220 million RMB). This decision later proved successful: after consolidation and reopening, the mining and attapulgite industries became much more profitable.[56] Compare these restructuring decisions with the corrupt approaches of Zhang Songjian (Mingguang) and Xu Shexin (Wuhe) described in the previous chapter.

The pro-growth aspects of local leader courage may have negative social consequences, as is apparent when looking at urban development and related land expropriations and housing demolitions. As discussed in more depth in Chapter 6, land expropriation is one of the greatest local threats to social stability, yet urban development requires land expropriation as well as housing demolition. Individual leaders have had transformative impacts (for better or worse) on local urban development. Jiang Guoxing in Suining came into office with a new requirement: "Urban areas are windows into a region, embodying a place's external image and the local investment environment. Suining has to rapidly build a premium city (*jingpin chengshi*, 精品城市) in order to boldly make the leap from a county-level small city to a medium-sized city" (He 2006). During Jiang's time in office, Suining was transformed, with no small degree of discontent due to expropriations and demolitions; the new urban development made the investment efforts of Jiang's successor, Wang Tianqi, much more effective (Interview JS115). In Xuyi, County Party Secretary Cai Duncheng was widely perceived as having a good sense of urban development and little constraint on his willingness to tear down old

[55] Ho, Bowles, and Dong (2003) study TVE privatizations in three counties in Shandong and Jiangsu, finding that within these provinces, the timing of reform varied across localities. They acknowledge that "the homogeneity of the privatization process within, and even across, the three counties indicates that central policies handed down from above were important in shaping, and forcing, the privatisation process," but highlight the different reform outcomes and speeds based on local decisions and conditions (a key concern of local cadres was that collective enterprises were being asset stripped).

[56] It also takes courage to reject certain investments. In Xuyi in the first half of 2002, a chemical industry project worth over 80 million RMB applied to invest, but was rejected because it was a polluting company. In the second half of 2002, a leather project worth over 100 million RMB was also rejected. Despite the negative impact to short-term industrialization and revenue, these decisions helped achieve tourism development goals and longer-term industrialization goals (Wang 2005, 113).

neighborhoods and develop new farmland. In contrast, the current Party secretary is recognized as having a good industrial sense but much less courage and more restraint when it comes to urban development (Interview JS133; Interview JS145). In Si County in Anhui, Jiangsu officials who accompanied me were openly distraught by the state of downtown, with crowded streets and small old buildings: "Where are all the tall buildings?" In the east of the city, the streets widen and new government buildings spring up everywhere, but this new government district is far from downtown, and the undeveloped downtown is perceived by locals (probably not the ones whose houses would be demolished) as a sign of the lack of courage of local leaders.

This Anhui lack of courage is acknowledged by scholars of Anhui's county development. In Bengbu, at Anhui Caijing University's County-level Economics Research Center (县域经济研究所), several scholars emphasized that the lack of courage in local leaders is debilitating, and that Anhui has tended to produce more county-level corruption, with the two connected.[57] In discussing the "law of avoidance" with a local official in Anhui, the official noted that most cadres would rather keep a low profile: "Outside cadres who come to County X don't dare be corrupt; but they also don't dare to do anything" (Interview AH164).

Conclusions

Throughout the administrative hierarchy, first Party secretaries are given extreme power. This power translates into an ability to affect local economic outcomes. Although the high degree of local control and influence held by county Party secretaries can be seen as problematic, making localities operate as difficult-to-control "independent kingdoms," the flip side of the coin is that hierarchical control of localities is actually enabled by this single node of control: if superiors can ensure compliance of county Party secretaries, then they can largely ensure compliance of counties. In the words of the former national head of the Organization Department, "The '*yibashou*' power is too great … if you correctly select and manage the '*yibashou*' this alone will solve most problems (Zhao and Zheng 2006).[58]

57 The higher level of county-level corruption in Anhui was mentioned as an observation, with no supporting data, but it confirms the leader biography data from the previous chapter that showed many more leader corruption cases in Anhui than in Jiangsu.

58 The former head says that when he took office in 1993, the goal was to successfully manage two "30s": 30 provincial Party secretaries and 30 provincial governors. The same logic applies to the county level.

County Party secretaries vary widely in their personal characteristics and pro-growth orientation. Some are more inclined and more capable, producing better growth paths. But what determines the capability and developmental approach and commitment of county Party secretaries? Why do the cadres in the Jiangsu case counties appear to outmatch their Anhui counterparts across all four pro-growth personal characteristics? How much do leader agency and initiative matter, and how much are leaders dependent on patronage for economic outcomes? The relationship between creativity, control, and courage is clear, and all involve local leadership initiative: bold leaders are more likely to attempt innovative policies and more likely to attempt to control their subordinates; creative leaders can develop ideas to ensure better control; leaders with control are more likely to successfully implement their ideas. Connections do not fit as neatly into this overlapping framework, and it is thus important to distinguish between connections and the other three Cs. The next chapter looks at the promotion incentives given to county leaders, and also argues that growth is based more on personal initiative than connections.

5

Paths to Promotion: The Inconsistent Importance of Economic Performance

Performance-based rewards can provide a key incentive for employees to work hard.

– *Horn (1995)*

"What gets measured is what gets done" is, perhaps, the most famous aphorism of performance measurement.

– *Behn (2003)*

Wang Tianqi served as Suining County Party secretary for four years from 2008 to 2011.[1] Of all the county Party secretaries serving in the six case counties since 1994, Wang achieved the best economic outcomes, with the county growing nearly 12 percentage points above the provincial average over the four years of his tenure. Wang also significantly deepened cadre reforms initiated under his predecessor Jiang Guoxing, as described in the previous chapter. He garnered a reputation for not only attracting industry and initiating rapid urban development, but also for controlling local cadres with a tight leash (the tautness of this leash was not always appreciated by interviewees). Wang was extremely career-minded, and his institutional innovation and economic success did not leave him fully satisfied, so to further his potential for promotion, Wang hired a local *fengshui* master to provide a suggestion as to how to boost both local growth and his own promotion prospects. The county government had already built a dragon-shaped walkway overpass in front of the county government headquarters, and the *fengshui* master said that this dragon needed a mountain. So, for an estimated 10 million RMB, Wang

[1] This paragraph is based on Interview JS230 and Interview JS115.

built a rock garden "mountain" directly behind the county government headquarters. Whether it was the economic success of the *fengshui* compliance or his successful institutional reforms and economic outcomes, in December 2011 Wang was sent to Suzhou City to serve on the Party Committee and head the Discipline Inspection Committee, and in May 2013 he became mayor of Suqian City.

There is much to learn from this simple story about the opaque and mysterious workings of county Party secretary promotion decisions. Despite common perceptions that economic success somehow "matters," conflicting perceptions about the importance of patron ties and luck abound. Describing the conditions for promotion, one official referred to a six-character idiom about "being in the right place at the right time with the right people" (*tianshi dili renhe,* 天时地利人和). The phrase was initially used by Mencius (孟子) and Sun Tzu (孙子) to indicate the prime conditions to go to war, but this official's interpretation was that to get promoted you need to be in the right place at the right time and know the right people; ability and achievements can position you well, but you also need a little bit of luck and personal connections (Interview JS254).[2]

This chapter argues that personnel management systems effectively transmit upper-level priorities. Having shown in Chapter 4 that county Party secretaries systematically influence local growth outcomes, this chapter shows that county Party secretaries are promoted based on local performance, although the criteria on which promotions are based differ between Jiangsu and Anhui and between counties in coastal and central provinces in general. Additionally, analyses below demonstrate that leadership initiative is more important for determining local economic outcomes than patron ties, implying that the personnel management system is itself partially responsible for growth outcomes.[3] In the case of Jiangsu, where officials are promoted based on growth outcomes, this implies the existence of a "tournament promotion hypothesis" by which political

[2] This is the same conclusion that Lampton (1986) finds in his study of six elite "paths to power" in an earlier generation.

[3] If leaders had a systematic influence, but growth resulted only from political connections (for instance in the form of greater fiscal transfers and/or preferential policies), then it is unclear whether *aggregate* provincial growth would be affected. For instance, there may be a fixed amount of total investment to distribute, so connection-based growth would imply redistribution rather than incremental growth. But local leaders have a systematic influence on local economic outcomes, so the perceived growth that higher levels base promotions on is not exogenous to leader ability and effort; a promotion regime that emphasizes growth thus has an impact on local conditions.

incentives to promote economic growth help explain overall high growth levels. In other words, in Jiangsu, promotion incentives help produce growth, an effect that fails to be felt in slow-growing Anhui.[4]

Institutional Development of Personnel Management

In a democratic system, downward accountability to the people defines how politicians act; the challenge in authoritarian regimes is to shape local political behavior with recourse only to mechanisms of upward accountability. In a system that maximizes the horizontal (*kuai*) power of local Party secretaries, control of these highly empowered local leaders by distant upper-level superiors becomes exceedingly problematic. With problems of information transmission, micromanagement of cadres above the county level is impossible (e.g., in the ways described at the sub-county level in the last chapter), so the methods and criteria for selection of these leaders determines the incentives and constraints that shape their behavior. This is a classic principal-agent problem that authoritarian regimes, China not excluded, have long struggled with. The basis of control and monitoring by upper-level principals shape the behavior of local agents, and depending on the goals such a system hopes to achieve, basing promotion decisions on patron-client ties or cadre achievement/ability may both be rational, with the former system capable of achieving political loyalty and the latter system more capable of mobilization towards specific goals.

With the world's largest political party and largest government bureaucracy set in an authoritarian polity, China faces particular difficulties in designing and implementing an effective personnel management system. China's cadre management system rationalizes and formalizes a massive hierarchical organization, setting out criteria for advancement for millions of Party and government positions. The system enables Party control on the basis of one-level-down management throughout administrative ranks, establishing multilevel upward accountability that enables the Party to maintain control over both the Party and state hierarchies. Such management of cadres helps to solve the principal-agent problems inherent in a hierarchical system built around delegation. Indeed, the "Party management of cadres" (*dangguan ganbu*, 党管干部) is a fundamental

[4] In the most recent years, Anhui has begun to grow quite rapidly, although this growth has been concentrated in Hefei and surrounding counties – most counties in the province, including the case counties, continue to grow quite slowly.

principle of the CCP. According to a former head of the national-level Organization Department, Zhang Quanjing, "If the Party did not manage cadres, how would the Party stay in charge? ... Giving up control would be tantamount to giving up leadership" (Zhao and Zheng 2006).

China's cadre management system over the past 30–40 years has undergone a succession of reforms towards greater formal institutionalization. This institutionalization has been most notable not in the methods of control, but in the methods of monitoring and evaluation. A formal cadre evaluation system was established as early as 1979, but the original system remained highly informal, dependent on broad guidelines set by the central government.[5] Since the mid 1980s the personnel management system has become much more institutionalized, particularly following a reform towards one-level down appointments that decentralized hierarchical control in 1983–1984. These reforms reduced the number of cadres directly appointed by the Center by upwards of 6000 people, and, consequently, the Center has attempted to regulate the promotion decisions that it no longer directly controls through formal rules and monitoring of officials' performance (Huang 1995, 828). Beginning in 1986, the Organization Department required that at year-end bureau-level (*juji,* 局级) and above officials must be given a performance summary (*gongzuo zongjie,* 工作总结) and an opinion poll must be conducted.[6] In 1988 this was extended to sub-bureau local levels.[7] A 1995 Organization Department "Notice" provided details on performance evaluation implementation in local areas, defining a framework with specific targets (and sub-targets), indicators, and measurement methods.[8] The "Regulation on Selection and Appointment of Party and Government Leading Cadres," first issued by the Central Committee in 1995 for trials and then updated and released in July 2002, was an attempt to "regularize party involvement in elite management, including

[5] See the Organization Department's 1979 "Circular on suggestions on implementing a system of cadre evaluation" (关于实行干部考核制度的意见的通知).

[6] See the Organization Department's 1986 "Circular on strengthening bureau-level cadre management at central Party and state institutions" (关于加强中共国家机关司局级干部管理工作的通知).

[7] Organization Department document No 7, issued in 1988, set annual guidelines for evaluation of Party secretaries and government executives at the county level, emphasizing that evaluations should serve as a basis for rewards, penalties, promotions, and demotions (Department of Organization 1989).

[8] See the translation of the Organization Department's 1995 "Notice on Strengthening and Improving the Evaluation of Practical Work Accomplishment of the Leadership Corps of Party Committees and Government at the County (Municipal) Level" by Wang (2008). For a discussion of the notice, see Chan and Gao (2008).

procedures with regard to appointment, transfer and demotion of cadres at county level and above" (Bo 2004). The Regulation included a four-step guideline for nominations (recommendation, screening, deliberation, and decision), outlined expected qualifications (at least five years' work experience, with two at the grass roots, at least two years at deputy positions; three years as chief before promotion to deputy at next level; at least a technical education; three months of training at party schools; healthy), and attempted to establish a system of avoidance (*diqu huibi*, 地区回避).[9] As late as January 2014, new regulations for local promotions and evaluations were still being introduced at the national level.[10]

All cadres and units are now evaluated, and many studies have analyzed the contents of these evaluations. National guidelines lay out broad general criteria. The 1988 Organization Document No. 7 set a format for quantitative evaluation with reliance on "social, economic, and cultural" targets; economic targets focused on industrial, fiscal, and agricultural conditions (Whiting 2004). Similarly, the 1995 Organization Department "Notice" highlighted "Party building, social development and spiritual civilization construction, and economic development" (Chan and Gao 2008). More recently, the 2006 "Scientific Outlook on Development's Pilot Methods for the Comprehensive Evaluation of Local Party and State Leading Groups and Cadres" lists additional statistical data to evaluate cadre performance, including local per capita GDP and GDP growth, fiscal revenue (and growth), urban and rural incomes, resource consumption, production safety, education outcomes, urban employment, social security, urban and rural "cultural life," family planning outcomes, arable land conservation, environmental protection, and science and technology innovation (Li, Ahluwalia, and Qiang 2013). In all of these documents, regional variation is allowed and indeed expected in determining specific targets, making the generalizability of local analyses of promotion criteria questionable. For instance, the 1995 Organization Department "Notice" explicitly contains a degree of flexibility to allow localities to

9 This included a rule that if a county secretary is elected in his home county, he must be transferred elsewhere after his first term. In June 1999, the Organization Department released a document concerning "The Regulation of Cadre Exchange," which argued that county and municipal leaders should not come from the same region, and county and municipal leaders should transfer to another area after ten years (Li 2004). Nationwide, the rotation/exchange system involved 96 percent of county Party secretaries and 97 percent of county magistrates from 1995 to 2001 (Zhang and Shan 2001).

10 For more on the institutionalization of personnel management and development of the target responsibility system (*mubiao zeren zhi*, 目标责任制), see Edin (1998), Whiting (2000), Tsui and Wang (2004), Zhuang (2007), and Chan and Gao (2008).

vary national guidelines to fit local conditions; localities can adjust the weights for each item to fit the local context (Chan and Gao 2008).

A system based on yardstick competition leads to high levels of competition as well as assumptions that evaluations help drive local behavior. Year-end evaluations explicitly note whether counties have hit their assigned targets and how they rank related to other counties.[11] Specific offices are dedicated to assuring that targets are hit, with a director assigned to "take care of rankings" (*fuze paiming,* 负责排名), and hitting targets becomes very stressful. As one county Investment Promotion Bureau chief notes, at the end of the year he cannot sleep from his stress-related headache: "I stay up late every night wondering how I can get investors to locate here" (Han 2011). However, there are reasons to expect that the sheer number of targets in different fields makes promotions based on uniform comparable criteria nearly impossible. According to one county Party secretary (Lu Qi, 鲁琦): "It's impossible not to evaluate. But it's extremely difficult to evaluate scientifically. The provincial and prefectural evaluations of us are too rigid (*yidaoqie,* 一刀切)" (Han 2011). Several studies have highlighted the problems of contradictory goals.[12] Given these difficulties, there is a perception that despite a plethora of targets, some targets are granted more importance in the de facto determination of promotions than indicated solely by their evaluation scores: in particular, avoiding veto targets and concentrating on GDP growth. Indeed, GDP emphasis or even GDP "worship" (*chongbai,* 崇拜) is often taken as a given in political economy analysis of China.

However, there is no guarantee that hitting *any* target ensures promotion; informal decision-making may dominate personnel evaluations. Indeed, the previous chapter highlighted differing levels of attention to economic targets at the sub-county level as well as informal personnel decisions made by the county Party secretary outside of the formal selection system. Failing to hit targets may result in being overlooked for promotion, but there is still a commonly perceived sense that patron ties, not performance, form the underlying basis for promotion. Pye (1981) and others have emphasized the political patronage networks required for advancement, and perceptions on the ground are often supportive of this view. For instance, of 1230 officials interviewed in Anhui in

[11] According to one Party secretary, good achievements alone are not enough; the important factor is whether other counties in the prefecture do better: "Regarding evaluations, sometimes the most difficult thing isn't fulfilling responsibilities, but rather winning a high ranking (*zhengqu hao de paiming,* 争取好的排名)" (Han 2011).

[12] See Chan and Gao (2008); Whiting (2000).

1998, 59 percent thought that demoted officials "lacked patrons above" (and 41 percent thought they did not "entertain or give gifts") (Anhui Provincial Organization Department 1998).[13] This contradicts another commonly held perception, one of meritocracy, and particularly meritocracy based on local GDP growth: "in China's Confucian tradition of meritocracy, a state should always strive for what's called '*shangshangce*,' or 'the best of the best' option by choosing leaders of the highest caliber" (Zhang 2012).[14] According to the "tournament promotion model" (*jinsheng jinbiao sai,* 晋升锦标赛), the cadre management system is not only meritocratic, but also leads to rapid economic growth through its emphasis on GDP growth (as well as potentially negative side effects, including environmental degradation and corruption).

Most likely, both meritocracy and patronage have some explanatory power, though many analyses assume an artificial separation between the two. Indeed, patronage still plays a role in highly formalized meritocratic bureaucracies in developed countries, and as Grindle (2012) has shown, patronage-based and meritocratic systems have tended across history to coexist and complement each other, rather than being an all or nothing. According to conversations with public administration experts in Jiangsu, three factors influence county leader promotion: county conditions (particularly economic growth), leader personal characteristics, and leader *guanxi* (Interview JS114; Interview JS279). Each of these factors is necessary, but the relative weights can differ. For instance, a highly successful leader might get promoted without a strong patron tie, while a leader with mediocre outcomes might get promoted if he has a powerful patron. This is similar to perceptions on the ground that patronage and ability both matter. Nor is this a new phenomenon, although emphases may have evolved: in his 1943 "How to Be a Good Leader," Zhou Enlai wrote that "Both political qualifications and work competence are indispensable criteria for selecting cadres, but political trustworthiness

[13] At the local level, Pei (2006) provides additional examples of such cadre perceptions: two-thirds of officials trained at one municipal Party school revealed that their promotion depended solely on the patronage of superiors, while only 5 percent thought their individual efforts could advance their careers; of 1150 officials in Harbin in 1997, 52 percent thought "personal connections determine cadre appointments"; and of 13,821 Party members in Sichuan in 1997, 40 percent complained that the system of selected cadres "lacks democracy and popular support."

[14] Indeed, there is intense competition for government employment: in 2013, according to China's State Administration of Civil Service, more than 1.38 million people applied for 20,000 vacancies in central authorities, implying an acceptance rate of less than 1.5 percent (Yang 2013).

takes precedence" (Zhou 1981). The relative importance of these dual promotion tracks determines whether China's system should be considered meritocratic, promoting qualified cadres up through the ranks, or a corrupt system of political patronage, only promoting well-connected (or well-paying) cadres regardless of personal accomplishments. If patronage dominates, with no attention to performance, then central control is weak and irrational/corrupt local behavior becomes more likely. In such a system, cadres would be more likely to benefit themselves at the sake of the public.[15] However, if patronage plays a role but is linked to performance, then the system is still meritocratic.

The body of evidence presented here suggests that despite institutionalization, the promotion system remains informal and subject to personal influence. This is especially true in looking specifically at county Party secretary promotions. Although performance evaluation management has become more rigorous and scholars have increasingly located specific targets and goals through documentary analysis, the relevance of these documents at the county leadership level is unclear. As with other cadres, county Party secretaries are evaluated based on the performance of their unit (the county) as well as their personal characteristics. All counties have targets they are meant to hit, and both provinces and prefectures produce annual rankings of counties across a variety of statistics. But the formal decision on county Party secretary promotions comes from the provincial Organization Department (OD), and the criteria these OD use to evaluate cadres are largely a black box. Moreover, as at the county level (discussed in the previous chapter), the preferences of higher-level authorities, particularly the provincial Party secretary, can de facto trump the de jure process. In other words, evaluations provide a basis upon which decisions *can* be made, but the OD and the higher-level authorities to which it answers may advance leaders based on other criteria. This suggests utility in analyzing actual promotions and cadre career paths rather than focusing only on documentary evidence. The following section describes career paths of county Party secretaries in Jiangsu and Anhui, focusing on broad descriptive statistics as well as specific outcomes from the case counties.

[15] For instance, Burns and Wang (2010) argue that "corruption opportunities have encouraged a perverse incentive alignment that allowed networks of superiors and subordinates to pursue their own private goals at the expense of the public."

Leadership Tenure, Career Paths, and Elite Mobility

County Party secretaries are highly upwardly mobile.[16] China's current general secretary, Xi Jinping, served as deputy county Party secretary and county Party secretary of Zhengding County, Hebei Province, from 1982 to 1985, before rising to much higher positions in Fujian Province. Bo (2009) has documented that of 31 provincial Party secretaries serving in March 2007, 12 had served as a county-level leader; of 31 provincial governors, 17 had served as a county-level leader. Of course, China has over 2000 county-level units, so most local cadres cannot expect to become general secretary or provincial Party secretary. However, although many cadres retire and others are transferred horizontally (i.e., neither promoted nor demoted), there is an unspoken rule (*qian guize,* 潜规则) in cadre management that if a cadre does not commit a major mistake he cannot be dismissed (Guo 2009). The worst a county Party secretary can expect is "semi" retirement into a relatively powerless position in local People's Congresses or People's Political Consultative Conferences.

Data on county Party secretaries in Jiangsu and Anhui over 1994–2010 provide a starting point for understanding leader biographies and career paths. These data include 276 county-leader combinations in Jiangsu and 333 in Anhui (note that several leaders serve in multiple counties, a phenomenon that enabled identification of systematic leader effects in Chapter 4). Leaders have similar age profiles in both provinces: in Jiangsu, county Party secretaries are 44.0 years old on average when they take office; in Anhui they are 45.6 years old; in both provinces, over 80 percent of cadres are hired in their 40s. Additionally, the "law of avoidance" (i.e., serving outside of one's hometown) has become more strictly enforced, as institutionalization would suggest; in 1994, 41 percent of Jiangsu county Party secretaries and 24 percent of Anhui county Party secretaries led the county in which they were born, but by 2010, this share had dropped to 4 percent in Jiangsu and 0 percent in Anhui. Similarly, while there is no law against serving within the prefecture-level administration in which one is born, the share of county Party secretaries leading counties within prefectures in which they were born has also dropped significantly.

Data on leader tenure length show that institutionalization of the personnel management system has not resulted in formalization of five-year

[16] Concerns of an acute hierarchical pyramid with few promotion options are not apparent at the level of the county Party secretary. See Burns and Wang (2010).

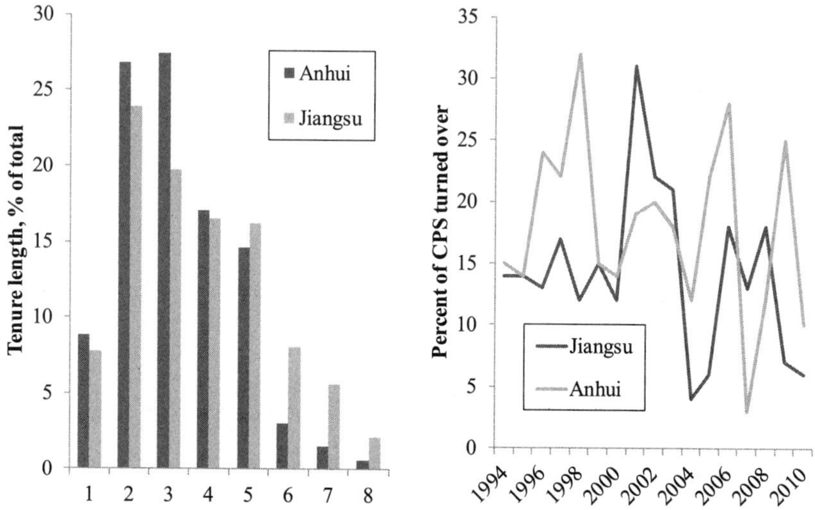

FIGURE 5.1. County Party secretary tenure length (left) and transition frequency (right)
Source: Biographical database; author's calculations.

terms; in Jiangsu, cadres serve on average 3.67 years before transitioning, while in Anhui they serve 3.20. The majority of county Party secretaries in both provinces leave after two or three years, with an additional one-third leaving after four or five years. On average, 24.6 percent of Jiangsu county Party secretaries and 29.4 percent of Anhui county Party secretaries are replaced each year. The distribution of tenure length and frequency across time is shown in Figure 5.1. This is very much in line with local perceptions: "successful" county Party secretaries try to get promoted to the city or provincial level within a year or two of taking office, because they see their future career options decreasing with each additional year spent at the county level (Interview JS254).[17]

At the end of their county terms, Party secretaries can move to another county, the prefecture/city, or the province, with no objective hierarchy among these paths (see Figure 5.2). Most county Party secretaries move to the city government within the same prefecture administrative area (54 percent in Jiangsu and 58 percent in Anhui). An additional 9 percent in Jiangsu and 6 percent in Anhui transferred to other prefecture

[17] Note that this phenomenon makes it difficult, if not impossible, to identify "political budget cycles" based on expected promotion dates, as Guo (2009) purportedly does. These tenure length averages are significantly below the advised five-year term.

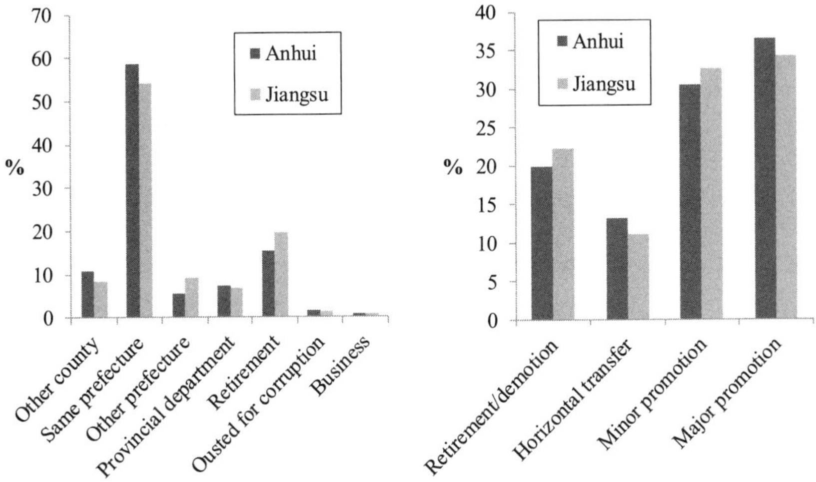

FIGURE 5.2. County Party secretary career paths
Source: Biographical database; author's calculations.

governments, while 8 percent in Jiangsu and 11 percent in Anhui transferred to become Party secretaries of other counties. In both provinces, 7 percent of county Party secretaries transferred to province-level departments, and 20 percent (Jiangsu) and 15 percent (Anhui) either officially retired or transferred to local People's Congresses and People's Political Consultative Conferences, which can be considered either retirement or demotion. In both provinces, only two cadres moved out of officialdom and into business.[18]

Both Jiangsu and Anhui exhibit high variation in promotion outcomes. As discussed in more depth below, promotions can take many forms, and differentiating between de facto and de jure transfers/promotions is difficult. Promotion identification is based on not only official rank, but also the specific job; some equally ranked locations and bureaus are "more equal" than others. For instance, while a transfer to another county may seem like a horizontal transfer, it might be a promotion if the leader

[18] Very few leaders leave the Party-state system, although it is known to happen. For instance, Xia Yisong (夏一松) left Lixin, Anhui, after serving for barely half a year. He was known for uncovering corruption cases and reporting attempted bribers, and apparently organized criminal organizations (*heishehui*, 黑社会) and corrupt officials threatened him until he resigned from government and entered business (Li 2001, Chapter 7). Although many county leaders are ousted for corruption later in their careers very few are kicked out while still in office; the general pattern is to move to a low-power position while the investigation goes on.

transfers to a more prosperous county or county-level city. Additionally, while officials in China very rarely leave officialdom, many county Party secretaries are transferred into relatively powerless positions (usually prefecture-level People's Congresses and People's Political Consultative Congresses), and it is not always clear when a "demotion" of this sort is a form of retirement and when it is actually a demotion.[19] Nevertheless, it is still possible to identify promotions. Based on local interviews, a clear indicator of promotion at the prefecture level (where most cadres go) is selection to the prefecture-level Party Committee, a selection that usually is matched with leadership of an important prefecture-level state or Party body: propaganda, organization, discipline inspection, or finance. These are "major promotions." Horizontal transfers consist of those cadres who move to other counties or county-level districts and cities. "Minor promotions" consist of other moves to the prefecture level; note that these "minor" promotions are frequently at the same level as the county position and often have less power; they are seen as horizontal transfers and even demotions at times.

Some county Party secretaries do very well, progressing beyond prefecture-level Party Committee membership and confirming the high degree of upward mobility. In Jiangsu, 23 county Party secretaries have become prefecture-level city mayors or Party secretaries or bureau heads at the provincial level; in Anhui, 17 have.[20] A handful were even more successful, becoming provincial deputy governors or even governors: Jiang Dingzhi (蒋定之) was Yangzhong county-level city Party secretary in the mid 1990s before heading the Jiangsu Provincial Organization Department and then serving as Wuxi Party secretary, vice chairman of the China Banking Regulatory Commission in Beijing, and eventually Hainan governor. Mao Weiming (毛伟明) headed Wujin (Jiangsu) in the early 2000s; after leading the Changzhou Politics and Law Committee, he became Taizhou mayor, Jiangsu Province development and reform commission head, and then deputy governor. Qiu He, discussed at length in the last chapter, became deputy governor of Jiangsu and deputy Party

[19] Li and Zhou (2005) note this problem at the provincial level: "Typically, provincial leaders do not retire in the full sense immediately after leaving office unless there are exceptional circumstances, such as poor health. Before retiring officially, they are often assigned, as a transition, to an honorary yet virtually powerless position ... Whatever gloss may be put on it, the loss of power is what marks the end of an official's political career." Because of the "subtle difference" between retirement and demotion, Li and Zhou group them together, as I do here.

[20] All six party secretaries of Kunshan County-Level City (Jiangsu) were part of this elite subset.

secretary of Yunnan before his downfall. In Anhui, Hua Jianhui (Wuhe) and Ni Fake (倪发科, Nanling) both became deputy governors.

Case Counties: Who Gets Promoted?

Promotion rules cannot be determined based on a small sample, but the career paths of the county Party secretaries from the sample counties are nevertheless of interest. Table 5.1 shows the basic career paths of all county Party secretaries in the sample. There is a wide range of career trajectories and outcomes, with several cadres becoming prefecture-level Party secretaries while others were pushed into low-power positions equivalent to early retirement (none were old enough to actually retire, and none left officialdom). Over the course of 1994–2011, each of the counties had either five or six county Party secretaries, with slightly longer average tenures than the Jiangsu and Anhui samples as a whole: 3.8 years in the three Jiangsu counties and 3.5 years in the three Anhui counties.

Leaders in Xuyi County in Jiangsu have had the most successful career outcomes, with four out of five promoted to the prefecture-level Party Committee (i.e., the "major promotion" noted above). The least successful and most recent county Party secretary, Cai Duncheng (蔡敦成), was also promoted, but only to Huaian City vice mayor. Along with promotion to the prefecture-level Party Committee, Xin Lizhong (1995–1997) also became the Huaiyin propaganda minister, and Wang Youfu (2001–2005) became the Politics and Law Committee secretary. Zhao Peng (赵鹏), whose innovative economic successes while in office from 1998 to 2000 were described in the previous chapter, became director of the Yancheng Organization Department before quickly being promoted to Yancheng mayor and then Yancheng Party secretary, an extremely successful career path. While Zhao was relatively young upon entering office (43 years old), his background had all been local, having served in the Huaiyin prefecture Organization Department and then as Xuyi mayor. In other words, he was not a cadre who had been groomed for quick promotion, implying that his successes gained attention. Growth during his time in office was over 9 percentage points above the provincial county average, an impressive outcome for a Northern Jiangsu county that early in the sample (Subei counties tended to improve their growth outcomes in more recent years relative to the south).

In Jiangsu's Sihong County, just to the north of Xuyi, Party secretaries have had somewhat less career success. The two county Party secretaries serving in the mid to late 1990s, Li Jiye (李继业) and Cai Yushui (蔡玉水), both transferred to powerless semi-retirement positions despite having just turned 50 (the Suqian Prefecture People's Congress and the Suqian Prefecture Government Office, respectively). The three county Party secretaries in the 2000s have all been promoted, but only Xie Hui (叶辉) had a "major promotion," becoming Suqian City propaganda minister and a Party Committee member. Qin Zhengbao (秦正宝) and Feng Yan (冯岩) became prefecture-level vice mayors. In terms of economic outcomes, none of the Sihong County Party secretaries had outstanding or terrible experiences; growth generally hovered around the provincial average.

In Suining, the Party secretaries serving in the 1990s and early 2000s only transferred to low-power positions in Xuzhou (People's Congress, Labor Bureau, Agriculture Bureau). These county Party secretaries reigned at a time of low growth, when Suining was known more for its petition (*xinfang*, 信访) output than its industrial output (see discussion in Chapter 6). The two more recent Party secretaries have had much more successful career paths. Jiang Guoxing's county branding may have been noticed and appreciated: he was helicoptered to the provincial level and became Jiangsu Province press and publication deputy director. Growth under Jiang was actually lower than the provincial average, although his urban development and reputational initiatives are seen as setting the stage for growth under his successor.[21] His successor, Wang Tianqi, was very successful: apparently his *fengshui* worked, or perhaps it was the reputation Suining gained from his institutional transparency initiatives, or maybe it was the fact that growth under him was over 11 percentage points above the provincial average – the highest of any leader in the case counties: he was promoted to wealthy Suzhou City to head the Party Committee for Discipline Inspection.

In the Anhui case counties, the criteria for promotion appear different. Of the county Party secretaries in Mingguang, two were convicted of corruption, cutting their careers short. The most successful, Song Weiping (宋卫平), served from 1996 to 1998. Growth was slightly above the provincial average, but Song was more known for rooting out the corruption that had become endemic during the Xue Xianzao administration that preceded him. Song had a background designed for the role, having spent the entire 1970s and 1980s working his way up the military hierarchy in the Beijing Military District. After Mingguang, Song was promoted to Chuzhou Prefecture Party Committee, vice mayor, then mayor, Anhui transportation minister, and Fuyang Prefecture Party secretary.

[21] His promotion to a high level non-*kuai* leadership position shows that he may have been rewarded without being given further economic responsibility.

Song's successor, Chen Bingbing, was seen as a groomed young cadre. He came in at only 37 years old and had significant economic success, but his subsequent promotion in 2002 was only to vice mayor, a "minor" promotion.[22] The corruption and terrible economic outcomes (growth 11 percentage points under the provincial average) under Zhang Songjian were discussed previously – he was jailed, not promoted.

Wuhe has been the most successful Anhui sample county in terms of leader career paths. Hua Jianhui (花建慧), the only female Party secretary in the six county sample, became deputy governor of Anhui in 2010, having served as Bengbu mayor and then Huaibei Prefecture Party secretary after leaving Wuhe. During her time in office, Hua gained a reputation for wielding an iron fist and turning towards urban development. Her economic reforms were successful – the county grew over 8 percentage points above the provincial average – but her local economic success was seen as secondary to her strict control over the local bureaucracy (Interview AH135; Interview AH184; Interview AH206). Zhu Yong (朱勇), Hua's successor from 1999 to 2001, became Huangshan Prefecture deputy Party secretary and then Anhui Province Petitions and Letters Bureau chief. His transfer to the provincial Petitions office is highly indicative; growth was below the provincial county average during his time in office, but he gained a reputation for calming things down. However, the two leaders succeeding Hua and Zhu failed to follow in their predecessors' footsteps; despite opposite economic outcomes (4 percentage points below and above the provincial average, respectively), both Zhang Guiyi (张桂义) and Xu Shexin (徐社新) were demoted/retired.

Finally, Si County has had no successful Party secretaries. The two most successful became prefecture-level vice mayors (of Suzhou and Bozhou). These were the two Party secretaries who had the worst relative economic outcomes (averaging 4.8 and 3.9 percentage points below the provincial county average). The most successful economically, Gao Degang (高德刚), held office in 2000 and 2001, when growth was 6.3 percentage points above the provincial county average; he was transferred to Suzhou Prefecture vice secretary (副秘书长), a demotion.

The different career paths in the case counties across the two provinces are interesting to compare. In Jiangsu, out of 16 county Party secretary promotions/demotions, three were demoted/retired, six transferred or had a "minor" promotion, and seven had a "major" promotion. The Anhui counties were slightly less successful: out of 13 career movements,

[22] Much later, in 2012, he became the Anqing Politics and Law Committee Secretary.

TABLE 5.1. *County Party secretary biographical data and local economic outcomes in case counties*

Name	Years in office	Age upon entry	Previous position(s)	Subsequent position(s)	Average annual GDP deviation (percentage points)
Xuyi, Jiangsu					
Chen Wei (陈伟)	1991–1994			Huaiyin Prefecture Party Committee	−14.6
Xin Lizhong (欣立忠)	1995–1997	45	Qingpu District Party secretary	Huaiyin Prefecture Party Committee and propaganda minister (convicted of corruption in 2000)	4.5
Zhao Peng (赵鹏)	1998–2000	43	Xuyi magistrate; Huaiyin Organization Department deputy chief	Yancheng Prefecture Party Committee and Organization Department chief; Yancheng mayor; Yancheng Party secretary	9.3
Wang Youfu (王友富)	2001–2005	49	Xuyi magistrate; Xiqiao Township Party secretary	Huaian Prefecture Party Committee and Politics and Law Committee Secretary	−3.7
Cai Duncheng (蔡敦成)	2006–2011	44	Xuyi magistrate; Luoma Lake Township Party secretary	Huaian Prefecture vice mayor	−1.1
Sihong, Jiangsu					
Li Jiye (李继业)	1993–1996	49	Sihong magistrate; Sihong Politics and Law Committee secretary	Suqian Prefecture People's Congress	−2.7

Cai Yushui (蔡玉水)	1997–1998	48	Shuyang magistrate; Shuyang Party school president; Shuyang propaganda chief	Suqian Prefecture Government Office director	4.1
Xie Hui (叶辉)	1999–2001	41	Daxing Township Party secretary	Suqian Prefecture Party Committee and propaganda minister	–0.7
Qin Zhengbao (秦正宝)	2002–2004	45	Sihong magistrate; Huaiyin Communist Youth League secretary	Suqian Prefecture vice mayor	–3.4
Feng Yan (冯岩)	2005–2011	40	Sihong magistrate; Shiling Township Party secretary	Suqian Prefecture vice mayor	–0.8
Suining, Jiangsu					
Lu Yongxin (吕永信)	1992–1994		Suining deputy Party secretary		8.6
Han Zhenmei (韩振美)	1995–1996	48	Suining magistrate; Xinyi deputy magistrate	Xuzhou Agriculture Bureau deputy chief	1.9
Wang Yuzhu (王玉柱)	1997–1999	49	Feng County magistrate	Xuzhou Municipal Labor and Social Security Bureau chief	–8.2
Guo Xizhong (郭希忠)	2000–2004	50	Xinyi Party secretary; Tongshan magistrate	Xuzhou Prefecture People's Congress vice chairman	–2.1
Jiang Guoxing (蒋国星)	2005–2007	50	Jurong (county-level) City magistrate	Jiangsu Province press and publication deputy director	–3.6
Wang Tianqi (王天琦)	2008–2011	40	Suining magistrate; Huaian Discipline Inspection Committee secretary	Suzhou City Committee for Discipline Inspection Secretary	11.7

(continued)

TABLE 5.1 (*cont.*)

Name	Years in office	Age upon entry	Previous position(s)	Subsequent position(s)	Average annual GDP deviation (percentage points)
Mingguang, Anhui					
Xue Xianzao (薛贤早)	1992–1995			Convicted of corruption	−3.8
Song Weiping (宋卫平)	1996–1998	42	Laian County deputy magistrate	Chuzhou Prefecture Party Committee; Chuzhou mayor; Anhui transportation minister; Fuyang Prefecture Party secretary	1.8
Chen Bingbing (陈冰冰)	1999–2002	37	Mingguang magistrate; Chuzhou Organization Department deputy chief	Chuzhou Prefecture vice mayor	5.2
Zhang Songjian (张松坚)	2003–2007	50	Nanqiao District Party secretary	Chuzhou Prefecture People's Congress vice chairman (convicted of corruption in 2011)	−10.7
Li Qingning (李庆宁)	2008-	48	Tianchang (county-level) City magistrate	*NA*	−5.8

Wuhe, Anhui					
Fan Zhonghua (范中华)	1992–1995				1.6
Hua Jianhui (花建慧)	1996–1998	41	Guzhen County Mayor; Guzhen Organization Bureau chief	Bengbu Prefecture deputy Party secretary; Bengbu mayor; Huaibei Prefecture Party secretary; Anhui Province deputy governor	8.4
Zhu Yong (朱勇)	1999–2001		Wuhe deputy Party secretary	Bengbu Prefecture Party Committee; Huangshan Prefecture deputy Party secretary; Anhui Province Petitions and Letters Bureau chief	−0.1
Zhang Guiyi (张桂义)	2002–2003	49	Wuhe magistrate	Bengbu Prefecture Grain Administration Bureau chief	−3.7
Xu Shexin (徐社新)	2004–2007	48	Wuhe magistrate; Bengbu Economic and Trade Committee deputy director	Bengbu People's Political Consultative Conference vice chairman	4.5
Hu Qiwang (胡启望)	2008-	40	Wuhe magistrate; Bengbu Agriculture and Forestry deputy bureau chief	*NA*	−4.0
Si, Anhui					
Tang Xinzhong (唐新忠)	1992–1996			Suzhou Prefecture People's Congress vice chairman	5.2

(*continued*)

TABLE 5.1 (*cont.*)

Name	Years in office	Age upon entry	Previous position(s)	Subsequent position(s)	Average annual GDP deviation (percentage points)
Wu Zhentang (吴贞堂)	1997–1999		Lingbi County magistrate	Bozhou Prefecture vice mayor	−4.8
Gao Degang (高德刚)	2000–2001		Si County magistrate	Suzhou Prefecture vice secretary (副秘书长); People's Political Consultative Conference vice chairman	6.3
Zhang Xu (张旭)	2002–2006		Si County magistrate	Suzhou Prefecture People's Congress vice chairman	1.0
Xu Guangbin (许广斌)	2007–2008		Si County magistrate	Suzhou Prefecture vice mayor	−3.9
Yan Jinxing (晏金星)	2009–2012	46	Si County deputy Party secretary; Si County Organization Bureau chief	Suzhou Prefecture vice secretary (副秘书长)	−3.3

five county Party secretaries were demoted/retired, five transferred or had minor promotions, and only three had major promotions. Looking at the three Jiangsu counties, the county Party secretaries who were seen as initiating successful local reforms or achieving high economic growth were promoted; those with negative outcomes or little impact were transferred to low-power positions. In Anhui, Hua Jianhui follows this pattern, but the other successful cadres had slow growth, and the four other county Party secretaries who presided over counties with growth more than 2 percentage points above the provincial county average did not have successful careers (including three who presided over growth 5 percentage points or more higher than the provincial county average, a considerable achievement). Consider only the most successful career-wise (those who reached prefecture mayor or Party secretary, or provincial minister level): in Jiangsu, Zhao Peng (Xuyi) and Jiang Guoxing (Suining) were known for innovative reforms, and Zhao Peng had the most successful growth in the entire sample with the exception of Suining's Wang Tianqi (who was also very successful in being promoted to Suzhou City). In Anhui, Song Weiping (Mingguang), Hua Jianhui (Wuhe), and Zhu Yong (Wuhe) have the honor. Song Weiping was known for controlling corruption, and Zhu Yong developed a reputation for handling societal dissatisfaction during a time of high rural discontent. Hua Jianhui achieved high economic growth, but her local reputation centers around her iron fist rather than her golden touch.

Does Economic Growth Predict Promotions?

Despite institutionalization of the personnel management system and many in-depth analyses of specific performance contracts, very little is known about the de facto promotion criteria for county leaders. The brief look at promotions within the case counties highlights economic success as a predictor of promotion in Jiangsu, but not in Anhui. This implies that promotion criteria may differ across provinces, as would be expected given central guidance promoting regional variation in evaluated targets. I explore the relationship between promotions and economic growth using the following equation:

$$Promoted_{it} = \alpha_1 \cdot Y_{it} + \delta \boldsymbol{PC}_{it} + \gamma_i + \varphi_t + \epsilon_{it} \tag{5.1}$$

Here, $Promoted_{it}$ is a dummy variable taking the value one for leaders who are promoted, Y_{it} is a measure of growth, γ_i are county fixed effects,

φ_t are year fixed effects, and ϵ_{it} is an unobserved error term. Equation 5.1 controls for a vector of leader personal characteristics ($\boldsymbol{PC}_{it}$), including gender, age, education level, and term length, as well as county and year fixed effects; a positive α_1 in a logit regression with promotion as a binary dependent variable indicates that higher economic growth is associated with a higher likelihood of promotion. Several definitions of economic growth and leader promotion can be employed, as can a varying set of controls.

Some additional background on county leadership career paths and identifying promotions is useful. As discussed above, promotions can be difficult to differentiate from horizontal transfers; subjectivity is often required to determine which bureau-leading position is a promotion and which is a demotion. A way around these coding difficulties is to only code clear promotions; for example, to look only at Party secretaries who become prefecture-level Party secretaries or mayors or the equivalent rank at the provincial level, or to mark as promotions only transfer to prefecture-level Party Committees and equivalent roles at the provincial level. Because of the coding complexity, a simple binary probit regression utilizing broad coding rules makes the most sense, enabling a differentiation between successful and unsuccessful leaders. This differs from many analyses (Li and Zhou 2005; Guo 2007; Choi 2012; Su et al. 2012) that use multinomial logit/probit regressions, differentiating between promotions, horizontal transfers, retirement, and demotions. Generating broad coding rules at the county level has both advantages and disadvantages as compared to the more rigorous coding at the provincial level. On the one hand, the data clearly mis-code certain promotions; for instance, when a Party secretary concurrently serves as a prefecture-level Party Committee member and remains on the Party Committee at the end of his county term, this is actually a transfer. On the other hand, highlighting only clear promotions removes a degree of subjectivity.

In the regressions in the following section, promotion is defined in two separate ways, both binary dummy variables. "Promotion Baseline" takes the value one when the Party secretary is promoted to a position at least equivalent to the prefecture-level Party Committee (in most cases, this position is the Party Committee itself, but in a few cases Party secretaries are promoted directly to equivalent or higher positions at the provincial level). The second definition, "Promotion All Star," takes value one only for leaders who move on to positions equivalent or equal to prefecture-level mayor. The relative frequencies of these promotion types are shown

TABLE 5.2. *Sample frequency by promotion definition*

	Promotion Baseline	Promotion "All Star"
Anhui	103/266 (38.7%)	17/266 (6.4%)
Jiangsu	89/246 (36.2%)	23/246 (9.3%)

in Table 5.2. While over one-third of leaders are promoted by the baseline definition, fewer than 10 percent become "all stars." It is important to note the high similarity in promotion distribution between the two provinces. If potential outcomes differed in frequency, this would imply different roles and potential for the county Party secretary position across provinces, which would complicate any comparison.

Table 5.3 and Table 5.4 present the marginal effects from a probit regression (Equation 5.1) on the Jiangsu and Anhui county samples, using both definitions of promotion. Table 5.3 uses annual observations and annual per capita GDP growth as the key right-hand side variable, including year fixed effects to control for growth trends across time. Alternatively, Table 5.4 instead uses only one observation per promoted/transferred Party secretary (i.e., excluding those still in office at the end of the sample) and calculates average growth deviations from the provincial average over the leader's tenure.[23] In the former regressions, by using annual observations the regressions over-sample leaders with longer tenures.[24] Because the two provinces have different cadre management systems, there is no reason to expect similar coefficients, and I run separate regressions to enable a comparison of provincial results (columns 2, 3, 5, and 6 in both tables). However, in order to evaluate and compare the

23 $YDiff_{iPS} = \sum_{t_0}^{t_0+N_{PS}} (Y_{it} - \bar{Y}_t) / N_{PS}$, where $YDiff_{iPS}$ is the average growth deviation for county Party secretary *PS* in county *i*; t_o is the year the county Party secretary takes office; N_{PS} is the county Party secretary tenure length, Y_{it} is GDP growth in year *t* in county *i*, and $\bar{Y}_t$ is the average growth across counties within the province. (Provincial subscripts are excluded, as the equation is calculated separately for Jiangsu and Anhui.)

24 Note also that these probit regressions exclude county fixed effects. Too many counties perfectly predict the dependent variable (i.e., all county Party secretaries within a county are either promoted or not promoted), and this perfect collinearity leads to nearly half of the observations being dropped (more for "all star" promotions). As a robustness check, I have confirmed that the magnitude and significance of the key independent variable remains the same when including county fixed effects (the magnitude increases in Jiangsu), but the results are not reported here.

different growth effects on promotion across the two provinces, columns 1 and 4 in both tables report results for a joint regression that includes an interaction term between a dummy variable for Jiangsu province and the relevant growth metric; this coefficient represents the different growth effect in Jiangsu relative to Anhui.

In Jiangsu, across all specifications and controlling for personal characteristics, higher growth predicts higher promotion probability. All promotion coefficients are significant at 1 percent. In Anhui, the coefficients are insignificant and negative, implying a weak effect of *lower* growth predicting *higher* promotion probability. The growth effect is significantly different between the two provinces (columns 1 and 4). Excluding the personal characteristic controls increases the observations but does not significantly alter the coefficients on growth (results not shown). The marginal effects show a range of magnitudes. In the average growth deviation baseline, 1 percentage point additional average growth translates into a 2.8 percent greater chance of promotion; in other words, growing 10 percentage points above average would lead to a nearly 30 percent greater chance of promotion, all else equal. In Anhui, personal characteristics also have their predicted sign: older cadres are significantly less likely to be promoted, and educated cadres (those with master's degrees) are significantly more likely to be promoted. Gender and tenure length have no predicted effect.

Before discussing challenges to this analysis and the different results for Jiangsu and Anhui, it is useful to conduct a broader analysis using nationwide county Party secretary tenure and transition data to generalize beyond Jiangsu and Anhui. Given data limitations, this broader nationwide analysis cannot control for biographical data beyond tenure length, and can only code promotions to prefecture-level mayors and Party secretaries (and not equivalents at the provincial level or any other promotion). To generate a sufficient sample, it is necessary to look at cadres who eventually reach these positions, not necessarily cadres who are immediately promoted, which may overemphasize the importance of their county tenure. In the sample, 185 county Party secretaries show up as future prefecture leaders.[25] The regression results shown in Table 5.5 and Table 5.6 are identical to those presented above, but include only the relevant growth measure and tenure length as right-hand side variables

[25] Of these, 25 are prefecture Party secretaries and 160 are mayors (although many of the mayors subsequently become Party secretaries). Most are not immediate transfers, but the position is high enough and the time period is short enough that any intermediate transfer also had to be a major promotion.

TABLE 5.3. *Growth and promotion probit regression results*

	(1)	(2)	(3)	(4)	(5)	(6)
Promotion type:	*Baseline*			*All–Star*		
	Combined	**Jiangsu**	**Anhui**	**Combined**	**Jiangsu**	**Anhui**
Jiangsu * annual growth (interaction)	0.00860***			0.0042***		
	(2.65)			(3.07)		
Annual growth	0.000207	0.0113***	−0.00114	−0.0000249	0.0061***	−0.000763
	(0.11)	(3.66)	(−0.52)	(−0.03)	(3.77)	(−0.78)
Female (d)	0.353***	0.126		0.120	0.0291	0.199
	(3.11)	(0.54)		(1.10)	(0.21)	(1.13)
Age	−0.00882**	−0.0110*	−0.00598	−0.0120***	−0.0132***	−0.015***
	(−1.99)	(−1.83)	(−0.88)	(−6.05)	(−4.22)	(−4.08)
Term length	0.0124	0.0196	0.00469	−0.00408	−0.00403	−0.00610
	(1.27)	(1.54)	(0.30)	(−0.94)	(−0.59)	(−0.69)
Masters (d)	0.123***	0.176***	0.0556	0.0195	0.0314	0.0132
	(3.46)	(3.66)	(1.04)	(1.25)	(1.26)	(0.45)
Jiangsu dummy (d)	−0.133***			0.00258		
	(−2.58)			(0.11)		
Observations	1101	586	507	1101	586	368

Marginal effects are reported; *t* statistics in parentheses; (d) for discrete change of dummy variable from 0 to 1. Annual growth refers to annual observations of per capita real GDP growth. All regressions include year fixed effects.

* $p < 0.10$, ** $p < 0.05$, *** $p < 0.01$

TABLE 5.4. *Growth deviations and promotion probit regression results*

	(1)	(2)	(3)	(4)	(5)	(6)
Promotion type:	*Baseline*			*All-Star*		
	Combined	**Jiangsu**	**Anhui**	**Combined**	**Jiangsu**	**Anhui**
Jiangsu*avg. growth dev. interaction	0.0321***			0.0184***		
	(2.97)			(3.40)		
Average growth deviation	0.0000838	0.0321***	0.0000051	−0.00205	0.0187***	−0.00157
	(0.02)	(3.25)	(0.00)	(−0.85)	(3.47)	(−0.77)
Female (d)	0.348**	0.227		0.241	0.294	0.203
	(2.11)	(0.82)		(1.12)	(0.83)	(0.78)
Age	−0.0133*	−0.0207*	−0.00550	−0.0211***	−0.0213***	−0.020***
	(−1.65)	(−1.82)	(−0.48)	(−5.15)	(−3.59)	(−3.58)
Term length	0.0279	0.0415	0.0119	0.0153	0.0172	0.0121
	(1.41)	(1.57)	(0.39)	(1.61)	(1.30)	(0.86)
Masters (d)	0.126**	0.169**	0.0806	−0.00266	0.00664	−0.0119
	(2.06)	(2.02)	(0.90)	(−0.10)	(0.16)	(−0.36)
Jiangsu dummy (d)	−0.0348			0.0405		
	(−0.57)			(1.33)		
Observations	318	163	152	318	163	155

Marginal effects are reported; *t* statistics in parentheses; (d) for discrete change of dummy variable from 0 to 1. Average growth deviation is average annual difference between county GDP growth and average county GDP growth within a province over the tenure of a Party Secretary.

* $p < 0.10$, ** $p < 0.05$, *** $p < 0.01$

TABLE 5.5. *National, coastal, and central growth and promotions*

	(1)	(2)	(3)	(4)	(5)
	Dependent variable = All-Star Promotion				
	National	Coast	Center	Jiangsu	Anhui
Per capita GDP growth	0.00016***	0.00091***	0.000015	0.0041***	−0.00039
	(3.20)	(3.71)	(0.11)	(3.81)	(−0.57)
Party secretary tenure	0.000584	0.00221	−0.00091	−0.00689	0.00298
	(0.88)	(1.20)	(−0.74)	(−1.27)	(0.48)
Year fixed effects	Yes	Yes	Yes	Yes	Yes
Observations	17,416	3836	5108	809	662

Marginal effects; *t* statistics in parentheses.

*** $p<0.01$, ** $p<0.05$, * $p<0.1$

(as well as year dummies when using annual growth). Five identical probit regressions are run on different samples: a national sample, an eastern province sub-sample, and a central province sub-sample, as well as the Jiangsu and Anhui samples for comparative purposes.[26] Columns 4 and 5 report the results for Jiangsu and Anhui, which confirm the findings above, justifying this more limited methodological approach: economic growth predicts promotions in Jiangsu, but not in Anhui. Columns 2 and 3 show that the relationship found in Jiangsu and Anhui holds more generally for eastern and central provinces, respectively. In eastern provinces, there is a significant positive relationship between growth and promotion, while there is a small and insignificant relationship in central provinces.

[26] The national sample excludes provincial-level municipalities and special administrative zones, leaving 22 provinces. Data for Sichuan (1996–2001) and Jiangxi (1996–2001) are also missing. Eastern provinces include Fujian, Guangdong, Jiangsu, Shandong, and Zhejiang. Central provinces include Anhui, Henan, Hubei, Hunan, Jiangxi, and Shanxi. The vast majority of China's population lives in eastern and central provinces. Counties in these provinces are very similar in size and population, but differences in wealth and growth outcomes are stark. Western provinces, on the other hand, are much larger and less populous, often have large minority populations, and have very diverse natural resource endowments, all of which make comparison both less feasible and less interesting.

TABLE 5.6. *National, coastal, and central average growth deviations and promotions*

	(1)	(2)	(3)	(4)	(5)
	Dependent variable = All-Star Promotion				
	National	**Coast**	**Center**	**Jiangsu**	**Anhui**
Avg. growth deviation	0.000254* (1.69)	0.00241** (2.46)	0.000905 (1.61)	0.0107*** (3.14)	−0.00058 (−0.28)
Party secretary tenure	−0.00216* (−1.70)	−0.00210 (−0.57)	−0.00223 (−1.15)	−0.0173* (−1.77)	−0.00900 (−1.07)
Year fixed effects	No	No	No	No	No
Observations	5406	1269	1731	238	266

Marginal effects; *t* statistics in parentheses.

*** p<0.01, ** p<0.05, * p<0.1

The growth and promotion regression results provide strong evidence for disparate cadre management criteria in Jiangsu and Anhui and in coastal and central provinces more broadly. The results for Jiangsu support the tournament promotion hypothesis, but the nonexistent effect in Anhui requires explanation. This is the focus of Chapter 6, which provides evidence that an alternative cadre management system stressing stability explains the results better than a patronage-based model that disregards performance.

Patron-Based Growth or Meritocratic Tournament Promotions?

An important question of causality arises: are Jiangsu cadres identified for their growth outcomes and therefore promoted, or are they pre-destined for greatness in the sense that patron ties got them not only the county Party secretary position but also the growth they were associated with on the job? Although the predominant patronage theory sees growth as exogenous to leader effects (e.g., Shih et al. 2012), another view of patron ties focuses on the positive economic effects of patronage (Interview JS197). The analysis above shows that high-growth cadres in Jiangsu are promoted, but if patronage itself leads to growth, then the underlying relationship is from patronage to promotion. An additional concern is that "favored" cadres are sent to counties with high growth potential.[27] The previous chapter's discussion of county Party secretary personal economic roles provided descriptive evidence that leadership impact on local economies can be felt through connections as well as individual initiative. Although connections can be developed and nurtured through skill, connections to leaders higher up the hierarchy are rightly seen as patronage. If leaders promote growth primarily through upper-level connections, this implies a patronage-based system; if leaders instead promote growth primarily through the other three Cs, this implies a largely meritocratic system. An ability-based meritocratic system can raise overall growth and efficiency, but a patronage system will redistribute potential growth from less favored to more favored localities.

This section shows that patron ties do not wholly determine local growth outcomes, implying that a tournament promotion hypothesis holds for Jiangsu. Literature has quantified the effect of state/Party connections on firm outcomes in China, but the effect of local leadership connections on economic growth has not been systematically explored.[28] Looking at a set of politically "favored" cadres to see whether they produce above-average growth outcomes can help explore this question. Although it is impossible to systematically uncover all patron-client ties and political connections given the informal nature of these ties, three sets of leaders seem to have clear connections. As evidenced by the Wang Daohan connection to Mingguang, geographic overlap with provincial leaders (provincial Party secretary and provincial governor), indicated by counties in which these leaders were born or worked, may give local leaders provincial *guanxi*. Additionally, two institutional norms shed light on the treatment of favored cadres: *dujin* (镀金) and *gaopei* (高配). *Dujin*, literally "to gilt," refers to cadres sent down for quick experience at the grassroots level, which will ostensibly round out, or "gild," their political careers.[29] There is an explicit assumption made in local interviews as well

[27] However, note that using lagged growth and county fixed effects as controls eliminates the possibility that they are just sent to counties with high growth over the whole period – the key must be growth potential. There is limited evidence for this reciprocal interaction between promotion and growth at the city level. Lin (2007) finds that the faster a leader is promoted, the more likely that he is to become a mayor of a rich city, and that these cities are themselves more likely to continue growing fast, in turn leading to greater chances for promotion based on growth performance.

[28] For government connections and firm performance, see Nee and Opper (2006), McNally, Guo, and Hu (2007), and Gu, Hung, and Tse (2008).

[29] The term originally applied to students who studied abroad to enhance their social status.

as various media that young cadres will be "parachuted" into counties for brief *dujin* experiences before getting elevated to higher positions at the city or province level. These officials are young and only serve for one or two years (more than that and the gilt may become more than skin deep).[30] *Gaopei* refers to "concurrent promotions," whereby county Party secretaries retain their local county leadership position while also joining the prefecture-level Party Committee in the city in which their county sits. Ostensibly, leaders on the prefecture-level Party Committee have strong institutional connections at that level, as seen from the Qiu He example in Chapter 4.

For all three sets of politically/institutionally favored leaders, the analyses below find no evidence that connections significantly predict economic growth outcomes. This does not mean that connections do not matter. As the discussion in Chapter 4 showed, at times connections can have clear positive effects on economic growth outcomes. Although part of the explanation for a nonexistent growth effect may be that these three "favored" sets of cadres are not representative of real connections or patron ties, a more likely explanation is that while connections *can* matter, they do not always matter; in other words, most leader impact is felt through leader characteristics and initiative rather than through patron ties. This implies that the tournament promotion hypothesis holds in Jiangsu, and means that the lack of economic basis for promotion in Anhui may itself be responsible for lower levels of economic growth.

Workplace and Hometown Connections to Provincial Leaders

Connections to provincial leaders, as discussed in Chapter 4, provide clear channels for increased investment and growth. But do counties with informal ties to provincial leaders typically perform better? Table 5.7 lists the hometown and work experience of all Anhui and Jiangsu provincial Party secretaries and governors over 1994–2011, highlighting when these leaders had previously lived or worked in counties or cities within the province. Because of the rule of avoidance and cadre rotation norms, many of the leaders have no prior living or work experience in the province they lead. Indeed, only one Anhui Party secretary or governor is originally from Anhui over this period.

[30] Youth and promotion potential clearly go together. For instance, Li and Bachman (1989) look at promotion speeds in their study of China's mayors, combining the city administrative level and mayoral age to identify slow, fast, and very fast cadres.

Using this information on provincial leader backgrounds, we can see whether ties through biographical history predict growth outcomes by regressing GDP growth (or investment growth) on a dummy variable taking the value of one when the concurrent provincial leader has previously spent time in the same county/city, along with a set of control variables:

$$Y_{it} = \alpha_1 \cdot ProvConnect_{it} + \beta X_{it} + \gamma_i + \varphi_t + \epsilon_{it} \qquad (5.2)$$

In the results reported in Table 5.8, all regressions include year fixed effects (φ_t) and county fixed effects (γ_i) as well as log GDP per capita and population as control variables (X_{it}). Results are reported for all potential dummy variables ($ProvConnect_{it}$): provincial governor versus Party secretary connection, shared county and/or city, and work history versus place of birth. Note that the Jiangsu results are more robust given the much larger sample size (219 county-year observations with a leader from the same county or city, versus only 48 for Anhui). Looking at the results, in none of the specifications does the leader connection predict greater growth or investment; indeed, many of the specifications indicate that growth is slower for these counties.[31] Similarly, if we make growth in earmarked fiscal transfers or general fiscal transfers the dependent variable, variables which the provincial leader could directly control, the results (not shown) still remain either insignificant or negative. In other words, ties to leaders seem to predict slower growth, if anything.[32]

This is a small sample, and it is easy to argue that the prefecture/city connections of provincial leaders would not benefit counties within these prefecture-level areas. Looking only at county connections yields too small a sample to give much power to the regression coefficients presented above. But a brief look at the specific "connected" counties supports the conclusions. In Jiangsu, four counties have direct connections to provincial leaders at some point during the sample period, and two had no county Party secretaries appointed during the relevant time frame.[33]

[31] Looking at dummy variables for place of birth or work history separately, the results (not shown) remain insignificant or negative.

[32] If this is true, it could imply that provincial leaders are worried about appearing to practice favoritism, and therefore take the other route.

[33] In Wu County, the home county of Zheng Silin, no county Party secretary was appointed during Zheng's time in office (1994–1998); Yu Funan (于福南) was already in office and stayed in office through 1998. Similarly in Haimen, the hometown of Ji Yunshi, no county Party secretary was appointed while Ji was in office (1999–2002): Xu Yongbing (徐永兵) was already in office and stayed in office until 2006 (one of the longest serving cadres in the sample). While Xu was in office, Haimen's GDP growth averaged 0.4 percentage points below the provincial average.

TABLE 5.7. *Hometown and within-province work experience of provincial leaders*

		Years in office	Home County (City)	Work County (City)
Anhui				
Party secretaries	Lu Rongjing	1994–1998	Lujiang (Chaohu)	(Tongling); (Ma'anshan)
	Hui Liangyu	1999	*NA*	*NA*
	Wang Taihua	2000–2004	*NA*	(Hefei)
	Guo Jinlong	2005–2007	*NA*	*NA*
	Wang Jinshan	2008–2009	*NA*	*NA*
	Zhang Baoshun	2010	*NA*	*NA*
Governors	Hui Liangyu	1994–1998	*NA*	*NA*
	Wang Taihua	1999	*NA*	(Hefei)
	Xu Zhonglin	2000–2002	*NA*	*NA*
	Wang Jinshan	2003–2007	*NA*	*NA*
	Wang Sanyun	2008–2010	*NA*	*NA*
Jiangsu				
Party secretaries	Chen Huanyou	1994–1999	(Nantong)	(Wuxi)
	Hui Liangyu	2000–2002	*NA*	*NA*
	Li Yuanchao	2003–2007	Lianshui (Huaian)	(Nanjing)
	Liang Baohua	2008–2010	*NA*	Taicang (Suzhou)
Governors	Zheng Silin	1994–1998	Wu (Suzhou)	*NA*
	Ji Yunshi	1999–2002	Haimen (Nantong)	(Lianyungang); (Suzhou)
	Liang Baohua	2003–2007	*NA*	Taicang (Suzhou)
	Luo Zhijun	2008–2010	*NA*	(Nanjing)

Source: Baidu; China Vitae.

Note: Counties are listed first; prefecture-level cities are listed in parentheses. "*NA*" indicates leader born outside the province or had no county experience.

TABLE 5.8. *Growth effects of geographical connections to provincial leaders*

	(1)	(2)	(3)	(4)	(5)	(6)
	GDP growth			*FAI growth*		
Connection:	*Full*	*Jiangsu*	*Anhui*	*Full*	*Jiangsu*	*Anhui*
PPS/PG, County & City	−2.184	−3.446***	−0.298	−9.190***	−10.02***	−11.49
	(1.472)	(1.277)	(3.546)	(2.938)	(2.653)	(6.947)
	"1"=267	"1"=219	"1"=48	"1"=267	"1"=219	"1"=48
PPS, County & City	−2.828**	−2.496**	−1.651	−7.685***	−4.518*	−8.448
	(1.307)	(1.070)	(2.974)	(2.446)	(2.381)	(7.291)
	"1"=148	"1"=103	"1"=45	"1"=148	"1"=103	"1"=45
PG, County & City	1.242	−1.795	3.674	−5.172	−10.73***	−14.19
	(1.776)	(2.025)	(6.232)	(3.690)	(3.619)	(17.10)
	"1"=130	"1"=122	"1"=8	"1"=130	"1"=122	"1"=8
PPS/PG, County	−3.870*	−2.548	−4.882***	−1.956	−7.052***	4.290
	(2.197)	(1.850)	(1.672)	(2.334)	(2.519)	(8.609)
	"1"=22	"1"=17	"1"=5	"1"=22	"1"=17	"1"=5
PPS, County	−7.777***	−5.195***		−6.440**	−7.942***	
	(2.253)	(1.277)		(2.851)	(1.005)	
	"1"=8	"1"=8	"1"=0	"1"=8	"1"=8	"1"=0
PG, County	−0.824	0.571	−4.882***	1.085	−4.275	4.290
	(1.382)	(1.675)	(1.672)	(3.296)	(5.845)	(8.609)
	"1"=14	"1"=9	"1"=5	"1"=14	"1"=9	"1"=5

Robust standard errors in parentheses. Number of dummy observations reported below standard errors ("1"=). *** p<0.01, ** p<0.05, * p<0.1
Note: All regressions include year and county fixed effects as well as log GDP per capita and population as controls. PPS=provincial Party secretary; PG=provincial governor; "County & City" is a dummy variable that takes value "1" for all counties in which a PPS/PG was born or had work experience.

In Lianshui County, the hometown of former Jiangsu Party Secretary Li Yuanchao, only one county Party secretary was appointed while Li was in office: Li Weiping (李卫平) was appointed in March 2006. Li Weiping had an impressive background – he previously headed the Zhenjiang City Trade bureau (镇江市贸易局局长) and had been an urban district Party secretary (镇江市润州区委书记) – and indeed he was perceived in the region as a "highly qualified" cadre whom Li Yuanchao had sent to the county specifically in order to boost local growth (Interview JS169). To provide extra authority, Li Weiping held a concurrent (*gaopei*) position on the prefecture-level Party Committee throughout his entire local tenure. In other words, Li had an economic background, he was perceived as qualified, he had institutional connections on the prefecture-level Party Committee, and he was sent to the hometown of the provincial Party secretary to turn things around. Yet growth averaged 0.4 percentage points *below* the provincial average while Li was in office (worse than two out of three of his predecessors, so the county fixed effect cannot be blamed). The ability he was selected for did not manifest, and connections could not turn the county around. Nor was he promoted very far, transferring to Zhenjiang City vice mayor in May 2012 – perhaps his lack of ability was discovered. Similarly, Taicang County, in which Jiangsu Governor and Party Secretary Liang Baohua previously worked, had only one leader appointed during 2003–2010, when Liang served as both governor and Party secretary of Jiangsu. Pu Ronggao (浦荣皋) was appointed in March 2006. Under him, growth averaged 1.0 percentage point *below* the provincial average (worse than both of his predecessors, so again the county fixed effect cannot be blamed), and after five years in office he was promoted to a city vice mayor position in October 2010. These two cases support the quantitative analysis: both Li Weiping and Pu Ronggao should have been expected to boost local outcomes due to their implicit connections to the concurrent provincial Party secretary, but neither achieved relative success in either local economic outcomes or personal career outcomes.

Dujin and Gaopei

Another way of attempting to quantify the role of connections is to look at "gilded" (*dujin*) cadres and the increasingly common phenomenon of "concurrent promotions" (*gaopei*, 高配) in which county Party secretaries serve concurrently as members of the prefecture-level Party Committee. There is not a strict definition for *dujin* cadres – the phenomenon is more along the lines of "you know it when you see it." The key is that cadres are young and sent down for short tenures. In the analyses below *dujin* cadres are defined as those in the bottom 10th percentile of the age distribution upon taking office (41 years old or younger in the sample) and having tenures of only one or two years. By this definition, 7.1 percent of Jiangsu county Party secretaries are *dujin*, as are 8.4 percent of Anhui county Party secretaries. Public administration and economics academics in Nanjing, Bengbu, and Beijing predominantly saw *dujin* in a cynical light, as patronage politics at its most blatant (Interview JS197, Interview BJ113, Interview AH293). In this telling, any future successful cadre needs grassroots experience, so they get "sent down" for a year or two early in their careers and simply try to avoid causing trouble. Interestingly, interviews in the Anhui and Jiangsu case counties demonstrated divergent conceptions of the role of the *dujin* process. According to one bureau director in Anhui, officials are sent to *dujin* "just so they can say that they've had some local experience. These officials don't care at all about growth. Really they just want to avoid mayhem (*luan*, 乱) so they can transition smoothly to their next post" (Interview AH106). Conversely, in Jiangsu, a bureau director believed that a reason for *dujin* was that "upper levels can really see your individual economic impact" in a situation in which you get to operate with full control (Interview JS281).

Gaopei is a more interesting institutional innovation that requires slightly more explanation. There is a disconnect between county Party secretary five-year term limits and a reality of three-year median tenures. Leaders seek quick transfers and perceive that staying beyond three years is a sign of being passed over for promotion.[34] There are clear negative consequences inherent in this system: if a county Party secretary is effective, this effect is unlikely to have much impact in only two years; and if a leader is effective, superiors may want him to stay in office. To combat the negative effects resulting from the juxtaposition of short tenures and career expectations, many provinces have experimented with *gaopei*, whereby a county Party secretary maintains his position but is concurrently elevated to a higher post, usually on the prefecture-level Party Committee.[35] Over the full 17-year sample, 52 Party secretaries in

[34] This perception was widely confirmed during fieldwork. See also Lian and Wu (2011); Chu (2012). According to Wang (2005), this phenomenon results in only 1 percent of county cadres filling their official term length.

[35] Here and in the exercises below I define *gaopei* as concurrent posts as county Party secretary and prefecture-level Party Committee. This misses leaders who hold other concurrent posts. In addition to the county-level leader database, the exercise depends on leader name lists for all prefecture Party Committees over 1994–2010, compiled from prefecture yearbooks.

Jiangsu served concurrently as prefecture-level Party Committee members or vice mayors out of a total 286 Party secretaries who served over this period. While *gaopei* has recently been given more attention and its frequency is increasing, it is not a new phenomenon. In 1996, only two Jiangsu county Party secretaries concurrently served on prefecture-level Party Committees, yet by 2008, 14 county Party secretaries did (nearly one-quarter of all county Party secretaries in Jiangsu that year).[36] On average, *gaopei* Party secretaries served 1.9 years before being concurrently elevated, and 2.7 years after being elevated; however, note that 17 of the 52 *gaopei* leaders entered their Party secretary terms already holding concurrent higher-level posts.

To analyze *gaopei* effects a distinction should be made between those leaders who are promoted after three or more years in office and those who are promoted upon entry or are promoted after only one or two years.[37] Given that their promotions preceded identifiable local growth outcomes, these latter cadres seem to have personal connections or some other path to promotion that is not contingent upon local performance. Below, the "core" *gaopei* sample corresponds to those leaders elevated after three or more years; the "rapid" sample are those elevated immediately or after one year. This "rapid" set of *gaopei* cadres who either enter office already on the prefecture-level Party Committee or who are concurrently promoted within one year of taking office clearly represent a different *gaopei* rationale that is not based on keeping them working locally based on performance outcomes. However, the rationale could be either patronage-based or meritocratic. In other words, these cadres may be seen as highly effective and thus sent to counties with the backing of the prefecture level, but they could also be groomed cadres.

In the case counties, perceptions were split on the actual rationale and effectiveness of *gaopei*: some saw the phenomenon as fulfilling its intended purpose by rewarding cadres who showed potential without making them

[36] In 1994, only one county Party secretary in Jiangsu concurrently served on prefecture Party Committees, yet by 2008, 17 did (nearly 30 percent of all Party secretaries). It is worth noting that this does not necessarily reflect a growing power of county interests in prefecture decision making. Party Committees at the prefecture level have grown increasingly large in Jiangsu, from an average of just over four members (plus nearly four deputy party secretaries) in 1996 to over eight members (plus 2–3 deputy party secretaries) in 2010. Overall, including the Party secretary and deputies, average Party Committee size has grown from under 9 in 1996 to nearly 12 in 2010. This dilution may partly offset the growing county voice.

[37] To understand this, recall the official rationale for *gaopei*: namely, rewarding high-performing county leaders while enabling them to continue working at the local level.

leave their posts. Unlike *dujin*, others saw "rapid" *gaopei* as a means of sending capable (and empowered) leaders to initiate change. This was particularly prominent in looking at Sunan (Jiangsu) cadres who were sent north. A comparison of growth under "core" *gaopei* leaders before and after their concurrent promotion allows us to examine whether the stated rationale of *gaopei* is evidenced and also potentially to identify an economic "patronage" effect. Ostensibly, leader capacity should not be affected by the concurrent promotion, yet superordinate connections are clearly improved; moreover, the Party secretary gains a voice in fiscal transfer and public investment decisions from the prefecture level, so if growth after *gaopei* is significantly higher than pre-*gaopei* growth, this implies a patronage effect. Below, I first regress growth on a *gaopei* dummy variable along with a set of controls, demonstrating that growth is higher under leaders who are eventually *gaopei* promoted. I then compare growth of *gaopei* cadres pre-*gaopei* and post-*gaopei* by comparing changes in average growth deviations from the provincial average:

$$DiffY_i = \alpha \cdot Gaopei_i + \beta \mathbf{X}_i + \gamma_i + \epsilon_i \tag{5.3}$$

Here, the differenced average growth deviation, $DiffY_i$, is equal to the difference between successive leaders of the average annual growth rate deviation from the provincial average, or $\sum_{t=1}^{n}\left(Y_{ijt} - \bar{Y}_{jt}\right)/n$, where n is equal to the term length of the leader, Y_{ijt} is the annual per capita GDP growth rate in county i in province j, and $\bar{Y}_{jt}$ is the average county per capita GDP growth rate in province j. For the subset of *gaopei* leaders, I treat their pre- and post-*gaopei* selves as two different leaders. $Gaopei_i$ takes value one for all *gaopei* leaders, and the coefficient α therefore identifies whether transitions to concurrent upper-level posts result in different growth outcomes than general transitions between leaders.

Table 5.9 compares growth before and after concurrent promotion. Similar to the exercises above, the first column analyzes whether "core" *gaopei* leaders have higher growth, demonstrating that their growth is above-expected, which supports the idea that *gaopei* cadres are recognized for their achievements, and also supports the general growth-promotion connection found for Jiangsu above. The results in column 2 look at whether the transition to concurrent promotion results in altered growth trajectories. The coefficient is positive but low in magnitude and insignificant, implying that pre- and post-*gaopei* leaders tend not to change systematically; the better superordinate *guanxi* and ability to target funds locally has no identifiable effect on growth. The results imply a weak or nonexistent relationship between patronage and growth. Core *gaopei* leaders produce above-average growth, but concurrent promotion itself has no effect on growth; while *gaopei* officials generally have higher economic growth, they do not have significantly improved economic performances post-*gaopei*. In other words, *gaopei* seems to be following its intended rationale – rewarding successful cadres through promotions while allowing them to stay in office and have a continued positive economic effect.

Analysis of growth outcomes and promotion prospects for both "rapid" *gaopei* and *dujin* county Party secretaries can help further distinguish between patronage and meritocracy growth effects. Are *dujin* and "rapid" *gaopei* cadres sent to high-growth counties, do they achieve better growth results, and do they have better promotion prospects? In the analysis below, I define *dujin* cadres as those in the bottom 10th percentile

TABLE 5.9. *"Core" gaopei growth effects in Jiangsu*

	(1)	(2)
	Annual PC GDP Growth	*Post – Pre* **Gaopei** *Provincial Growth Differential*
"Core" *gaopei*	3.10**	1.29
	(1.17)	(0.88)
Population	−0.21	−0.01
	(0.13)	(0.01)
Log PC GDP	22.13***	−0.82
	(6.71)	(0.70)
1yr lag DV	−0.13	
	(0.09)	
2yr lag DV	−0.06	
	(0.04)	
3yr lag DV	−0.07	
	(0.05)	
Constant	−187.4**	7.89
	(71.57)	(7.07)
County fixed effects	Yes	No
Year fixed effects	Yes	No
Observations	740	251
R-squared	0.30	0.01

Robust standard errors in parentheses.

*** p<0.01, ** p<0.05, * p<0.1

of the age distribution upon taking office (41 years old or younger) and having tenures of only one or two years. "Rapid" *gaopei* county Party secretaries are those who are already concurrently on the prefecture-level Party Committee when they enter office or rise within one year. To answer the three questions just posed, three equations are necessary, following from the basic approach of Equation 5.1 and Equation 5.2:

$$PredecessorY_{it} = \alpha_1 \cdot Connection_{it} + \beta X_{it} + \gamma_i + \varphi_t + \epsilon_{it} \quad (5.4)$$

$$Y_{it} = \alpha_1 \cdot Connection_{it} + \beta X_{it} + \gamma_i + \varphi_t + \epsilon_{it} \quad (5.5)$$

$$Promoted_{it} = \alpha_1 \cdot Connection_{it} + \delta PC_{it} + \gamma_i + \varphi_t + \epsilon_{it} \quad (5.6)$$

Here, $PredecessorY_{it}$ refers to growth under the previous county Party secretary; $Connection_{it}$ is a dummy variable indicating the leader connection and taking value one for *dujin* or "rapid" *gaopei* cadres, depending on the regression. All other variables are defined as before.

Table 5.10 below shows results from these six regressions (three equations for both *dujin* and "rapid" *gaopei* cadres), including year and county fixed effects as well as population and log per capita GDP controls. The regression results imply that in both Jiangsu and Anhui, *dujin* county Party secretaries are significantly more likely to become "all star" cadres, although the effect is stronger in Jiangsu (columns 5 and 6). However, these *dujin* cadres do not have strong growth effects in either province (columns 3 and 4), and they do not get sent to counties with significantly different recent growth patterns (columns 1 and 2). In contrast, the "rapid" *gaopei* county Party secretaries have significant growth relationships in Jiangsu: they are sent to counties that have experienced significantly worse growth in recent years (column 1), and during their tenures growth is significantly higher (column 3); they are then significantly more likely to have highly successful career paths (column 5). In Anhui, these "rapid" *gaopei* cadres are undistinguished: sent to average counties, achieving average growth, and not having significantly higher promotion prospects.

The *dujin* results suggest that certain young cadres are groomed for success, with their "sent down" experience much in line with local perceptions: they need local experience for their resumé for a few years, but the local outcomes are irrelevant. The Jiangsu interview perspective of an "economic ability testing ground" may have been too optimistic – the key may simply be not screwing up. These results argue against the

TABLE 5.10. Dujin *and* gaopei *growth and promotion outcomes*

	(1)	(2)	(3)	(4)	(5)	(6)
	GDP growth under predecessor		**GDP Growth**		**"All-star" promotion**	
	Jiangsu	*Anhui*	*Jiangsu*	*Anhui*	*Jiangsu*	*Anhui*
Dujin	1.426	−2.494	0.560	0.655	1.866***	0.958**
	(1.496)	(1.899)	(1.258)	(1.770)	(0.486)	(0.481)
"Rapid"	−4.188***	0.260	4.178**	0.258	1.550***	0.0828
gaopei	(1.379)	(1.418)	(1.598)	(1.310)	(0.376)	(1.068)

Standard errors in parentheses. *** p<0.01, ** p<0.05, * p<0.1

Note: Growth regressions in columns 1, 2, 3, and 4 are all fixed effects regressions including county and year fixed effects as well as per capita GDP and population controls, and robust standard errors. The promotion regressions in columns 5 and 6 use a logit model. *Dujin* CPS are those who serve for only 1- or 2-year terms and enter office at age 41 or lower (10th percentile). "Rapid" *gaopei* CPS are those who are already concurrently on the prefecture-level Party Committee when they enter office or rise within one year. "All star" promotion is defined as above in the text.

patronage-to-growth hypothesis. There is a consensus that *dujin* cadres are favored, and the evidence on their future growth potential is clear. If growth stemmed from patron assistance, we would expect these cadres to have very high growth outcomes.

The rapid *gaopei* results tell a different story, one that highlights the Jiangsu provincial emphasis on economic growth. A subset of cadres is selected (either for perceived ability or because of patron ties) and sent to poorly performing areas (e.g., Sunan cadres sent to Subei), where either due to their ability, or because of their connections, they boost local outcomes and are then rewarded with promotions. No doubt the "rapid" *gaopei* cadres have good connections that help growth, but as discussed in the previous chapter, these connections are not necessarily patron ties. Indeed, the key for many Sunan cadres who are sent north is having connections to specific industrial firms. In this telling, highly capable, well-connected cadres are sent to poor-performing areas with additional institutional strength behind them through their prefecture-level representation. This connection may give them more resources as well as more courage and local control. They achieve positive economic results and then move on to bigger and better positions. This supports the argument that Jiangsu has a provincial system of cadre management that emphasizes economic growth outcomes. Regardless of which interpretation is accepted – connections allow high growth for "rapid" *gaopei* or "rapid" *gaopei* are initially selected for high ability – the difference between Jiangsu and Anhui is interesting.[38] If connections allow high growth, then we must assume that connections in Anhui focus on non-growth outcomes.

Combined with the empirically nonexistent connection between provincial leader ties and growth, this section implies that while connections *can* have a positive impact on local outcomes, they do not systematically explain enhanced growth outcomes: the relationship between leaders and growth has stronger roots in local initiative than in patron-based assistance. The results also imply that China, or at least Jiangsu, may have a dual-track system for promotions: a select elite are promoted regardless of performance, likely as a consequence of strong patron ties, while the majority of less connected cadres appear to be promoted based on performance. We cannot ignore the role of patronage for elite promotions, but performance-based promotions appear to be the norm.

Conclusion

This chapter has provided evidence that county Party secretaries in Jiangsu and coastal provinces more broadly are promoted based on economic growth outcomes during their tenures. This growth appears to result from some aspect of "ability" rather than from luck or patronage, which therefore supports a tournament promotion hypothesis that attributes a portion of rapid economic growth to the competition induced between local leaders. In Anhui and central provinces more broadly, county Party secretaries who are promoted tend to have slightly lower economic growth during their tenures. Assuming a "norm" of performance-based promotions in Jiangsu, what does the lack of a significant relationship between economic outcomes and promotions in Anhui imply? One possibility is that patronage dominates, and that Anhui has a nonmeritocratic system, but a more convincing argument is that county Party secretaries in Anhui are promoted based on other criteria. To explain the negative correlation between economic outcomes and promotions, the nonmeritocratic criteria or the meritocratic nongrowth criteria should be negatively correlated

[38] With the *dujin* results in mind, the selection-on-ability hypothesis makes more sense.

with growth, which would imply that the previous regressions suffered from omitted variable bias. The next chapter explores the hypothesis that excessive stability maintenance is correlated with low growth, and that Anhui county cadres are rewarded largely for their success in maintaining stability.

6

Ignoring Growth: The Institutional and Economic Costs of Maintaining Stability

> *Across the border [in Jiangsu], growth is "number one." Here, growth is secondary to stability. That's why we have no leaders with any courage.*
>
> – *County government official, Anhui (Interview AH138)*

> *The Mingguang leaders aren't at fault for poor growth. They're very constrained. The biggest problem in Mingguang is that Anhui itself takes no initiative, but rather simply implements government policies. In Jiangsu, the provincial government takes central policies and adjusts them. It does everything it can that won't truly offend the upper levels.*
>
> – *County government official, Anhui (Interview AH104)*

In 2009 and 2010, Si County in Anhui and Sihong County in Jiangsu made (unwelcome) national news. In Si in 2009, the authorities demolished a nearly 1000-year-old temple (*shijiasi*, 释迦寺), despite local opposition as well as a complaint by the local Culture Bureau to the national Culture Bureau.[1] According to one journalist's investigation, in July 2007 the county leaders had directly pressured the land bureau to auction off 25 *mu* (4.1 acres) that included the temple area, which ended up selling for 11.5 million RMB. The county-level Culture Bureau was not consulted, and when it found out in 2008 it raised objections, including to the provincial- and national-level Culture Bureaus. In the end, however, the local bureau could not withstand local government pressure and the temple was razed. A month after national news (Beijing's *Xinjing Bao*, 新京报) published an exposé of the demolition, the local government

[1] The following account is based on local discussions as well as Li (2010) and Xin'an Evening News (2010).

changed positions and fined the developer 400,000 RMB for the illegal demolition while also making the developer pay for a new temple on the original site. The magistrate at the time received internal Party discipline (*dangnei jinggao chufen,* 党内警告处分) and promised that "from now on, we'll strengthen our awareness of the rule of law and will establish a section-level (*zhengkeji,* 正科级) cultural protection bureau." But most of the blame was put on the county Party secretary, whose career was basically ended: he was removed from office and demoted to a prefecture-level deputy secretary (*mishu,* 秘书).

In Sihong in 2010, county authorities closed and demolished a forestry station (*linye zhan,* 林业站) despite rallying and petitioning by its 68 employees and 30,000 netizen complaints. In October 2009, the county government had planned to demolish the station, which had been built in 1966. The forestry unit (*danwei,* 单位) had become an "un-loved" (*niangniang buteng, jiujiu buai,* 娘娘不疼、舅舅不爱) unit that the county government wanted to close. Following a closure plan that upset the employees, they sent a notice to upper authorities in February 2010 claiming that the closure was illegal. Jiangsu provincial authorities took notice, making the employees optimistic, but then they slowly lost hope as the county did not change its intended actions. On March 12, at a large county meeting, the employees were given a warning not to rally or obstruct the destruction. They did not cooperate. Within a week, 30,000 netizens had taken notice and news had spread provincially and nationally. The county still had no intention of changing its plans, and quickly followed through, to much local dismay.

Soon after this incident, Sihong's pyramid informal finance problem became national news.[2] This incident also happened in 2010–2011 under the same Party secretary, Feng Yan (冯岩). The pyramid scheme reached 2 billion RMB, with thousands of locals involved. Moreover, government employees were themselves instigators and recipients of many of the loans; the illegal financing was happening with the direct support of local authorities.[3] The situation eventually blew up, making national news, including the cover story of Money Weekly (理财周刊), but the Party leadership, rather than condemning the informal lending, instead continued to argue that the lending had had a positive influence on local growth. Perhaps because of this, penalties were not harsh: all

[2] See Money Weekly (2011).

[3] According to an employee of the local PBOC, lots of government officials were participating in the high lending, so supervision existed in name only (*jianguan xingtongxushe,* 监管形同虚设) (Tu 2011).

500 suspected ringleaders who were brought in were released. The Party secretary at the time of both the informal lending bubble and the forestry station demolition, Feng Yan (冯岩), was not punished, nor were his promotion prospects negatively affected by the two incidents. In November 2011 he became Suqian City vice mayor, a moderate promotion.

The Si and Sihong cases hint at different approaches to potentially "destabilizing" incidents in Jiangsu and Anhui: in Si County, the Party secretary involved in a major incident was removed from office and demoted, and the county issued an apology and was forced to make institutional changes. Conversely, in Sihong, the county Party secretary overseeing two incidents that became national news was promoted, and he justified his actions by arguing that they were pro-growth.

This comparison represents a larger phenomenon. The findings in the previous chapter suggest that Jiangsu, a wealthy coastal province, and Anhui, a poorer inland province, emphasize different criteria in their evaluations of county Party secretaries. Despite publicized changes in emphasis away from growth "quantity" and towards growth "quality," Jiangsu continues to promote its county Party secretaries on the basis of economic success. Anhui, which needs all the growth it can get, instead seems to disregard or even penalize fast-growing counties. This chapter argues that this at-first-glance surprising anomaly is actually a direct consequence of differential implementation of the two primary central Party-state mandates: growth and stability. The center rewards Jiangsu (and other wealthy province) leaders who pursue and achieve economic growth, and rewards Anhui (and other poor/central province) leaders who maintain stability. While the central Party-state no doubt would *rather* have growth *and* stability in both regions, its risk averse strategy has been to continue to let some regions develop first. As a consequence of this incentive structure, local leaders and governments in Anhui and other central provinces have been less innovative institutionally, have had worse governance, have made less bold economic decisions, and have achieved worse economic outcomes. Summarizing this hypothesis, a cadre in Anhui succinctly explained why his county failed to grow while the neighboring county in Jiangsu was a model of success: "[In Jiangsu], growth is number one. Here, growth is secondary to stability. That's why we have no leaders with any courage (*poli*, 魄力)" (Interview AH138). One Anhui county head of the local Economic and Information Technology Committee agreed that Anhui saw stability and growth as equal, while Jiangsu saw growth as more important, noting that this played out particularly in hitting investment promotion targets – he and others were given targets, but actually hitting them was irrelevant.

This chapter continues in three parts. First, I provide evidence that Anhui and central provinces are more likely to emphasize stability in promotion decisions. No proxy for county stability publicly exists to enable a quantitative analysis similar to that in the last chapter, but anecdotal evidence from local news sources, county yearbooks, and field visits provide considerable support for an Anhui emphasis on stability that differs from the Jiangsu emphasis. An emphasis on maintaining stability really refers to an emphasis on avoiding instability – as *most* places achieve this outcome, there is less differentiation to base evaluations on, leading to a larger role for informal patron ties in promotion decisions. A look at the biographical histories of county leaders demonstrates that Anhui is significantly more likely to promote party leaders with organizational, public security and law, or propaganda backgrounds, while Jiangsu promotes significantly more cadres from the economic bureaucracy, further implying an Anhui government emphasis on stability over growth. Second, the chapter explores reasons for this focus on stability. Given the high levels of social discontent surrounding demolitions, land conversion, restructuring, and other actions associated with China's growth model, rapidly reforming high growth counties have greater potential for instability; residents of slow-growing counties may be generally dissatisfied with slow growth, but simmering ennui may not spur them onto the street or the petitions office. Finally, the chapter explores the consequences of this stability focus in terms of economic outcomes, looking at approaches to governance and fiscal decisions and arguing that a stability priority has antigrowth consequences: leaders in Anhui and central provinces fear institutional innovations that could constrain local bureaucracies and prevent government failures, and their economic policies and fiscal decisions reflect a risk-averse attitude that prioritizes preventing discontent rather than boosting local growth.

Regional Variation in Promotion Criteria: Stability Maintenance

There is both documentary and anecdotal evidence that poorer central regions emphasize stability more than their coastal counterparts. Stability maintenance (*weiwen,* 维稳) has long been noted as an important criterion in cadre performance evaluations, particularly following the Tiananmen

Square incident in 1989.[4] Several studies have focused on "veto targets" (*yipiao foujue,* 一票否决), i.e., those targets whose failure nullifies any and all other successes.[5] Over time, five veto categories have been highlighted: clean Party building and anticorruption (*dangfeng lianzheng jianshe,* 党风廉政建设), petitions (*xinfang,* 信访), family planning (*jihua shengyu,* 计划生育), comprehensive control (*zonghe zhili,* 综合治理), and production safety (*anquan shengchan,* 安全生产). The biggest concern for many bureaucrats are petitions (*xinfang,* 信访), frequently referred to as the "sword of Damocles" hanging over cadres' heads (Han 2011).[6] The negative effect of petitions on promotion prospects has long been observed.[7] Cao Guoying, a former head of the national Ministry of Civil Affairs Petition Office (民政部信访办公室), puts it plainly: "The central complaints bureau can assign points to major local cadres, based on the number of appeals from the locality, the number of cases it has resolved, and the outcome of the settlement. If too many points are deducted, the career of local officials may be affected" (Jiang 2002). At the local level, the apparent incentive structure leads to efforts to avoid petitions and obstruct petitioners rather than respond to the content of the complaints, largely because problems that are solved pre-petition do not enter into evaluations.[8] This makes the work of the petition offices themselves relatively unimportant to local leaders: according to Cao, the former head of the national Civil Affairs Petition Office, "in the eyes of many leaders, petition bureaus are just decoration (*xinfang bumen zhishi yige baishe,* 信访部门只是一个摆设)," making effective work nearly impossible (Jiang 2002).[9] At the same time, localities spend more and more to

[4] Following the Tiananmen Square incident, in 1991, the Ministry of Public Security lobbied to have social stability added to cadre evaluations; ever since, public security heads at the local level have been more likely to be the heads of the political-legal committee rather than courts or procuratorate head (Minzner 2013).

[5] See, for example, Heimer (2006).

[6] For an overview of the petitions system, see Minzner (2006).

[7] See, for example, O'Brien and Li (1995).

[8] Lieberthal (2004, 298) tells a story from Jilin Province in 1993, when a village party chief stopped a peasant and asked for "bicycle tax." The peasant secretly wrote a letter to the county Party secretary to complain, and the county Party secretary then admonished the village chief for not intercepting the letter before it was sent, "noting that they would all have been in trouble if the peasant had written to the provincial level." The village chief then made an example of the peasant, having local police beat him to death in front of a meeting of the village.

[9] Cao Guoying headed the Civil Affairs Petition Office from 1998 to 2000, and describes the difficulties he faced as, "Right now there are very few good people (*haoren shaole,* 好人少了) working in petitions bureaus; they've all left" (Jiang 2002). His department had seven people to handle 10,000 annual petitions – this was more than most departments, which

avoid petitions and intercept petitioners.[10] Nevertheless, there has been increasing pressure from the top not to use repressive authoritarian tactics. For instance, at the National People's Congress in 1999, Zhu Rongji asserted that local governments "must solve contradictions at the initial stage, must not use simple and rude methods to escalate conflicts, and must not use 'means of dictatorship' to deal with people and the masses" (Chen 2012). In sum, as Ying Xing of the China University of Political Science and Law highlights, "The petitions system is full of contradiction. On one hand, the state consistently emphasizes the need to break bureaucratic obstruction of petitioners ... but on the other hand, the state consistently requests that all problems be handled at the grass-roots levels and emphasizes the need to decrease the volume of 'level-skipping' petitions (*yueji*, 越级上访) ..." (Jiangnan Times 2004).

This strong stability focus in evaluations of local governments seems to conflict with findings of pro-growth promotion incentives, but a potential explanation is that sub-provincial level case studies and documentary analysis have overlooked regional variation. Most studies in the local "promotion incentives" field focus explicitly on wealthier regions. The findings and research of Edin and Whiting have been extremely (and justifiably) influential, but these authors themselves admit that their findings of strong pro-growth local incentives for promotions cannot be generalized to less developed regions. Whiting (2004) looks at Shanghai suburbs, some of the wealthiest in all of China. Whiting (2000) compares townships in Zhejiang (Yueqing), Shanghai (Songjiang), and Jiangsu (Wuxi), all of which were within counties that ranked within the top 5 percent of counties in terms of tax revenue. Edin (1998) focuses on townships and counties in Jiangsu, Shandong, Beijing, and Zhejiang, admitting that, "This study focuses on the economically successful areas in the eastern part of China and can thus not be generalized to the poorer areas in western and central China."

Alternatively, studies in less developed regions have often highlighted the contradiction between economic and stability goals, and have focused

often only had one person. Most petitions were sent back down for the local government to handle, but many just sent the problems back up again. According to another high-level complaint bureau official: if a local government ignores the decision of a petitions bureau, then the case is referred to the higher-level petitions bureau, and then progressively up the ladder (Cai 2004).

[10] A People's Congress official from Sichuan estimates that it costs 10,000 RMB to take back a single petitioner who goes to Beijing, and Chen (2012) notes that one city in Hunan spent 100,000 RMB controlling a single petitioner in 2002.

on the need for stability and the prevalence of nonmeritocratic promotion criteria. Gao (2009) in his case study of a western county (Zhouzhi County in Shaanxi) finds much less emphasis on economic indicators: in 2007, the county developed a total of 1143 indicators to measure whether local officials had fulfilled functional targets: of these, 292 (25.5 percent) related to public service provision, 257 (22.5 percent) to economic development, 197 (17.2 percent) to Party building, 193 (16.9 percent) to bureaucratic institution-building, 170 (14.9 percent) to stability, and 34 (3 percent) were unclassifiable. Above these functional targets, the county prioritized four common "veto" targets that had to be hit: population control, production safety, handling of public complaints, and maintaining social stability. In other words, less than a quarter of the technical targets were related to economic development, and "stability"-related criteria accounted for all veto targets. Additionally, local studies outside of the wealthy east often find a much larger role for patronage in county-level and sub-county-level promotions. Two-thirds of township officials in Anhui believed that promotions were based solely on connections (Zhong 2003).[11] If avoidance of veto targets is the most important criterion for promotion, then yardstick competition becomes more difficult (as *most* cadres in any given year will succeed on the binary scale), which in turn makes patronage politics more likely. In other words, added importance of patronage is an expected consequence of a focus on maintaining stability: promotion-minded officials in stability-focused areas concentrate on not making mistakes rather than having positive achievement records, and the lack of outcome comparability increases the importance of informal criteria.

Tied into and supporting this divergent regional promotion criteria hypothesis, the consequences of instability (mass incidents) for leaders in poorer provinces seem to be more negative than in richer provinces, as the comparison at the beginning of the chapter implied.[12] Unfortunately,

[11] Additionally, one case study on the reasons for corruption in Fuyang City (Anhui) concludes that in economically backwards regions like Northern Anhui, the only promotion shortcut (*shengqian jiejing,* 升迁捷径) is to bribe the locality's *yibashou* who controls the cadre promotion market, or literally "black hat distribution power" (*wushamao pifaquan,* 乌纱帽批发权) (Zhang 2007).

[12] We would also expect to find different regional trends in government responses to protests and mass incidents, and there is indeed some evidence that responses are similar within regions but not across regions. Chen (2012, 220) finds that "there exists little systematic variation in petitioning strategies and government responses among most inland provinces," concluding that the findings for Hunan "are largely applicable to at least most inland provinces of China." Similarly, Lee (2007) compares China's "rustbelt"

there are no systematic data on county-level mass incidents to enable rigorous comparison across regions.[13] However, internet searches on Baidu provide nonsystematic evidence that the consequences of mass incidents for leaders differ across regions. As the Si County example highlighted at the beginning of the chapter, mass incidents in poor provinces are bad news for local Party secretaries. The "6.17" incident in Shishou (county-level city) in Hubei in 2009 was a large public protest and riot following the suspicious death of a young local chef. The death was officially deemed a suicide, but local crowds suspected foul play and took to the streets to protest. Within a month of the incident, the local Party secretary was removed from his post for weakly (*buli,* 不力) handling the incident – he was not removed due to any indication of personal knowledge or involvement in the initial cause of the discontent (Xin 2009).[14] Similarly, after tens of thousands of locals gathered to protest the Pubugou dam project in Hanyuan County, Sichuan, the local Party secretary, Tan Zhengyu, was quickly dismissed (Mertha 2008). Local discontent largely centered on the authoritarian approach to relocation taken by Tan's predecessor as Party secretary, and Tan himself was not accused of any actual wrongdoing, nor was the Pubugou project that was being protested his idea or even a county-level project, but rather a provincial-level project with national backing.

In wealthier provinces, mass incidents do not seem to automatically spell doom for local Party secretaries. Consider the "4.10" incident in Dongyang (county-level city) in Zhejiang in 2005. In response to county authorities opening the Zhuxi Chemical Industrial Park and relocating polluting factories there, thousands of residents from 10 villages encamped by the chemical park entrance, forcing the factory to shut. On April 10, the county authorities sent in 1500 local cadres and public security personnel. Conflict ensued, with over 100 police officers and 200 villagers injured. After drawing national attention and a Beijing investigation, the Dongyang authorities admitted to wrongdoing – the industrial park had been built on illegally requisitioned land – and closed 11

versus "sunbelt" protests, lumping together provinces in these two regions, and Hurst (2009) also looks at cross-regional variation in government responses to protests.

13 "Mass incidents" are also a problematic term – referring to a wide range of phenomena, many of which are ostensibly not destabilizing and some of which are actually pro-government. Although they are still "unauthorized" gatherings, and thus meet the definition. For a long discussion on the inconsistent definition of "mass incident," see www.zonaeuropa.com/20061115_1.htm.

14 This was not the end of his career, but his promotion prospects were shattered – less than a year later he was appointed as Jingzhou City (荆州市) deputy secretary (*mishu,* 秘书).

factories. After the incident, the county Party secretary, Tang Yong (汤勇), was promoted to minister of propaganda and Party Committee member of prefecture-level Jinhua City (why he was seen as having a good grasp of rhetoric or public relations is entirely unclear).[15] Closer to the sample counties, Jiangning District (Nanjing) Party Secretary Wang Jianhua was very controversial, and in 2004 he was under investigation for illegal land conversions – but these problems did not hurt his career prospects: in August 2008 he was directly promoted to Lianyungang City Party secretary, a multilevel promotion.

Regional Differences in County Party Secretary Career Backgrounds

The explicit focus on noneconomic criteria for promotions in Anhui is also supported by an analysis of the career backgrounds of county leaders. Considerable evidence from political, psychological, and managerial disciplines highlight the experiential determinants of leader behavior.[16] According to "upper echelons theory," backgrounds determine leader psychology which determines leader behavior and actions: "The central premise of upper echelons theory is that top executives view their situations – opportunities, threats, alternatives and likelihoods of various outcomes – through their own highly personalized lenses. These individualized construals of strategic situations arise because of executives' experiences, values, personalities and other human factors. Thus, according to the theory, organizations become reflections of their top executives" (Hambrick and Mason 1984).[17] A similar vein of thought comes from bureaucratic politics, and particularly Allison and Zelikow (1999), summarized by "where you stand depends on where you sit": organizations themselves influence how their members behave.

[15] Or consider the experience of Party Secretary Gao Yongyuan (高永远) in Wuchuan county-level city, Guangdong, in February 2006. In February 2006, a fight broke out between villagers from Dameichen and Xiaomeichen villages. Gao went to the scene but was completely ignored and required a police escort to get away. He was not punished for the incident, and in 2008 was promoted a level (to *futingji*, 副厅级) while keeping his current position.

[16] On the experiential and psychological determinants of US Presidential behavior, see Barber (1972). Lasswell (1930) develops a broader framework of personality types of political actors based on their developmental experiences and Freudian psychology. According to Lasswell: "Political science without biography is a form of taxidermy"; hopefully this book is not reading like a stuffed pigeon.

[17] See also Finkelstein, Hambrick, and Cannella (2009).

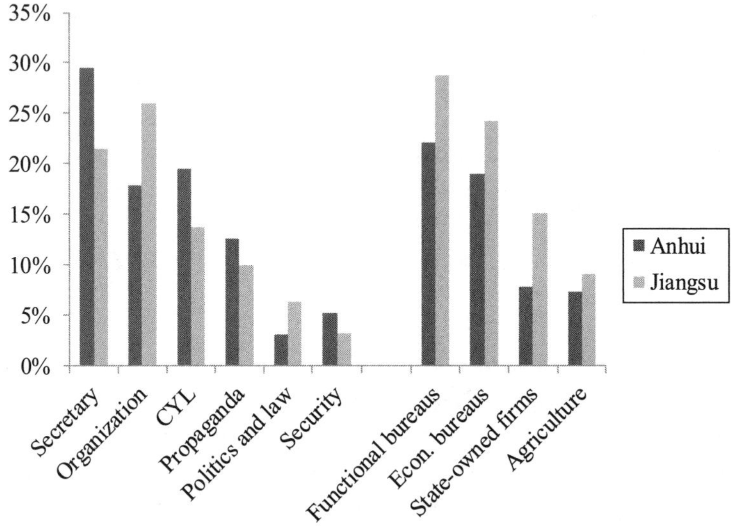

FIGURE 6.1. County Party secretary work history in Jiangsu and Anhui
Share of county Party secretaries by previous work experience
Source: Biographical database; author's calculations.

All of this suggests that the backgrounds of leaders are important for determining their behavior and policy emphases while in office, and this conclusion is no doubt recognized by the provincial Organization Department as it selects county leaders; in other words, the provincial authorities will select cadres who have backgrounds deemed relevant for the work they are expected to undertake. It is therefore interesting to compare biographical histories of county Party secretaries in Jiangsu and Anhui using the biographical data compiled for the analyses in Chapter 5. Doing so, it is clear that in Jiangsu, cadres in economic bureaus are more likely to be promoted to county leadership positions, while Anhui is more likely to promote leaders with administrative, security, or propaganda backgrounds.[18] Overall, 47 percent of Anhui county Party secretaries have an economics background while 62 percent of Jiangsu county Party secretaries have an economics background; conversely, 72 percent in Anhui have an administrative, security, or propaganda background, compared

[18] These categories are broadly defined. Economic background here is defined to include work experience in economic, financial, planning, and industrial bureaus, as well as in SOEs. Administrative backgrounds include secretary (*mishu*, 秘书), organization department, Communist Youth League, and politics and law (*zhengfa*, 政法). Security includes petitions, civil affairs (*minzheng*, 民政), public security, and military.

to 56 percent in Jiangsu. A more granular distribution of backgrounds is shown in Figure 6.1, which demonstrates that the aggregate does not reflect a bias in only one economic category; rather, Jiangsu cadres have more economic experience across categories. It is important to emphasize that all Party secretaries in the sample have risen up through the system. Only a few have backgrounds in SOE work, and the remainder have all worked in Party-state organizations at the county, prefecture, or province level, or as township-level Party secretaries. Anhui and Jiangsu both have similar and robust economic and noneconomic government offices. In other words, the background discrepancies do not occur as an artifact of larger relative economic samples to choose from in Jiangsu.[19]

The lower incidence of economic backgrounds of Anhui cadres will likely manifest in less economic focus and less economic ability of local leaders, and their appointment implies less focus on economic growth more broadly by the provincial authorities; if a province desired more rapid economic growth, it would select cadres based on their performance on this metric, as we see in Jiangsu. Promoting noneconomic officials implies a focus on noneconomic criteria. Further, assuming that priorities are sent down the administrative hierarchy, then this divergent sub-provincial approach to promotions implies that the national level CCP may emphasize different promotion criteria across different regions in its evaluations of province-level authorities.

Stability versus Growth in Anhui and Jiangsu Provincial Promotions

Studies of the determinants of promotion for provincial leaders have come to conflicting conclusions, with many identifying a role for economic growth in determining promotions and others implying that informal patron ties are themselves determinant (see discussion in Chapter 5). A possible reason for the inconsistent results of these studies may be that provincial leaders are selected based on regionally determined criteria; some provinces may be incentivized to focus on growth, while others may be incentivized to focus on stability. If this is the case, then the province is an unsuitable level of analysis for uncovering univariate

[19] However, the possibility remains that Jiangsu's economic bureaucracies have relatively more power given the greater economic success in Jiangsu, and that this greater relative power translates into greater promotion potential. I cannot discount this alternative explanation, but the fact that Party secretaries with economics backgrounds declined somewhat in Jiangsu during Jiangsu's most rapid period of economic growth (the 1990s), implies that the effect may not be great.

promotion incentives (e.g., looking only at the effect of economic growth on promotions). A useful analysis could differentiate coastal and central provinces with interaction terms on two variables of interest, one representing economic outcomes and one representing stability outcomes, but to analyze this growth/stability tradeoff, we need a proxy for stability. The current best practice for determining local stability seems to be from the volume of petitions, legal cases, or protests. Petitions, or "visits and letters" (*xinfang,* 信访), received at each official administrative level in China and seen as an alternative to the legal system, can serve as a measure of stability and discontent, and may indeed be the metric used by authorities in evaluations of stability maintenance, as highlighted above.[20] Given limited petition data, I focus here only on Jiangsu and Anhui provincial leaders, analyzing the promotions of four Anhui Party secretaries (Hui Liangyu, Wang Taihua, Guo Jinlong, and Wang Jinshan) and three Jiangsu Party secretaries (Chen Huanyou, Hui Liangyu, and Li Yuanchao).[21] These seven provincial Party secretaries, as well as their tenures, average petition and growth outcomes, and subsequent positions (promotions or demotions) are shown in Table 6.1.[22]

Looking at the promotion results as well as the petition and growth outcomes provides an indication of different central emphases in the promotion of provincial leaders. This is a limited sample, so no rigorous results are possible, but the general trend is clear: in Anhui, better petition performance (identified by negative values, or below-average growth) leads to better promotion prospects, regardless of GDP growth, while in Jiangsu, better growth performance leads to better promotion prospects, regardless of petition growth. Figure 6.2 illustrates this result graphically.

[20] See discussion in Minzner (2006). Petition data is sensitive but still more accessible than other data from Provincial Security Bureaus that could proxy for "instability" or societal discontent (Chen 2010).

[21] Petition data is not available at the county level, and only exists publicly for selected provinces in selected years, covering only eight provinces in central and eastern China: in the east, Fujian, Guangdong, Jiangsu, Shandong, and Zhejiang; and in the center Anhui, Henan, and Jiangxi. The data are collected from annual editions of provincial almanacs from 1991 to 2011 (i.e., covering data from 1990 to 2010). The "sample average" referred to in the comparisons references this full eight-province sample.

[22] The promotion/demotion categorizations are somewhat subjective. For instance, Guo Jinlong's lateral move to Beijing Mayor could technically be seen as a demotion, but in reality seems to be a promotion that groomed him for more power (in 2012 he became Beijing Party secretary as well as a Politburo member). Chen Huanyou's move to Jiangsu Provincial People's Congress Chairman was clearly a positional demotion, but it could have come mostly as a result of his age (he turned 65 in the year of his promotion). Most other codings are more objective.

TABLE 6.1. *Provincial Party secretaries, growth, and petitions*

Party secretary	Province	Tenure	Petitions[a]	PC GDP[b]	Subsequent post
Hui Liangyu	Anhui	1998–1999	−10.1	−1.3	Promotion (Jiangsu Party secretary)
Wang Taihua	Anhui	2000–2004	6.9	−0.5	Demotion (national propaganda vice min.)
Guo Jinlong	Anhui	2005–2006	−3.4	−2.9	Promotion (Beijing mayor)
Wang Jinshan	Anhui	2007–2009	−0.4	2.8	Demotion (NPC Rural Affairs Dep. Dir.)
Chen Huanyou	Jiangsu	1994–1999	1.5	−0.7	Demotion (JS People's Congress Chairman)
Hui Liangyu	Jiangsu	2000–2002	4.0	1.0	Promotion (Politburo)
Li Yuanchao	Jiangsu	2003–2007	−6.8	1.0	Promotion (Politburo)

[a] Petition growth rate over tenure minus average sample growth rate.
[b] Real per capita GDP growth rate over tenure minus average sample growth rate.

The upper left quadrant represents Party secretaries whose terms coincided with below average per capita GDP growth and higher than average petition growth: in other words, they underperformed across both economic and stability dimensions. Both of these Party secretaries, one from each province, were demoted. The Party secretaries on the right side of the graph experienced above-average growth. In Jiangsu, these two cadres (Hui Liangyu and Li Yuanchao) were both promoted to the Politburo, even though petitions rose much faster than the sample average under Hui. However, the most successful Party secretary in terms of average growth, Wang Jinshan in Anhui, was demoted, while the two Anhui Party secretaries in the lower left quadrant representing below-average economic growth and better petition performance were both promoted. Hui Liangyu personally demonstrates the provincial contrast: after a two-year term in Anhui he was promoted to Jiangsu for a three-year

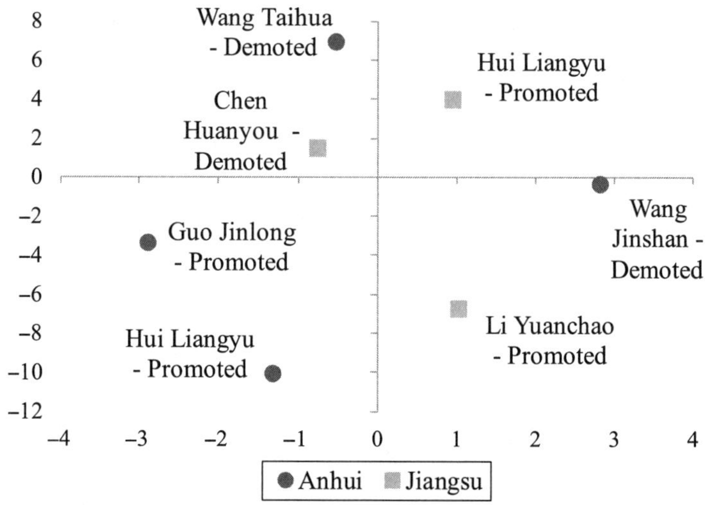

FIGURE 6.2. Growth versus stability outcomes and provincial promotions
Petition growth difference (y axis) versus per capita GDP growth difference (x axis)
Note: Petition growth and per capita GDP growth refer to difference between the average growth rate over leader tenure and the sample average.
Source: Provincial almanacs; China Statistical Yearbook, various years; author's calculations.

term.[23] In Anhui, his term coincided with lower-than-average growth but a huge decline in petitions. In Jiangsu, growth was above-expected, but petition volume increased significantly. In both cases, he was "rewarded" with promotion.

This apparent difference in provincial promotion criteria necessitates a rethinking of the importance of provincial leadership personalities in setting overall provincial development strategies, and it implies that provincial emphases transmitted to counties are actually determined by the national-level CCP. This challenges the idea that provincial incentives to counties are a rational response to conflicting goals set by the center (i.e., the idea that poor provinces may simply be less capable of producing growth, so their rational response is to focus on stability instead). Rather, it appears that the center itself varies promotion decisions across provinces. This has implications for how we perceive provincial leadership personalities. Many provincial leaders in advanced coastal provinces are

[23] Technically this is a horizontal transfer, but given Jiangsu's vastly greater size, such a transfer is widely recognized as a promotion.

identified as "reformers," while provincial leaders in central and western provinces are often identified as being cautious in reform and focused on stability. For instance, Hu Chunhua, or "Little Hu" (i.e., younger protégé of Hu Jintao) was appointed as Guangdong Party secretary in 2012 and now has developed the reputation of being a reformer, but his background in Inner Mongolia, Hubei, and Tibet showed instead a willingness to strictly quell instability: in response to concerns that Hu had overreacted to protests in Inner Mongolia, Hu told the Financial Times, "When we deal with mass incidents, there is no question we will take compulsory measures ... We will be tough when we need to be tough, and we will be soft when we need to be soft."[24] The implication is that provincial Party secretaries are constrained by "institutional momentum" (Cohen 2012); in other words, the center has selected some provinces to grow and reform and other provinces to maintain stability, and selected leaders reflect these emphases.

Let Some Places Get Rich First

Regional variation in promotion criteria content and the selection of leaders without economics backgrounds support the conclusion that poorer central provinces emphasize stability while richer eastern provinces emphasize economic growth. How do we explain this result, which contradicts the "conventional wisdom" of "GDP worship" (*chongbai*, 崇拜) across Chinese local governments? Part of a focus on stability over growth may be a "stages of development" problem, whereby the center has determined that poorer places may not have the capacity or leisure to focus on growth, with more pressing problems at hand. There is indeed an indication that as counties and provinces develop, the economic criteria for promotion become more important. In a sense, this follows from Barrington Moore's hypothesis that as development increases, political

[24] This conclusion follows Cohen (2012), who writes regarding Wang Yang and Hu Chunhua: "This trend should also give us some pause before rooting for Wang or Hu as reformers – neither of their records shows particularly bold action before traveling to Guangdong, so to some extent Wang's liberal policies in the southern province may simply reflect institutional momentum. In fact, besides his time in Tibet, Little Hu initiated a harsh crackdown at the first signs of protests in Inner Mongolia in the spring of 2011." Wang Yang is seen as a major reformer who pioneered a "Guangdong model of development"; indeed, he oversaw important reforms when heading both Chongqing and subsequently Anhui. But Wang rose up in Anhui (Tongling City and then the provincial government office), where the focus was entirely different.

decision making becomes based more on rational-technical criteria, an idea that Stewart et al. (1972) found had validity across regions within the Soviet Union.[25] For instance, there is an indication that in the mid 1990s Subei counties were focused on veto targets rather than economic growth. Jiang Guoxing, the former Suining County Party secretary, recalls the difference between Subei and Sunan counties that he realized while still Party secretary of Jurong county-level city in Southern Jiangsu, before transferring north to Suining:

> I remember at a "Three Represents study meeting" with all the province's county Party secretaries, Li Yuanchao asked, "As secretaries, what do you most want to accomplish, what are the most intractable issues, what problem do you most want to solve?" One cadre's response left the biggest impression: "put the one-child policy first." Right after he said it, everyone laughed out loud, but I also realized then that northern Jiangsu still had a county like Suining. Personally, I said to concentrate on investment attraction, which was well received and cadres asked me to speak longer. (Wang 2006)

But as this quote shows, while in some sense poor Subei counties had similar nongrowth foci, leadership was incentivized to change this state of affairs. When Jiang arrived in Suining, "We therefore immediately implemented the 'four firsts': development is the first task, investment attraction is the first matter, industrialization is the first plan, government service is the first responsibility" (Wang 2006). Even in Southern Jiangsu, there may have been a shift in county development emphases over time. In a 1996 interview, a different former Party secretary of Jurong (county-level) City discussed the importance of petition work, saying it was the first issue he focused on when in office: "grasping petitions means grasping stability, and grasping the entire situation; petition work isn't the work of the petitions department, but rather the work of every leader" (Zhu and Wen 1996). Consequently, this Party secretary made petition volume the foundation (*yiju*, 依据) of township and department *yibashou* evaluations.[26]

[25] Stewart et al. (1972, 1283) find that in the least developed *oblasti*, links with Politburo-Secretariat members explains over 14 percent of variance in mobility, while in developed *oblasti* industrial performance explains a larger share of mobility variation, leading to a conclusion that "when the post-Stalin era is analyzed as a whole, the most important variable in each region is essentially that predicted by applying Moore's proposition to different levels of development within the Russian republic."

[26] This was effective: In the first year of his initiative, petitions to the province level fell by 33 percent, making Jurong the best performing county in Zhenjiang prefecture.

Indeed, in this sense, the Anhui emphasis on stability has the potential to evolve into an emphasis on growth, and this may already have begun, particularly in and around the capital, Hefei. Smith (2009) refers to interviews at the Anhui Academy of Social Sciences to conclude that, "Taking their cue from Zhejiang and Jiangsu, since 2005 the Anhui provincial government has exerted pressure on county leaders to attract private and government investment." And in a similar vein to the "stages of development" idea, there is evidence that poorer provinces may be more likely to emphasize city development over county development. Recall the growth regressions in Chapter 2, which showed that across China, county growth rates were negatively correlated with the growth rate of the prefecture urban core. In that sense, there is a possibility that the stability emphasis is just a county phenomenon. For instance, Xuzhou City in Subei does seem to emphasize county growth more in recent years, likely as a result of the provincial emphasis on Subei counties catching up: see the 2010 introduction to "100 strong" counties and Xuzhou plans for changing from a "strong city weak county" model to a "strong counties make Xuzhou strong" model, and also the 2005 Xuzhou Yearbook, which highlights as a key annual development that county industrial value added exceeded city industrial value added for the first time. However, it is not clear that this is just a poor province versus rich province dichotomy – central Jiangxi has one of the most county-focused developmental strategies in all of China. Nor is it clear that city and county growth must be mutually exclusive.

More broadly, the "stages of development" idea has been explicit in national development plans throughout the reform era: the CCP has a long history of "letting some places get rich first." The center is able to directly affect local development outcomes by directing investment and preferential policies that allow certain regions to benefit at the expense of others. This was particularly apparent in the Mao era and Deng era. During the Mao era, a planned economy made economic intervention by the center easier, and industrialization of China's northeast and the "Third Front" were explicit regional development foci. In the Deng era, certain regions were given preferential policies in terms of relaxation of government price and regulatory controls and tariffs as well as beneficial province-center fiscal arrangements. This was done intentionally, with recognition that certain regions would prosper before others: at a meeting with a business delegation from the United States in 1985, Deng Xiaoping uttered one of the most (selectively) quoted lines of China's reform era: "Let some places and some people get rich first, leading and helping other places and other people to progressively achieve joint prosperity." Note the direct inclusion of "some places" (*yibufen diqu,* 一部分地区) as well as "some people" (*yibufen ren,* 一部分人).[27] Policies in the 1980s and early 1990s explicitly allowed certain areas to have pro-growth preferential policies and special economic zones. The best discussion of these preferences is in Wang and Hu (1999), whose title is self-explanatory: *The Political Economy of Uneven Development*. The findings here update their conclusions: as explicit policy and fiscal preferences have largely equalized between regions (or at least started to converge), the central Party-state has continued to encourage uneven development through the incentives it provides to cadres in different regions. The rationale for Deng in the 1980s was to concentrate efforts in a small place and let these first movers "lead and help" (*daidong he bangzhu,* 带动和帮助) the backwards areas. But mostly these areas have led and helped themselves, and they continue to do so.

Beyond a "stages of development" perception that sees central provinces as incapable of growth, the relationship between economic growth and social instability provides a likely context for the dichotomous central emphases. The center has adopted a "some regions first" strategy as a way to maximize both national growth as well as national stability. In the economic growth literature, many papers identify a negative effect of instability on growth, but the more relevant relationship here is instead the effect of economic growth on instability.[28] Olson (1963) and Huntington (1968) were among the earliest social scientists arguing that growth itself causes instability. Olson notes that the poor are as unlikely to start a revolution as the rich, quoting Hoffer that there is a "conservatism of the destitute as profound as the conservatism of the privileged." Rather, those whose place in the social order is changing might resort

[27] In both English and Chinese the aphorism has simply become "let some people get rich first" (*rang yibufen ren xian fuqilai,* 让一部分人先富起来), although this exact combination of words was never actually uttered by Deng. Searching Google in English for "let some people get rich first" (in quotes) yields 158,000 results; combined searches for "some people and some places get rich first," "some places and some people get rich first," and "some places and people get rich first" yield a total 4231 results. Searching in Chinese enables searches for the untranslated exact quote, which yields 1,090,000 results for "一部分人可以先富起来" versus 193,000 results for the full "一部分地区、一部分人可以先富起来."

[28] For the negative effects of instability on economic growth, see Alesina et al. (1996) and Hibbs (1973).

to revolution. Not only does growth uproot and destabilize traditional social and political structures, but there are a significant number of losers and increases in various forms of unemployment – in China this is most clearly seen in the loss of 40 million jobs as SOEs restructured in the late 1990s and early 2000s.[29] Huntington argues that when the development of political institutions lags behind social and economic change, instability and violence may result. Accepting this argument, a logical explanation for the dichotomous coastal/central cadre management foci is that the CCP fears that an emphasis on growth in undeveloped regions will result in instability; a response is to let some first-movers get rich and make sure that stability reigns elsewhere.

As domestic concerns of instability have mounted, allowing certain places to develop first may therefore be a rational decision. Issues associated with rapid development tend to lead lists of the causes of instability: in particular, land expropriation and environmental degradation result from industrialization and urban development. As one county official bemoaned, "when things get done, bad things can happen," concluding that this explained why local leaders in Anhui did not implement bold economic reforms (Interview JS192). At the local level in particular there seems to be a contradictory relationship between economic development and social stability. County officials recognize the contradictory nature of the goals they are assigned. In Jingbian County (Shaanxi), Chan and Gao (2009) argue that this recognition leads county officials to be more tolerant of township officials not hitting targets (helping to explain the lack of demotions); in other words, in this poorer region, while economic and stability targets coexist, the economic targets are trumped, similar to the Anhui case county experiences described above.[30]

The causes of social discontent have evolved, with important regional implications. In the 1990s, discontent stemmed from SOE/TVE restructuring and agricultural taxation (and other rural problems confronting agriculture, the countryside, and peasants, i.e., the *sannong wenti*, 三农问题). Chen (2012) documents the increase in worker welfare and enterprise restructuring disputes over the 1990s in central China, leading to three times as many petitions in that period as land expropriation. But in the 2000s, environmental concerns and particularly land problems

[29] Note that it might be more accurate to term this job loss as a "reduction in employment," as a significant portion of the lost jobs were due to voluntary and forced early retirement.

[30] Chan and Gao (2009) highlight this contradiction in the targets given to officials in Jingbian, arguing that growth leads to increased migration to the county seat, which leads to increased crime (migrants are responsible for 60 percent of local criminal cases).

became more contentious and important.[31] Land is now the most important source of state-society conflict and discontent, with as many as 65 percent of mass incidents in China stemming from land issues.[32] There are important regional implications of this evolution in state-society conflict. Rural conflicts focusing on tax burden disputes were mainly a central China phenomenon, while land-rights disputes take place more in developed regions that have needed the land for urbanization and industrialization (Yu 2007).[33] This has resulted in a shift from the concentration of mass incidents in central China to a concentration in coastal China: in the 1990s, central China had relatively more "instability," but in recent years the coastal region has.[34] Additionally, different sources of conflict have different consequences: according to Yu (2007): "... in the past, peasants mainly resorted to *shangfang* (petitioning high-level government authorities to appeal against unfair local government behavior), or propagandizing their cause and refusing to pay taxes. In land-rights disputes, however, they choose demonstrations, parades, or other forms of civil disruption including sit-ins (*jingzuo*) at the doorstep of government buildings or on highways and railways to obstruct the flow of key transportation." This implies that land expropriation may be a more problematic concern for overall stability than rural issues.

Although the central focus on letting some regions grow first may be rational, it is short-sighted from both an economic *and* a stability perspective. Economic growth can have destabilizing consequences, but the implied Huntington relationship does not remain linear and positively sloped forever; rather, initial stages of economic growth may be destabilizing, but at a certain point continued growth should become a socially stabilizing force. If we accept the Huntington argument, then

[31] See the 2012 Mass Incident Research Report (2012, 年群体性事件研究报告) for a breakdown of current sources of conflict. Some land-based discontent arises from legal expropriation, meaning that land-rights conflicts stem from both legal and implementation problems (Chen 2006).

[32] A rural problems research task force at the Chinese Academy of Social Sciences found that in the first six months of 2004, of 62,446 phone complaints to central media, 15,312 reflected rural land issues (24.5 percent of the total) – much higher than the share for any other category – and of 623 petitioners who came to Beijing and were successfully interviewed from 6/14/2004 to 7/15/2004, 463 dealt with land issues (73.2 percent). In the first half of 2004, of 130 mass incidents, 87 (66.9 percent) were based on land issues.

[33] Yu (2005) finds that in terms of petition frequency, the majority of land problems are concentrated in economically advanced coastal regions.

[34] Wedeman (2009) uses a locational coefficient in his dataset of mass incidents to identify the relative frequency of regional mass incidents, finding that while in the 1995–1999 period, the center had over twice as many relative incidents (central region locational

petition volume should rise in tandem with economic growth before leveling off and falling when state capacity suffices. Already in China, there are some indications that the instability in coastal regions has begun to peak, with new (and potentially less tumultuous) causes of state-society conflict.[35] An example from Xuyi County, Jiangsu, highlights the potential inverted-U relationship between growth and stability. Wang Youfu served as Xuyi County Party secretary from December 2000 through June 2006, a period in which Xuyi took off economically through industrialization and urban development. As discussed in Chapter 4, Wang was known for his boldness and direct style: he was the Party secretary with the trademark phrase "act first, discuss later" (*bulun xiangan*, 不论先干) (Wang 2005). Naturally, this style created enemies and detractors as well as supporters. In 2002, Wang's second full year in office, during a period of rapid economic transformation and growth, petitions grew almost three-fold year-on-year.[36] In subsequent years, however, they rapidly fell, and Wang is now remembered as a bold reformer rather than a socially destabilizing leader.[37] Similarly, when Suining County's economic reforms picked up the pace in the early and mid 2000s, the county was known for its societal discontent: the "label" (*biaoqian*, 标签) by which Suining was most famous to outsiders was "Suiningers are litigious" (*suiren haogong*, 睢人好讼), referring to the high volume of local petitions and lawsuits (M. Yang 2010). But after several years of rapid growth, in recent years petitions have declined and Suining has become known more for institutional reforms than local litigiousness.

Using provincial data on petitions and per capita GDP, the expected inverted-U relationship between growth and petitions holds. This brief analysis uses the same petitions data as discussed above. As the simple univariate regression results in Table 6.2 and the chart in Figure 6.3 show,

coefficient of 1.60 versus 0.64 for the coastal region), by 2005–2009 the relative regional frequencies had reversed (coastal region locational coefficient of 1.29 versus 0.82 for the central region).

35 For instance, Fewsmith (2013, 12–13) finds that in poor Sichuan Province state-society friction generally arises between impoverished peasants and local cadres over land requisition and taxation, while in wealthy Zhejiang Province, "a growing entrepreneurial class, particularly those who are party members, has increasingly argued that its views need to be taken into account."

36 Xuyi Almanac, various years.

37 This was the same general path that Qiu He experienced in Shuyang County, as indicated by the previously quoted local citizen who initially engaged in frequent petitions before determining that "It seems that at that time, I was backward. I couldn't see as far as Qiu He" (quoted in Fewsmith 2013).

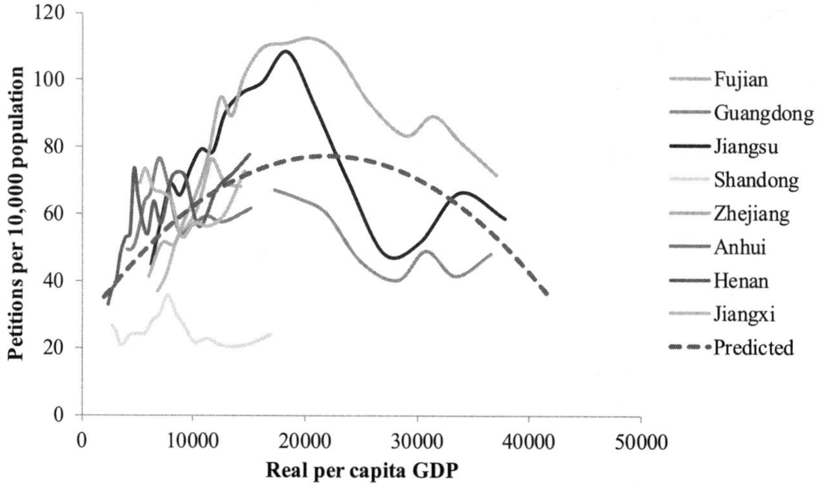

FIGURE 6.3. Visualizing petition frequency and economic development
Source: Provincial Almanacs, various years; author's calculations.

there is a strong negative quadratic relationship between per capita GDP and petition volume. Regardless of whether year and/or province fixed effects are included, petition volume seems to peak between 20,000 and 25,000 RMB per capita (in 2000 constant RMB). All central provinces remain below this inflection point (Anhui per capita income reached only 15,072 by 2010), implying that, for them, increased growth may indeed go hand in hand with instability. The predicted values in the graph below come from the fixed effect model with year dummies. The rich coastal provinces are all in red, while the poorer central provinces are in yellow. All of these poorer central provinces are still on the upward part of the curve: more growth can be expected to lead to more discontent.

Given the inverted-U relationship between economic development levels and discontent, as well as the varying growth/promotion relationships in richer eastern and poorer central provinces, it is reasonable to expect that the central Party-state provides a different set of incentives to leaders of the two sets of provinces. But this is short-sighted: the central Party-state no doubt expects all provinces to develop at some point, and getting over the "instability hump" sooner rather than later might be more effective. By focusing more on stability in poorer regions, the center delays and lengthens this process, and in the meantime incentivizes less

TABLE 6.2. *Regression results: petition frequency and economic development*

	(1)	(2)	(3)	(4)
	Petitions Per 10,000 Provincial Residents			
Real per capita GDP (1000 RMB)	4.655***	3.733***	3.361***	3.224*
	(0.869)	(0.652)	(0.942)	(1.892)
Real per capita GDP squared	−0.106***	−0.0892***	−0.0703***	−0.0697**
	(0.0221)	(0.0140)	(0.0223)	(0.0285)
Constant	26.14***	19.49**	15.35***	16.05
	(5.465)	(8.512)	(2.691)	(34.91)
Province FE	No	Yes	No	Yes
Year FE	No	No	Yes	Yes
Observations	109	109	109	109
R-squared	0.251	0.720	0.351	0.835
Implied inflection point (RMB per capita)	21,958	20,925	23,905	23,128

Robust standard errors in parentheses.

*** p<0.01, ** p<0.05, * p<0.1

attention to economic outcomes in these provinces that in turn results in worse institutional and governance outcomes.

Consequences of Stability-Based Promotion Incentives

The contention here is not that poor provinces are incentivized to prevent economic development, but rather that the incentive to ensure stability inadvertently conflicts with pro-growth development strategies. An emphasis on stability maintenance in the promotion of local leaders leads to poor governance and to low growth. Low-growth provinces and counties therefore remain poor and continue to emphasize stability maintenance in promotion decisions. The emphasis on stability maintenance has two immediate effects: it disincentivizes local leaders to implement creative and/or courageous ideas, and it enhances the importance of patronage in promotion decisions for the reasons highlighted earlier, namely the inability for sufficient yardstick comparison of leader achievements across a binary yes/no stability maintenance variable. As identified in Chapter 4, low degrees of creativity and lack of courage will prevent the emergence of good governance through innovative and or/bold institutional reforms. Without institutional reforms and with leaders' lack of courage to "shake things up" locally, localities will not develop high degrees of control over local cadres; combined with the added importance of patronage in promotion decisions, this incentivizes (or at least fails to disincentivize) further corruption. A lack of pro-growth policies leads directly to lower growth, and poor governance leads indirectly to lower growth through lower levels of investment and firm efficiency, as highlighted in Chapter 3. Most of these processes have been analyzed already in the book: the lower degree of cadre control and higher incidence of corruption in Anhui was a focus of Chapter 3, as were the effects of poor governance on growth; Chapters 3 and 4 also highlighted lower levels of institutional innovation in Anhui; and Chapter 4 demonstrated leader effects on local economic policies. Below, I provide additional evidence that Anhui and noncoastal provinces are less innovative and bold with regard to institutional reforms, and that they select economic policies and fiscal priorities that do not maximize growth.

Regional Differences in Levels of Institutional Innovation and Reform

Chapter 4 argued that a key ingredient for local development arose from bold innovations of the county Party secretary. Jiangsu has produced its fair share of courageous leaders who pursue economic growth and development without regard for local opinion. For instance, Wang Tianqi in Suining instituted bold, nationally recognized institutional reforms to control local cadres, limit corruption, and increase government transparency. This reform, as well as other institutional/administrative reforms that successfully rein in cadre behavior, have the potential to improve pro-growth governance, local investment, and growth.

China's decentralized growth model in the reform era has emphasized the importance of local experimentation: some of this experimentation is directly sanctioned and encouraged by the central government: for example, the Shanghai Free Trade Zone that has gotten so much press in 2013/2014. Other experimentation is locally driven, with successful experiments subsequently adopted more broadly.[38] There is a debate on whether less or more developed areas are more likely to experiment with institutional reforms. Fewsmith (2013) concedes that, "Local authorities

[38] This locally driven experimentation can be driven by local governments as well as forced onto local governments by local citizenry.

do not experiment with political reform in places where heightened tensions are such that the experiments might spin out of control," but then argues that Sichuan used political reform as a provincial strategy to gain recognition from the center: "because the province was too poor to impress central authorities through economic growth, political reform became an alternate strategy." Similarly, Saich and Yang (2003) note that while it is generally accepted that institutional innovations are more likely to occur once a certain degree of economic development has been attained, poor localities have often experimented with reforms as a consequence of local crisis: "it is interesting to note that a number of key innovations in China since the 1970s have occurred in less economically developed areas" (Saich and Yang 2003, 186).[39] One important example is Provincial Party Secretary Wan Li's decision to eliminate communes in post-Mao Anhui.

The conventional wisdom is correct: while poorer areas have indeed initiated some institutional and political reforms, such reforms seem to have predominantly been a developed region phenomenon. A likely explanation is that for every successful reform, other reforms may go "too far" or backfire; risk-averse officials in less developed areas that focus on stability do not want to take the risk. Beyond the discussions in Chapters 3 and 4 that identify higher levels of institutional innovation in the Jiangsu case counties than the Anhui case counties, there are many additional examples of innovative reforms at the local level in developed regions, often initiated by local leaders trying to gain notice or improve local outcomes. These include some of the most radical institutional/political reforms in China: county-level participatory budgeting (Wenling, Zhejiang), marketization (Shunde, Guangdong), the Service Promise System (Yantai, Shandong).[40] Additionally, administrative

[39] They analyze experimentation in 1998 with direct elections in three townships, two in Sichuan and one in Shenzhen. As additional evidence they cite the household responsibility system and the villagers' committee elections, with the former initiated in Anhui and the latter begun in Guangxi. Their explanation is that: "First, local governments in many poor areas lack the revenue to meet basic public needs or to respond to crises. This can create the need to innovate with existing institutions ... Second, local communities in poorer areas may be less riven by interest groups and the forces of pluralism. This may facilitate consensus building about alternative solutions. Third, innovation initiated by government might be accepted more readily. Local societies might not have much information about alternatives, especially if migration is not particularly significant. Under these circumstances the combination of remoteness would allow for more experimentation ..."

[40] Wenling County in Zhejiang has been at the forefront of participatory budgeting, with experimentation in Xinhe (新河镇) and Zeguo (泽国镇) townships. Zeguo randomly

reforms are often initiated by the need for smoother economic operations, and these types of concerns are often more relevant in more advanced economic regions. Zeguo's Party secretary admitted with regard to the participatory budgeting experiment: "Although I gave up some final decision-making power, we gained more power back because the process has increased the legitimacy for the choice of projects and created public transparency in the public policy-making process. Public policy is therefore more easily implemented" (He 2011). Similarly, Foster (2006) describes the impetus for Service Promise System reforms in Yantai as a way to prevent the phenomenon of "hard to get in the door, hard to deal with the bad attitude of officials, and hard to get things done." This was part of the "administrative openness" (*zhengwu gongkai,* 政务公开) movement that had become popularized at the turn of the millennium as a way to promote more efficient administrative (Huang 2000).

Data on the Local Governance Innovation Awards (discussed in Chapter 3) enables a more rigorous look at the regional distribution of local institutional reforms. Every two years since 2000, the China Center for Comparative Politics and Economics, the Comparative Research Center for the Party of the Central Party School, and the Center for Chinese Government Innovations of Peking University have jointly given out local governance innovation awards (*zhongguo difang zhengfu chuangxin jiang,* 中国地方戏横幅创新奖). The topics for innovation include "political transparency, civil society organizations, democratic elections, self-governance, integrity, public hearings, poverty alleviation, political participation, administrative services, and etc." Winners are awarded 50,000 RMB, and public agencies from the township level and higher can apply. Looking at the regional distribution of these awards, it is clear that the awards have been given predominantly to local governments on the coast, even controlling for population and number of county-level units (the central and Western regions have more county-level units than the coast as well as larger overall populations). This is seen in Figure 6.4. The contrast between coastal and central China is particularly stark; while 67 coastal-region governments were awarded or nominated for prizes between 2000 and 2010, only 11 central-region governments were. Moreover, according to Yang

selects citizens to oversee capital construction project decisions. See Fewsmith (2009); Cabannes and Ming (2013). For Shunde reforms, see Xu (2011). See also a 2003 Wenzhou (Zhejiang) campaign to "improve the way in which bureaucrats treat citizens" (Foster 2006, 221).

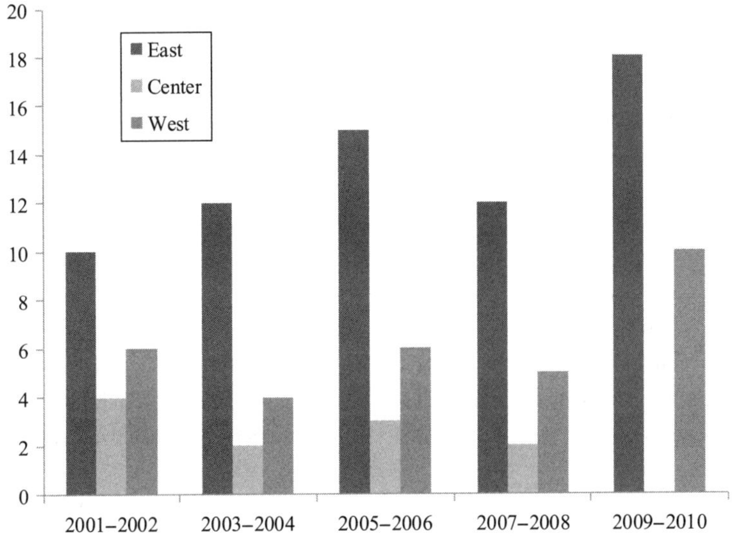

FIGURE 6.4. Governance innovation concentrated on east coast
Number of winners and nominees of "Chinese Local Governance Innovation Prize"
Source: Innovations & Excellence in Chinese Local Governance (中国地方政府创新奖), 2013 handout; author's calculations.

(2013), the majority of these local government "innovators" see the goal of governance innovation as boosting local government efficiency, and 23 out of 92 finalists involving innovations in public administration specifically focused on attracting outside capital and improving the local economy, the largest of any category. In other words, local governance innovations are concentrated in coastal China and they are seen primarily as a way to boost local government capacity in the pursuit of economic efficiency. This supports the divergent findings in the Anhui and Jiangsu case counties.[41]

Regional Differences in Economic Policy Choices

Stability-based promotion incentives also inadvertently result in policy choices that are less explicitly pro-growth. Indeed, at the most basic

[41] This analysis has conflated innovations that can be reasonably considered "political reforms" and innovations that aim to reduce local tensions or enhance local efficiency by providing some new service. Many of the innovations discussed here in coastal areas fall into this latter category, while innovations in poorer provinces (e.g., Sichuan) have perhaps been more focused on genuine political reform. I thank an anonymous reviewer for this insight.

level, a focus on stability may prevent cadres even from doing their own work: one township deputy mayor in Sichuan, another poor province, notes that "I'm not a 'stability maintenance expert' … but stability maintenance takes up most of my energy. From my own experience, every year I spend four months on stability maintenance (*weiwen*, 维稳), two months preparing inspection materials, and two months in meetings and studying, which leaves at most four months to do real work (*gan zhengshi*, 干正事)" (Xiao 2013). More systematically, the case county examples demonstrate the lack of pro-growth policies in Anhui, where local cadres and businesses identified a cadre environment that involved simply implementing provincial decisions and not pushing the envelope. For instance, with regard to investment promotion work, one interviewee explained that this work started very late in Anhui (officially not until 2001 in every county throughout the province). In 2004 the center allowed every county to have a province-level development zone, which were then developed over the next few years – but again there was no local decision or initiative (Interview AH104). Although one would think that every county getting a development zone at the same time would lead to massive competition that could determine county winners and losers, the interviewee said that while there was some competition, for the most part investment relies on city-determined "policy directions" (*fazhan dingwei*, 发展定位). For instance, Mingguang focuses on refrigerators and other white goods as a result of Chuzhou City policies, whereas counties in Wuhu City all focus on car parts. In Jiangsu, counties were much more likely to take the initiative on new strategic directions.

More compelling cross-county evidence comes from fiscal decisions. Fiscal decisions directly reflect local government developmental priorities. If counties/provinces are more concerned with stability and less concerned with economic growth, we should expect to see fiscal expenditure concentrated relatively more on categories that prevent local discontent and fiscal revenue sourced from areas that do not cause discontent. For instance, as discussed above, land expropriation and environmental protection are two of the most important sources of local mass incidents. Governments concerned about stability should therefore invest relatively more in environmental protection and rely relatively less on revenues from land expropriation.

County-level fiscal data can help determine if fiscal priorities differ between Jiangsu and Anhui by running the following two regressions on a set of expenditure and revenue categories:

$$ExpCat_{it} = \alpha_1 \cdot Anhui_i + \beta ExpTot_{it} + \beta \mathbf{X}_{it} \left(+\varphi_t\right) + \epsilon_{it} \qquad (6.1)$$

$$RevCat_{it} = \alpha_2 \cdot Anhui_i + \beta RevTot_{it} + \beta \mathbf{X}_{it} \left(+\varphi_t\right) + \epsilon_{it} \qquad (6.2)$$

Here, a separate regression is run for each expenditure (6.1) and revenue (6.2) category as a share of GDP, $ExpCat_{it}$ and $RevCat_{it}$, respectively. $Anhui_i$ is a dummy variable taking value one for Anhui province counties; $ExpTot_{it}$ and $RevTot_{it}$ are total expenditure and revenue as a share of GDP. $\mathbf{X}_{it}$ refers to a set of additional control variables, and φ_t are year fixed effects.[42] Year effects are included whenever possible, but for certain expenditure categories data only exist for one year (2007). The coefficients of interest, α_1 and α_2, demonstrate the magnitude and significance of the Anhui dummy variable. In determining how relative fiscal priorities differ between Jiangsu and Anhui, it is essential to control for both total expenditure and revenue as well as per capita income. If national or provincial governments have minimum expenditure requirements on the environment, for instance, then we would expect poor governments to spend "more" on the environment.[43] In the regressions below, I include both log per capita GDP and population as additional controls. Regressions were also run controlling for the industrial share and urbanization rate: the results were very similar and are not reproduced here.

The discussion here implies that local governments in stability-focused regions will concentrate revenue collection on areas less likely to spark discontent (e.g., state asset revenue rather than land conversions or agricultural taxes and fees), and they will focus expenditure on areas that may limit discontent (e.g., environmental spending, agricultural support). Specifically, county fiscal categories of interest include expenditure on environmental protection and revenue from land transactions,[44]

42 Note that we cannot use county fixed effects as this would make the Anhui dummy perfectly collinear and therefore prevent analysis of the variable of interest.

43 A natural objection is that Anhui and poorer central provinces were seen as the foci of rural discontent, leading to abolition of the agricultural tax. But note that this may conflate a wealth-correlated result with regional variation – poor agricultural counties were concentrated in the center and thus more likely to have agricultural taxation. In analyzing county expenditure priorities and revenue sources, cross-provincial variation will arise from both county-level decisions and provincial decisions; national mandates on social expenditure should have constant effects by wealth.

44 Note that at the county level, the title deed (or contract) tax (*qishui*, 契税) is the only regularly reported revenue from land transactions, which covers taxation from all transfers of fixed assets. Other land-related taxes and fees, including the urban land use tax (*chengshi tudi shiyong shui*, 城市土地使用税), land value-added tax (*tudi zengzhi shui*,

TABLE 6.3. *Anhui and Jiangsu county differences in revenue and expenditure categories*

	(1)	(2)	(3)	(4)	(5)
	Expenditure	Revenue	Revenue	Revenue	Revenue
	Environ. Protection	*Land transactions*	*Administrative fees*	*Penalties*	*State assets*
Anhui dummy	0.113***	−0.0674***	0.178**	−0.0700**	0.144*
	(3.84)	(−3.76)	(2.05)	(−2.38)	(1.77)
Expend./GDP	0.00685*				
	(1.74)				
Revenue/GDP		0.0493***	0.0611***	0.0200***	0.0847***
		(18.49)	(3.12)	(6.47)	(5.08)
Log PC GDP	0.00596	0.0133	−0.158***	−0.109***	0.0584
	(0.35)	(1.11)	(−3.77)	(−6.53)	(1.04)
Population	0.0321	−0.0291**	−0.129	−0.0652**	0.0909*
	(1.33)	(−2.19)	(−1.40)	(−2.28)	(1.68)
Constant	−0.151	0.0908	2.110***	1.497***	−1.207*
	(−0.58)	(0.63)	(2.99)	(5.81)	(−1.86)
Years	2007	2005–2007	2007	2007	2007
Year FE	No	Yes	No	No	No
Observations	113	339	111	113	113
R-squared	0.225	0.592	0.268	0.285	0.289

Robust standard errors; t statistics in parentheses.

*** $p<0.01$, ** $p<0.05$, * $p<0.1$. Note that the time periods vary, as the *National Prefecture and County Finance Statistics Yearbooks* do not consistently include the same categories, and post-2007 no longer include granular fiscal categories. All regressions include the maximum number of years with available data.

administrative fees, penalties/confiscations, and state assets (and SOEs).[45] If local governments in Anhui attempt to prevent discontent, even at the expense of economic growth, then environmental protection expenditure should be relatively high and land-based revenue should be relatively low.

土地增值税), arable land occupation tax (*gengdi zhanyong shui,* 耕地占用税), and land transfer fee (*tudi churang jin,* 土地出让金), are not reported at the county level.

45 To look at state asset and SOE revenue, I combine the operation income of state-owned assets (*guoyou xiben jingying shouru,* 国有资本经营收入) and income from the use of state-owned resources (*guoyou ziyuan (zichan) youchang shiyong shouru,* 国有资源（资产）有偿使用收入). Note that I do look at public security expenditure. Public security expenditure includes spending on public security (and state security), procuratorate, courts, and justice. So although we would expect public security spending itself to be relatively higher in Anhui, the other included categories should increase with institutionalization and the rule of law, which would imply higher relative spending in Jiangsu.

Anhui counties would be expected to earn *less* from potentially contentious penalties/confiscations and *more* from potentially growth-reducing red tape (administrative fees). Similarly, they should earn more from state assets due to less privatization and restructuring of local state firms (due to both fear of unemployment as well as diminished incentives to reap the economic efficiency gains from restructuring).

Table 6.3 reports regression results for all of these fiscal variables. The coefficient for the Anhui dummy is presented in the first row. The results support the story. As expected, controlling for total expenditure/revenue shares of GDP, per capita income, and population, Anhui counties spend more on environmental protection, and their revenue relies less on land transactions and penalties and more on administrative fees and state assets. In other words, Anhui counties spend more money on a category with high potential for public disturbance, and they collect less revenue from categories that could ignite public discontent (land and penalties), depending instead on red tape (administrative fees) and existing state assets.

Conclusions

This chapter has demonstrated that the counterpart to a lack of pro-growth incentives for promotions in Anhui and central China can be found in stronger promotion incentives for stability maintenance. This stability maintenance incentive is transmitted down the administrative hierarchy from the central Party-state, and it results in less courageous and less innovative local leadership as well as fewer pro-growth economic and fiscal policy choices. Consequently, this focus on stability over economic growth has weakened local governing capacity and lowered the potential for political reform and innovative governance, although it has also had positive effects (e.g., greater efforts at environmental

Indeed, the sample counties spend very similar expenditure shares on this category (between 4 and 7 percent of total expenditure in all six case counties), although slightly larger in the three Jiangsu case counties (5.9 percent versus 4.6 percent). Much of this has to do with greater institutionalization in Jiangsu, which has more courts and more cases handled, rather than more attention to local policing and public order management. For instance, Jiangsu in 2010 had over twice as many registered lawyers (11,903 versus 5019), as well as many more mediators (226,714 versus 139,366). Additionally, most criminal cases are larceny (over 75 percent in both provinces): disturbing public order accounts for less than 1 percent of total cases in both provinces: 6528 in Jiangsu and 5710 in Anhui. (All of the data in this paragraph are from the Jiangsu and Anhui 2011 provincial yearbooks.)

protection). Moreover, the focus on stability may not even be effective. Without the growth incentive spurring efforts to improve local investment environments, local corruption becomes more likely, undermining efforts to win local support. Indeed, local citizens appear more dissatisfied with local governments in Anhui than in Jiangsu, despite fiscal decisions that seemed designed to effect the opposite outcome.[46]

[46] Of course, there are many disgruntled people in Jiangsu as well. One local taxi driver referred to the local Party secretary as "a central Party dog," and when I told him I was studying economic development at the county level, he told me (twice): "Don't listen to anything they tell you, understand?"

7

Conclusion: A New Political Economy of Uneven Regional Development

We are now ready to answer the questions posed in the first chapter: *What is the role of county Party secretaries in determining local governance and growth outcomes?* China's county-level economic growth is highly capital-intensive and dependent on successful investment attraction efforts. These efforts are contingent on local pro-growth governance that helps firms by reducing the costs of government failures and by ameliorating market failures. County Party secretaries wield high degrees of local control, and their efforts largely determine local governance and investment attraction outcomes. County Party secretaries use *connections* to senior government officials and outside firms to attract investment and preferential policies; they ensure pro-growth governance through *control* over the local bureaucracy; and they initiate institutional reforms and county marketing tactics that require *creativity* and *courage*.

Why do county Party secretaries emphasize particular developmental priorities? China's personnel management systems, built on upward accountability, successfully transmit upper-level priorities down to the county level and largely shape the behavior of local leaders. In provinces that emphasize stability in their counties, county Party secretaries concentrate their efforts on preventing destabilizing incidents. In provinces that emphasize economic growth in their counties, county Party secretaries concentrate their efforts on policies and institutional reforms that will attract investment and boost growth.

In terms of the two provinces selected for in-depth analysis, Jiangsu, a wealthy coastal province, and Anhui, a poorer inland province, emphasize different criteria in their evaluations of county Party secretaries. Despite publicized changes in emphasis away from growth "quantity" and towards growth "quality," Jiangsu continues to promote its county Party secretaries on the basis of economic success. Anhui, which needs all the growth it can get, instead promotes county leaders based on stability maintenance. These promotion emphases are a direct consequence of differential implementation of the two primary central Party-state mandates: growth and stability. The center has rewarded Jiangsu (and other wealthy province) leaders who pursue and achieve economic growth, and it has rewarded Anhui (and other poor/central province) leaders who maintain stability. Although the central Party-state no doubt would *rather* have growth *and* stability in both regions, its risk-averse strategy has been to continue to let some regions develop first. As a consequence of this incentive structure as well as the relationship between leaders and growth and between governance and growth in China's counties, county leaders and governments in Anhui have been less innovative institutionally, have had worse governance, have made less bold economic decisions, and have achieved worse economic outcomes; counties in Jiangsu have vastly outperformed their Anhui counterparts since the mid 1990s. The argument can be summed up in Figure 7.1 and Figure 7.2, representing the vicious and virtuous circles resulting from different promotion emphases.

This book makes contributions across several areas of study: the relationship between local governance and local growth, the role of local

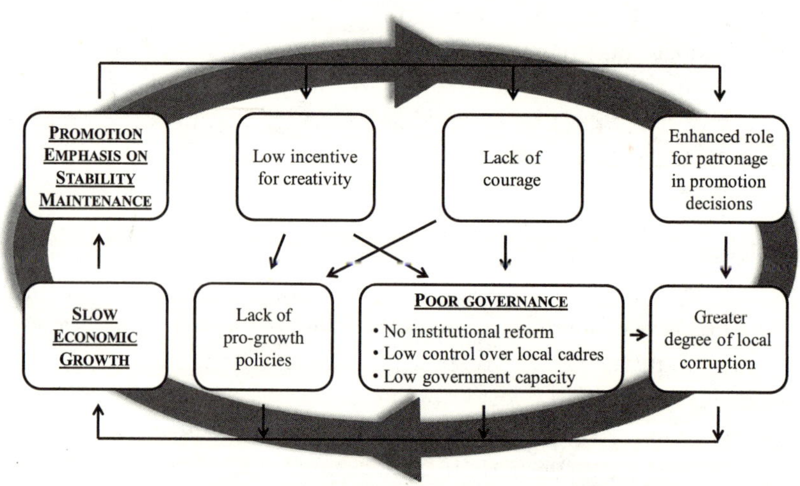

FIGURE 7.1. The vicious circle of stability-based promotion incentives, poor governance, and low growth

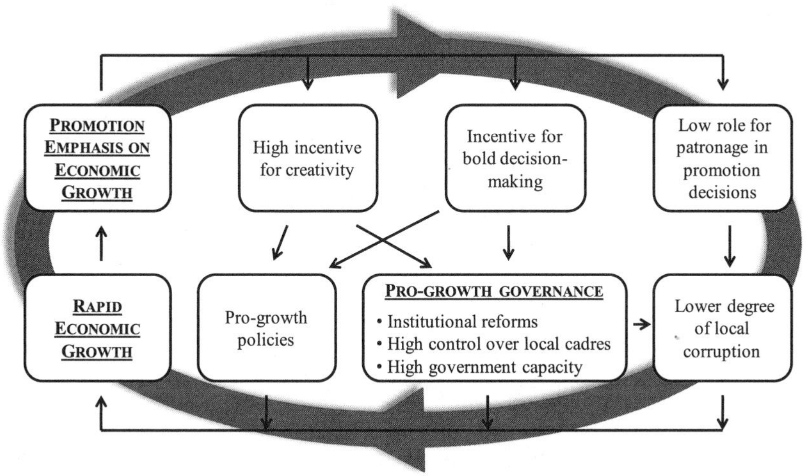

FIGURE 7.2. The virtuous circle of growth-based promotion incentives, good governance, and high growth

leaders in economic and institutional development, and the developmental efficacy of upward accountability. There are several additional implications. For the China studies field, it is important to note that the cliché of GDP growth at all costs is not universal; in identifying regional differences, the book both confirms and challenges the assumption that GDP growth is at the top of all local official rankings. Moreover, although the pursuit of GDP does have many unintended negative consequences, it may also have unintended positive consequences. Additionally, there are important implications for understanding central-local relations: China has a functioning meritocracy that effectively transmits policies and developmental priorities down the administrative hierarchy. For studies of economic development more broadly, there are important implications regarding the determinants of pro-growth governance as well as implications for the developmental capacity of upwardly accountable local autocracies: China's Party-state has achieved many of its intended objectives through meritocratic promotions, although the adaptability of the current system is not clear.

This research both challenges and confirms the assumption of "GDP worship" that pervades the study of China's economic growth and local politics. The cliché of the "blind pursuit of GDP growth" at all costs is not universal; it holds in some regions but not all. In enabling an identification and comparison of one province that has growth-based promotion incentives and one province that does not, this book sheds important light on a long-running debate over the consequences of GDP worship in an upwardly accountable political environment. As suggested by the conventional wisdom, growth-based incentives have many unintended negative consequences; however, such growth-based incentives also have unintended positive consequences, and it is unclear if alternative promotion criteria or even downward accountability would have been able to achieve similar social and developmental outcomes, to say nothing of growth outcomes.

The pursuit of GDP growth enshrined in an upwardly accountable system results in many local pathological behaviors and potentially sub-optimal social outcomes. Minzner (2009) puts the problem aptly: "China's leaders' existing strategy for addressing the principal-agent problems at the heart of the Chinese bureaucracy is itself the cause of many governance problems that they seek to address." Demonstrating the lack of attention to local citizenry, one popular saying in Anhui in the 1990s went: "Your promotion does not depend on my begging; my begging does not affect your promotion" (Zhou 1996).[1] Many studies of social problems arising from cadre behavior focus on the pursuit of GDP growth: for instance, Bernstein and Lu (2003, xv) note that peasant burdens "were the product of a well-entrenched approach to development that set performance targets irrespective of local capacities to meet them ... and that rewarded officials for achievement, not questioning the methods used." Similarly, Fan et al. (2009) find that social welfare is missing in bureaucrats' promotion formula and that education and health care are "sacrificed" to prop up local GDP. Poor environmental outcomes are also associated with the GDP focus. Several studies have found that economic incentives for local officials lead to large local implementation gaps in the enforcement of environmental regulations, contributing to China's growing environmental challenges (He et al. 2012; Ran 2013). Indeed, the fiscal analysis in Chapter 6 showed that where pro-growth promotion incentives were replaced by pro-stability incentives, expenditure on environmental protection rose. The existence of "race to the bottom" tax policies due to interjurisdictional competition to boost

[1] "So long as officials are only responsible to their superiors and not the people they supposedly serve, and as long as the people have no means to attain justice for themselves through democratic elections as stipulated in the constitution, nor oversight from the National People's Congress or an independent judiciary, a bottom-up system of self-government will not replace the top-down performance evaluation system, and the rights of Chinese citizens will continue to be arbitrarily violated by those wielding power over the public" (Zhang 2010).

growth has resulted in lower local revenue, which further hurts social outcomes through lower social expenditures.[2]

Yardstick evaluation based on GDP growth also leads to economic pathologies, particularly over-investment at the expense of consumption. China's growth model has been based on excessive domestic investment, and an intended switch to domestic consumption as a source of growth has thus far proved fairly elusive; part of the difficulty has been aligning local government incentives to pursue consumption rather than investment. As Zhu Hanqing from the Quzhou Party School notes, the "Chinese characteristics tournament promotion model" dictates that GDP competition will be based on boosting investment rather than consumption, leading to an "excessive (*jigao,* 畸高)" investment rate (Zhu 2011). Officials in the counties I visited referred to the "three disorders (*san luan,* 三乱)" in investment attraction: every investment is sought out, even those that have already failed locally (*luan zhaoshang,* 乱招商); if investment comes from outside, accept it no matter what (*zhao luanshang,* 招乱商); and accept all possible investments to boost evaluations (*zhaoshang luan,* 招商乱). Such overinvestment leads to inefficient allocation and bubble-type euphoria. In Xuyi, for the price you could buy a downtown apartment just a few years ago, you now cannot even rent for a year, and plans are underway to build a 300-meter skyscraper and a five-star hotel (Interview JS207). Consequently, worries of a bubble based on excessive debt have started to grow. Since the central crackdown on lending, locals have started to worry, and there are now upwards of 50,000 square meters of empty unsold apartments in Xuyi. In Suining, several recent investments seem to have been "over-euphoric," including a factory built to resemble the White House and a chateau built to resemble a European castle. One mover and shaker in the informal finance field (self-described as working in "private finance") assured me that everything I saw (cars, houses, factories, etc.) was bought on debt, and it "will not end well" (Interview JS262). Such debt is also frequently (and correctly) attributed to growth-based promotion competitions (Zhang 2011).

[2] A "race to the bottom" and regulatory arbitrage to attract investment ironically hurts overall potential for revenue generation even while benefiting individual localities – in other words, tax breaks and cheap land make sense for local growth and revenue collection, as they may lead to lower short term revenue but will bring industrial investment and future revenue – so it is rational for each locality to engage in this race to the bottom. Break (1967, 23–24) argues that in an environment in which local governments compete for business, governments will not set tax rates higher than in surrounding areas, or will decrease effort in tax collection: "Active tax competition, in short, tends to produce either a generally low level of state-local tax effort or a state-local tax."

These frequently identified problems with the pro-growth incentive structure are acknowledged by the research here, but the book also suggests unexpected positive impacts on local governance and institutional reform. Some complaints levied against the growth model go too far. For instance, corruption is often blamed on the growth pursuit, but whereas China's political system with upward accountability enables corruption, the results here imply that the pursuit of GDP may not result in higher levels of corruption than a pursuit of stability: indeed, counties studied here that pursued GDP growth tended to have lower levels of corruption that often reflected government-business collusion, while counties that pursued stability instead tended to have more prosecuted cases of corruption, which more frequently related to the buying and selling of offices and did more to undermine trust in the system.[3] More importantly, the growth pursuit appears to have incentivized local leaders and local governments to improve local investment climates through governance improvements. Many of these improvements are private goods available only to a subset of firms, but other institutional improvements benefit the broader public. Chen and Xu (2011) controversially argue that in China's early development phase, a tournament competition that made economic growth the basis of competition was not only good for growth, but actually was the governance model with the most potential to increase social welfare. This is because public good preferences were weak and also because asymmetric/incomplete information problems arose as a consequence of undeveloped channels for public expression.[4] Although this book does not focus on local public goods provision, it does demonstrate much higher levels of fiscal revenue and expenditure in growth-pursuing counties, which undoubtedly helped boost social welfare and likely improved social outcomes compared to alternative promotion criteria.

This has implications for the debate on China's capacity for administrative adaptation or atrophy. The findings in this book implies that central capacity to control local outcomes (or at least developmental emphases) remains strong, and also that a pro-growth incentive has resulted in

[3] This is of course not to say that upward accountability is better than downward accountability for preventing corruption. Indeed, a large body of evidence has shown that elections can serve as a disincentive to corruption (Ferraz and Finan 2008, 2011; Banerjee et al. 2010). However, even in democracies, decentralized developing economies often experience collusive rent-seeking between local business elites and politicians that harms nonconnected and weaker portions of the local population (Duflo et al. 2006).

[4] Chen and Xu (2011) further argue that in more recent years a change to a model of public provision of social welfare/insurance requires a shift in the tournament promotion model towards competition based on "harmony" (*hexie*, 和谐).

Appendix 1: Interview Methodology

The fieldwork conducted for this project consisted of six months of fact-finding interviews from October to December 2012 and April to June 2013. In addition to interviews with local officials and citizens, case study analysis also benefited from the collection of local documents and media related to finance, local economic conditions, and government work plans. Interviews with think tanks, professors, and research institutes in Nanjing (Jiangsu), Bengbu (Anhui), and Beijing helped provide greater context and theory. In the case counties, interviews were predominantly ethnographic in approach rather than journalistic, "soaking and poking" rather than targeting pointed questions.[1] All interviews were conducted in Chinese (local dialects in the case counties are mutually intelligible with standard Mandarin). A total of 97 interviews/conversations were conducted: 55 with government officials, 33 with private sector investors and businesses, and 9 with academics and think tank researchers. These interviews were complemented by numerous informal conversations with local citizens. Interviews consisted of both formal open-ended interviews and more informal conversations, including many held during meals. Most of the 55 government interviews were conducted with officials in economic or industrial bureaus: finance, taxation, investment promotion, industry, and urban management. Others were conducted with finance- and investment-related officials within functional bureaus (e.g., culture, transportation). The interviews were predominantly held with county

[1] As described by Leech (2002, 665): "The journalistic style tries to verbally pin the respondent down by appearing to know everything already. The questions are direct and directed toward a particular outcome. The ethnographic style of interviewing instead tries to enter the world of the respondent by appearing to know very little."

officials, although I also interviewed a handful of township and village officials. In terms of level of access, I interviewed many bureau chiefs, but no Party secretaries themselves (a deputy magistrate and a deputy Party secretary were the highest positions with whom I interacted). Problems arising from a lack of direct access to county Party secretaries were mitigated by access to local documents and local media, including speeches and interviews using the county Party secretaries' own voices. Due to the sensitivity of many interviews, all are coded and assigned randomly generated values between 101 and 299, which are reported along with the province, Jiangsu (JS), Anhui (AH), or Beijing (BJ), for example JS146 or AH279.

Appendix 2: Data Description

Quantitative analyses at both the national and regional level are based on five sets of county-level data: general economic data, detailed fiscal data, census data, geographic data, and county leadership biographies. The extent of these data is unique. At the national level, basic economic data come from annual editions of the *China County-Level Socio-Economic Data Yearbook* 《中国县(市)社会经济统计概要》. These data, over the years 1996–2010, have been compiled for easy download by the China Data Center at the University of Michigan. County-level economic data for Jiangsu and Anhui come from annual editions of provincial statistical yearbooks, with data for 1993, 1994, and 1995, as well as data on fixed asset investment, sourced from annual editions of the Anhui Almanac, Jiangsu Almanac, Anhui Statistical Yearbook, and Jiangsu Statistical Yearbook. Except where noted, all economic data are deflated using provincial GDP deflators from annual editions of the China Statistical Yearbook, and quantities are presented in 2000 constant *renminbi* (RMB). Provincial petitions (*xinfang*, 信访) data used in Chapter 6 are found in annual editions of provincial yearbooks over 1990–2010.

Fiscal data comes from editions of the *National Local Public Finance Data* 《全国地市县财政统计资料》, and includes detailed revenue, expenditure, and fiscal transfer data for every county-level administrative unit in China. This volume is published annually, but only in hard copy. For this reason, relatively few economic analyses have made use of the full data.[1] Collection of these data were limited to Jiangsu and Anhui

[1] Zhang and Shih (2008) and Zhang (2006) include multiple years of analysis based on the full data.

TABLE A.1 *Biographical summary statistics*

	Observations (Mean, Std.Dev.)		
	Total	Anhui	Jiangsu
Unique County – Year	2023	1037	986
Unique County – county Party secretary	637	351	286
Unique county Party secretary[a]	606	333	273
Gender (0=Male, 1=Female)	471 (0.03, 0.16)	239 (0.03, 0.16)	232 (0.03, 0.17)
Age	446 (47.2, 4.2)	225 (46.2, 3.9)	221 (48.2, 4.2)
Master's Degree (1=yes)	405 (0.44, 0.50)	197 (0.36, 0.48)	208 (0.51, 0.50)
Home Province (1=same as employment)	407 (0.90, 0.30)	197 (0.89, 0.32)	210 (0.91, 0.28)
Home Prefecture (1=same as employment)	407 (0.58, 0.49)	197 (0.48, 0.50)	210 (0.67, 0.47)
Home County (1=same as employment)	365 (0.09, 0.28)	183 (0.04, 0.19)	182 (0.14, 0.35)
Previous Post	522	281	241
Subsequent Post	598	313	285

Note: Biographical data observations are listed per unique county-leaders only.

[a] Several Party secretaries serve in multiple counties.

over 1995–2007 (the 2008–2009 yearbooks have been released, but they have very limited data categories, and more recent yearbooks had not been released as of 2013).

Census and geographic data come from the *China Fifth Population Census Data* 《中国2000年第五次县级人口普查数据》. The census data for 1982, 1990, 2000, and 2010 includes detailed population and employment data for all counties in China. The matched geographic data include county land area, as well as county distance from economic centers, from borders, and from the coast. The data are available on CD and are easily manipulated using ArcGIS software.

Finally, and most importantly, biographical data cover all counties and county-level cities in Jiangsu and Anhui over 1994–2010, sourced from a combination of online databases, national, provincial, prefecture/city, and county almanacs (*nianjian*, 年鉴) and statistical yearbooks (*tongji nianjian*, 统计年鉴), in addition to comprehensive internet searches using both Baidu and Google.[2] In addition, for 22 provinces in China (all provinces excluding autonomous regions and province-level municipalities), basic data consisting of the names and tenures of county leaders (Party secretaries and magistrates) have been compiled based on annual provincial yearbooks.[3] The year 1994 is selected as a starting point because of the fiscal and administrative reforms of the early 1990s. Insufficient data are available pre-1994 to enable a comparison of these two broadly defined reform era periods, so starting in 1994 maximizes the time period over which we would expect to observe a relatively stable tournament promotion system. In total, the Jiangsu and Anhui database consists of 2023 county-year observations of county Party secretaries between 1994 and 2011. This covers every available county-year for which economic data exist.[4] Biographical data include age, gender, ethnicity, year of Party entry, hometown, education, previous employment experience, and subsequent employment. Descriptive statistics are shown in Table A.1. Overall, there are 637 uniquely matched county and county Party secretary observations, 286 in Jiangsu across 58 counties, and 351 in Anhui across 61 counties. Note that these are not unique leader observations, as Jiangsu has 13 Party secretaries who serve in multiple counties during the sample and Anhui has 18. While every county-year has a leadership observation, biographical observations are less complete; for instance, data on subsequent positions exist for 94 percent of the sample, but data on hometown and education are only available for 64 percent. Given that more successful cadres are more likely to have their biographies available online, this missing data will have a bias towards less successful leaders.

[2] I also acknowledge the generosity of Dr. Bo Zhiyue for allowing me to check my own promotion codings against his database of Jiangsu leader promotions, which was particularly helpful for early years in the sample.

[3] This national tenure and turnover data was compiled in collaboration with Dr. Monica Martinez-Bravo with help from research assistants at Johns Hopkins SAIS. Additional data on prefecture-level leaders for the *gaopei* analysis in Chapter 6 come from Jiangsu and Anhui prefecture/city yearbooks.

[4] In the cases when a county or county-level city became a county-level district over the sample period (1994–2011), I only include the observations prior to the administrative reclassification.

To my knowledge, no other research has used similarly detailed and complete county-level economic and biographical data. National county name data has only been used by Guo (2007, 2009), and this was over a shorter period.[5] In addition to the longer time coverage, this dataset improves on Guo (2007) in two important ways. First, and most importantly, the inclusion of biographical information rather than just office-holder name allows for the inclusion of a more robust set of control variables and more detailed information on employment history and promotion results. Second, the provincial almanac name lists tend to record office-holders as of December 31st of the previous year. The natural standard is to assume that the leader in the year *t* yearbook served in year *t-1*. Yet given turnover dates distributed throughout the year, this rule misidentifies leaders in nearly half of all cases.[6] The data here consider a leader-year observation as one in which a leader serves for over half the year. In the case where no leader serves for over half a year (e.g., one Party secretary is replaced in May and his successor does not take office until August), the year is "given" to the Party secretary who spends more time in office.

5 Guo looked at 1997–2002, excluding Tibet, Sichuan, and Chongqing.

6 Party secretary terms are most likely to start in November–April (66 percent), corresponding with national and provincial Party and People's Congresses. Over 43 percent begin their terms in the second half of the year, and 15 percent begin their terms in December.

Bibliography

Abrams, Scott, and Fergus Murphy. 2005. "The Design and Implementation of Local Development Strategies: The Case of Central and Eastern Europe." In *Local Governance and the Drivers of Growth*, 232–264. Paris: OECD Publishing.

Acemoglu, Daron, and James Robinson. 2012. *Why Nations Fail: The Origins of Power, Prosperity, and Poverty*. New York: Crown Business.

Acemoglu, Daron, and Melissa Dell. 2010. "Productivity Differences between and within Countries." *American Economic Journal: Macroeconomics* 2 (1): 169–188.

Acemoglu, Daron, Simon Johnson, and James A. Robinson. 2001. "The Colonial Origins of Comparative Development: An Empirical Investigation." *The American Economic Review* 91 (5): 1369–1401.

Adams, Renee B., Heitor Almeida, and Daniel Ferreira. 2005. "Powerful CEOs and Their Impact on Corporate Performance." *The Review of Financial Studies* 18 (4): 1403–1432.

Aidt, Toke S. 2009. "Corruption, Institutions, and Economic Development." *Oxford Review of Economic Policy* 25 (2): 271–291.

Akai, Nobuo, and Masayo Sakata. 2002. "Fiscal Decentralization Contributes to Economic Growth: Evidence from State-Level Cross-Section Data for the United States." *Journal of Urban Economics* 52: 93–108.

Alesina, Alberto, Suze Ozler, Nouriel Roubini, and Phillip Swagel. 1996. "Political Instability and Economic Growth." *Journal of Economic Growth* 1 (2): 189–211.

Allison, Graham, and Philip Zelikow. 1999. *Essence of Decision: Explaining the Cuban Missile Crisis*, second edition. New York: Longman.

Almond, Gabriel, and Sidney Verba. 1963. *The Civic Culture: Political Attitudes and Democracy in Five Nations*. Princeton University Press.

Alperovich, Gershon. 1984. "The Economics of Choice in the Allocation of Intergovernmental Grants to Local Authorities." *Public Choice* 44: 285–296.

Alt, James E., and Kenneth A. Shepsle. 1990. *Perspectives on Positive Political Economy*. Cambridge University Press.

Anhui Provincial Organization Department. 1998. "A Research Report on Improving the System to Promote and Demote Party and Government Officials (推进党政领导干部能上能下问题研究报告)." In *Selected Essays on Organizational Work, Part I (组织工作研究文选)*, 335.

Anhui Provincial Party Committee and Anhui Provincial Government. 2008. "Opinions on Implementing the Scientific Development Concept to Promote Faster and Better County Economic Development (关于贯彻落实科学发展观促进县域经济又好又快发展的若干意见)." *Anhui Provincial Government Reports, 2008, #10*. May 3. 15–18.

Armstrong, John A. 1959. *The Soviet Bureaucratic Elite: A Case Study of the Ukrainian Apparatus*. New York: Praeger.

Bagehot, Walter. 2009 [1867]. *The English Constitution*. Oxford University Press.

Bai, Chong-en, Yingjuan Du, Zhigang Tao, and Yueting Sarah Tong. 2004. "Local Protectionism and Regional Specialization: Evidence from China's Industries." *Journal of International Economics* 63 (2): 397–417.

Bai, Yihua. 1995. *Reform and Exploration of China's Grassroots Governance (中国基层政权的改革与探索)*. Beijing: China Social Press.

Bailey, Stephen. 1999. *Local Government Economics: Theory, Policy, and Practice*. Basingstoke, UK: Macmillan.

Bao, Yonghui, and Shousong Xu. 2009. *Political Path: Ten Years of Qiu He (政道：仇和十年)*. Hangzhou: Zhejiang People's Press.

Bao, Zhongsun, Yanpeng Zhang, and Wei Wang. 2000. *The 1998 (Wuxi) Research Report: A Survey on Medium- and Small-Scale Enterprises in South Jiangsu, China*. Jiangsu Academy of Social Sciences and EIM Small Business Research and Consultancy.

Barber, James David. 1972. *The Presidential Character: Predicting Performance in the White House*. Englewood Cliffs, NJ: Prentice-Hall.

Bardhan, Pranab. 1984. *The Political Economy of Development in India*. Oxford: Basil Blackwell.

Bardhan, Pranab, and Dilip Mookherjee. 2006. *Decentralization and Local Governance in Developing Countries: A Comparative Perspective*. Cambridge: MIT Press.

Baretti, Christian, Bernd Huber, and Karl Lichtblau. 2002. "A Tax on Tax Revenue: The Incentive Effects of Equalizing Transfers: Evidence from Germany." *International Tax and Public Finance* 9 (6): 631–649.

Barghoorn, Frederick C. 1966. *Politics in the USSR*. Boston: Little Brown.

Barnett, Doak A. 1967. *Cadres, Bureaucracy, and Political Power in Communist China*. New York: Columbia University Press.

Barro, Robert. 1997. *Determinants of Economic Growth: A Cross-Country Empirical Study*. Cambridge: MIT Press.

1991. "Economic Growth in a Cross Section of Countries." *Quarterly Journal of Economics* 106 (2): 407–443.

Barro, Robert, and Xavier Sala-I-Martin. 1995. *Economic Growth*. Cambridge: McGraw-Hill.

Baum, Richard, and Alexei Shevchenko. 1999. "The 'State of the State'." In *The Paradox of China's Post-Mao Reforms*, edited by Merle Goldman and Roderick MacFarquar, 334–360. Cambridge: Harvard University Press.

Behn, Robert. 2003. "Why Measure Performance? Different Purposes Require Different Measures." *Public Administration Review* 63: 586–606.

Bernstein, Thomas, and Xiaobo Lu. 2003. *Taxation Without Representation in Contemporary Rural China*. New York: Cambridge University Press.

Bertrand, Marianne, and Antoinette Schoar. 2003. "Managing with Style: The Effect of Managers on Firm Policies." *Quarterly Journal of Economics* CXVIII: 1169–1208.

Besley, Timothy. 2007. *Principled Agents? The Political Economy of Good Government*. Oxford University Press.

Bhagwati, Jagdish N. 1982. "Directly Unproductive, Profit-seeking (DUP) Activities." *Journal of Political Economy* 90 (5): 988–1002.

Bian, Zhu. 2009. "Decoding Post-Qiu He County Party Secretaries: Too Much High Profile Cadre Risk Taking (后仇和时代县委书记解读:官员行事高调风险太大)." *Xinmin Weekly*, April 15. http://news.sina.com.cn/c/sd/2009-04-15/175017616302.shtml.

Bird, Richard, and Michael Smart. 2002. "Intergovernmental Fiscal Transfers: International Lessons for Developing Countries." *World Development* 30 (6): 899–912.

Blanchard, Olivier, and Andrei Shleifer. 2001. "Federalism With and Without Political Centralization: China Versus Russia." *IMF Staff Papers* 48.

Blecher, Marc. 1991. "Development State, Entrepreneurial State: The Political Economy of Socialist Reform in Xinju Municipality and Guanghan County." In *The Chinese State in the Era of Economic Reform: The Road to Crisis*, edited by Gordon White, 265–291. Armonk, NY: M.E. Sharpe, Inc.

Blecher, Marc, and Vivienne Shue. 1996. *Tethered Deer: Government and Economy in a Chinese County*. Stanford University Press.

Bo, Zhiyue. 2002. *Chinese Provincial Leaders: Economic Performance and Political Mobility Since 1949*. Armonk, NY: M.E. Sharpe.

2004. "The Institutionalization of Elite Management in China." In *Holding China Together: Diversity and National Integration in the Post-Deng Era*, edited by Barry Naughton and Dali Yang, 70–100. New York: Cambridge University Press.

2009. "Political Mobility of County Leaders in China: The Case of Jiangsu." *Provincial China* 1 (2): 76–96.

Boex, Jameson, and Jorge Martinez-Vazquez. 2005. "The Determinants of the Incidence of Intergovernmental Grants: A Survey of the International Experience." *Andrew Young School of Policy Studies Research Paper Series, Working Paper 06-52*.

Boyne, G. A., O. James, P. John, and N. Petrovsky. 2007. "Happy consumers, loyal voters: Voter reaction to incumbent performance in English local governments, 1999–2006." *57th Political Studies Association Annual Conference*. Bath.

Brady, David, and Michael Spence. 2010. *Leadership and Growth*. Washington, DC: The World Bank.

Bramall, Chris. 2006. *The Industrialization of Rural China*. Oxford University Press.

2008. "Rural Industrialisation and Spatial Inequality in China, 1978–2006." *Economic and Political Weekly* 43 (52): 43–50.

Brandt, Loren, and Xiaodong Zhu. 2000. "Redistribution in a Decentralized Economy: Growth and Inflation in China under Reform." *Journal of Political Economy* 108 (2): 422–439.

Break, George. 1967. *Intergovernmental Fiscal Relations in the United States*. Washington, DC: The Brookings Institution.

Brender, Adi, and Allan Drazen. 2005. "Political Budget Cycles in New versus Established Democracies." *Journal of Monetary Economics* 52 (7): 1271–1295.

Brennan, Geoffrey, and James M. Buchanan. 1980. *The Power to Tax: Analytical Foundations of a Fiscal Constitution*. London: Cambridge University Press.

Brodsgaard, Kjeld Erik. 2010. "Governing Capacity and Institutional Change in China in the Reform Era." *The Copenhagen Journal of Asian Studies* 28 (1): 30–35.

Brzezinski, Zbigniew K., and Samuel P. Huntington. 1964. *Political Power: USA/USSR*. New York: Viking.

Bulman, David, and Aart Kraay. 2012. "Thirty Years of Growth in China: Accumulation, Reallocation, and TFP Growth, 1978–2008." In *Background paper for China 2030: Building a Modern, Harmonious, and Creative Society*, edited by World Bank. Washington, DC: World Bank.

Bunce, Valerie. 1981. *Do New Leaders Make a Difference? Executive Succession and Public Policy Under Capitalism and Socialism*. Princeton University Press.

Burns, John P., and Xiaoqi Wang. 2010. "Civil Service Reform in China: Impacts on Civil Servants' Behaviour." *The China Quarterly* 201: 58–78.

Cabannes, Yves, and Zhuang Ming. 2013. "Participatory Budgeting at Scale and Bridging the Rural-Urban Divide in Chengdu." *Environment and Urbanization* 26 (1): 1–19.

Cai, Fang, Dewen Wang, and Yang Du. 2002. "Regional Disparity and Economic Growth in China: The Impact of Labor Market Distortions." *China Economic Review* 13 (2–3): 197–212.

Cai, Hongbin, and Daniel Treisman. 2005. "Does Competition for Capital Discipline Governments? Decentralization, Globalization and Public Policy." *American Economic Review* 95 (3): 817–830.

2006. "Did Government Decentralization Cause China's Economic Miracle?" *World Politics* 58: 505–35.

Cai, Hongin, Hanming Fang, and Lixin Colin Xu. 2005. "Eat, Drink, Firm, Government: An Investigation of Corruption from Entertainment and Travel Costs of Chinese Firms." *NBER Working Paper 11592*.

Cai, Jane. 2006. "Minimum Prices for Industrial Land to Rise Next Year." *South China Morning Post*, December 29. www.scmp.com/article/576876/minimum-prices-industrial-land-rise-next-year.

Cai, Yongshun. 2004. "Managed Participation in China." *Political Science Quarterly* 119 (3): 425–51.

Cao, Dagong. 2008. "Mingguang City Passes Delegate Proposal: All Three-Wheeled Vehicles Banned (明光市扎实办理代表议案——正三轮车全部被取缔)." *Jianghuai Law Journal (江淮法治)* 7: 34–35.

Chan, Hon S., and Jie Gao. 2008. "Performance Measurement in Chinese Local Governments." *Chinese Law & Government*, 41 (2–3) 4–9.

2009. "Putting the Cart before the Horse: Accountability or Performance?" *Australian Journal of Public Administration* 68 (Suppl. 1): S51–S61.
Chandler, Alfred Jr. 1962. *Strategy and Structure*. New York: Doubleday.
Chang, Ha-Joon. 2008. *Bad Samaritans: The Myth of Free Trade and the Secret History of Capitalism*. New York: Bloomsbury Press.
Che, Haigang. 2010. "Trial in Making County Committee Power Transparent Expanded Nationally (县委权力公开透明运行试点推向全国)." *Study Times*, November 29. http://theory.people.com.cn/GB/13345388.html.
Chen, Ge. 2006. *One Hand Blocks the Sky: The Cautionary Tale of 18 Fallen County Party Secretaries (一手遮天: 18名县委书记垮掉的警示)*. Beijing: Xinhua Publishing House.
Chen, Guidi, and Chuntao Wu. 2006. *Will the Boat Sink the Water? The Life of China's Peasants*. New York: Public Affairs.
Chen, Guoquan, and Zhenwei Huang. 2010. "Hot Topics in Local Governance Innovation Research and a Preview of Theories." *Zhejiang University Journal (Social Science Version)* 14–25.
Chen, Xi. 2010. "State-generated Data and the Study of Contentious Politics in China." In *Chinese Politics: New Methods, Sources and Field Strategies*, edited by Allen Carlson, Mary E. Gallagher, Kenneth Lieberthal, and Melanie Manion, 15–32. New York: Cambridge University Press.
2012. *Social Protest and Contentious Authoritarianism in China*. Cambridge: Cambridge University Press.
Chen, Xin. 2012. "Government Aims to Close Income Gap with Steady Wage Hike." *China Daily*, February 9. http://usa.chinadaily.com.cn/business/2012-02/09/content_14567594.htm.
Chen, Xiwen. 2006. "Conflicts and Problems Facing China's Current Rural Reform and Development." In *China's Agricultural Development: Challenges and Prospects*, edited by Xiao-yuan Dong, Shunfeng Song, and Xiaobo Zhang, 33–42. Hampshire: Ashgate Publishing.
Chen, Ye, Hongbin Li, and Li-An Zhou. 2005. "Relative Performance Evaluation and the Turnover of Provincial Leaders in China." *Economics Letters* 88 (3): 421–425.
Chen, Zhao, and Tong Xu. 2011. "Moving Towards 'Competition Based On Harmony': Changing Central and Local Governance Models Under Tournament Promotions (走向"为和谐而竞争": 晋升锦标赛下的中央和地方治理模式变迁)." *The Journal of World Economy (世界经济)* 9: 3–18.
Choi, Eun Kyong. 2012. "Patronage and Performance: Factors in the Political Mobility of Provincial Leaders in Post-Deng China." *The China Quarterly* 212: 965–981.
Coase, Ronald H. 1937. "The Nature of the Firm." *Economica* 4 (16): 386–405.
1964. "The Regulated Industries: Discussion." *American Economic Review* 54: 194–197.
Cohen, David. 2012. "The New Hu in Town." *The Diplomat*, December 20. http://thediplomat.com/2012/12/the-new-hu-in-town/.
Colander, David C., ed. 1984. *Neoclassical Political Economy: The Analysis of Rent-Seeking and DUP Activities*. Cambridge, MA: Ballinger.
Cumberland, John H. 1981. "Efficiency and Equity in Interregional Environmental Management." *Review of Regional Studies* 10 (2): 1–9.

Dabla-Norris, Era, and Paul Wade. 2002. "The Challenge of Fiscal Decentralization in Transition Countries." *IMF Working Paper WP/02/103*.

Davoodi, Hamid, and Heng-fu Zou. 1998. "Fiscal Decentralization and Economic Growth: A Cross-Country Study." *Journal of Urban Economics* 43 (2): 244–257.

De Brauw, Alan, and Scott Rozelle. 2008. "Migration and Household Investment in Rural China." *China Economic Review* 19: 320–335.

DeLong, J. Bradford, and Lawrence H. Summers. 1991. "Equipment Investment and Economic Growth." *Quarterly Journal of Economics* 106 (2): 445–502.

Denizer, Cevdet, Daniel Kaufmann, and Aart Kraay. 2013. "Good Countries or Good Projects? Macro and Micro Correlates of World Bank Project Performance." *Journal of Development Economics* 105: 288–302.

Department of Organization. 1989. "Circular on Provisional Implementation of the System of the Annual Performance Evaluation of Party and Government Cadres (中共中央组织部关于实行地方党政领导干部年度工作考核制度的通知)." In *Selection of Documents on Personnel Work, vol. 11 (人事工作文件选编)*, edited by Ministry of Personnel, 119–120. Beijing: Xueyuan Publishing House.

Dickson, Bruce. 2008. *Wealth Into Power: The Communist Party's Embrace of China's Private Sector*. Cambridge University Press.

Dimitrov, Martin K. 2013. "Internal Government Assessments of the Quality of Governments in China." *CDDRL Working Papers Number 126*.

Djilas, Milovan. 1957. *The New Class: An Analysis of the Communist System of Power*. New York: Praeger.

Dong, Weihong. 2013. "Benchmark Land Price in China: Present State and Outlook." *FIG Working Week 2013*. Abuja, Nigeria: International Federation of Surveyors.

Dong, Xueqing, Heping Zhang, and Zeyuan Zhang. 2005. "Who Are We? Interviews with County Party Secretaries (我们是谁？县委书记采访录)." *Outlook Weekly (瞭望新闻周刊)*, November 7.

Downs, Anthony. 1967. *Inside Bureaucracy*. Boston: Little, Brown.

Drazen, Allan. 2001. "The Political Business Cycle after 25 Years." In *NBER Macroeconomics Annual 2000, vol. 15*, edited by Ben Bernanke and Kenneth Rogoff, 75–117. Cambridge: National Bureau of Economic Research.

Duckett, Jane. 1998. *The Entrepreneurial State in China: Real Estate and Commerce Departments in Reform Era Tianjin*. New York: Routledge.

Duflo, Esther, and Raghabendra Chattopadhyay. 2004. "Women as Policy Makers: Evidence from a Randomized Policy Experiment in India." *Econometrica* LXXII: 1409–1443.

Easterly, William, and Ross Levine. 2003. "Tropics, Germs, and Crops: How Endowments Influence Economic Development." *Journal of Monetary Economics* 50 (1): 3–39.

Edin, Maria. 1998. "Why Do Chinese Local Cadres Promote Growth? Institutional Incentives and Constraints of Local Cadres." *Forum for Development Studies* 25 (1): 97–127.

Etzioni, Amitai. 1961. *A Comparative Analysis of Complex Organizations: On Power, Involvement, and Their Correlates*. New York: The Free Press.

Evans, Peter. 1995. *Embedded Autonomy: States and Industrial Transformation*. Princeton University Press.

Evans, Peter, and James E. Rauch. 1999. "Bureaucracy and Growth: A Cross-National Analysis of the Effects of 'Weberian' State Structures on Economic Growth." *American Sociological Review* 64 (5): 748–765.

Fair, Ray C. 1978. "The Effect of Economic Events on Votes for President." *The Review of Economics and Statistics* 60: 159–173.

Fan, C. Cindy. 1997. "Uneven Development and Beyond: Regional Development Theory in Post-Mao China." *International Journal of Urban and Regional Research* 21 (4): 620–639.

Fan, Joseph P. H., Jun Huang, Randall Morck, and Bernard Yeung. 2009. "The Visible Hand Behind China's Growth." *Paper prepared for the Joint NBER-CUHK Conference on Capitalizing China.*

Fei, Guangsheng. 2009. "Impact of Financial Transfer Payment on the County's Economy———Empirical Analysis Based on Cross-Section Data of Anhui Province (财政转移支付对县域经济的影响——基于安徽省截面数据的实证分析)." *Journal of the Gansu Administration Institute (甘肃行政学院学报).*

Feng, Juncheng, Rui Hao, Yang Li, and Kezhong Zhang. 2012. "The Effect of Leadership Transition on Government Expenditure: Evidence from China." *Annals of Economics and Finance* 13 (1): 97–118.

Feng, Shao. 2011. "Introducing a Public 'Happiness Index' into Government Performance Appraisals." *Decision Making and Information* 314: 58.

Ferlie, Ewan, Lynn Ashburner, Louise Fitzgerald, and Andrew Pettigrew. 1996. *The New Public Management in Action.* Oxford University Press.

Fewsmith, Joseph. 2006. "Promotion of Qiu He Raises Questions about Direction of Reform." *China Leadership Monitor* 17.

2009. "Participatory Budgeting: Development and Limitations." *China Leadership Monitor* 29: 1–14.

2013. *The Logic and Limits of Political Reform in China.* Cambridge University Press.

Finkelstein, S., D. C. Hambrick, and A. A. Cannella. 2009. *Strategic Leadership: Theory and Research on Executives, Top Management Teams, and Boards.* New York: Oxford University Press.

Fisman, Raymond, and Roberta Gatti. 2002. "Decentralization and Corruption: Evidence across Countries." *Journal of Public Economics* 83 (3): 325–345.

Flinders, Matthew, and Felicity Matthews. 2007. "Rebuilding Strategic Capacity? Multi-Level Governance, Leadership and Public Service Agreements in Britain." In *Public Governance and Leadership: Political and Managerial Problems in Making Public Governance Changes the Driver for Re-Constituting Leadership*, edited by Rainer Koch and John Dixon, 175–206. Wiesbaden: Deutscher Universitäts-Verlag.

Fornasari, Francesca, Steven Webb, and Heng-Fu Zuo. 2000. "The Macroeconomic Impact of Decentralized Spending and Deficits: International Evidence." *Annals of Economics and Finance* 1 (2): 403–433.

Foster, Kenneth W. 2006. "Improving Municipal Governance in China: Yantai's Pathbreaking Experiment in Administrative Reform." *Modern China* 32 (2): 221–250.

Franzese, Robert J. 2002. "Electoral and Partisan Cycles in Economic Policies and Outcomes." *Annual Review of Political Science* 5 (1): 369–421.

Fried, Morton H. 1953. *Fabric of Chinese Society: A Study of the Social Life of a Chinese County Seat.* New York: Frederick A. Praeger, Inc.

Friedman, Edward, Paul Pickowicz, and Mark Selden. 2005. *Revolution, Resistance, and Reform in Village China.* New Haven: Yale University Press.

Fukuyama, Francis. 2013. "What Is Governance?" *Center for Global Development Working Paper* 314: 1–18.

Gamble, Sidney D. 1954. *Ting Hsien: A North China Rural Community.* New York: International Secretariat, Institute of Pacific Relations.

Gao, Jie. 2009. "Governing By Goals and Numbers: A Case Study in the Use of Performance Measurement to Build State Capacity in China." *Public Administration and Development* 29: 21–31.

Gerschenkron, Alexander. 1962. *Economic Backwardness in Historical Perspective.* Cambridge: Harvard University Press.

Giguere, Sylvain. 2004. "The Drivers of Growth: Why Governance Matters." In *Local Governance and the Drivers of Growth*, 11–38. Paris: OECD Publishing.

Giles, John, Albert Park, and Fang Cai. 2006. "How has Economic Restructuring Affected China's Urban Workers?" *The China Quarterly* 185: 61–95.

Gilley, Bruce. 2004. *China's Democratic Future: How It Will Happen and Where It Will Lead.* New York: Columbia University Press.

Gong, Ronggang. 2000. "Current Situation and Development Measures of Mingguang City Township and Village Enterprises (明光市乡镇企业的现状及发展对策)." *Rural Economy (乡镇经济)* 1: 44–45.

Gradstein, Mark. 2004. "Governance and Growth." *Journal of Development Economics* 73: 505–518.

Greenstein, Fred. 1969. *Personality and Politics.* Chicago: Markham Publishing Company.

Grindle, Merilee. 2012. *Jobs for the Boys: Patronage and the State in Comparative Perspective.* Cambridge, MA: Harvard University Press.

Grossman, Phillip J. 1994. "A Political Theory of Intergovernmental Grants." *Public Choice* 78: 295–303.

Gu, Flora F., Kineta Hung, and David K. Tse. 2008. "When Does Guanxi Matter? Issues of Capitalization and Its Dark Sides." *Journal of Marketing* 72: 12–28.

Guo, Gang. 2007. "Retrospective Economic Accountability Under Authoritarianism: Evidence from China." *Political Research Quarterly* 60 (3): 378–390.

2009. "China's Local Political Budget Cycles." *American Journal of Political Science* 53 (3): 621–632.

Hall, Peter A., and Rosemary C. R. Taylor. 1996. "Political Science and the Three New Institutionalisms." *Political Studies* XLIV: 936–957.

Hall, Robert E., and Charles I. Jones. 1999. "Why Do Some Countries Produce So Much More Output Per Worker Than Others?" *The Quarterly Journal of Economics* 114 (1): 83–116.

Hambrick, Donald C., and Phyllis Mason. 1984. "Upper Echelons: The Organization as a Reflection of Its Top Managers." *Academy of Management Review* 9: 193–206.

Han, Sun Sheng, and Clifton W. Pannell. 1999. "The Geography of Privatization in China, 1978–1996." *Economic Geography* 75 (3): 272–296.

Han, Yong. 2011. "Cadre Year-End Evaluations (官员政绩年终考)." *China Newsweek (中国新闻周刊)* 12: 10.

Han, Zhenmei. 1995. "Cultivating Backbone Financial Resources is Key to a Public Finance Virtuous Circle (培植骨干财源是财政良性循环的关键)." *Public Finance* 11 (364): 32–33.

He, Baogang. 2011. "Civic Engagement through Participatory Budgeting in China: Three Different Logics at Work." *Public Administration and Development* 31: 122–133.

He, Baogang, and Youxing Lang. 2000. "Predicament in Buyun: A Study of the First Direct Election of a Township Head in China." *Twenty-First Century* 64: 125–136.

He, Guizhen, Yonglong Lu, Arthur P. J. Mol, and Theo Beckers. 2012. "Changes and Challenges: China's Environmental Management in Transition." *Environmental Development* 3: 25–38.

He, Haifeng. 2006. "JIangsu Suining County Party Secretary Jiang Guoxing Strongly Breaks Suining's Difficulties (江苏睢宁县委书记蒋国星力破睢宁困局)." *Decision-making* 10: 26–28.

He, Zengke. 2007. "Political legitimacy and innovations in Chinese local government: a preliminary empirical study." *Yunnan Public Administration College Journal* 2: 8–13.

Heilmann, Sebastian. 2008. "From Local Experiments to National Policy: The Origins of China's Distinctive Policy Process." *The China Journal* 59: 1–30.

2008. "Policy Experimentation in China's Rise." *Studies in Comparative International Development* 43 (1): 1–26.

Heimer, Maria. 2006. "The Cadre Responsibility System and the Changing Needs of the Party." In *The Chinese Communist Party in Reform*, edited by Kjeld Erik Brodsgaard and Yongnian Zheng, 122–138. New York: Routledge.

Hibbs, Douglas. 1973. *Mass Political Violence: A Cross-Sectional Analysis.* New York: Wiley and Sons.

Hicks, John Richard. 1932. *The Theory of Wages.* New York: St. Martins.

Ho, Samuel P. S. 1994. *Rural China in Transition.* Oxford: Clarendon Press.

Ho, Samuel P. S., Paul Bowles, and Xiaoyuan Dong. 2003. "'Letting Go of the Small': An Analysis of the Privatisation of Rural Enterprises in Jiangsu and Shandong." *Journal of Development Studies* 39 (4): 1–26.

Holmberg, Sören, and Bo Rothstein. 2012. *Good Government: The Relevance of Political Science.* Cheltenham: Edward Elgar.

Hood, Christopher. 1991. "A Public Management for All Seasons?" *Public Administration* 69: 3–19.

Hook, Brian, Dick Wilson, and Michael Yahuda. 1979. "Quarterly Chronicle and Documentation." *The China Quarterly* 77: 157–216.

Hoover, Edgar M., and Joseph L. Fisher. 1949. "Research in Regional Economic Growth." In *Problems in the Study of Economic Growth*, 173–250. New York: National Bureau of Economic Research.

Horn, Murray J. 1995. *The Political Economy of Public Administration: Institutional Choice in the Public Sector.* Cambridge University Press.

Hsu, Robert. 1991. *Economic Theories in China, 1979–1988*. Cambridge University Press.

Hsu, S. Philip, and Jhih-Wei Shao. 2014. "The Rule-Bound Personnel Turnover of China's Provincial Leaders, 1993–2010." In *Choosing China's Leaders*, edited by Chien-wen Kou and Xiaowei Zang, 97–123. New York: Routledge.

Hsueh, Tien-tung, and Qiang Li. 1999. *China's National Income: 1952–1995*. Boulder: Westview Press.

Hu, Angang, and Yong Guo. 2001. "Comprehensive Strategies of Corruption Control and Institutional Design During Transition (转型期防治腐败的综合战略与制度设计)." *Management World (管理世界)* 6: 44–55.

Hu, Qiwang. 2010. "Comrade Hu Qiwang Speech at the County Investment Promotion Work Meeting (胡启望同志在全县招商引资工作调度会上的讲话)." Wuhe, Anhui, October 2. www.wuhe.gov.cn/DocHtml/1/2012/5/24/201205241525464 65.html.

2012. "Comrade Hu Qiwang Speech at the Opening Meeting of the Wuhe County 16th People's Congress (胡启望同志在五河县第十六届人民代表大会第一次会议闭幕式上的讲话)." 1: 9. www.ahwhedu.com/include/content.php?id=18449.

Hu, Qiwang, interview by Xinhua Anhui Channel (新华网安徽频道). 2012. *Wuhe County Party Secretary Hu Qiwan Discusses "Striving to Become Northern Anhui's Development Pacesetter" (五河县委书记胡启望谈"争当皖北发展排头兵")* (April 10). http://ah.wenming.cn/rwft/201204/t20120410_602788.shtml.

Huang, Bihong, and Kang Chen. 2012. "Are Intergovernmental Transfers in China Equalizing?" *China Economic Review* 23: 534–551.

Huang, Delin. 2000. "Initial Exploration into 'Administrative Openness' ("政务公开"：初探)." *China Administrative Management (中国行政管理)* 1: 28–29.

Huang, Kai-Ping., and Karen Y. Wang. 2011. "How Guanxi Relates to Social Capital? A Psychological Perspective." *Journal of Social Sciences* 7 (2): 120–126.

Huang, Yasheng. 1995. "Administrative Monitoring in China." *The China Quarterly* 143: 828–843.

1996. *Inflation and Investment Controls in China: The Political Economy of Central-Local Relations During the Reform Era*. New York: Cambridge University Press.

Huntington, Samuel P. 1968. *Political Order in Changing Societies*. New Haven: Yale University Press.

Hurst, Jeremy, and Melissa Jee-Hughes. 2001. "Performance Measurement and Performance Management in OECD Health Systems." *OECD Labour Market and Social Policy Occasional Papers* 47.

Hurst, William. 2009. *The Chinese Worker after Socialism*. New York: Cambrdige University Press.

Jacobs, A. J. 2003. "Devolving Authority and Expanding Autonomy in Japanese Prefectures and Municipalities." *Governance* 16 (4): 610–623.

Jacobs, Bruce J. 1999. "Uneven Development: Prosperity and Poverty in Jiangsu." In *The Political Economy of China's Provinces: Comparative and Competitive Advantage*, edited by Hans Hendrischke and Feng Chongyi, 113–154. London: Routledge.

Jian, Da. 2003. "Corruption from Following the Leader's Example (唯'一把手'马首是瞻的腐败)." *People's Daily*, October 29. www.people.com.cn/GB/guandian/1033/2157280.html.

Jiang, Yihe. 2002. "Cao Guoying: The key is to have feeling (曹国英: 关键要有感情)." *Newsweek (新闻周刊)*, April 1.

Jiangnan Times. 2004. "Reform of the Petitions System Starts With Difficulty: "Intercepting Petitioners" Results from Perfromance Evaluation Pressures (信访制度改革艰难启航"劫访"背后是政绩压力)." *Jiangnan Times (江南时报)*, November 16.

Jin, Hehui, Yingyi Qian, and Barry Weingast. 2005. "Regional Decentralization and Fiscal Incentives: Federalism, Chinese Style." *Journal of Public Economics* 89 (9–10): 1719–1742.

Johnson, Chalmers. 1982. *MITI and the Japanese Miracle: The Growth of Industrial Policy, 1925–1975*. Stanford University Press.

1987. "Political Institutions and Economic Performance: The Government-Business Relationship in Japan, South Korea, and Taiwan." In *The Political Economy of the New Asian Industrialism*, edited by Frederic C. Deyo, 136–164. Ithaca: Cornell University Press.

Jones, Benjamin F., and Benjamin A. Olken. 2005. "Do Leaders Matter? National Leadership and Growth since World War II." *Quarterly Journal of Economics* 120 (3): 835–864.

Jorgenson, Dale W. 1991. "Productivity and Economic Growth." In *Fifty Years of Economic Measurement: The Jubilee of the Conference on Research in Income and Wealth*, edited by Ernst R. Berndt and Jack E. Triplett, 19–118. University of Chicago Press.

Joseph, William A., ed. 2014. *Politics in China: An Introduction*, second edition. Oxford University Press.

Kang, David. 2002. *Crony Capitalism: Corruption and Development in South Korea and the Philippines*. Cambridge University Press.

Kaufmann, Daniel, Aart Kraay, and Pablo Zoido-Lobatón. 1999. "Governance Matters." *World Bank Policy Research Working Paper 2196* 1–61.

Kaufmann, Daniel, and Aart Kraay. 2002. "Growth Without Governance." *World Bank Policy Research Working Paper No. 2928*.

Kaufmann, Daniel, and Shang-Jin Wei. 1999. "Does 'Grease Money' Speed Up the Wheels of Commerce?" *World Bank Policy Research Working Paper No. 2254*.

Keefer, Philip. 2007. "Governance and Economic Growth." In *Dancing with Giants: China, India, and the Global Economy*, edited by L. Alan Winters and Shahid Yusuf, 211–242. Washington, DC: The World Bank.

Keen, Michael, and Maurice Marchand. 1997. "Fiscal Competition and the Pattern of Public Spending." *Journal of Public Economics* 66: 33–53.

Keng, Shu. 2010. "Developing into a Developmental State: Explaining the Changing Government-Business Relationships behind the Kunshan Miracle." In *Dynamics of Local Governance in China During the Reform Era*, edited by Tse-Kang Lang and Yun-han Chu, 225–272. Lanham, MD: Lexington Books.

Kennedy, John James. 2007. "From the Tax-for-Fee Reform to the Abolition of Agricultural Taxes: The Impact on Township Governments in North-west China." *The China Quarterly* 189: 43–59.

Khan, Mushtaq. 2008. "Governance and Development: The Perspective of Growth-Enhancing Governance." In *Diversity and Complementarity in Development Aid: East Asian Lessons for African Growth*, edited by GRIPS Development Forum, 107–152. Tokyo: GRIPS Development Forum/ National Graduate Institute for Policy Studies.

King, Gary, Robert Keohane, and Sidney Verba. 1994. *Designing Social Inquiry: Scientific Inference in Qualitative Research.* Princeton University Press.

Klitgaard, Robert. 1988. *Controlling Corruption.* Berkeley: University of California Press.

Knack, Stephen, and Philip Keefer. 1995. "Institutions and Economic Performance: Cross-Country Tests Using Alternative Institutional Measures." *Economics and Politics* 7: 207–227.

Kreuger, Anne. 1990. "Government Failures in Development." *Journal of Economic Perspectives* 4 (3): 9–23.

Krueger, Anne. 1974. "The Political Economy of the Rent-Seeking Society." *The American Economic Review* 64 (3): 291–303.

Krugman, Paul. 1994. "The Myth of Asia's Miracle." *Foreign Affairs* 73 (6): 62–78.

Kuhn, Robert Lawrence. 2010. *How China's Leaders Think: The Inside Story of China's Past, Current and Future Leaders.* Singapore: Wiley.

Lal, Deepak, and Hla Myint. 1996. *The Political Economy of Poverty, Equity, and Growth: A Comparative Study.* Oxford: Clarendon Press.

Lam, Tao-chiu. 1999. "Institutional constraints, leadership and development strategies: Panyu and Nanhai under reform." In *Cities in China: Recipes for Economic Development in the Reform Era*, edited by Jae Ho Chung, 256–295. London: Routledge.

Lampton, David M. 1986. *Paths to Power: Elite Mobility in Contemporary China.* Ann Arbor: University of Michigan Press.

1987. "Chinese Politics: The Bargaining Treadmill." *Issues and Studies* 23: 11–41.

1992. "A Plum for a Peach: Bargaining, Interest, and Bureaucratic Politics in China." In *Bureaucracy, Politics, and Decision Making in Post-Mao China*, edited by Kenneth G. Lieberthal and David M. Lampton, 33–58. Berkeley: University of California Press.

2014. *Following the Leader: Ruling China, from Deng Xiaoping to Xi Jinping.* Berkeley: University of California Press.

Landry, Pierre F. 2008. *Decentralized Authoritarianism in China: The Communist Party's Control of Local Elites in the Post-Mao Era.* Cambridge University Press.

Lardy, Nicholas R. 2014. *Markets over Mao: The Rise of Private Business in China.* Washington, DC: Peterson Institute for International Economics.

Lasswell, Harold D. 1930. *Psychopathology and Politics.* New York: Viking Press.

Lee, C. K. 2007. *Against the Law: Protests in China's Rustbelt and Sunbelt.* Berkeley: UC Press.

Lee, Peter N. S. 2000. "Informal Politics of Leadership Succession in Post-Mao China." In *Informal Politics in East Asia*, edited by Lowell Dittmer, Haruhiro Fukui, and Peter N. S. Lee, 165–182. Cambridge University Press.

Leech, Beth L. 2002. "Asking Questions: Techniques for Semistructured Interviews." *PS: Political Science and Politics* 35 (4): 665–668.

Leff, Nathaniel H. 1964. "Economic Development Through Bureaucratic Corruption." *American Behavioral Scientist* 8 (3): 8–14.

Li, Changping. 2001. *Speaking Truth to the Premier (我向总理说实话)*. Beijing: Guangming Daily Press.

Li, Cheng. 2004. "Political Localism versus Institutional Restraints: Elite Recruitment in the Jiang Era." In *Holding China Together: Diversity and National Integration in the Post-Deng Era*, edited by Barry J. Naughton and Dali L. Yang, 29–69. Cambridge University Press.

Li, Cheng, and David Bachman. 1989. "Localism, Elitism, and Immobilism: Elite Formation and Social Change in Post-Mao China." *World Politics* 42 (1): 64–94.

Li, Guangming. 2010. "Accepting money to give out official positions: Anhui office-selling party secretary sold out all posts in six years (收钱给"官帽"安徽卖官书记6年卖光所有"官帽")." *Legal Daily (法制日报)*, July 22. http://unn.people.com.cn/GB/21674/21717/12218963.html.

Li, Hongbin, and Li-an Zhou. 2005. "Political Turnover and Economic Performance: The Incentive Role of Personnel Control in China." *Journal of Public Economics* 89 (9–10): 1743–1762.

Li, Jian. 2010. "Si County Demolishes Song Dynasty 1000 Year Old Ancient Temple to Construct Commerical Housing (安徽泗县拆北宋近千年古寺建商品房)." *Beijing News (新京报)*, August 17. http://news.sina.com.cn/c/2010-08-17/015317973384s.shtml.

Li, Linda Chelan. 2005. "Differentiated Actors: Central and Local Actors in China's Rural Tax Reforms." *Modern Asian Studies* 40: 151–174.

Li, Qiang. 2010. "What Type of Place is Suining? (睢宁是个什么地方?)." *Commerce Weekly (商周刊)* 26: 90–91.

Li, Shaomin, Shuhe Li, and Weiying Zhang. 1998. "Cross-Regional Competition and Privatization in China." *MOCT-MOST: Economic Policy in Transitional Economies (Economics of Planning)* 9 (1): 75–88.

Li, Shaomin M., and Judy J. Wu. 2010. "Why Some Countries Thrive Despite Corruption: The Role of Trust in the Corruption-Efficiency Relationship." *Review of International Political Economy* 17 (1): 129–154.

Li, Xiaoyun, Sanjeev Ahluwalia, and Dong Qiang. 2013. *Lessons In Public Sector Reform from China*. Washington, DC: The World Bank. http://siteresources.worldbank.org/EXTGOVANTICORR/Resources/3035863-1289428746337/Lessons_PSR_China.pdf.

Lieberthal, Kenneth G. 2004. *Governing China: From Revolution through Reform*, second edition. New York: W.W. Norton & Company.

Lieberthal, Kenneth G., and David M. Lampton. 1992. *Bureaucracy, Politics, and Decision Making in Post-Mao China*. Berkeley: University of California Press.

Lin, Justin Yifu, Mingxing Liu, and Ran Tao. 2013. "Deregulation, Decentralization, and China's Growth in Transition." In *Law and Economics with Chinese Characteristics: Institutions for Promoting Development in the*

Twenty-First Century, edited by David Kennedy and Joseph E. Stiglitz, 467–490. Oxford University Press.

Lin, Tingjin. 2007. "Economic Logic of Political Promotion: Prefectural Mayors of China." *Public Management Research* 5: 45–68.

Linden, Carl A. 1966. *Khrushchev and the Soviet Leadership: 1957–1964*. Baltimore: Johns Hopkins.

Lipset, Seymour Martin. 1959. "Some Social Requisites of Democracy: Economic Development and Political Legitimacy." *The American Political Science Review* 53 (1): 69–105.

Liu, Junjie. 2005. *Development of County Economy and Construction of Small Towns (县域经济发展与小城镇建设)*. Beijing: Social Science Documentation Publishing House (社会科学文献出版社).

Liu, Mingxing, Ran Tao, Fei Yuan, and Guangzhong Cao. 2008. "Instrumental Land Use Investment-Driven Growth in China." *Journal of the Asia Pacific Economy* 13 (3): 313–331.

Londregan, John B., and Keith T. Poole. 1990. "Poverty, the Coup Trap, and the Seizure of Executive Power." *World Politics* 42 (2): 151–183.

Long, Guoying, and Mee Kam Ng. 2001. "The Political Economy of Intra-Provincial Disparities in Post-Reform China: A Case Study of Jiangsu Province." *Geoforum* 32: 215–234.

Lu, Yinqiu, and Tao Sun. 2013. "Local Government Financing Platforms in China: A Fortune or Misfortune?" *IMF Working Paper WB/13/243*.

Lucas, Robert E. 1988. "On the Mechanics of Economic Development." *Journal of Monetary Economics* 22: 3–42.

Ma, Jun, and Zhibin Zhang. 2009. "Remaking the Chinese Administrative State Since 1978: The Double-Movements Perspective." *Korean Journal of Policy Studies* 23 (2): 225–252.

Manion, Melanie. 2004. *Corruption by Design: Building Clean Government in Mainland China and Hong Kong*. Cambridge: Harvard University Press.

Martinez-Bravo, Monica, Gerard Padro i Miquel, Nancy Qian, and Yang Yao. 2011. "Do Local Elections in Non-Democracies Increase Accountability? Evidence from Rural China." *NBER Working Paper 16948*.

Martinez-Vazquez, Jorge, Baoyun Qiao, and Li Zhang. 2007. "The Role of Provincial Policies in Fiscal Equalization Outcomes in China." *GSU International Studies Program Working Paper 07-05*.

Maskin, Eric, Yingyi Qian, and Cheng-Gang Xu. 2000. "Incentives, Information, and Organizational Form." *Review of Economic Studies*, 67 (2): 359–378.

Mauro, Paolo. 1995. "Corruption and Growth." *The Quarterly Journal of Economics* 110 (3): 681–712.

McChesney, Fred S. 1987. "Rent Extraction and Rent Creation in the Economic Theory of Regulation." *Journal of Legal Studies* 16: 10–18.

McCubbins, Mathew, and Thomas Schwartz. 1984. "Congressional Oversight Overlooked: Police Patrols vs. Fire Alarms." *American Journal of Political Science* 28: 165–179.

McNally, Christopher, Hong Guo, and Guangwei Hu. 2007. "Entrepreneurship and Political Guanxi Networks in China's Private Sector." *East-West Center Working Papers* 19.

Menard, Claude, and Mary M. Shirley. 2008. *Handbook of New Institutional Economics*. Berlin: Springer-Verlag.

Mertha, Andrew. 2005. "China's 'Soft' Centralization: Shifting Tiao/Kuai Authority Relations." *The China Quarterly* 791–810.

2008. *China's Water Warriors: Citizen Action and Policy Change*. Ithaca: Cornell University Press.

Migdal, Joel. 1988. *Strong Societies and Weak States: State-Society Relations and State Capabilities in the Third World*. Princeton University Press.

Milgrom, Paul, and John Roberts. 1992. *Economics, Organization and Management*. New York: Prentice-Hall.

Ming, Ying. 1998. "Analysis of the Mingguang Corruption Nest Case (明光窝案透析)." *Supervision in China* 1: 20–22.

Minzner, Carl. 2006. "Xinfang: An Alternative to Formal Chinese Legal Institutions." *Stanford Journal of International Law* 42 (103): 1–92.

2009. "Riots and Cover-Ups: Counterproductive Control of Local Agents in China." *Washington University Faculty Working Paper Series, Paper No. 09-11-01*.

2013. "The Rise of the Security State." *Association for Asian Studies Annual Conference*. San Diego, CA.

Moe, Terry M. 1984. "The New Economics of Organization." *American Journal of Political Science* 28 (4): 739–777.

Money Weekly. 2011. "Investigation into the Collapse of Sihong's High-Interest Loan Market (泗洪高利贷崩盘调查：受害人不敢报案只能苦等)." *Money Weekly (理财周刊)*, August 8. http://bank.eastmoney.com/news/1174,20110808154243037.html.

2011. "Investigation into the Sihong High-Interest Loan Crash: Victims Don't Dare Report, Only Suffer (泗洪高利贷崩盘调查: 受害人不敢报案只能苦等)." *Money Weekly (理财周刊)*, August 9.

Montinola, Gabriella, Yingyi Qian, and Barry R. Weingast. 1995. "Federalism, Chinese Style: The Political Basis for Economic Success in China." *World Politics* 48 (1): 50–81.

Moore, Barrington. 1954. *Terror and Progress USSR: Some Sources of Change and Stability in the Soviet Dictatorship*. Cambridge: Harvard.

Munday, Max. 1990. *Japanese Manufacturing Investment in Wales*. Cardiff: University of Wales Press.

Musgrave, Richard A. 1959. *The Theory of Public Finance: A Study in Public Economy*. New York: McGraw-Hill.

Myrdal, Gunnar. 1968. *Asian Drama: An Inquiry Into the Poverty of Nations*. New York: Pantheon.

Nathan, Andrew. 2003. "Authoritarian Resilience." *Journal of Democracy* 14 (1): 6–17.

Naughton, Barry. 1987. "The Decline of Central Control over Investment in Post-Mao China." In *Policy Implementation in Post-Mao China*, edited by David M. Lampton, 51–79. Berkeley: University of California Press.

2003. "How Much Can Regional Integration Do to Unify China's Markets?" In *How Far Across the River? Chinese Policy Reform at the Millennium*, edited by Nicholas Hope, Dennis Yang, and Mu Yang Li, 204–232. Stanford University Press.

Naughton, Barry, and Dali Yang. 2004. *Holding China Together: Diversity and National Integration in the Post-Deng Era*. Cambridge University Press.

Nee, Victor, and Sonja Opper. 2006. "China's Politicized Capitalism." In *Background paper for Dancing with Giants: China, India, and the Global Economy*. Washington, DC: Institute for Policy Studies and the World Bank.

Ning, Jiayao, Jun Li, and Bin Tian. 2012. "Sub-provincial Fiscal Decentralization and Inter-governmental Relations: A Discussion of "Province Managing County" (省以下财政分权与政府间关系 – 兼论省直管县)." *Sub-National Fiscal Research (地方财政研究)* 2: 30–36.

Niskanen, William A. 1971. *Bureaucracy and Representative Government*. Chicago: Aldine Press.

North, Douglass. 1990. *Institutions, Institutional Change and Economic Performance*. Cambridge University Press.

North, Douglass, John Joseph Wallis, and Barry R. Weingast. 2009. *Violence and Social Orders: A Conceptual Framework for Interpreting Recorded Human History*. Cambridge University Press.

O'Brien, Kevin, and Lianjiang Li. 1995. "The Politics of Lodging Complaints in Rural China." *The China Quarterly* 143: 756–783.

O'Donnell, Guillermo. 1998. "Horizontal Accountability in New Democracies." *Journal of Democracy* 9 (3): 112–126.

Oates, Wallace E. 1972. *Fiscal Federalism*. New York: Harcourt Brace Jovanovich.

Obstfeld, Maurice. 1998. "The Global Capital Market: Benefactor or Menace?" *Journal of Economic Perspectives* 12 (4): 9–30.

O'Donnell, Guillermo. 1999. *Counterpoints: Selected Essays on Authoritarianism and Democratization*. University of Notre Dame Press.

OECD. 2003. *Managing Decentralisation: A New Role for Labour Market Policy*. Paris: OECD Publications.

Oi, Jean C. 1992. "Fiscal Reform and the Economic Foundations of Local State Corporatism in China." *World Politics* 45 (1): 99–126.

1999. *Rural China Takes Off: Institutional Foundations of Economic Reform*. Berkeley, CA: University of California Press.

Oldenburg, Philip. 1987. "Middlemen in Third-World Corruption: Implications of an Indian Case." *World Politics* 39 (4): 508–535.

Olson, Mancur. 1963. "Rapid Growth as a Destabilizing Force." *The Journal of Economic History* 23 (4): 529–552.

Pan, Xinming. 2012. "Sihong: "Three Concentrations" Are in the Rapid Advance Phase (泗洪："三个集中"，正是满帆快进时)." *Suqian Daily (宿迁日报)*, August 17. www.sihong.gov.cn/art/2012/8/17/art_2637_97516.html

Pande, Rohini. 2011. "Can Informed Voters Enforce Better Governance? Experiments in Low Income Democracies." *Annual Review of Economics* 3: 215–237.

Parish, William, and Martin King Whyte. 1978. *Village and Family in Contemporary China*. University of Chicago Press.

Parkinson, Michael. 2004. "Local Strategies in a Global Economy: Lessons from Competitive Cities." In *Local Governance and the Drivers of Growth*, edited by OECD, 135–174. Paris: OECD Publishing.

Pei, Minxin. 1994. *From Reform to Revolution: The Demise of Communism in China and the Soviet Union*. Cambridge: Harvard University Press.

2006. *China's Trapped Transition: The Limits of Developmental Autocracy*. Cambridge: Harvard University Press.

Peng, Guohua. 2006. "Analysis of the Craze of Visiting Ministries to Lobby for Money and of Lobbying for Official Appointment (对"跑部钱进""跑官"成风的分析)." *People's Daily*, August 18: 9.

Ploss, Sidney. 1965. *Conflict and Decision-Making in Soviet Russia: A Case Study of Agricultural Policy, 1954–1963*. Princeton University Press.

Pollitt, Christopher, and Geert Bouckaert. 2011. *Public Management Reform: A Comparative Analysis of NPM, the Neo-Weberian State, and New Public Governance*. Oxford University Press.

Porter, Michael. 1990. *The Comparative Advantage of Nations*. London: Macmillan.

Posner, Richard A. 1975. "The Social Costs of Monopoly and Regulation." *Journal of Political Economy* 83 (4): 807–827.

Pratt, John W., and Richard Zeckhauser. 1991. *Principals and Agents*. Boston: Harvard Business School Press.

Prud'homme, Remy. 1995. "The Dangers of Decentralization." *The World Bank Research Observer* 10 (2): 201–220.

Przeworski, Adam, Susan C. Stokes, and Bernard Manin,. 1999. *Democracy, Accountability, and Representation*. Cambridge University Press.

Pye, Lucian. 1981. *Dynamics of Chinese Politics*. Cambridge, MA: Oelgeschlager,Gunn & Hain.

Qi, Kan. 1996. "Things That Were Caused by Evaluation and Ordering (由评价、排序而引起的……)." *China Statistics* 4: 18.

Qi, Xiangdong. 2013. "Development Zone Three Platforms Help Suining SMEs Develop (睢宁经开区三大平台助中小企业发展)." *China County Times (中国县域经济报)* 98. www.xyshjj.cn/bz/xyjj/lb/201312/67988.html.

Qian, Yingyi, and Gerard Roland. 1998. "Federalism and the Soft Budget Constraint." *The American Economic Review* 88 (5): 1143–1162.

Qian, Yingyi, Gerard Roland, and Cheng-Gang Xu. 2006. "Coordination and Experimentation in M-Form and U-Form Organizations." *Journal of Political Economy* 114 (2): 366–402.

Qian, Yingyi, and Barry Weingast. 1997. "Federalism as a Commitment to Preserving Market Incentives." *Journal of Economic Perspectives* 11 (4): 83–92.

Qian, Yingyi, and Cheng-Gang Xu. 1993. "The M-form hierarchy and China's economic reform." *European Economic Review* 37 (2–3): 541–548.

Qin, Wangcheng. 2009. "Resarch and Reflections on Transforming the Rural Labor Force in Suining County (对睢宁县农村劳动力转移的研究与思考)." *China New Technologies and Products (中国新技术新产品)* 4: 122.

Ran, Ran. 2013. "Perverse Incentive Structure and Policy Implementation Gap in China's Local Environmental Politics." *Journal of Environmental Policy & Planning* 15 (1): 17–39.

Reed, Bradly W. 2000. *Talons and Teeth: County Clerks and Runners in the Qing Dynasty*. Stanford University Press.

Riker, William H. 1964. *Federalism: Origin, Operation, Significance*. Boston: Little, Brown.

Rodriguez-Pose, Andres, and Roberto Ezcurra. 2011. "Is Fiscal Decentralization Harmful for Economic Growth? Evidence from the OECD Countries." *Journal of Economic Geography* 11 (4): 619–643.

Rothstein, Bo. 2013. "Understanding the Quality of Government in China: The Cadre Administration Hypothesis." *CDDRL Working Papers Number 133*.

Rozelle, Scott. 1994. "Decision-Making in China's Rural Economy: The Linkages Between Village Leaders and Farm Households." *China Quarterly* 137: 99–125.

1994. "Rural Industrialization and Increasing Inequality: Emerging Patterns in China's Reforming Economy." *Journal of Comparative Economics* 19: 362–391.

Sachs, Jeffrey D., John W. McArthur, Guido Schmidt-Traub, Margaret Kruk, Chandrika Bahadur, Michael Faye, and Gordon McCord. 2004. "Ending Africa's Poverty Trap." *Brookings Papers on Economic Activity* 35 (1): 117–240.

Sah, Raaj Kumar, and Joseph Stiglitz. 1986. "The Architecture of Economic Systems: Hierarchies and Polyarchies." *American Economic Review* 76: 716–727.

1991. "The Quality of Managers in Centralized versus Decentralized Organizations." *Quarterly Journal of Economics* 106: 289–295.

Saich, Tony. 2002. "The Blind Man and the Elephant: Analyzing the Local State in China." In *East Asian Capitalism: Conflicts, Growth and Crisis*, edited by Luigi Tomba, 75–99. Milan: Feltrinelli.

2013. "The Quality of Governance in China: The Citizen's View." *CDDRL Working Papers Number 129*.

Saich, Tony, and Xuedong Yang. 2003. "Innovation in China's Local Governance: 'Open Recommendation and Selection'." *Pacific Affairs* 76 (2): 185–208.

Sartori, Giovanni. 1970. "Concept Misformation in Comparative Politics." *The American Political Science Review* 64 (4): 1033–1053.

Schneider, Ben Ross. 1999. "The Desarrollista State in Brazil and Mexico." In *The Developmental State*, edited by Meredith Woo-Cumings, 276–305. Ithaca: Cornell University Press.

Seawright, Jason, and John Gerring. 2008. "Case Selection Techniques in Case Study Research: A Menu of Qualitative and Quantitative Options." *Political Research Quarterly* 61 (2): 294–308.

Seckington, Ian. 2007. "County Leadership in China: A Baseline Survey." *The University of Nottingham China Policy Institute, Discussion Paper 17*.

Segal, Adam, and Eric Thun. 2001. "Thinking Globally, Acting Locally: Local Governments, Industrial Sectors, and Development in China." *Politics & Society* 29 (4): 557–588.

Shah, Anwar. 2006. "A Comparative Institutional Framework for Responsive, Responsible, and Accountable Local Governance." In *Local Governance in Industrial Countries*, edited by Anwar Shah, 1–40. Washington, DC: The World Bank.

Shambaugh, David. 2008. *China's Communist Party: Atrophy and Adaptation*. Washington, DC: Woodrow Wilson Center Press.

Shangguan, Jiaoming. 2010. "Crawfish Life and Death (小龙虾生死劫)." *Southern Metropolis Daily (南方都市报)*, September 30. www.nbweekly.com/news/china/201009/12768.aspx.

Shen, Liren, and Yuanchen Dai. 1992. "Formation of 'Dukedom Economies' and Their Causes and Defects." *The Chinese Economy* 25 (4): 6–24.

Sheng, Ruoyu. 2011. "Holiday Anti-Corruption: Why Do "Yibashou" Get in Trouble So Much? The Center Explores Limiting Power (节日防腐："一把手"易"出事"根子在哪？中央探索限权)." *People's Daily (人民日报)*, February 15. http://politics.people.com.cn/GB/30178/13918581.html.

Shih, Victor, Christopher Adolph, and Mingxing Liu. 2012. "Getting Ahead in the Communist Party: Explaining the Advancement of Central Committee Members in China." *American Political Science Review* 106 (1): 166–187.

Shirk, Susan. 1992. "The Chinese Political System and the Political Strategy of Economic Reform." In *Bureaucracy, Politics, and Decision Making in Post-Mao China*, edited by Kenneth G. Lieberthal and David M. Lampton, 59–91. Berkeley: University of California Press.

1993. *The Political Logic of Economic Reform.* Berkeley: University of California Press.

Shleifer, Andrei, and Robert W. Vishny. 1993. "Corruption." *The Quarterly Journal of Economics* 108 (3): 599–617.

2002. *The Grabbing Hand: Government Pathologies and Their Cures.* Cambridge: Harvard University Press.

Sihong County Government. 2013. "Sihong Key Enteprise Management Assitance Service Overview Table (泗洪县重点企业帮办服务一览表)."

Sihong Development Zone Regulatory Committee. 2013. "Sihong County Invesment Promotion Advantages – Service Environment (泗洪县招商引资优势--服务环境)." Sihong County. www.shkfq.gov.cn/zsyz/zsyz/135.aspx.

Sihong Economic Development Zone Regulatory Commission. 2013. *Sihong Investment Promotion Advantages: Service Environment (泗洪县招商引资优势--服务环境).* Sihong, Jiangsu: Sihong Economic Development Zone Regulatory Commission. www.shkfq.gov.cn/zsyz/zsyz/135.aspx.

Sihong News Agency. 2013. "Sihong Initiates 96 Major Projects: Total Investment of 17.6 Billion Yuan (泗洪96个重大项目集中开（竣）工 总投资176.05亿元." July 30. http://leaders.people.com.cn/n/2013/0730/c356819-22382499.html.

Sirkin, Harold L., Michael Zinser, and Douglas Hohner. 2011. *Made in America, Again: Why Manufacturing Will Return to the U.S.* The Boston Consulting Group. www.bcg.com/documents/file84471.pdf.

Skocpol, Theda. 1982. "Bringing the State Back In." *Items* 36 (1–2): 1–8.

Smith, Graeme. 2009. "Political Machinations in a Rural County." *The China Journal* 62: 29–59.

Snow, Edgar. 1971. "A Conversation with Mao Tse-Tung." *Life,* April 30: 4

Snyder, Richard. 2001. "Scaling Down: The Subnational Comparative M *Studies in Comparative International Development* 36 (1): 93–110

Song, Guangyong, and Yong He. 2003. "What a Chinese Mayor Learned from 'Engaging in Politics' in US (中国市长美国'从政'心得)." *People's Daily*, October 27.

Stein, Ernesto. 1999. "Fiscal Decentralization and Government Size in Latin America." *Journal of Applied Economics* 2 (2): 357–391.

Steinfeld, Edward. 1998. *Forging Reform in China: The Fate of State-Owned Industry*. Cambridge University Press.

Stewart, Philip D., Robert L. Arnett, William T. Ebert, Raymond E. McPhail, Terrence L. Rich, and Craig E. Schopmeyer. 1972. "Political mobility and the Soviet political process: A partial test of two models." *American Political Science Review* 66 (4): 1269–1290.

Stigler, George. 1957. "The Tenable Range of Functions of Local Government." In *Federal Expenditure Policy for Economic Growth and Stability*, edited by Subcommittee on Fiscal Policy, US Congress Joint Economic Committee, 213–219. Washington, DC: Government Printing Office.

Su, Fubing, Ran Tao, Lu Xi, and Ming Li. 2012. "Local Officials' Incentives and China's Economic Growth: Tournament Thesis Reexamined and Alternative Explanatory Framework." *China & World Economy* 20 (4): 1–18.

Suining Investment Promotion Office. 2012. "Suining Guide (睢宁指南)."

Suining Party Committee and Suining Government. 2012. "Suifa No. 1: Suining Party Committee and Suining Government Notice on the Publication of "Suining County Investment Promotion Preferential Policies" (睢发[2012] 15号: 中共睢宁县委 睢宁县人民政府关于印发《睢宁县招商引资优惠政策》的通知)." February 19.

Suliman, Osman, ed. 1998. *China's Transition to a Socialist Market Economy*. Westport, CT: Quorom Books.

Swinburn, Gwen. 2006. *Local Economic Development: Quick Reference*. Washington, DC: The World Bank.

Swinburn, Gwen, Soraya Goga, and Fergus Murphy. 2006. *Local Economic Development: A Primer – Developing and Implementing Local Economic Development Strategies and Action Plans*. Washington, DC: The World Bank.

Tai, Junyong. 2004. "The Cause of Development: Changes in Siyang's Political Situation (温饱之困：泗阳政局变迁)." *Xiaokang Magazine*, December 2. http://news.sina.com.cn/c/2004-12-02/15215103470.shtml.

Tao, Ran, Fei Yuan, Mingxing Liu, and Heng-fu Zou. 2007. ""Race to the Bottom" Competition by Negotiated Land Leasing: an institutional analysis and empirical evidence from Chinese cities." *China Economics and Management Academy Working Paper* 294.

Theil, Henri. 1967. *Economics and Information Theory*. Chicago: Rand McNally.

Thießen, Ulrich. 2003. "Fiscal Decentralisation and Economic Growth in High-Income OECD Countries." *Fiscal Studies* 24 (3): 237–274.

Thun, Eric. 2006. *Changing Lanes in China: Foreign Direct Investment, Local Governments, and Auto Sector Development*. Cambridge University Press.

Tian, Suisheng, Hui Luo, and Wei Zeng. 2005. *The Introduction to Chinese Administration Divisions (中国行政区划概论)*. Beijing: Peking University Publishing.

Tiebout, Charles M. 1956. "A Pure Theory of Local Expenditures." *The Journal of Political Economy* 64 (5): 416–424.

Treisman, Daniel. 2000. "The Causes of Corruption: A Cross-National Study." *Journal of Public Economics* 76 (3): 399–457.

Tsai, Kellee. 2002. *Back-Alley Banking: Private Entrepreneurs in China*. Ithaca, NY: Cornell University Press.

2004. "Off Balance: The Unintended Consequences of Fiscal Federalism in China." *Journal of Chinese Political Science* 9 (2): 1–26.

2006. "Adaptive Informal Institutions and Endogenous Institutional Change in China." *World Politics* 49: 116–141.

2007. *Capitalism Without Democracy: The Private Sector in Contemporary China*. Ithaca: Cornell University Press.

Tsui, Kai-yuen, and Youqiang Wang. 2004. "Between Separate Stoves and a Single Menu: Fiscal Decentralization in China." *The China Quarterly* 177: 71–90.

Tu, Chonghang 涂重航. 2011. "Jiangsu Sihong Citizen High-Interest Loans: Losses After the Collapse (江苏泗洪全民放高利贷 崩盘后遭受损失)." *Beijing News (新景报)*, August 1. http://news.sina.com.cn/c/sd/2011-08-01/035722910541.shtml.

Tullock, Gordon. 1965. *The Politics of Bureaucracy*. Washington, DC: The Public Affairs Press.

UNDP. 1999. *Decentralization: A Sampling of Definitions*. Joint UNDP-Government of Germany Working Paper. http://web.undp.org/evaluation/documents/decentralization_working_report.PDF.

Urio, Paolo. 2012. *China, the West and the Myth of New Public Management: Neoliberalism and Its Discontents*. New York: Routledge.

Vernon, Raymond. 1966. "International Investment and International Trade in the Product Cycle." *Quarterly Journal of Economics* 80: 190–207.

Vogel, Ezra. 1990. *One Step Ahead in China: Guangdong under Reform*. Cambridge: Harvard University Press.

von Mises, Ludwig. 1944. *Bureaucracy*. New Haven: Yale University Press.

Walder, Andrew G. 1995. "Career Mobility and the Communist Political Order." *American Sociological Review* 60 (3): 309–328.

1998. *Zouping in Transition: The Process of Reform in Rural North China*. Cambridge: Harvard University Press.

Walker, Richard M., and Jiannan Wu. 2010. "Future Prospects for Performance Management in Chinese City Governments." *Administration & Society* 42 (1): 34S–55S.

Wang, Alex. 2013. "The Search for Sustainable Legitimacy: Environmental Law and Bureaucracy in China." *Harvard Environmental Law Review* 37: 365–440.

Wang, Bingchun, and Huaibei Hui. 2010. "Sixian's Development Zone Promotes Economic Development Potential (泗县开发区着力提升经济发展能力)." *Daybreak News (拂晓报)*, April 1.

Wang, Fei-Yue, Daniel Zeng, James A. Hendler, Qingpeng Zhang, Zhuo Feng, Yanqing Gao, Hui Wang, and Guanpi Lai. 2010. "A Study of the Human Flesh Search Engine: Crowd-Powered Expansion of Online Knowledge." *Computer* 43 (8): 45–53.

Wang, Feng. 2006. "Sunan Cadres Sent North: Jiang Guoxing Tells It As It Is (苏南干部下苏北，蒋国星实话实说)." *South Reviews (南风窗)*, July.

Wang, Peilin. 2013. "江苏上收土地收储出让权 防止无序和超规模融资." *First Financial Daily*, September 26. www.yicai.com/news/2013/09/3027799.html.

Wang, Qingyun. 2003. *County Economic Development Theory and Practice (县域经济发展的理论与实践)*. Beijing (北京): Commercial Press (商务印书馆).

Wang, Shaoguang. 2003. "The Problem of State Weakness." *Journal of Democracy* 14 (1): 36–42.

2004. "For National Unity: The Political Logic of Fiscal Transfer in China." In *Nationalism, Democracy and National Integration in China*, edited by Leong H. Liew and Shaoguang Wang, 221–246. London: RoutledgeCurzon.

Wang, Shaoguang, and Angang Hu. 1999. *The Political Economy of Uneven Development: The Case of China*. Armonk, NY: M.E. Sharpe.

Wang, Ted. 2008. "Notice on Strengthening and Improving the Evaluation of Practical Work Accomplishment of the Leadership Corps of Party Committees and Government at the County (Municipal) Level." *Chinese Law and Government* 41 (2–3): 10–22.

Wang, Wei. 2005. "A Summary of Research on Local Governance Innovation in China." *Public Administration Journal* 177: 64–69.

Wang, Weibo, Xian Liu, and Quanbao Wang. 2010. "Reforming County Power: Control the Party Secretary (县权改革——管住县委书记)." *China Newsweek (中国新闻周刊)*, December 16.

Wang, Wenfei Winnie, and C. Cindy Fan. 2006. "Success or Failure: Selectivity and Reasons of Return Migration in Sichuan and Anhui, China." *Environment and Planning* 38 (5): 939–958.

Wang, Xiaodong, Changrong Qu, Yuefeng Ma, Jianwei Xie, and Ke Yan. 2011. "A Day in the Life of a County Party Secretary (县委书记的一天)." *People's Observer (人民观察)*, February 12. http://cpc.people.com.cn/GB/64093/117005/13898887.html.

Wang, Youfu. 2005. *Act First, Discuss Later: The Practice and Reflections of a County Party Secretary (不论先干：一个县委书记的实践与思考)*. Beijing: People's Daily Press.

Wang, Youhua. 2005. "1% Implementation Rate: Why is Cadre "Term of OFfice System" Failing (执行率仅1% 官员"任期制"缘何失灵)." *People's Daily*, March 21. http://politics.people.com.cn/GB/1026/3256257.html.

Wedeman, Andrew. 2002. "State Predation and Rapid Growth: Politicization of Business in China." In *Political Business in East Asia*, edited by Edmund Gomez, 155–181. New York: Routledge.

Wei, Houkai, Jie Liu, Minliang Zhou, Dali Yang, and Wuxian Hu. 1997. *Regional Development in China: Economic Growth, Institutional Transition and Regional Inequality (中国地区发展——经济增长、制度变迁与地区差异)*. Beijing: Business Management Publishing House.

Wei, Houkai, Yeqiang Wang, and Mei Bai. 2013. *The Micro-Analysis of Regional Economy in China: A Perspective of Firm Relocation*. Singapore: World Scientific.

Wei, Yehua Dennis, and Sunwoong Kim. 2002. "Widening Inter-County Inequality in Jiangsu Province, China, 1950–95." *The Journal of Development Studies* 38 (6): 142–164.

Weingast, Barry R. 1993. "Constittutions as Governance Structures: The Political Foundations of Secure Markets." *Journal of Institutional and Theoretical Economics* 149 (1): 286–311.

1995. "The Economic Role of Political Institutions: Market-Preserving Federalism and Economic Development." *Journal of Law, Economics, & Organization* 11 (1): 1–31.

Weng, Shiyou. 2006. "Xuyi Party Secretary Wang Youfu: Using Marketing Strategies as a Party Secretary (江苏盱眙县委书记王友富：用营销的方式当书记)." *Decision Making*, January 9. http://news.sina.com.cn/c/2006-01-09/17408816567.shtml.

Whiting, Susan. 2000. *Power and Wealth in Rural China: The Political Economy of Institutional Change.* Cambridge University Press.

2004. "The Cadre Evaluation System at the Grass Roots: The Paradox of Party Rule." In *Holding China Together: Diversity and National Integration in the Post-Deng Era*, edited by Barry Naughton and Dali Yang, 101–119. New York: Cambridge University Press.

Whyte, Martin King. 2010. *Myth of the Social Volcano: Perceptions of Inequality and Distributive Injustice in Contemporary China.* Stanford University Press.

Wildavsky, Aaron. 1964. *The Politics of the Budgetary Process.* Boston: Little, Brown & Co.

1968. "Budgeting as a Political Process." In *International Encyclopedia of the Social Sciences, vol. 2*, edited by David L. Sills, 192. New York: Crowell, Collier, Macmillan.

Williamson, Oliver E. 1975. *Markets and Hierarchies, Analysis and Antitrust Implications: A Study in the Economics of Internal Organization.* New York: The Free Press.

Winston, Clifford. 2006. *Government Failure versus Market Failure: Microeconomics Policy Research and Government Performance.* Washington, DC: Brookings Institution Press.

Wolfers, Justin. 2002. "Are Voters Rational? Evidence from Gubernatorial Elections." *Stanford GSB Working Paper No. 1730.*

Wong, Cecilia. 2002. "Developing Indicators to Inform Local Economic Development in England." *Urban Studies* 39 (10): 1833–1863.

Wong, Christine. 2009. "Rebuilding Government for the 21st Century: Can China Incrementally Reform the Public Sector?" *The China Quarterly* 200: 929–952.

Woo, Jung-en. 1991. *Race to the Swift: State and Finance in Korean Industrialization.* New York: Columbia University Press.

Woo, Wing Thye. 1999. "The Real Reasons for China's Growth." *The China Journal* 41: 115–37.

Woo-Cumings, Meredith. 1999. *The Developmental State.* Ithaca: Cornell University Press.

World Bank. 1997. *China 2020: Development Challenges in the New Century.* Washington, DC: The World Bank.

/orld Development Report 2009: Reshaping Economic Geography. ıington, DC: The World Bank.

"How to Note: A Framework for the Assessment of Fiscal Decentralization stem." *Social Development Notes: Community Driven Development and Local Governance*, February 13.

ɔ14. *Urban China: Toward Efficient, Inclusive, and Sustainable Urbanization.* Washington, DC: The World Bank.

Wu, Jing, Yongheng Deng, Jun Huang, Randall Morck, and Bernard Yeung. 2013. "Incentives and Outcomes in China's Environmental Policy." *NBER Working Paper 18754*.

Wu, Jingsheng, and Xiu Wang. 2013. "Develop Grace, Cultivate Public Trust, and Set Sail to Lead the Convoy for Investors (展风采 树公信 为投资者扬帆护航)." *China Reform Daily*, January 30.

Wu, Lan. 2010. "Mingguang City Former Party Secretary Zhang Songjian On Trial: Accused of Accepting 4.34 Million in Bribes (安徽明光市委原书记张松坚受审 被控受贿435万)." *China News Service*, April 14. http://leaders.people.com.cn/GB/11361711.html.

Wu, Yanrui. 2009. *Capital Stock Estimates By Region And Sector In China's Integration With The Global Economy.* Cheltenham, UK: Edward Elgar Publishing Limited.

Wu, Yiping, and Jiangnan Zhu. 2011. "Corruption, Anti-corruption, and inter-county income disparity in China." *The Social Science Journal* 48: 435–448.

Wu, Yu-Shan. 2002. "Chinese Economic Reform in a Comparative Perspective: Asia vs. Europe." *Issues & Studies* 38 (4): 93–138.

2003. "Institutions and Policies Must Bear the Responsibility: Another Case of Nonantagonistic Competition." *Issues & Studies* 39 (2): 24–40.

Wuhe County Government. 2009. "Wuhe County City Plan (2009–2030) (五河县城市规划（2009–2030））."

Wuhe Government. 2012. *Preferential Policies (Summary) (优惠政策（摘要））.* Wuhe: Wuhe Government. www.wuhe.gov.cn/DocHtml/1/2012/6/8/6121656114631.html.

2013. "Economic Strengths (经济实力)." Wuhe. www.wuhe.gov.cn/SortHtml/1/238369539.html.

Xia, Ming. 2000. *The Dual Developmental State: Development Strategy and Institutional Arrangements for China's Transition.* Brookfield, Vermont: Ashgate.

Xiao, Hui. 2013. "Deputy Township Mayor Posts Online Resignation: Four Months of Stability Maintenance Work Leaves Four Months for Real Work (副镇长网上发辞职感言:4个月维稳剩4个月干正事)." *Beijing News (Xin Jing Bao)*, July 5. http://news.xinhuanet.com/2013-07/05/c_124959920.htm.

Xie, Danyang, Heng-fu Zou, and Hamid Davoodi. 1999. "Fiscal Decentralization and Economic Growth in the United States." *Journal of Urban Economics* 45 (2): 228–239.

Xin, Bing. 2009. "Hubei Shishou City Party Secretary Sacked for Weak Handling of Mass Incident (湖北石首市委书记处置群体性事件不力被免职)." *IPTV (荆楚网)*, July 25. http://news.xinhuanet.com/local/2009-07/25/content_11770011.htm.

Xin'an Evening News. 2010. "Announcement of the Resolution of the Si County Shijia Temple Destruction: Relevant Leaders are Punished (泗县释迦寺被破坏事件处理结果公布：相关领导受到处分)." *Xin'an Evening News (新安晚报)*, September 17. http://ah.anhuinews.com/system/2010/09/17/003356388.shtml.

Xinhua News. 2013. *Chinese county's fake economic data exposed.* September 5. Accessed September 18, 2013. http://news.xinhuanet.com/english/china/2013-09/05/c_132695215.htm.

Xu, Changliang. 2013. "Three Concentrations: Turn Sihong's Countryside into a Field of Hope (三集中：让泗洪乡村成希望田野)." *Xinhua News*, April 10. www.sihong.gov.cn/art/2013/4/10/art_2637_97545.html.

Xu, Chenggang. 2011. "The Fundamental Institutions of China's Reforms and Development." *Journal of Economic Literature* 49 (4): 1076–1151.

Xu, Weihua, and Lixin Wang. 2000. "Analysis of the Formation and Evolution of Power Corruption in Chinese Society (试析当前我国社会中权力腐败的形成与演变)." *Journal of Hubei Adult Education Institute* 3: 16–21.

Xu, Xianxiang, Xianbing Wang, and Yuan Shu. 2007. "Local Officials and Economic Growth, (地方官员与经济增长——来自中国省长、省委书记交流的证据)." *Economic Research (经济研究)* 9: 18–31.

Xu, Yaotong. 2011. "Shunde's 'Earth-Shattering' Bureau System Reforms (顺德大部制改革"石破天惊")." *Tongzhou Gongjin (同舟共进)* 9. http://theory.people.com.cn/GB/15501429.html.

Yang, Dali. 2004. *Remaking the Chinese Leviathan: Market Transition and the Politics of Governance in China.* Palo Alto: Stanford University Press.

2006. "Economic transformation and its political discontents in China: Authoritarianism, unequal growth, and the dilemmas of political development." *Annual Review of Political Science* 9: 143–164.

Yang, Fuxiang. 2012. "Export Labor and Attract Back Productive Strength: A Survey of the Situation of Mingguang City's Returning Ventures (输出劳动力引回生产力——明光市返乡创业情况调查)." *Decision-making* 4: 6–7.

Yang, Min. 2010. "The Comprehensiveness of Suining's Reforms (睢宁改革的前后左右)." *Decision-making* 9: 19–24.

Yang, Xuedong. 2001. "Region, Individuals and Institutional Innovation: A Case Study of Qindu District, Xianyang City in Shaanxi Province (地域、个人与制度创新—对陕西省咸阳市秦都区改革的个案分析)." In *Further Discussion of the Transformation from the Pressurized System to the Democratic System of Cooperation (再论从压力型体制向民主合作体制的转变)*, edited by Jingben Rong, 189–245. Beijing: Central Compilation and Translation Press.

2013. "Local Government Reform in China in the Past Ten Years: An Evaluation based on the Chinese Local Governance Innovation Awards." *CDDRL Working Papers Number 137.*

Yang, Yi. 2013. "Civil service recruitment registration begins in China." *Xinhua News*, October 16. http://news.xinhuanet.com/english/china/2013-10/16/c_132804605.htm.

Yao, Yang, and Muyang Zhang. 2012. "Subnational Leaders and Economic Growth." *Peking University, China Center for Economic Research Working Paper.*

Yao, Yongkang. 2010. *Research on Accelerating the Transformation of County-Level Economic Development Patterns (加快转变县域经济发展方式研究)*. Zhenjiang, Jiangsu: Jiangsu University Press.

Yep, Ray. 2004. "Can 'Tax-for-Fee' Reform Reduce Rural Tension in China? The Process, Progress, and Limitations." *The China Quarterly* 177: 42–70.

Yi, Lili, and Haifeng He. 2012. "Difficulties and Solutions in Creating County Party Committee Power Transparency (县委权力公开透明运行的困境与出路)." *New Horizon (新视野)* 2: 81–84.

Yin, Heng, and Hong Zhu. 2011. "Research on County Level Public Finance Productive Expenditure Bias (县级财政生产性支出偏向研究)." *China Social Sciences (中国社会科学)* 1: 88–101.

Young, Alwyn. 2000. "The Razor's Edge: Distortions and Incremental Reform in the People's Republic of China." *Quarterly Journal of Economics* 115 (4): 1091–1135.

2003. "Gold into Base Metals: Productivity Growth in the People's Republic of China during the Reform Period." *Journal of Political Economy* 111 (6): 1220–1261.

Yu, Jianrong. 2005. "Land problems have become the focal point of rural rights resistance (土地问题已成为农民维权抗争的焦点)." *Chuangzao* 6: 79.

2007. "Social Conflict in Rural China." *China Security* 3 (2): 2–17.

Yuan, Peng. 2000. "Institutional Innovation and Structural Adjustment in TVEs (乡镇企业的体制与结构调整)." In *The Analysis and Forecast of China's Rural Economic Situation: 1999–2000 (1999–2000年: 中国农村形势分析与预测)*, edited by Rural Development Research Institute of China's Academy of Social Sciences and Rural Social and Economic Survey Team of the State Statistical Bureau, 97–121. Beijing: Social Science Documentation Publishing House.

Yuhui District People's Court. 2005. "2005 Document 4: Zhang Guiyi Embezzlement and Bribery Case (2005禹刑初字第14号: 张桂义挪用公款、受贿案)." Criminal Judgment Document (刑事判决书), Bengbu City.

Zang, Xiaowei. 2004. *Elite Dualism and Leadership Selection in China*. London: RoutledgeCurzon.

Zhai, Nianxiang, and Guangqing Xiang. 2007. "An analysis of China's current land acquisition system and policy implications (中国土地征用体制分析及政策建议)." *Chinese Public Administration* 3: 9–12.

Zhai, Tianshan. 2009. "A study of how to improve the system of civil servant performance evaluation." In *Good Governance in China – A Way Towards Social Harmony: Case Studies by China's Rising Leaders*, edited by Mengkui Wang, 40–49. London: Routledge.

Zhan, Jing Vivian. 2011. "Explaining Central Intervention in Local Extra-Budgetary Practices in China." *Asian Survey* 51 (3): 497–519.

Zhang, Guang. 2009. "Exploration of the Causes and Effects of Provincial Fiscal Decentralization Differences (财政分权省际差异 ，原因和影响初探)." *Journal of Public Administration (公共行政评论)* 1: 133–158.

Zhang, Guohua, and Erzhen Zhang. 2008. *Kunshan's Way in Reform and Opening (改革开放的昆山之路)*. Beijing: People's Publishing House.

Zhang, Han, and Yun Lan. 2009. "Suining County Government Advertisement Attracts Heated Debate (江苏睢宁县政府登悬疑广告推介城市引热议)." *Beijing News (新景报)*, March 10. http://society.people.com.cn/GB/1062/8933605.html.

Zhang, Jun, Yuan Gao, Yong Fu, and Hong Zhang. 2007. "Why Does China Enjoy So Much Better Physical Infrastructure?" *Economic Research Journal* 3: 4–19.

Zhang, Kun. 1997. "The Mingguang Corruption Nest Case." *Inside and Outside of Court (法庭内外)* 12 (85): 34–35.

Zhang, Peng, and Mann Xu. 2011. "The View from the County: China's Regional Inequalities of Socio-Economic Development." *Annals of Economics and Finance* 12 (1): 183–198.

Zhang, Pengfei, and Victor Shih. 2008. "Deficit Estimation and Welfare Effects after the 1994 Fiscal Reform in China: Evidence from the County Level." *China & World Economy* 16 (3): 22–39.

Zhang, Qianfan. 2010. "Performance or Petitions?" *Caixin*, October 20.

Zhang, Qinghua, and Heng-fu Zou Zou. 2007. "Returns to Education, Productivity, and Economic Growth in China." *Journal of Comparative Policy Analysis* 9 (3): 293–308.

Zhang, Tao, and Heng-fu Zou. 1998. "Fiscal Decentralization, Public Spending, and Economic Growth in China." *Journal of Public Economics* 67 (2): 221–240.

Zhang, Weiwei. 2012. "Meritocracy Versus Democracy." *The New York Times*, November 9. www.nytimes.com/2012/11/10/opinion/meritocracy-versus-democracy.html?partner=rss&emc=rss&pagewanted=all&_r=2&.

Zhang, Wenjun. 2011. "Promotion Game, Performance Assessment and Local Government Debt Expansion (晋升博弈、政绩考核与地方政府债务扩张)." *Journal of Shanghai Finance University (上海金融学院学报)* 5 (107): 72–77.

Zhang, Xiaobo. 2006. "Fiscal decentralization and political centralization in China: Implications for growth and inequality." *Journal of Comparative Economics* 34: 713–726.

Zhang, Xinguang. 2007. "Analysis of the Systemic Roots of China's Local Governance Deterioration (中国地方政权退化现象的体制根源探析)." *Journal of Jiangxi University of Finance and Economics* 5: 74–77.

Zhang, Xiusheng, ed. 2009. *China County-Level Economic Development (中国县域经济发展)*. Wuhan: China University of Geosciences Publishing House.

Zhang, Yan, and Xiangqian Shan. 2001. "Organization Department: National Cadre Personnel System Reform Makes Great Progress (中组部：全国干部人事制度改革取得重大进展)." *People's Daily*, June 25. http://news.sina.com.cn/c/285425.html.

Zhao, Lei (赵蕾), and Yan (郑焰) Zheng. 2006. "中组部前部长直言高官管理：非常反感跑官要官." *南方周末*. November 10. http://news.xinhuanet.com/legal/2006–11/10/content_5311550.htm.

Zhao, Shukai. 2005. *Township reform: reflections and perspectives – a survey on 20 townships (Xiangzhen gaige: jiantao yu zhanwang – shisheng ershi xiangzhen diaocha)*. Beijing: Development Research Center, State Council.

Zhao, Xiaojian, and Yan Li. 2003. "The secrets of the income tax reform (所得税改革玄机)." *Caijing Magazine*, January 14.

Zheng, Yongnian. 2007. *De Facto Federalism in China: Reforms and Dynamics of Central-Local Relations*. Hackensack, NJ: World Scientific.

Zhong, Yang. 2003. *Local Government and Politics in China: Challenges from Below*. Armonk, NY: East Gate.

Zhou, Enlai. 1981. *Selected Works of Zhou Enlai, vol. 1*. Beijing: Foreign Languages Press.

Zhou, Jialai, Daocai Zhu, and Shijie Zhang. 2012. *Anhui County Economic Competitiveness Report 2010–2011 (安徽省县域经济竞争力报告)*. Beijing: China Business Press (中国商业出版社).

Zhou, Katie Xiao. 1996. *How the Farmers Changed China: Power of the People*. Boulder, CO: Westview Press.

Zhou, Qingzhi. 2004. *The Structure and Operation of China's County-Level Administration: A Sociological Investigation of County W (中国县级行政结构及其运行: 对W县的社会学考察)*. Guizhou: Guizhou People's Press.

Zhu, Hanqing. 2011. "Systemic Roots of China's High Investment Rate: A Framework for Analysis Based On Local Official Promotion Tournaments (中国高投资率的制度根源 ---- 基于地方官员晋升锦标赛的分析框架)." *Journal of Nanjing Party Institute of CPC (中共南京市委党校学报)* 4: 35–40.

Zhu, Jiangnan. 2008. "Why are Offices for Sale in China? A Case Study of the Office-Selling Chain in Heilongjiang Province." *Asian Survey* 48 (4): 558–579.

Zhu, Jieming. 2004. "Local Developmental State and Order in China's Urban Development During Transition." *International Journal of Urban and Regional Research* 28 (2): 424–447.

Zhu, Kaibao, and Yancai Wen. 1996. "Interview with Jiangsu Jurong City Party Secretary Guo Lirong (一字一句总关情：记江苏省句容市委书记郭礼荣心系信访二，三事)." *Secretary Work (秘书工作)* 4: 36–37.

Zhu, Lijia. 2011. "County Government Transparency Paves the Road to Democracy (县政公开为民主铺路)." *Study Times*, May 9. http://theory.people.com.cn/GB/14588926.html.

Zhuang, Guobo. 2007. *Leadership Cadre Performance Evaluation Theory and Practice (领导干部政绩评价的理论与实践)*. Beijing: China Economics Press (中国经济出版社).

Zou, Le. 2011. "Disguised Offices Lobby for Funding and Privileges." *Global Times*, September 21. www.globaltimes.cn/DesktopModules/DnnForge%20-%20NewsArticles/Print.aspx?tabid=99&tabmoduleid=94&articleId=676226&moduleId=405&PortalID=0.

Zweig, David. 1997. "Institutional Constraints, Path Dependence, and Entrepreneurship: Comparing Nantong and Zhangjiagang, 1984–1996." *Hong Kong University of Science and Technology Working Papers in the Social Sciences, No. 15*.

2002. *Internationalizing China: Domestic Interests and Global Linkages*. Ithaca: Cornell University Press.

Zysman, John. 1983. *Governments, Markets, and Growth: Financial Systems and the Politics of Industrial Change*. Ithaca: Cornell University Press.

Index